Walking Softly
in the Wilderness

Walking Softly in the Wilderness

The Sierra Club Guide to Backpacking

John Hart

Sierra Club Books
San Francisco

The Sierra Club, founded in 1892 by John Muir, has devoted itself to the study and protection of the nation's scenic and ecological resources—mountains, wetlands, woodlands, wild shores, and rivers. All club publications are part of the nonprofit effort the club carries on as a public trust. There are over 50 chapters coast to coast, in Canada, Hawaii, and Alaska. Participation is invited in the club's program to enjoy and preserve wilderness everywhere. Adress: 530 Bush Street, San Francisco, California 94108.

Library of Congress Cataloging in Publication Data

Hart, John, 1948—
    Walking softly in the wilderness.

    Includes index.
    1. Backpacking. I. Sierra Club. II. Title.
GV199.6.H37   796.5   76-21620
ISBN 0-87156-191-3

Illustrations by Bonnie Laurie Russell
Book design by Jon Goodchild
Printed in the United States of America
10   9   8   7   6   5

Acknowledgments

I OWE THANKS TO MANY PEOPLE for assistance on this book.

At the top of the list are the readers, who worked through the entire manuscript or reviewed selected chapters: Michael McCloskey, Jim Watters, Allen Smith, and Wendy Goldwyn, all of the Sierra Club; John Stanley, of the Club's Wilderness Impact Study team; Jim Owens of the Smilie Company (camp and trail gear); George D. Davis of the Wilderness Society; Phil Ward of the National Park Service; Bill Devall and his sociology students at Humboldt State University, Arcata, California; Gilbert Roberts, M.D.; Norman A. Wilson, snow consultant; Mike Hughes, George Malanson, Bill Riebsame, and Nick Van Pelt; and my parents.

Many others gave information and advice. Among them are Jim Absher, Gordon Benner, M.D., Garrett De Bell, Ann Dwyer, Michael J. Franzblau, M.D., Willi Fuller, Gaynor Franklin, Larry Gaudreau, Iris Noble, Tom Pillsbury, Harry Reeves, Alan Schmierer, Jerry South, Steve Ziman. Also Stephanie Atwood, Jordan Fisher-Smith, Christie Hakim, Lelia Loban Lee, Bob Schneider, Sari Sommarstrom, and Shirley Taylor; Don M. Deck of the Boy Scouts of America; Mike Harding of Mountain Traders; W. M. Harlow of the State University of New York; O. Granger of the University of California, Berkeley; Reuben Rajala of the Appalachian Mountain Club; George H. Stankey and Carl Westrate of the U. S. Forest Service; Floyd Wilson of the Wilderness Education Foundation; and MacPherson Brothers of San Francisco, tannery agents.

Numerous offices of the National Park Service and the U.S. Forest Service also were of help in this research.

—J.H.

Acknowledgment is made for permission to reprint
material from the following sources:

Anabasis by St.-John Perse, translated by T.S.
Eliot. N.Y.: Harcourt, Brace Jovanovich, Inc. Copy-
right © 1938, 1949 by Harcourt, Brace & Co.
A Wizard of Earthsea by Ursula LeGuin. N.Y.:
Ace Books. Copyright © 1968 by Ursula K. LeGuin.
By permission of the author.
Gerard Manley Hopkins, Poems and Prose edited
by W.H. Gardner. N.Y.: Oxford University Press.
Copyright © 1953, 1963 by W.H. Gardner.
Mount Analogue by Rene Daumal, translated by
Roger Shattuck. Baltimore, Md.: Penguin Books.
Copyright © 1952 by Librairie Gallimard.
Reprinted by permission of Random House, Inc.
Oregon Winter by Jeanne McGahey. Andes, N.Y.:
Woolmer/Brotherson Ltd. Copyright © 1973 by
Woolmer/Brotherson Ltd.
*Patterns of Wilderness Use as Related to
Congestion and Solitude* by George H. Stankey *et
al.* Published by the U.S. Forest Service, Inter-
mountain Forest and Range Experiment Station.
Round River by Aldo Leopold. N.Y.: Oxford
University Press. Copyright © 1953 by Oxford
University Press
This is Dinosaur by Wallace Stegner. N.Y.:
Alfred A. Knopf, Inc. Copyright © 1955 by Wallace
Stegner. By permission of the author.
*The War between the Rough Riders and the
Bird Watchers* by Wallace Stegner. Reprinted from
the **Sierra Club Bulletin** (May, 1959) by permission
of the author.
Wilderness Forever by Howard Zahniser, from
Wilderness: America's Living Heritage. Copyright
© 1961 by the Sierra Club.

Contents

Note to the reader

My impression of books in the backpacking field is that
they are insufferably bossy. *Walking Softly in the Wilderness* cannot be entirely an exception, for no book of manageable length and decent clarity can explore *all* the
possible choices in wilderness gear and methods. Instead, a
book must simplify. It must select. Often it must present
only one way of doing things when there may be others
just as good. And the effect cannot fail to be one of
arbitrariness.

   Much of what is said in this book may come, in time, to
seem wrong to you, or inefficient, or outdated. That is as it
should be. Every backpacker finds a personal style; your
style in the wilderness will be your own.

   However, I hope that you will be slow to discount
what this book has to say about *low-impact* methods in the
wilderness: about the skills of using but not injuring the
vulnerable land. For these are not merely points of "backcountry manners" or "wilderness etiquette." Not after-
thoughts. Not optional finishing touches. Low-impact
methods are the new necessities. And while there are
legitimate disagreements about some of the details, the
outlines are clear enough. There is little doubt about the
things each hiker needs to know and do.

   I hope you will help.

The Land Beyond the Roadhead

Where do the six trails go?
What are the mountains named
That are colored like Iroquois?
—Jeanne McGahey

1:
The Land Beyond the Roadhead

THERE IS A COLD, sky-colored lake in Colorado, three days' walk from any road, unchanging in the wilderness of stone and timberline.

There is a volcanic mountain in Washington that glistens all year long with snow and the lasting ice of glaciers. You reach it by hiking miles of trail through some of the greenest forest country in the world.

In Florida there is a horizon of jungle and sawgrass, full of unfamiliar beasts and brilliant birds. The swift, calm gliding of your canoe does not disturb them.

In Utah there is an unscarred canyon, a red, sunken world cut into a mile-high desert plateau.

On the New Jersey coast there is a barrier island, a line of dunes between quiet marshes and the noisy sea, reached by no bridge, traversed by no highway.

These, and a thousand like them, are the places we call *wilderness*. They are the unaltered landscapes of America, the places we have not reshaped with our machines, not stamped with our straight lines. They are the last survivals of the wildness beyond the old frontiers: the wildness that once was a continent wide.

When we learned to value these places—to recognize the benefits, practical and subtle, that we get from them—it was almost too late. It was almost too late when we realized that we actually *needed* them, that, in some important way, we cannot do without them. Nor is it a lesson we have truly learned. While some of our wild places have official labels and official protection—in federal wilderness units, in parks, in wildlife refuges—many others are unlabeled, unprotected. They have remained what they are only by fortunate accident. These wild places are disappearing fast and steadily: there was more wild country in America last year than there is today. Next year there will be, inevitably, somewhat less. And while the wilderness shrinks, the need for it and the public demand to know and enjoy it are steadily growing. Just how long the shrinking goes on and just how much wilderness is finally preserved depend on what Americans want and what they ask loudly for.

Wilderness belongs to everyone: it is a national possession. Its value is not only for those who make direct and obvious use of it. But wild country does inevitably have a particular meaning, a further meaning, to those who make the effort to go into it. It belongs, in a certain sense, to that very large yet very distinctive group: the backpackers.

Today there are millions of them, heading out from the roadheads. They are the people who don't mind walking, who are willing to carry moderate loads on their backs, who find a luxury in self-sufficiency. The backpackers earn their pleasure and would not find it so pleasant if it were not earned.

And yet the entry to the world of the trails is not hard. There are few Americans who are physically prevented from making the effort that the wilderness requires. There are many—indeed, the large majority—who have so far not tried. Some just aren't attracted and find the idea foreign. Others genuinely can't afford the gear. Others are content to have their wilderness secondhand, in books and photographs. But still others—who knows how many?—stay home because they simply don't know how to start or have an exaggerated idea of the difficulties, the discomforts, the expense.

Wilderness travel is not free—but it is, for most people,

reasonably inexpensive.

Wilderness travel is not effortless—but it is, if you choose to make it so, quite easy.

Wilderness travel is not entirely without discomforts—but these are slight enough beside the rewards.

Wilderness travel is probably not for everyone. But it may be for a good number of people who have not yet found it out. There seems to be in many people a kind of hunger for wilderness, which, once aroused, is never to be satisfied by any substitute. And judging by the rate at which backpacks are selling, this hunger is more widespread than anyone a few years ago imagined.

The wilderness boom

It wasn't so long ago that Americans were labeled a sedentary people: car-bound, television-sitting, never doing, always looking on. But if that image ever reflected a

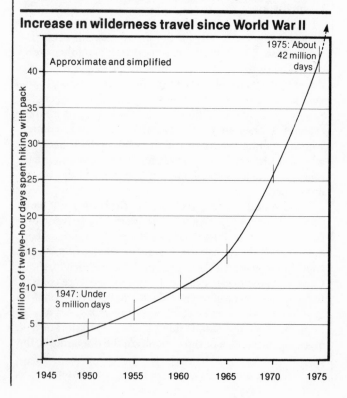

Increase in wilderness travel since World War II

1975: About 42 million days

Approximate and simplified

1947: Under 3 million days

Millions of twelve-hour days spent hiking with pack

40 — 35 — 30 — 25 — 20 — 15 — 10 — 5

1945   1950   1955   1960   1965   1970   1975

truth, it needs revision now. Our national style is changing. We are turning, by the millions, to recreation outdoors, and the crowds that seek the footpaths of America are growing fastest of all.

In 1975, by the best estimate, Americans spent some forty-two million days hiking in the nation's wild and semi-wild places—a sixteen-fold increase since 1945. Wilderness hiking has grown five times as fast as the population, and three times as fast as auto camping—though the camp-grounds, too, have seen a postwar "boom."

The makers of backpacking gear are selling about $400 million worth of packs, shelter, clothing, food, and gim-micks every year. Nearly one and three-quarter million backpacks were sold in 1973 alone. On the graphs, all the curves are rising, with as yet no sign of a leveling off.

For those who have loved the wilderness all along, who have worked and fought to defend it from logging, mining, the endless thrusting-forward of the roads, this rush to wild places is a very hopeful sign. It suggests that the value of our wilderness may at last be fully recognized. It suggests that there may be more people every year asking that we save what can still be saved.

The impact problem

But along with this hope has come a stirring of alarm. As more and more people seek out the wilderness, some of that wilderness is suddenly, unmistakably, *crowded.* Cer-tain especially popular places are getting the worked-over look of run-down city parks.

In New Hampshire use of the White Mountains back-country doubled from 1968 to 1972, and is well on its way to doubling again. More than 60,000 people every year take the trail into Tuckerman Ravine on the slopes of Mount Washington. In Yosemite National Park the use of the roadless sections has nearly tripled since 1968.

At Cascade Pass in northern Washington, as many as 300 people have been counted at one time on the tiny summit meadow.

In the Appalachians from the Smokies to the Catskills, the woods around popular campsites have been stripped of young growth by hikers hunting for fuel.

At popular lakes in any western range you may find

shorelines trampled bare and spotted all around with
blackened fire-rings.

On the famous High Peaks of the Adirondacks the
trampling of thousands of boots is destroying the moist
alpine tundra that makes these peaks so much of another
world. In Colorado's Rocky Mountain National Park, similar damage may take hundreds of years to reverse itself.

And so it is, on even the greatest mountains. The Forest
Service has had to limit use of the trail up Mount Whitney
in California, highest in the forty-eight lower states. And
on 20,300-foot McKinley in Alaska, where any ascent is an
expedition, there are campsites buried in decades of
accumulated junk.

The danger signs are everywhere, most obvious in the
East and in the Far West, where wild lands lie closest to
great cities, but spreading fast to the remoter ranges of
mid-continent. Today, in almost every well known wilderness, there are places where the fabric of the land has vis-
ibly begun to fray.

About the permanent damage to the land—the long-
term impairment of natural systems—ecologists tend to be
somewhat reassuring. The genuinely spoiled places, they
say, are (so far) small and few. But "wilderness" is a word
that means not just the country itself but also our experience of that country. And this experience is, in its own
way, a fragile, vulnerable thing.

When backpackers are asked what they desire most of
all from wild places, the answer comes back: *solitude.* Not,
to be sure, the total solitude of the single traveler: most
backpackers travel in groups of two, three, or four, and
like it that way. "Solitude," for them, means that they
should meet few other groups; that they should meet no
large parties at all; and that they should have no company
at camp. Four or five meetings a day, for many, begins to
spoil the experience. (This is not to say that larger groups
have no place in the wilderness, but there is little question
that the larger parties are resented by the smaller.)

Damage to the land, injury to the experience: these are
the two dimensions of the "impact problem." If every
hiker were scrupulously careful to make no mark on the
land, to intrude on others as little as possible, the twofold
problem would be far less difficult to solve. Unfortunately,

16

too many backpackers are still relying on old methods, still maintaining outdated habits, still acting like lonely pioneers in an empty mountain world. Their weight on the land is heavy. It takes only a few of them to make a crowd.

The rise of the rules

It is not only the backpackers who are troubled by the changes they see in the backcountry. Government agencies manage our protected wilderness, and it is their charge to keep it truly wild. But that means that the door to the wilderness cannot be endlessly, limitlessly open. Already, the authorities are moving to regulate use as never before. "Wilderness permits" are more and more often required. At the moment only a few highly-visited roadheads have actual daily quotas, but the time may come when it will be common to find, at the edge of wilderness, a "Come back tomorrow" sign.

It is hard to be comfortable with such restrictions. One of the chief pleasures of the land beyond the roadhead has always been the independence of the traveler and his freedom from formal rules. Quotas, certainly, should be a last resort. There is reason to complain, in some instances, that other, gentler methods have not been properly tried.

But for all that, there seems little chance that formal controls can be dispensed with now. And there is little logic in resenting them. Indeed, when the reasoning behind the limitations is made clear, most backpackers seem to accept them willingly. For more about the problems of wilderness management, see Chapter 32.

One thing is unmistakable. Restriction will come soonest, and in the most annoying form, in the places where the hikers themselves have failed. As an official at Yosemite National Park put it, "We have to plan everything with the *worst* backcountry user in mind." The job of protecting wilderness belongs largely to us who enjoy it. Each of us has the power to make the problem less.

First, each backpacker must make certain that his own way in the wilderness is a gentle and a thoughtful way. There is neither need nor excuse for adding new scars to the land. It is time to make a game, an ethic, a matter of pride, of walking softly in the wilderness world. We have to grasp the fact that no change we inflict on the changeless wilderness is trivial: each of us, now, is a thousand.

Second, we can seek out the less-known, less-used, and less-regulated areas. Even in such crowded regions as the High Sierra and the Adirondacks you can find relatively empty lands. Crowding is still the exception, not the rule; it's easy enough to avoid the busy trails, the lakeshores and trailside camps, the busy days of the week, the busy times of the year.

And there is a third contribution that some may want to make. The demand for wilderness is great and growing— so much greater, then, the need to protect our only, irreplaceable, supply. Each of us has the chance to speak out for wilderness. Each can lend some small individual weight to the cause of protecting what is unprotected now. If every second or third backpacker did so, the future of the wilderness would be immeasurably brighter. For more on this, see Chapter 30.

If wilderness has an essence, that essence is *room*. The more wilderness we have, the roomier it will be.

Going light: first points

This book is not just about backpacking. It is about that special kind and style of backpacking called "going light."

A few years ago, when you spoke of "going light," you were probably thinking of the poundage in your pack. "Going light" was the skill of paring down the load, of leaving at home every ounce that could be spared. And that is still an excellent thing to do.

But today "going light" has an additional meaning. Today you go light to spare the land. You choose your route, your gear, your destination with the welfare of the wilderness in mind. You camp and travel by the rules of "low impact."

Those principles are not complex. There are, indeed, different problems from region to region, as the landscape changes. There are questions which the different experts answer differently. Yet the main points are clear. Unfortunately, no more than a minority of today's backpackers seem to have heard even the most constantly repeated slogans of low impact. Before this book goes further, some of these points should be stated once more.

The go-light backpacker doesn't camp on meadows.

This is a hard one; it seems to run against some instinct out of the Stone Age. The novice hurries to camp on the grass at the edge of the water or—a second choice—on the grass at the edge of the forest. But meadows, and especially high, moist meadows, are exceedingly fragile (they are also damp, cold, and full of mosquitoes). No matter how inviting that lakeside lawn appears, try for a camp in the woods or on barer, higher ground. Even in steep terrain three or four people can usually find a flat and pleasant spot.

The go-light camper avoids camps at timberline. Whether in Oregon or in Maine, the plants of timberline— the tiny stunted trees, the heathery, ground-pressed flowers—are already fighting to survive. It may take decades of short summers to bring measurable growth, and any damage you do will last a very long time. Try to plan your camps lower down, where living things have more margin, or higher up, where the rock and snow are barren.

Go-lighters take the landscape as they find it. The perfect camp is found, not made. If you want a laid-out campsite, choose an established one. If you pitch a tent, find a site with natural drainage. Don't cut limbs, dig ditches, pound nails, pile stones. The game is preservation, not pioneering.

Thoughtful backpackers carry out all their trash. Hikers are very conscientious these days about outright litter, but many still think it good practice to bury the junk they cannot burn. *Don't do it.* In most wild places the soils are shallow; animals and erosion often dig up what you bury. Whatever isn't burned should go out the same way it arrived—in your pack.

The go-lighter is sparing with fire. This is one of the more complicated matters: see Chapter 19. But note that in many wild areas fires are allowed only at certain sites or in certain zones. A light, portable stove gives you much more freedom to camp where you like.

The modern backpacker goes along with agency rules. In designated parks and wilderness areas, you may need a *wilderness permit:* see Chapter 14. With it you will get a list of regulations and suggested practices. Follow these, no matter what you may have read or what differing conclusions you may have formed. The agency workers aren't just hassling you: they are the people who watch the land; they see the changes, good and bad. Some of their rules are experimental, but the experiments have to be made. Play along—or go them one better in your efforts to spare the land.

Backpackers are anxious to do the right thing. In fact, as studies show, it would be hard to find another group of people so conscientious. It is misinformation, not any vandalistic instinct, that keeps bad habits going. To change those habits, the friends and users of America's wilderness need only to know why. And that is perhaps the most hopeful fact of all.

The freedom of the wilderness

We look back with something like sorrow to the days of the Great Wild: when Thoreau at Walden, a day's ride from Boston, could test the uses of utter isolation—when Muir could set out into the unknown Sierra, sleeping on beds of cut boughs, with no further provisions than a loaf of bread, a warm coat, and a billycan. That condition of the world could not last. But it is a pity that we have gone so far in the other direction—that we have pushed so far beyond what might have been the healthy balance point of civilized and wild.

Yet the wilderness we have—even that shrunken wilderness—is grand beyond description. And if it is no longer large enough to absorb and nullify whatever abuses we pour into it, it can be large enough for the delight of everyone who comes to visit it. It can be—if we can learn the self-restraint that makes it possible, in this our crowded world, to be free.

2:
Breaking In

Whoever you are, the way is open.

Wilderness travel is not for the experts only, nor for the well-to-do, nor for the young. It is not only for the people who love to travel hard and count the miles behind them. It is not a competition. It is not a proving ground.

The way is open; yet it can be hard to know just where and how to begin. Some people choose to hurry themselves and make their first trip a considerable mountain journey. Others prefer to take it in slower stages.

The easy first step: *start hiking close to home.* You need not walk far, nor seek out rugged terrain: just start taking short walks, as easy as you like, on any available parkland trail. You will need no special gear at the beginning, and later only a light daypack and a pair of boots. If you would like to go with a group, get in touch with a local hiking club. These are found all over the country: the Appalachian Mountain Club and its chapters, the Mazamas, the Mountaineers, the Carolina Mountain Club, the Colorado Mountain Club, and endless others. The Federation of Western Outdoor Clubs and the Appalachian Trail Conference (see addresses in the appendix *Resources*), can give you information on their member organizations. The Sierra Club has chapters all over the United States and in much of Canada; most of these run local outings. Inquire also at the nearest backpacking store.

There are advantages to hiking with a group. For one thing, it hooks you into a grapevine, with the constant chatter about gear, experiences, places to go, problems encountered and solved. For another, you can watch how more experienced hikers handle themselves. And though most backpackers eventually choose to travel in family-sized parties, these group sessions are good social fun.

Now, as gradually as you like, begin building up your stock of gear and the skills that go with it. A good pair of boots will be about the first on your list. As soon as you have them, set out to break them in. Wear them for short distances, then for long, until boot and foot have adapted each to the other. Try out the combinations of clothes you have in mind to wear on later overnight trips. When you buy your pack, try loading it and carrying it on a day-hike.

Spend time working with a compass and a topographic map on local, familiar ground; learn to translate from map to land and from land to map. This is important: even if you never plan to step off plain trails, you are bound to find places where you need to do a little navigation, and you might conceivably find yourself someday in a situation where map and compass could save your life.

If day-hiking is Step One, Step Two (which many skip) is the organized, overnight backpacking trip. Most hiking clubs run these; in national parks you will find such trips run by concessioners as well. In such a group you have the support of experienced people, and if you've arrived without some small, crucial object, you can just about count on the party having a spare.

These sizable organized groups have a very special function. Many people never need them; some frankly detest them; but for many hikers they are the indispensable bridge into a wilderness that seems at first a bit strange and incalculable. Organized groups, some studies suggest, have more middle-aged people than you find elsewhere in the wilds, and more children; unlike smaller parties, they are made up about equally of men and women.

Step Three, for those who wish to make it, is the first independent trip with family or friends. The first time you head out, you may want to choose a well-known corner of the wilderness; inquire around the grapevine or check one of the trail guides sold in backpacking stores and in most general bookstores (see also Chapter 11). With that first trip behind you, you have known real self-sufficiency; you are no longer "breaking in." You are on your way.

Do you have to "get in shape"?

It depends.

Hiking with a pack is not, of itself, very hard. Anybody who is reasonably active at home can turn to the trails with no special preparation. But to people who have accustomed themselves to a life of physical leisure beyond the limits of what is healthy, backpacking can seem hard. To those who have spent years behind their desks—even though they golf or ski on weekends—it can seem hard. To the muscular man who regards himself as strong, yet seldom hikes or bicycles or swims, it may come harder than he expects.

There are several ways in which one can be "fit." But there is just one kind of "fitness" that matters on the trail: the kind known variously as "stamina," "cardiovascular conditioning," or just plain "wind." This is not a matter of bulging muscles but a matter of efficient heart and lungs. When you are fit in this way, your heart will beat relatively slowly, even when you are working hard; you will be taking deep, satisfying breaths; you won't feel pressed for air. You get this stamina from lots of walking, lots of cycling, or from briefer periods of running or swimming. Anything that makes the heart and lungs work will strengthen them. Peak effort isn't important. The long haul is.

Now you won't catch many backpackers "training" for a trip. Why should they? They're not athletes. It's fun they're after. If you're in good enough shape to climb a few flights of stairs without collapsing, you're in good enough shape for an easy start on the trail. But if you don't have even a small reserve of stamina, then it's worth the effort to build some before you head for the hills.

It goes without saying that you need a doctor's advice if you suspect that something more than inertia is wrong with you; older people in particular should start slowly and keep the doctor posted on what they're undertaking. But the chances are good that your physician will enthusiastically approve. The backpacker's kind of fitness is the

kind that doctors most welcome in their patients, and
nobody basically healthy needs to deny himself the pleasure of the trails.

Some hikers quite unconcernedly allow themselves to
grow soft between outings and schedule a couple of easy
days at the start of a lengthy wilderness trip to recover
their wind. But if you plan a short, ground-covering weekend trip, you need to be somewhat in shape at the beginning. So keep on hiking near home between adventures. Or
if you're short of time and it appeals to you, jog.

Gearing Up

B

Naturally, we also carried all the standard mountain climbing equipment: cleated shoes and nails of all kinds, ropes, screw rings, hammers, snap hooks, ice axes, crampons, snowshoes, skis and all accessories, as well as instruments for observation like compasses, clinometers, altimeters, barometers, thermometers, range-finders, alidades, and cameras. And arms: rifles, carbines, revolvers, short sabers, dynamite—in other words, enough to face any foreseeable obstacle.

—René Daumal

3:
Gearing Up

No MATTER HOW GRADUALLY you begin, you will soon have to start locating gear—*objects*, and quite a few of them. Even the lightest pack will contain seventy or eighty separate items. The novice, looking at a list like the one on the next few pages, sees a sizable job ahead.

Exhibit: A Typical Packlist for Dry-Summer Mountains

(For one person in a party of three. No price shown for items found at home.)

Item	Weight in pack	Cost
Clothing, worn		
stout cotton pants	—	—
belt	—	—
underpants	—	—
net undershirt	—	7.00
cotton shirt	—	—
hat	—	4.50
sunglasses	—	6.50
inner socks	—	1.50
outer socks	—	3.50
hiking boots	—	40.00

Item	Weight in pack	Cost
Clothing, packed		
spare socks, one set	13 oz.	6.00
hiking shorts	10 oz.	11.50
rain chaps	5 oz.	5.50
spare sunglasses	2 oz.	2.50
knit cap	4 oz.	2.50
down vest	10 oz.	30.00
light wind-shell	9 oz.	23.00
poncho, packboard style	21 oz.	20.00
Sleeping gear		
mummy sleeping bag in stuffsack	46 oz.	110.00
Ensolite pad	8 oz.	4.50
groundsheet, 7' x 9'	9 oz.	10.00
Shelter (group)		
tarp (12' x 10')	44 oz.	30.00
Kitchen and basic tools (individual)		
flashlight	3 oz.	2.80
spare batteries, bulb	2 oz.	1.00
matches	1 oz.	1.00
cup	3 oz.	1.70
spoon	1 oz.	—
knife	4 oz.	8.00
bandannas, two	2 oz.	2.00
50' nylon cord	4 oz.	1.50
candle	1 oz.	—
Kitchen (group)		
stove	15 oz.	20.00
windscreen	3 oz.	5.00
two pots	16 oz.	18.50
gripper	1 oz.	.70
quart fuel can	6 oz.	4.50
funnel		
eyedropper	1 oz.	1.50
Consumables (group)		
food (three people, four days)	384 oz.	42.00
reserve food	48 oz.	7.00
fuel	18 oz.	.40
water	—	—
Emergency, first aid, repair		
rigid container for medical kit		
gauze pads		
Band-Aids		
roll gauze		
Ace bandage		

Item	Weight in pack	Cost
aspirin		
painkiller (prescription)		
antibiotic (prescription)		
razor		
adhesive tape		
snake bite kit		
first aid booklet		
spare matches		
spare pencil		
whistle	11 oz.	16.00
sew and repair kit	2 oz.	1.00
Office		
notebook, pencils	2 oz.	.50
maps	2 oz.	3.50
natural history guides	4 oz.	3.00
compass	1 oz.	5.00
cheap watch	—	—
Personal		
toothbrush, etc.	1 oz.	—
toilet paper	1 oz.	—
lip balm	1 oz.	1.50
suncream	2 oz.	2.00
Haulage		
pack	60 oz.	60.00
stuffbags	5 oz.	5.00
plastic bags and closures	2 oz.	1.50
quart water bottle	4 oz.	1.50

Weight of pack and contents
  Personal gear: 16 pounds
  One third of group gear: 1 pound 13 ounces
  One third of consumables: 9 pounds 6 ounces

  Total: **27 pounds 9 ounces**

Costs of pack and contents
  Personal gear: $407.00
  One third of group gear: 26.75
  One third of consumables: 16.50

  Total: **450.25**

Take a moment to scan this list. It allows something more than minimum comfort on a trip in hospitable western mountains in a hospitable season, late summer. Humidity is low, water plentiful, weather pleasant, trails plain.

Such conditions are by no means the rule in the American wilderness. This list is *not* a model to go by but only an illustration of the way one party packed for a particular journey. It is meant to show something of the *logic of gear*.

What do you need to travel safely and in comfort?

You need *clothing:* garments to protect you from sun, from wind and cold, from rain and snow, from scratching brush and irritant plants, from mosquitoes and stinging flies.

You need *sleeping gear* for warmth at night and *shelter* to keep you dry.

You need *water and food,* and the tools of cooking and eating (unless you choose to rely on no-cook meals).

You need a *knife,* a *flashlight,* plenty of *matches,* and a good length of *cord.*

You need *emergency, medical,* and *repair* gear for problems major and minor.

You need *navigation tools*—usually just maps and a compass.

You need *personal items*—toilet paper and a toothbrush at the minimum.

And you need *containers*—mostly bags, big and little, and a pack to put it all in.

One of the minor pleasures of wilderness travel is the comfortable feeling of dealing with good gear. You come to know that collection of objects almost like a language: the uses of each item, its faults, its limitations, the location in which it should be packed to be most easily at hand when you require it. This familiarity *can* lead to a kind of obsessive fussiness. It can also produce the "gear freak," the zealot who is restless when lacking the very latest innovation in every department. But for all that, the pleasure of gear is a genuine pleasure.

In buying gear, there's a Rule Number One: *Go slowly.* There is no reason to purchase everything at once, and unless you are unusually sure of yourself you should not try to. Borrow and rent equipment whenever you can. Make do with what you have on hand. Some expensive items— like stoves and tents—are shared, so you can rely at first on your companions; or you can begin with organized trips where these items are part of the package. It is almost never a mistake to put off buying equipment. The longer

you delay, the better chance you have to find out what
truly suits you.

Where to buy

If you can, get the help of a backpackers' specialty
shop—or of several. There are now many of these nationwide. Department stores, surplus outlets, and general
sporting goods stores also carry wilderness gear, but they
seldom can answer the questions you need to ask.

Take a look in the Yellow Pages: first under "backpacking and mountaineering," then under "camping,"
"skiing," and "sporting goods." If you are lucky, you may
have several competing specialty shops in your area. Use
all of them. Consider. Shop around. No need to stay home
while you're considering: many stores also rent packs,
tents, and sleeping bags. And renting is not a waste of
money—it's a valuable series of lessons in the merits of
different brands and designs.

The salespeople in most of the specialty shops are
knowledgeable, easy to talk to, and generous with their
time. Don't feel you're imposing on them: the time they
spend on you is reflected in the prices they charge. They
always have opinions, and there is almost always disagreement from store to store; compare the versions, and
you learn a good deal. A few backpacking stores are larger,
somewhat cheaper, and less personal: take your pick. But
there is something reprehensible about gathering all your
advice from the smaller stores only to do all your buying at
the larger ones.

If you don't have access to specialty shops, there's
always mail order. You should collect the catalogs of the
major outfits, in any case, for the information they contain.
Some very good lines of gear are sold primarily by mail.
But there is truly no substitute for seeing and handling the
gear yourself.

In the last few years the choices in gear have doubled
and redoubled. For every type of equipment there are not
just competing brands but competing, fundamentally
different, designs; and every one of them seems to have
been tested on a trek across the Sahara, or on some vast
and terrible mountain wall in Asia. The days are gone
when a mere backpacker can keep track of the changing

technological scene. This makes the advice of the sales-people, biased though it often is, more important than ever.

For more help, you can turn to equipment rating articles published in such magazines as *Backpacker* and *Wilderness Camping* (see *Resources*). *Backpacker* has assembled a number of its studies into the book *Backpacking Equipment*, a sort of Consumer's Guide to the most debated items of wilderness gear. These ratings are not beyond dispute. You must also keep in mind that a negative report on a product often causes the manufacturer to alter the design—thus all such studies tend to become rapidly dated. Nonetheless, they can help the buyer navigate the equipment labyrinth.

Faced with these complexities, some backpackers become obsessed with gear. They spend endless energy in the search for some pack or tent or sleeping bag that strikes them as "the ideal." While it's good to take your time, it's also good to remind yourself frequently that gear is only a set of tools: a means to an end. The backpacker does the work, not the backpack. And when you get out into the field, you're likely to find that different, competing models, if equally well-made, do the job about equally well.

How much will it cost?

What about the first weekend trip? How *little* can you spend and still be safe and comfortable in the wild?

This depends, of course, on where you are going, how much useful junk you have around, and how many people you have with you to share common expenses. By renting some of the major pieces of gear and buying the cheapest adequate versions of other items, you can probably reduce the tab to a little over $100 the first time you go out. Lower than that it is difficult to go.

The cost of successive trips will depend on what new items of equipment you buy each time. The shopping never stops entirely; there are always minor objects to add or replace. Once you are past such major purchases as pack and boots, however, you will find yourself spending much less: seldom over $50 a trip, and often only a fraction of that.

What about the total cost of building your permanent stock of good equipment? It can no longer be said that backpacking gear is cheap. A pretty complete set of well-made summer gear is likely to set you back something like $400, in 1976 prices, before you are through (but remember that this expense will be spread out over several years). More than half of the price tag will be for four major items—your *boots* (Chapter 4), your *pack* (Chapter 5), your *sleeping bag* (Chapter 6), and your *stove* (Chapter 9). If you need a *tent*—but you may not—that is the fifth major purchase (Chapter 7). There are also some very expensive items of wilderness clothing to be had—items which, however, you may well be able to do without (Chapter 8).

Minimum cost of first weekend trip

Individual

rent pack	$ 5
rent sleeping bag	7
buy cheapest boots	25
2 sets socks	10
pad, groundcloth	8
poncho, chaps, hat	25
other items	10
food	10
individual total	**100** (plus any restaurant meals)

Group

rent tent (?)	7
rent stove	2
fuel	1
pans or billy cans	(found at home)
group total	**11** (plus shared auto costs)

There are ways of beating down this entry price. A few stores handle secondhand gear; many have bulletin boards where sellers advertise. Then again, you may be able to find *seconds*—items that come from the factory with harmless imperfections. These are sold at reduced prices, either at factory outlets or in special "seconds shops." At present, seconds are most easily found in the West, where a disproportionate share of the manufacturing is done. Inquire at local stores.

If you're pretty sure of what you need, you can pick up excellent bargains at the seasonal sales which gear stores hold. Too, stores which rent gear eventually sell those items at cut prices.

Military surplus stores (many of which are not surplus at all but merely discount houses) have some good prices on good gear. They also stock flimsy products: go carefully here. The same goes for department stores, general sporting goods stores, and the like.

If you can't handle the prices that well-made items generally fetch, you have another, quite legitimate choice: you can spread your money further on cheaper, mass-production items. These products may look much like the costlier versions, but by and large, and with some delightful exceptions, they just don't hold up as well. If you buy such items, consider it a form of renting. (In the long run you may be wasting both a certain amount of money and the natural resources that go into the manufacture of "disposable" equipment.) It should be noted that both J. C. Penney and Sears Roebuck market fairly adequate lines of wilderness gear at attractive prices.

Whether you buy high or low, don't spend money needlessly on gear that's intended for heavier use than you plan to give it. Some shoppers look by reflex at the "top of the line." They buy the weightiest, costliest, most nearly "expeditionary" sleeping bags, packs, boots, tents, jackets. For almost all of them this is an error. The sleeping bag you could use on the North Slope of Alaska is only hot and clammy in a normal wilderness summer. And a Himalayan-scale backpack is a poor container for a weekend's worth of gear.

The prices in this book

The prices of the things backpackers need have been heading—very rapidly—higher. Some items have increased more than once during the preparation of this book. A typical annual increase seems to be six to ten per cent.

So please bear in mind that *all* prices given here are both approximate and liable to change. They reflect the situation at the end of 1976. It isn't just probable that you will find higher price tags when you go out to buy: it is certain.

How much will it weigh?

Let's say you have a packload without too many extras:

no paperback novels, no ropes, no cameras, no Monopoly games. Assume your load is for a lightweight summer trip. Forget for a moment about water, food, and fuel. And forget about shelter, stove, pots—the gear you will be sharing among companions.

Thus limited, the *basic dry weight* of your pack—including clothing, bedding, first aid kit, various oddments, and the pack itself—should be somewhere between sixteen and eighteen pounds. This does not count your boots or the clothes you start out wearing, but it does include clothes for rain and moderate cold which will, with luck, be stowed away much of the time.

To get a notion of what the rest of the packload will weigh, you can apply these rules of thumb:

●For food, figure on two pounds per person per day. With expensive freeze-dried foods and an average appetite, you may find yourself happy with less. Most women eat less, most teenagers a good deal more.

●Add one pound for each pint of water you normally carry.

●Add twelve ounces for each pint of white gas or kerosene. A typical if economical allowance is one-quarter cup, or 1.5 ounces, per person per day: see Chapter 12.

●If your group will use a tent or tents, figure about three pounds per person. But allow just one pound per person if shelter is a tarp or tarps.

●Finally, a group of two or three hikers will carry two to three pounds of cookware and stove.

So, if two of you were heading out for five summer days, in, say, the Adirondacks; if you carried, as you should for that trip, both stove and tent; and if each of you had a pint of water in a canteen, your theoretical share of the load would be something like this:

> 17 lbs. of personal kit
> 10 lbs. of food
> 1 lb. of water
> 1.5 lbs. of cooking gear
> 8 ozs. of fuel (1.5 oz. per person per day)
> 3 lbs. of shelter

for a theoretical total of thirty-three and a half pounds.

This, like the detailed list a few pages back, is merely an illustration. But it makes the point: on a trip of less than a week in a place and month not extraordinarily hostile, you won't need a load of more than thirty-five pounds.

But how much can you comfortably carry?

An old rule of thumb says you can carry a third of your body weight. And indeed, if you have to, you can; climbers often wind up toting that or more. But for most people on today's trails—people who come for the simple fun of it— that is far too much. With light, modern gear, it should be possible to limit your pack to a fifth of your own weight on trips of a few days.

So a 200-pound man might have a comfortable limit of 40 pounds; a 110-pound woman, by this formula, would be limited to 22. With loads of this order, an experienced hiker may almost be able to forget that he has a load on his back. (But note: if you are overweight, your built-in extra poundage doesn't entitle you to a heavier pack.) If you hike in a group, as most people do, you can split up food, fuel, and community gear according to body weight. As to your personal gear, you're stuck with it. If you travel alone, your pack will include all "community" gear and ride a little heavier.

The one-fifth rule is only a starting point. It is possible to cut down this standard load, easier still to build it up. Every hiker makes his own compromise between the advantages of a light pack and the advantages (if any) of the extra gear.

Going light: old style and new

You will hear the most drastic advice about cutting the weight in your pack. People really do cut handles off toothbrushes. Whether or not this deadpan game makes a practical difference, it's true that the overloaded hiker gets ingenious at finding objects to leave home.

But "going light," that familiar slogan, has undergone a subtle change in meaning. Today it refers less to the load in your pack than to the weight—the impact—of your passage on the land. And in adopting this version of "going light," backpackers have learned to accept a few more ounces of weight on their shoulders.

The heaviest of the new necessities is the stove. Nobody should travel in today's wilderness without one.

Don't put yourself in the position of *having* to kindle a fire when conditions are wrong. (Sometimes there is no down, dead wood to be had. Sometimes fires are not permitted, or permitted at certain sites only. In other cases your fire would leave ugly and unnecessary scars.) And a stove gives you a much wider choice of campsites—much more freedom to revise your plans.

Extra water containers, too, are carried more often now. In well-watered mountains like the Cascades or the Adirondacks, it may seem odd to keep more than a sip in your canteen. But if you have bottles you can fill toward evening, you no longer have to cling to stream and trail. You can, for instance, work your way up some lofty ridgeline and camp where dawn will strike you early and alone.

And of course you never plan to save weight at the expense of the land—by building, for instance, shelters of green branches. That was fine for the mountain men of the 1860s, but it has no place in the wilderness today. As for the famous natural foods to be found in the hills, they're there, all right, but you find them undisturbed only because not many people have yet thought of looking for them. Enjoy that trout, enjoy those huckleberries or wild onions, but count them as luxuries. "Living off the land" is an idea whose time has passed. This development is ironic and yet quite logical: the stronger our wish to preserve the wild places, the less we can meet them on their own terms; the more sophisticated, civilized, and complex become the gadgets we must bring into them.

The wilderness regions and the gear you take

From region to region and season to season, rules change. One list of gear won't serve for all landscapes, all weathers, all the different demands of the American wilderness.

Some places are dry in summer; some are wet. In the dry-summer mountains of the West, shelter and raingear can be simple and light; the occasional thunderstorm is more an entertainment than a piece of serious weather. But in the Smokies or the North Cascades, summer rain is real, and much can be said for carrying a tent.

Humidity counts, too. If the air is dry between rains, cotton clothing and down sleeping bags are efficient. But in the Catskills or the Blue Ridge, even a cool, clear night may be damp enough to saturate your down and chill your cotton clothes. In such places wool clothes and synthetic-filled sleeping bags have their advantages.

In the deserts, and on some ridge routes in less arid ranges, water is the factor that limits you. Springs and streams may be far apart, and unreliable at that. In Death Valley, for instance, two-thirds of your load may be water.

In areas where winter brings snow, a whole new kind of wilderness, a white and challenging wilderness, appears with the first cold storm.

Problems with gear

Catalogs often contrive to give you the impression that wilderness gear is indestructible and perfect. Of course (as you'll find out soon enough) this isn't so. Some items and some brands hold up better than others; none are invariably trouble-free. Sleeping bags and tents get torn. Stoves balk and have to be tinkered with. Waterproofing wears off and has to be renewed. Zippers fail. On cheap packs—and even on some very costly ones—inadequate stitching may fray. As for flashlights, they fail about as often as they work.

Wilderness gear is indeed better made, on the average, than other consumer goods today. Yet much of it is made less well than it could be. When you shop for gear, pay special attention to the detail of construction: durability is perhaps the greatest virtue of all. (The gear industry began as a collection of tiny, independent makers. Now, like other fields of commerce, it is in the process of sorting out into a handful of big conglomerates. This may affect the quality of gear.)

Many minor repairs, of course, can be done on the trail. And when the problem is too large for that, most reputable shops and manufacturers are very good about repairing items that were faulty to begin with. Some stores will do additional repairs very cheaply on items purchased from them. Shoemakers will sew on leather patches, replace hooks, D-rings, and grommets, and handle many other problems with leather and heavy fabric. And one equipment outlet, Eastern Mountain Sports, runs a nationwide mail-order repair service for most kinds of gear.

4:
Boots

Smooth-trail and rough-country boots

SOONER OR LATER—and probably sooner, because this purchase is one of the hardest to put off—you will have to pick out a pair of hiking boots. The choice is wide. In fact, for easy shopping, it is *too* wide. Some seventy different manufacturers make hiking boots, and every one of them claims special virtue for its product. You can get lost in the clamor of competing features and learned arguments for this or that cunning arrangement of leather.

And yet there are just two things you really require from a boot. First, you need a boot that is heavy enough and stiff enough for the kind of hiking you want to do—and not one ounce heavier. Second—and all important—you need a boot that *fits*. Remember these needs, pursue them, and you can't go very far wrong. Having satisfied these requirements, you may find that only one make and model of boot is left on your list. If you still have alternatives, that's the time to start comparing the other selling points of the competing brands—and low price is the best selling point of all.

Most (not all) boots suitable for hiking with a pack are quite alike in basic design. The sole is usually of tough, high-carbon synthetic rubber (the common brand is Vibram) molded in a pattern of projecting, beveled *lugs*. Above this lug sole is a *midsole* of one or several layers, and above that an *insole* on which your foot actually rests. These soles are stitched, by varying methods, to the *upper*. The leather of the upper boot may be stiff or pliable, but toe and heel are always stout and hard.

The lightest boots weigh as little as three pounds in a size 8 or 9; the heaviest can run seven pounds or even more. (Special boots intended for women only are sized differently. Few women use these, though; boots are unisex.) What you gain with greater weight and stiffness is *protection*. A boot shields the foot from sharp, bruising rocks, from moisture, and from cold. If you're walking on a flat, gentle trail on a temperate day, you need little protection. For scrambling cross-country over hard, broken rock, you need a good deal more.

How heavy a boot do you need?

We can divide the range of backpacking boots into approximate thirds.

Smooth-trail boots are the lightest, thinnest, and most flexible. They are more comfortable than heavier boots and easier to break in. They are fine for backpacking on well-surfaced trails if the climate is not too cold—and many backpackers do most of their hiking in just such gentle landscapes. Typical weights, for a middle-range size, lie between three and four pounds the pair. Some hikers ignore the manufacturer's advice and wear these lighter boots on rugged trails and even on cross-country travel, but the uppers are too soft to give the kind of ankle support you really need for such hiking. Prices presently run from under $30 to over $40 (see *Shopping for boots* below).

Rough-country boots are heavier, more solid, and stiffer. They can be waterproofed far better than smooth-trail boots; in general they serve more purposes. But there's a penalty in comfort and in weight: they range from about four pounds to almost five pounds the pair. Prices run from about $40 to $60, and they are rising all the time.

Mountaineering boots begin at about five pounds and go on up—way up. Their leather is very strong, thick, and rigid. The heavier ones have extra-thick midsoles, and some have totally rigid soles which make them great for certain kinds of climbing but terrible for ordinary walking. Most hikers need to know about these massive constructions only to guard against buying them by mistake. But if you plan to do a great deal of cross-country travel in rugged places, one of the lighter mountaineering boots may be worth the $50 to $70 it will cost you.

Along with these boots of the standard design, there are special boots for special purposes; these will be noted later.

Now, which do you want?

The best boot is the lightest boot that will serve your purpose. A pound on your feet, army research shows, is as hard to move as five pounds on your back. The over-equipped backpacker usually has too much leather on his feet and has paid too much for it. Flexibility is another important advantage. While stiff boots are sometimes needed, they can be hard on the feet. Especially vulnerable is the Achilles tendon -the big cord that runs from calf to heel, just under the skin. Many people who wear massive boots have trouble with painful, inflamed Achilles tendons, caused by the incessant bruising of the flesh against the top of a rigid boot-heel.

Unless you mean to do very rough hiking, and to do it soon, be slow to buy *any* pair of boots that weighs over four and a half pounds in a size 8 or 9. And if you expect to hike on smooth trails for a while, it's best to begin with one of the lightest and cheapest models. You may actually wear it out before you want anything sterner. If not, old boots sell readily at backpacking stores that handle this sort of business. Or you can hang onto the light pair—it will certainly be useful, and most backpackers eventually own a whole row of diverse clodhoppers.

Lugs: a question of impact

"This trail has become an eroding gully, torn up by the trampling of thousands upon thousands of lug-soled hiking boots." It is common, these days, to read such statements as this. There is growing feeling that the lugs of the typical bootsole, projecting like so many saw-teeth, do more than

40

their share of damage to the land.

It does seem clear that lug soles disturb moist ground more than flat soles do. Lugs dig in and grip—that's their great advantage. They also tend to break up the soil surface, leaving fragments that runoff can carry away in times of rain. So the problem is certainly real, particularly in the eastern states, where the soil remains damp all year. What is not clear yet is the magnitude of the damage done. Is this a minor issue, or a major one? Some thorough research now being undertaken in various places should bring better answers soon.

Some claim that lug soles, regardless of their possible impact, are essential for sure-footedness. In certain situations this is doubtless true. But on the trails that most of us walk, most of the time, almost *any* kind of sole would do.

The main problem with flat soles is that you can't find them—at least not in the specialty shops. Outside of these stores, you have two possibilities. First is the common department store work boot, an inexpensive model that works fine in easy travel. Many backpackers have never used anything else. Second is the army's "general combat" boot—much stouter, but (in the opinion of many who have used it) brutally uncomfortable. Beyond that, there's nothing. The gear industry simply does not make a boot for rugged hiking with anything other than a lugged sole.

Impact isn't the only consideration here. On certain types of terrain, flat-soled boots actually serve you better. On loose, gravelly ground for instance—a surface often encountered in cross-country desert travel—lug soles are a nuisance, because the indentations get packed with debris. The ideal boot here would combine a smooth sole and a solid, middle-weight upper. But no one in the industry is building such a boot. (You do have the option of changing to another type of sole when your original lugs wear out. Be prepared, though, for raised eyebrows at the shoemaker's.)

Shopping for boots

If you have to, you can order boots by mail. Many people do and are quite satisfied. But first make a real attempt to locate the pair that suits you in local stores. As with most gear, the case is good for shopping in the specialty outlets; their buyers screen out boots that are down-right flimsy or ill-made, so you don't have to be on your guard. You can concentrate instead on the two essentials, proper weight and proper fit.

There are a few bargains outside the backpacking stores, however, that you should consider. Almost any store selling shoes will offer two types of light boots that you see on easy trails. The ordinary "work boot," with a slick leather surface and a crepe sole, is mentioned above; it's an excellent bargain at $20 to $30. Less suitable is the "waf-flestomper," a cheap shoe designed to look like a hiking boot. Most have suede uppers and some sort of lugged sole, cemented on rather than stitched on, and are quite fragile.

The GI regular combat boot is also a bargain, if you find it sufficiently comfortable: at around $22 in surplus stores it is comfortable in price, at least. These stores also carry a lighter, ventilated "tropical combat" boot for about $15; these are much favored for travel in warm, wet places, such as low-lying regions of the South.

If you need a rough-country boot, bargains are harder to find. A few backpacking stores sell used hiking boots, or take commissions for helping the owners sell them. Such boots go for between a third and two-thirds of new prices and have this extra advantage: they need little breaking in.

Finding a fit

When you go shopping, make up your mind to insist on a good fit. When in doubt, don't buy. If you are one of the lucky people, you may find your boot quickly. If you aren't, brace yourself for quite a few sessions of trying boots on.

Wear the combination of socks you plan to wear when you hike (see *Socks* below). Tell the salesperson your street shoe size and let him take it from there. (You need help on this—sizing is anything but standard—but the specialty store employees know their stock.)

Slide on your candidate pair. They should feel a good bit roomier than normal shoes—at least half an inch longer than your stocking foot, but less than an inch. Before you lace up, push your foot forward inside the boot as far as it will go. You should just barely be able to fit an index finger all the way down between your heel and the back of the boot. (Two fingers is too much room.)

Now kick back in the boot to settle the heel into the socket and lace the boots tightly. (If the laces draw the sides of the closure so close together that they almost touch, the boot is too loose for you.) Have the salesperson hold your heel to the floor and do your best to lift the back of your foot. The heel should rise no more than an eighth of an inch inside the boot. (That's not much. It should feel very firm.)

To check the fit of the toe, hook your heel over a rock, a wooden shoe-rack, or a street curb, so that your toe points sharply downhill. Kick forward inside the boot. If your toes feel stubbed against the tip, the boot is too short. (You can also kick against something hard, if the store will let you—some say it's bad for the boot.) You must be able to wriggle your toes freely when you wear the boot, or you risk cutting off the circulation of blood in your foot.

To make sure the boot is not too wide, have someone hold the boot to the floor and try to rotate your foot inside it. The ball of your foot shouldn't shift noticeably sideways. Don't worry if the sides of the boot feel tight—boots loosen up in this dimension. (But they don't get longer or shorter—heel and toe are crucial.)

You may hear it said that it is better to have a boot too large than too small, on the theory that you can always add socks. But don't count too much on this. A boot that is sloppy in the store will only get sloppier. And a loose heel is almost bound to give you blisters. Even moleskin or an athletic-style heel cup may not help much.

If the boots seem to pass these various tests, make sure you have them laced up tightly and spend a few minutes "hiking" around the store. Don't just stroll: speed up, slow down, go up and down stairs, swivel, do knee bends. Watch again for a feeling of tightness in the toes or of sloppiness in the heels.

Most stores allow you to take boots home with you and walk around indoors until your mind is made up—then, if you must, return them for a refund. A very few stores will allow you to make a better test by walking on dry city streets. Or you can climb up and down stairs in a city building. If you find nothing that fits you properly in a particular store, go elsewhere. Keep looking. Different brands of boots can be *very* different in configuration. (Boots are built on standardized patterns called "lasts." A last is nothing but a model foot—a theoretical, average foot. Somewhere out there, somebody is probably building boots on a last that matches your foot-shape reasonably well.)

Some people have unusual trouble finding a satisfactory fit. Many Americans have narrow heels and wide toes; most boots made in the United States, or specifically for the American market, respect this anatomy. Sometimes you can get the shop to stretch the leather to eliminate cramped spots, depending on where they are and how serious, after you buy the boot. If you have a high arch, so that the foot presses unpleasantly against the tongue of the boot, you can skip one pair of eyelets or hooks when you lace up; sometimes it helps. And there are various ways of building up the inside of a boot that fits sloppily. None of these methods are very satisfactory, though; if you have a really unsolvable fitting problem, you may have to go to a shoemaker.

Buying by mail

The key thing, as every catalog will tell you, is to send an outline of your stockinged foot. (One foot is usually the larger: trace that one, or both.) It's a good idea to list several choices from the brands offered, so that the mail-order people can choose the "last" that best fits your foot-outline. It makes sense to deal with the large houses, like Recreational Equipment and Eastern Mountain Sports, because of their wide selection. When the boots arrive, do as you would with a pair you brought home yourself: test the fit, wear them inside, and send them back for replacement or refund if you aren't satisfied. And don't be satisfied too easily.

Finer points of boots

So much for the basics of boots. The subject doesn't stop there. No kind of gear has quite so many angles, features, and gimmicks to judge and juggle.

In one thing the boot-buyer is fortunate: there seem to be few downright rip-offs in this market. There are flimsy boots at very low prices—and some good boots as well; there are excellent boots that are overpriced; but no specialty store is going to sell you something that will fall apart.

In the store one difference will jump out at you. Some boots have a rough, felt-like surface; others are smooth and shiny. These are called "rough-out" and "smooth-out" surfaces. There is little practical difference between them. Pay no attention to looks—all boots look alike after the first few journeys.

Much more important is the distinction between *top-grain* and *split-grain* leather. The tanned skin of the cow is thicker than it needs to be for boot leather. So, in the factory, it is split, and the layers pulled apart. The outer layer, the layer next to the hair, is rugged, pliable, naturally oily, and sheds water. The lower layers, split-grain leathers, are permeable and not so strong. Most hiking boots are made of top-grain material. Some of the best bargains, however, are lightweight boots of split-grain leathers. Such boots are excellent for trail hiking where water is not a problem. They do stretch and get a lumpy look, and they wear out more quickly than boots of top-grain leather.

There are other differences among leathers. Some pieces are tougher and cost more. Large chunks also cost more. Some boots are made from many pieces of leather and so have many seams; some are made of a single piece, with just one seam. These one-piece boots are the most expensive, the most durable, the easiest to waterproof, and the hardest to break in. Some mountaineers insist on them; backpackers can almost ignore the question.

Most boots have at least some foam padding around the foot, between the main leather wall and a thin inner liner. Padded boots are easy to break in. They are, however, hard to keep dry in wet climates, because the padding soaks up water.

There are several different ways of closing off the spaces between the tongue and the rest of the upper. Unless you hike where it is almost always dry, you should make sure there is *something* there. Often it will be a "bellows" of thin, flexible leather; or it can be two flaps under the tongue which overlap.

Lacing varies, too. There may be grommeted *eyelets*, *D-rings* that rivet onto the leather, or *hooks*. Most often there is some combination. Eyelets break less often than

45

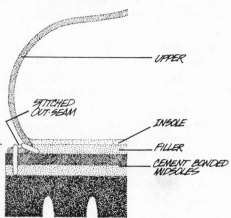

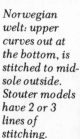

Norwegian welt: upper curves out at the bottom, is stitched to midsole outside. Stouter models have 2 or 3 lines of stitching.

UPPER

STITCHED OUT-SEAM

INSOLE

FILLER

CEMENT BONDED MIDSOLES

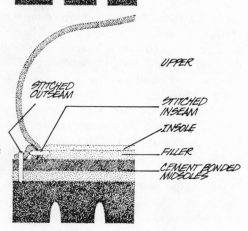

Goodyear welt: upper is stitched to a strip of material which is stitched to midsole.

UPPER

STITCHED OUTSEAM

STITCHED INSEAM

INSOLE

FILLER

CEMENT BONDED MIDSOLES

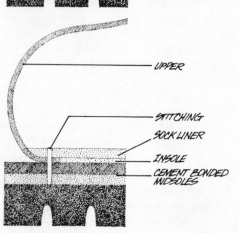

Littleway welt: upper curves inward, is stitched to midsole inside foot compartment. Better boots have double line of stitching.

UPPER

STITCHING

SOCK LINER

INSOLE

CEMENT BONDED MIDSOLES

46

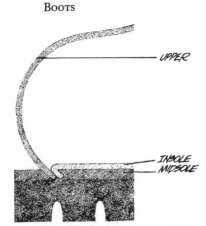

Injection molding: upper penetrates mid-sole and is bonded without stitches.

the others but are a little harder to lace, especially with cold hands. Rings and hooks tend to break off, but any shoemaker can repair them for a small charge. Sometimes, midway in a row of hooks, one pair of normal hooks is replaced by a pair of "clinch hooks" or other devices that grip the laces and prevent them from sliding through. Using these, you can, in theory, tighten the laces firmly on one side of the clinch hook while leaving them loose on the other.

Many heavier boots have leather or plastic collars sewn on around the top of the ankle opening. The idea is to keep the tiny rocks of "scree" from bouncing into your boots. These collars don't seem to accomplish their main purpose very well. The scree collar does have another function, however, at least on a rigid boot: it cushions the sensitive Achilles tendon. (Some boots lack collars but give you some extra padding above the heel.)

In the sole there are more variations. There is one thing that matters considerably: all boots suitable for back-packing have a *midsole*, a separate layer (or layers) between the lug sole and the upper. If the midsole is miss-ing, there is a little cushion between foot and ground, and the boot cannot usually be resoled.

There are four ways in which the upper can be fas-tened to the midsole. When you see visible stitching around this junction, you are looking either at a *Norwegian welt* or at a *Goodyear welt*. If you see more than one row of stitching, or if the boot is an import, you can be sure it is

Norwegian. The Goodyear, used on many American boots, is not so sturdy, but it's acceptable for typical backpacking use. You can recognize this welt by the separate band of leather or plastic that runs around the groove.

If there are no visible stitches around the sole, it may mean that the stitching is inside (the *Littleway* method). There's quite a controversy beween Norwegian and Littleway fans, but both methods, in truth, are good. On some mountaineering boots the absence of visible stitching may indicate that another acceptable process, called *injection molding*, was used. (Again, always make sure there is a midsole.)

Boots which have outside stitching also have a sole that is wider than the upper. Inside-stitched or injection-molded boots are flush with the sole. If you are a rock-climber, the flush edge is useful. If you aren't, don't worry about this; in fact, the wider sole may give better support.

Other types of boots

Alongside the three basic types—smooth-trail boots, rough-country boots, and mountaineering boots—there are perhaps a dozen different kinds of specialized shoes. *Rock-climbing boots* come in various types; they are light, tight, fragile, and generally unsuited for plain walking. *Shoepacs* are high boots with waterproof rubber around the foot and leather rising up the ankle; they are much used for winter travel in the East (see Chapter 23). *Cross-country ski boots*

Shoepac

are just the things—for cross-country skiing. Lighter than the lightest regular hiking boot, they are built to fit onto skis with light, simple three-pin bindings. *Ski mountaineering boots* are heavier models for much more rugged skiing.

Recently the padded, specially constructed *running shoe* has been suggested as an alternative to the standard hiking boot. Some experts contend that these light, flexible shoes are in fact the ideal for trail hiking in a warm climate. They are easier on the feet than "true" hiking boots, and this—so it is argued—is well worth a certain lack of protection. Some hikers, encouraged by such advice, have taken to wearing running shoes even in rugged cross-country travel.

What about socks?

Ask ten people, get ten answers. Most people start by wearing two pairs: a thinnish wool or cotton inner pair (say a medium-weight athletic sock) and a thick wool outer. Then, if they like, they experiment. If you blister easily, try wearing a very thin white sock—as thin as a normal dress sock but *not* made of nylon, which is hot—inside the others. There are many variations, but either they make no difference, or they make a different difference to everyone.

Accessories

There are plenty of extras (aren't there always?) that you can take for your feet. The real necessity is *moleskin* or *molefoam,* sheets of protective padding, sticky on one side, that you can buy in any drugstore. Apply moleskin whenever you suspect you have a blister coming. (Some people find plain adhesive tape works just as well—try both.) A few hikers take *foot powder* to fight both blisters and athlete's foot; a very few take *rubbing alcohol. Soft shoes*—tennis shoes, moccasins, or whatever—are sometimes taken to use around camp: for comfort, of course, but also because they disturb the ground less than Vibram soles. (Light shoes are also sometimes useful for crossing streams.) *Booties* ($11-22) are loose, high-topped slippers stuffed with insulation. Not needed in summer, they can make the difference between achingly cold feet and luxuri-

ously warm ones on a cold winter night. *Spare laces?* Use
your general-purpose cord. *Gaiters* ($6-20) are fabric col-
lars that fasten around the tops of your boots when you
slog through snowbanks or wade through ankle-deep scree.
On muddy trips you may need a wire brush: see below.

Taking care of boots

Any good boot—except a work boot, or the bargain
kind built of split leathers—should last five years or more.
But unless you get the habit of taking care of your boots,
they will fall apart long before they need to.

Leather is a marvelous material. It's like waterfowl
down—nothing we can make works quite as well as the
original. But leather is also fragile. There are three things
in particular that damage it: too much heat, too much
moisture, and too much drying-out. Repeated wetting and
drying is the worst of all.

First treatment

After you choose your boots, be sure to find out
whether they are made of *chrome-tanned* or *oil-tanned*
leather. (The manufacturer's catalog should tell you, if the
salesperson can't. Chrome-tanning is much more common.
"Dry-tanned" and "mineral-tanned" are the same as
"chrome-tanned." "Vegetable-tanned" means that oil was
used.) Neither method is clearly better—there's a debate, of
course—but the differently-tanned leathers must be treated
differently. Oil-tanned boots can be oiled, in moderation;
chrome-tanned boots soften unduly when oiled, and lose
the natural porosity that allows the evaporation of moisture from your feet.

When you get your boots home (and know they are
right for you), give them their first coat of conditioner. If
oil-tanned, rub them thoroughly with a good boot grease
or boot oil. If chrome-tanned, you have a choice of several
waxy compounds, solid or liquid, some of which contain
silicone. If your next trips are to be in summer, especially
in a dry climate, it makes little difference which you use,
and you need not apply the conditioner thickly—its function is to preserve the leather, not to keep the water out.

For winter boots, though, and whenever water repel-
lency is crucial, the best compound is the wax-and-silicone

preparation called Sno-Seal. Sno-Seal (shoestores and specialty shops should have it) comes in two forms: a paste, sold in a round metal can, and a liquid version in a plastic jar. To apply solid Sno-Seal, melt it first, setting the can on the stove in a shallow pan of water. Rub the resulting liquid into the leather with your hands or a rag, scrubbing hard enough to keep the leather warmed by the friction. The sealant must sink right in; the waxy surface film that forms does little good. If you are planning your next trip in rain or snow, better put on several coats.

If you're using Sno-Seal in the ready-made liquid form, the operation is a little simpler, but essentially the same. Rub long. Rub hard.

Both oils and silicone preparations are sometimes accused of damaging the welt and sole of boots to which they are applied. If you're cautious, you can paint the junction of sole and upper with shellac or silicone-free wax. It may be a good idea to coat exposed stitches with epoxy glue. Some hikers apply a clear liquid shoe polish *inside* the boot, especially at the heel, to prevent the deterioration of sweat-soaked inner surfaces.

Breaking in

This is a job you should start right away. The original oil or wax treatment you gave your boots will help soften them. Light and flexible boots, especially those with lots of inside padding, may shape themselves to your feet in a few miles. With heavier boots it will take ten miles for the first stiffness to disappear and fifty miles before the adjustment is complete. Allow several weeks for this. Start with easy walks and short distances. Don't be surprised if you get blisters—better now than later. You may find that you can help tender skin to toughen by massaging it with rubbing alcohol every day; walking barefoot, when you can, also helps. Try leaving the upper hooks or eyelets in the lacing pattern unused for the first miles; this may help to prevent heel blisters. Be sure to have at least ten miles of break-in hiking behind you before you head out on a more considerable journey.

If you don't have time for this method, there are various shortcuts. This one comes most highly recommended: *Fill your boots with hot tap water; empty them immedi-*

ately; then put them on over dry socks and hike until they are dry. Be careful, though: this treatment can give you a crop of blisters, and if you're leaving on a big trip tomorrow, you don't want *that.*

When you first start wearing your boots, make sure that the tongue lies straight under the lacing. If it gets twisted or lopsided at this stage, it will have a tendency to stay that way—forever.

On the trail

As much as you can, keep your boots dry. On some trips, obviously, this is hard. Take them off when you can; keep them under cover at night. When they're seriously wet, the quickest way of drying them is to wipe them inside and then wear them with a pair of dry socks. The foot is a very good heater. In the winter try to keep your damp boots from freezing; often you must take them inside your sleeping bag with you (in a plastic bag).

Don't dry your boots at the edges of a campfire. Don't even leave them in the hot sun any longer than you can help. Leather is tender to heat and ultraviolet—as tender as human skin. Cooked boots fall apart like cooked meat. The uppers can dry out, crack, shrink, and twist; the various layers in the sole can split apart; the seams can fail. Don't chance it.

Don't leave mud caked on a boot. As mud dries, it draws out the natural moisture from leather, and it can damage the glues in the sole. If you plan a muddy trip, it's worth taking a small, stiff wire brush.

Between trips

When you get home, clean your boots thoroughly with a stiff brush, a sponge, and a little cool water. (Saddlesoap is good, used inside and out.) Then let them dry very thoroughly. If the boots are quite wet, or if the air where you store them is very humid, stuff them with newspapers to draw the dampness out. A little Lysol sprinkled inside will keep mildew from forming.

When the boots are dry, give them another rubdown. This time, use wax or silicone compound for both oil-tanned and chrome-tanned models: too much oiling of any boot will soften the leather more than you need or want.

(But note this exception: oil-tanned boots must continue to be oiled if the main object is to keep water out, as in winter camping. Further, you should rub oil into any spot on any boot—oil-tanned or chrome-tanned—that shows signs of drying out and cracking.)

If you will be storing boots for a month or more, it's a good idea to put them in a sealed plastic bag. By inserting a pair of cheap department-store shoetrees—strips of springy metal with knobs on the ends—you can keep the soles from curling. Some people go further and store their boots on rigid ski-boot racks.

Resoling and repairs

A trail hiker doesn't need to have his boots resoled until the rubber lugs are worn almost flat—unless his feet start hurting because of the diminishing cushion of the sole. But don't let the soles wear so thin that the *midsole*—the second layer up—is exposed, or resoling will become much more difficult. A climber, of course, wants his friction and resoles more frequently; so does a winter hiker, who needs every possible millimeter of rubber between his warm foot and the cold snow.

Any boot with a midsole can be resoled. The price is currently $17 to $20—probably less than half the cost of your boot and very much worth it; even the lightest boot is likely to make it through two soles.

Neoprene-rubber lug soles come in many brands; Galibier and Vibram are the most familiar ones, but all are good. They also come in different patterns. Vibram calls its shallow-cleated, softer, thinner sole the *Roccia;* the deeper-cut and harder version is the *Montagna.* Most boots near the light end of the scale come with Roccia soles. It's a well-kept secret, but Vibram also manufactures a *lugless* hard-rubber sole, called the *Silvato.* It has small corrugations, for traction, but no deep-cut teeth. By the time you wear out a set of regular lugs, you'll be in a position to judge how badly you need them; maybe you should ask for a flat Silvato the second time around. If, on the other hand, you have a real need for lugs, you should probably order the Montagna style, or its equivalent in another brand. Thicker soles wear longer, and cost no more.

53

5:
The Pack

THE PACK MAKES THE BACKPACKER. Without it you remain
a hiker, confined to a circle with a car at its center and a
radius as long as you can walk in half a day. But with your
pack on your back, you are a *traveler on foot;* you can go
for a week or longer, and cover, if you wish, several hundred wilderness miles. There is something formal, almost
ceremonial, in the way an experienced packer hoists his
load on the first morning of a trip.

And that moment should be a pleasant one. *A properly
fitted pack is comfortable.* Nobody, on a wilderness trip of
normal length and difficulty, should have to feel like a
pack animal, struggling forward under a painful burden.
While any pack is likely to seem heavy at the end of a long
day, no pack should make you groan sincerely when you
put it on (some people groan for show). If it does, something is wrong. Either you've filled the pack too full, or
you have it wrongly adjusted, or—just possibly—you have
the wrong pack in the first place.

There are hundreds of different models of packs on the

market. New designs are turning up each year. Many are just *summit packs* or *daypacks*—hiker packs built for minor loads. If you take only the bare necessities and strap your sleeping bag on the outside, you *can* make a large daypack do for an easy weekend trip. But sooner or later you will want to put out the money for a full-sized pack, and here the complexities begin.

Buying a full-sized pack

In buying a pack you have to watch out for some inferior products. Packs by "reputable manufacturers" (who's reputable? See *Resources* for a partial listing) are usually well built. The specialty shops, not surprisingly, are your safest source. While sporting goods shops often stock fine brands, they aren't always able to fit you properly, nor can they give you experienced advice. Department stores, with some exceptions, are risky places to purchase a pack. They often carry models which, though they may look quite decent, are actually neither comfortable nor strong: such packs have been known to fail the first time out. You can spot these imitations most easily by their price. No acceptable pack now sells for less than $30, and $50 is a much more typical price. Some large, elaborate designs go for $100 or more. The cheapest packs that are worth buying are marketed by Recreational Equipment, Inc.; J. C. Penney and Sears Roebuck also carry inexpensive but adequate models.

Even among the "reputable" brands, don't *assume* quality. *Look* for it. Sewing, particularly, is not always what it should be. This will be discussed later.

Some people buy their first pack quickly, taking the first model that seems to fit them well. Others like to dwell on the decision. Both methods work, but there is something to be said for going slowly. This is a big purchase, and chances are you'll be traveling with the thing for many years.

Many gear stores have packs for rent. Take advantage of this if you can. Only experimenting on the trail permits you to know for sure what you like best, especially if you are deciding between a soft backpack and a frame pack, or between two sharply different styles of frame. (A typical three-day rental fee is $5.) Check the stores you can reach for the lines they carry; read the catalogs; but trust nothing so much as your own comfort and convenience.

Frame pack or soft backpack?

Modern full-sized backpacks are a genus with two species. First, there are the familiar *frame packs:* large, compartmented packbags attached to rigid frames. Second, and much newer on the scene, are the large *soft backpacks:* these lack any outwardly visible skeletons.

Both types can be traced back to designs in use before World War II. But all the packs of that period had the same fault: they were supported entirely by the shoulders. The upper body carried the whole load. In fact, the upper body is not well-adapted to supporting weight. No pack which hangs off the shoulders, without any other point of support, is comfortable with a load of more than fifteen to twenty pounds; and the packs of that period—compressing the spine and dragging at the back—were uncomfortable indeed by current standards.

The full-size packs developed since World War II solve this problem. They contrive, by one means or another, to shift the pressure down from the weak shoulders to the powerful muscles of the thighs and buttocks.

The frame-style pack was the first to change. Just after the war, two makers—Kelty and Camp Trails—began combining a long, rigid packframe with a weight-supporting *hip belt.* This was the key. When a load is carried on a frame thus equipped, the weight bears down on the frame, and via the hip belt, on the lower body. The shoulders take only a small share of the burden. More than any other factor, this innovation made wilderness hiking infinitely more pleasant, and the wilderness a place where almost anyone could go. For twenty years and more, the belted frame pack was absolutely standard on the trails.

But that is no longer the case, for the design of packs without external frames has been advancing as well. Many, now, are made so that they divide the load between shoulders and hips, as frames do. And quite a few of these well-designed soft backpacks are comfortable enough to give the frames some competition.

What are the practical differences?

Frames are completely or almost completely rigid.

They tend to bounce and swing whenever the wearer makes a quick motion. Soft packs ride closer to the body and flex somewhat as you move. They don't lurch so much on your shoulders when you swing around a corner, jump down from a log, or stumble on rough ground; so they have special advantages for travel off the trail. On the other hand, frame packs generally hold more gear. And they have a considerable advantage in warm weather: standing well out from the back, except at the points of the support, they give sweat plenty of chance to evaporate. Soft packs, pressing closer to the body, can make you feel hot and sticky on a summer day.

What about the essential thing, comfort under a load? There is plenty of disagreement here, but the slowly-emerging consensus would seem to be this: soft packs are excellent for light or average loads but don't handle over-loads as well as do the frames.

You might summarize the pros and cons like this:

• If you expect to carry loads of a fifth of your body weight or less on most of your trips, and if you plan to do most of your hiking on plain trails, as most people do, then either a soft pack or a frame pack makes sense. Personal preference must decide. All you can do is rent each kind for a trial and trust your experience.

• If you plan to carry much heavier loads quite often, on these same trails, you will probably find a frame pack more comfortable than a soft pack.

• If you plan to spend much time *off* the trail, going cross-country, especially over rugged ground; if you want to use the pack for scrambling or for climbing; or if you want a pack that you can carry when skiing, the choice is clear: the soft pack, with its flexibility and closer fit, is almost certainly for you. For snowshoeing, too, a soft pack is preferable, though a frame can be used.

• Yet even to this there is an exception. People who carry *very* large loads, say fifty pounds and over, often prefer frames even off the trails. Despite the incessant lurching of a rigid pack during rough travel, some find the weight easier to handle that way. (Other packers disagree.) If you plan to carry loads on this order, rent the alternatives, then decide.

The frame pack

The frame pack has three parts. First is the frame itself, a framework of metal tubing commonly shaped like an H with several crossbars. (Sometimes the H is closed off at top or bottom or both.) Second, wide supporting straps over the shoulders and around the waist carry the weight and steady the load. Finally, the packbag—tall, flat, and box-like—is attached to the frame, generally by metal pins. You almost always buy frame and packbag as a unit; you can't ordinarily mix and match different brands. But shoulder straps and waistbelts can be exchanged.

Most frames have a slight double curve to match the shape of the spine. Sometimes the tubing is aluminum, sometimes an alloy of magnesium. Very recently, frames of molded plastic have been introduced. Joints are sometimes fused, sometimes mechanical. Quite a few models are built to be adjustable for different wearers. Both plastic and adjustable models are somewhat less rigid than the other types.

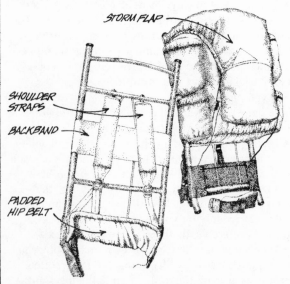

STORM FLAP

SHOULDER STRAPS

BACKBAND

PADDED HIP BELT

If you'd like to hear the arguments for all these variations, ask a salesperson or consult the catalogs.

When you wear a properly-fitted frame, none of the tubing touches your body. The three parts of the pack that actually touch you are the shoulder straps, the hip belt, and the backbands.

Shoulder straps typically attach to the frame near the top, on one of the upper cross-bars. They then diverge to pass over the shoulders and run down the sides of the body to attach at the two lower points of the H of the frame. A buckle in front of the shoulder adjusts them for length. They are padded where they rest on your skin.

The hip belt—it should be a single band of tough cotton or nylon—attaches at those same two points, the bottom tips of the H, and runs around the waist, buckling securely at the front. Some belts are padded, some aren't—experiment to find out which you like best (plain belts $2.50, padded belts under $10).

When a frame pack is properly worn, the two shoulder straps may do little more than hold the pack upright and steady on your back. (To convince yourself of this, try on a loaded frame pack with the hip belt cinched up tight; then unbuckle the belt so that all the load comes onto the shoulder straps. You'll instantly feel the backward-and-downward drag.)

Across the frame are stretched one or two fabric backbands, the points at which the pack rests against your back. There is usually one backband just above the small of the back, a second just below. Some are of solid nylon or cotton; some of stout mesh; a few are padded. There is usually an adjustment—a metal turnbuckle or just criss-crossed cords—so that each backband can be tightened as it begins to stretch, or loosened for sliding to a more comfortable position. (On some packs the bands cannot be shifted, which makes fit especially important.) Solid fabric backbands do trap sweat, so extra wide ones don't make much sense, unless they are made of open net.

The wrap-around version

Five companies are now marketing a variation of the standard H-shaped frame. In these models the frame curves sharply forward at the bottom, so that the two vertical tubes end right beside the hipbones (rather than on your back well behind the hip). Or else the frame sprouts metal extensions forward. Either way the point is the same: the shoulder straps and the hip belt attach to the frame much farther forward than with the standard H. The idea is to bring a still larger proportion of the total load onto the hips, leaving still less hanging from the shoulders.

Does it work? Some users are enthusiastic, others unimpressed. One frequently-voiced opinion is that wrap-around packs may make light weights more comfortable, but they do little good with very heavy loads. Indeed, some say that heavy loads ride *better* on the standard frame. The new design does have some interesting features. Wrap-around packs will stand up by themselves (if you set them on flat ground). If you sit down wearing one, the hip belt won't jerk up out of place, as always happens with a standard frame.

More important, these packs don't seem to lurch so much on a rough trail. But some wearers complain that they feel overbalanced by the load whenever they head steeply up or down.

Several things are clear. First, the new design works best for people with broad hips. Second, with such a pack you must pay careful attention to finding the right fit— there is little margin of error regarding comfort. Third, if you are interested in the design, you should definitely rent at least one wrap-around model before you buy. These packs, definitely very right for some people, are very wrong for others.

The packbag

You wouldn't think there could be so many different ways to build a bag to haul a few pounds of gear in. Shape, size, fabric, zippers, compartments, closures, features: the list goes on and on. Fortunately, only a few of these distinctions matter all that much. It comes down to personal preference, convenience, and even to style.

Most packbags are made of a smooth, tightly-woven nylon duck. (Cotton is okay too. It's cheaper but heavier and less resistant to water.) Others have a rougher nylon called "cordura." Cordura is very handsome, but its loose weave makes it somewhat liable to catch and tear on anything sharp—something to consider in cross-country travel. Almost all manufacturers now make their bags with water-proofed fabric. You can recognize it by the glossy inner surface. Waterproofing, by itself, won't keep your gear dry in wet snow or heavy rain, but every little bit helps. (For really wet conditions, a waterproof pack cover is essential.)

How *big* a packbag do you need? Full-size bags vary from under 2,000 cubic inches capacity to more than 6,000 cubic inches, though the really big bags fit only on long frames worn by long people. For comparison, a standard brown supermarket bag holds about 1,400 cubic inches.

For summer trips of a week or less, the smaller pack-bags should do fine. A small load rides more neatly in a small bag than in a big one. (The sleeping bag, remember, is generally strapped on outside.) Most wilderness trips are quite short—a few days, a few miles. You don't have to have a warehouse on your back.

For very long trips; for remote climbing trips; and for winter trips of more than a few days, even very large packs can become astonishingly full. But packs with a capacity of more than 5,000 cubic inches are really meant for expeditions, and most backpackers who buy them are spending too much money for too much pack.

Most packbags are *three-quarter length*—shorter than the frames on which they are mounted. The sleeping bag, stuffed in a storage sack and strapped to the lower cross-bars of the frame, fills the remaining space. Some bags are so designed that you can shift the bag up or down to change the center of gravity (a high-riding load is best for trail travel, a low center of gravity helps in cross-country scrambling).

How is the packbag *divided*? In the commonest design there is a large upper compartment, held open at the top by a light metal frame. A long fabric *storm flap* pulls over the top opening and part way down over the front of the pack (that is, down the side away from your back). Underneath this top compartment there is commonly a smaller bottom chamber, with a zipper. Then there are zippered outside pockets, at least two, one on each side of the pack, and often many more (the more, the handier: it's a nuisance to have to dig too deep into the pack for things you need during the hiking day).

There are endless variations on this simple design. Some bags aren't divided inside but have a single deep compartment. This is less convenient for getting at things, easier for packing bulky or odd-shaped items. One model

61

has a zip-out divider so that you can have it either way. Several have sewn-in dividers but leave corner gaps so you can stick long objects down through. One model has four horizontal compartments, like floors in a building, each opened by a zipper.

Zippers, these days, are mostly made of hard nylon. Often they run straight across the tops of the compartments they open (you still have a usable space if a zipper breaks). But on some packs the zippers are vertical or arc-shaped; they're easier to pack and unpack. On some models the whole front of the pack zips out, so that you can pack it like a suitcase. There's no advice to give but this: suit yourself.

Fitting a frame pack

A pack, like a pair of boots, must fit you. Fortunately, by comparison with the problems of fitting boots, the fitting of a pack is easy. The key thing is the length of the frame. Some models adjust, but most come in three or four sizes to match the body length from shoulder to waist. A salesperson can help you locate the right size and make

Correct fitting of frame pack:
shoulder straps rise over
shoulders, hip belt rides on hip bone

obvious adjustments to the hip belt and shoulder straps. Next, load the pack with not less than thirty pounds. Most stores offer you sandbags or climbing ropes, but some sources claim that only a realistic packload, with both heavy items and light bulky ones, really shows you how the pack will ride.

Get the pack on your back and tighten the hip belt firmly. It should lie just below the upper edge of the hipbone, and the lower of the two backbands (if there is one) should fit snugly just beneath the small of your back. As you tighten the hip belt, the whole pack should shift upward on your back so that the shoulder straps actually *rise* just slightly from your shoulders. You'll feel the weight come onto your waist. If this doesn't happen, the pack is probably too short for you.

Next, tighten or loosen the shoulder straps to make them firm but not tight—you should be able to slide a couple of fingers between the strap and your shoulder with no trouble. Then take an indoor hike with your load. Climb stairs, bend, sit down, stride. Make sure that the hip belt is comfortable and that it shows no sign of slipping up or down from its proper position (except when you sit). Satisfy yourself that the metal tubing of the frame doesn't touch your back at any point. Check that the buckles on the shoulder straps don't slip (on some cheap models they may). The waistbelt closure—there are several types—must also grip very securely. If it seems inclined to loosen in the store, it will be far worse on the trail.

What about fitting one of those wrap-around packs? The tests are much the same (though there's no lower backband). You must make very sure that the hip belt stays in place. If it has any tendency to slip up into the hollow of the waist or down much below the point of the hip, reject the pack. People with narrow hips often find they cannot wear packs of this design.

Checking for quality

There are several things you should take time to look for, even in the best of the packs. You can always get a bad specimen of a generally reputable brand. And it is rare to see a pack that is nicely built in every important detail.

What about the frame? Some frames are built so

strongly that you could use them for ladders. For normal purposes you don't need such high technology, and most frames, except the suspiciously cheap ones, are strong enough. If you want to check, set the pack up with one "foot" on the floor, one raised, and press down from the upper opposite corner. This crosswise pressure catches the frame at its weakest. Don't overdo it, or you might damage a weak frame. If you see the frame even beginning to distort under the pressure, let up quickly, and find another store.

Packbags can be attached to their frames in several ways. Most commonly you see stout metal pegs poking through holes in the metal and through grommets in the packbag. These "clevis pins" are held in place by metal lock-rings. Some packs clip on with fabric tabs. Tabs should be reinforced, grommets stout. There should be at least three such points of attachment on each side.

Feel the padded parts of the shoulder straps. The pads should be firm, almost hard, not soft and compressible.

Frankly, it seems to be hard to find a packbag that is as well-sewn as it should be. Prestige is no guarantee, though some brands are more consistent than others. The stitches should be small and numerous, not widely spaced. The rows should be straight and neat, and if you see much double or triple stitching, you've got a prize. Look at the end of each line of stitches. It should be bar-tacked—the line should finish in a dense bar of stitches one almost on top of another. If there's no bar-tacking at all, seams may begin to unravel as soon as you leave the store. Examine carefully the sewing at the bottom of the pack and on and around the pockets. In the very best packs there will be multiple stitching and perhaps an extra layer of fabric at places which take special stress, like the "root" of the storm flap and the ends of zippers.

If you find all that, you're in luck.

The soft pack: general

Soft packs vary more than frame packs. Here we deal with several basic designs, not just one. The packs that are suitable for basic backpacking, though, have this in common: they contrive, by one means or another, to put most of the weight on the hips, as a frame does.

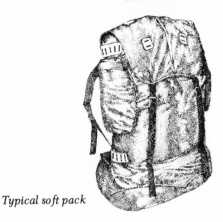

Typical soft pack

To do that, a pack must have a waistbelt, and it must be fairly rigid. Most soft packs use internal supports of some kind: flexible metal bars, molded plastic shells, and the like. One of the most interesting designs uses no such stays at all. Rather, the load itself—packed carefully and firmly in two side-by-side vertical compartments—becomes the rigid "frame." The sleeping bag is stuffed balloon-tight into a wrap-around bottom compartment with a belt and buckle at the front.

The various designs have selling points too complex to go into here. If you buy the double-tube-and-wrap-around style, you need to make sure that your sleeping bag can actually be stuffed into the bottom compartment. Some variants of the design give you more room than others; a really bulky bag, especially with synthetic filler (see Chapter 6), will be hard to cram into any of them.

Soft packs tend to be smaller than frame packs, but several have enough volume for frame-sized loads (soft packs are often used in winter mountaineering, which requires voluminous gear). If you aren't sure a pack has a big enough capacity for you, try to rent it, or at least something of similar size, before you make up your mind to buy.

Most soft packs have just one big compartment. Some open at the top, with a zipper or drawstrings and straps. On others the whole front of the pack unzips for easy loading. Some models have several outside pockets—always useful. Side pockets may be detachable. There may or may not be "ski sleeves" down each side to hold your skis or anything long and thin. The variations (and the discussions concerning them) go on and on.

Fitting

Some soft packs come in just one size but offer several adjustments. Others come in several sizes with fewer movable buckles and straps. Whatever is most comfortable for you is, of course, the right thing, but the simpler the design you choose, the fewer things there are to go wrong.

To test the fit, do about as you would with a frame pack. Get a salesperson's help in locating the closest size or making the main adjustment. Load the pack heavily and get it on your back. The hip belt, as with any pack, should ride just under the point of the hipbone. Tighten the belt firmly; then lengthen or shorten the shoulder straps to put

Hiker wearing soft pack

most of the weight on the belt while still holding the pack firm. (The closer it rides, the less it will drag your shoulders backwards.)

Most soft packs have special lift straps. These connect the main shoulder straps to the top edge of the pack. As you tighten the lift straps, they raise the shoulder straps and help shift the weight to the hips. On one-size-fits-all packs, the shoulder straps converge on an anchor (perhaps an adjustable metal bar) which you can slide up or down to suit the length of your torso. The more adjustments your model allows, the longer you need to spend working out the arrangement most comfortable for you.

When you have the right combination, the hip belt should be snug and firm; the shoulder straps should be high enough so that one shoulder can droop without the pack swinging off on that side; and the weight should distinctly be coming to bear on your lower body. When in doubt between sizes, go to the larger one.

The points of weakness

In a soft pack, waist and shoulder straps must attach directly to the pack bag, and these attachments are crucial. Sometimes the straps are sewn in place; sometimes they are held in place by pins that penetrate the packbag and attach to the internal frame. If the straps are sewn on, look for double and triple stitching and strong bar-tacking— several inches of the strap should be sewn down. Look for leather pads, rivets, extra fabric, or other reinforcements at these critical points. Get the store to tell you about the strap attachments on the packs it carries.

What about daypacks?

Long before you buy a full-sized pack, you will need a *daypack*—a small, uncomplicated rucksack just big enough to carry a lunch, a camera, a canteen, and the essential safety items you should never leave behind (see list, Chapter 15). You use such a pack, of course, for trips near home but also on long wilderness trips if you want to be able to shuck your main pack and take off on a side excursion.

The purchase of a daypack is easy. There are, of course, competing brands and features, but, when you get right down to it, a daypack is too simple a thing to argue about. A tough fabric bag and a couple of wide shoulder straps, and you've got it. The basic daypack should weigh no more than a pound, cost no more than $20, and handle loads up to about 20 pounds.

The packbag can be of nylon or cotton (the nylon is usually waterproof). Some bags open and close with zippers, variously placed; others use straps. Some have outside pockets, others don't. A useful daypack will be not less than twelve inches wide, not less than a foot deep, and perhaps six inches thick. Since a loosely loaded bag fits more comfortably to the back than one stuffed to the limit, be generous. And please note: a "summit pack" for climbing must be much larger than a pack for simple day-hikes; many packs sold as summit packs are far too small to carry the gear that a safe climb requires.

The shoulder straps should have buckles for adjustment, and they should be wide enough not to cut into your flesh when the pack is heavily loaded. (Some packs use padded straps.) You will sometimes find a stabilizing strap that buckles across the chest to keep the load from bouncing on your back. Whatever the variation, look for good sewing and reinforcement where the straps are sewn to the packbag.

Not all daypacks ride on the back. There's also the *fanny pack*, really a big belt with a pouch in the back. Skiers prefer them to shoulder packs on short trips because they don't bounce so much. A daypack can also serve as a backpack for a child. For more on baby-carriers and small packs for kids, see Chapter 24.

For somewhat heavier loads there are *framed rucksacks;* these are more elaborate and expensive than daypacks and have rigid internal supports. They handle big loads better than simple daypacks, but not nearly so well as the full-sized packs which shift the weight to the hips. Except for certain special uses, the old-style framed rucksack is now a design to avoid.

Accessories

If you buy a frame with a small packbag, or any but the largest of the soft packs, you may find yourself cramped for space if you take a trip of unusual length. But many things can be done to make a smallish pack carry a big load.

To a frame pack you can add a *frame extension:* a U of metal tubing which rounds off the top of the original H to give you more stowing room. You can tie objects to the tubing, or store them under the stormflap, supported by the extension. The price is about $3.50.

Then there are *tie-on patches,* squares of thick leather with two slits (about $1 each at gear stores). You sew these to the pack wherever you need an attachment; then, running thin nylon webbing through the slits, you can fasten objects securely. (You can do your own stitching with an awl, but a shoemaker does a much neater job for about 50¢ a patch.) Whenever objects have to be tied on, elastic *shock cords* are invaluable. Extra *pack pockets* can also be purchased and sewn on.

For hiking in extended rain or in long, wet snowstorms, you will just about have to have a waterproof *pack cover* ($10); for short summer storms, a multi-purpose poncho will serve nicely ($13 to $30). Pack covers are simple nylon shells that snap on over the pack. Once on, they're a nuisance because they block access to the outer pockets, but items inside stay dry. Wet-weather hikers may also paint *seam sealant* on the seams of their packbags—water gets in at these points no matter how waterproof the cloth. Then there's the old-timer who packs every item of gear in a plastic bag, inside his otherwise unprotected packbag, and troubles himself no further.

Bags and carriers

After the main pack itself, the most common gear containers are cloth stuffbags and plastic bags in various sizes. Take plenty of the latter, especially where it's wet.

A useful accessory is the *beltbag,* a rectangular cloth pouch with a zipper that rides on the belt. You can use it for ski waxes; for film and small camera accessories; for pencil and paper; for lunch; for anything you need close at hand, and don't want to shift from pocket to pocket every time you add or subtract a layer of clothing. Beltbags run $2 to $5. Then there's the belt-hung *bottle carrier,* $2 to $3, which turns any water bottle into an accessible canteen.

If you carry a camera, you may want a set of elastic slings to hold it steady and accessible against your chest. There are several sorts available at camera shops and some gear stores ($9 to $10)—or you can rig your own, if you are ingenious, with shock cord and webbing. None of the commercial ones seem to hold the camera as firmly as one would like.

Packs and low impact: the question of color

When you buy your pack, you encounter the troublesome question of *color*. Wilderness gear is sold today in every shade, bright or subdued: various blues; reds and yellows and explosive iridescent oranges; leaf-greens and olive-greens, rust-browns and earth-browns and compound colors in between. Color is part of the pleasure of handling good gear, and one of the things that gives a stack of fine equipment that curiously *valuable* look.

But there's more than personal taste to consider when you choose a color. There's a question of impact as well. Simply put, do you want to stand out or blend in? Unless you're hiking in the eastern woodlands in October, a bright pack makes you highly visible. Indeed, it makes you *too* visible: the more fellow hikers you see and are seen by, the more crowded the wilderness landscape must appear. This is a problem everywhere but doubly so above timberline. A dozen hikers in an alpine basin, carrying gear in muted colors, may give you no hint of their presence—three with packs in "international orange" can make the same place seem busy. For low impact, then, you choose the soft shades; you choose to blend in.

There is a counterargument, however, and that is safety. Maybe you do a lot of traveling in popular hunting areas at just the wrong time of year and *want* to be seen. Or maybe you're thinking about a time when you could conceivably need to be rescued. Standing out as it does, bright gear can draw searchers to a lost or injured hiker, especially if the search is from the air.

Every backpacker must find his own balance between arguments of safety and the pleasures of unobtrusiveness. If you're very concerned about the rescue angle, I would suggest this compromise: carry something brightly colored in your pack—raingear, perhaps, or a ground cloth. This you can spread on the ground, or drape on your pack, whenever you need to be seen. But a pack made of a vivid fabric is like a light you can never turn off.

6:
The Bedroll

Mummy-style sleeping bag

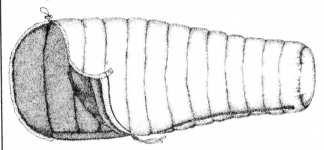

Boots and packs, Lord knows, are expensive enough these days. But the chances are good that pack and boots together will cost you little more than your third major purchase: your sleeping bag.

How do you set about choosing the right bag? Once more, as with every major item of gear, there are certain distinct questions to ask yourself. In buying a sleeping bag, you need to know *how warm* a bag you need; *what kind of insulating material* you want in it; and *what shape and design* are best suited to your use. Then there are certain features you should look for in any bag.

How much bag do you need?

First things first. How cold will it get where you plan to go? People tend to buy heavier and costlier models than they actually need. The bag you choose should be about right for the temperatures you expect to encounter frequently during the next few years. Don't think in terms of an eventual dream trip to Alaska. Don't even buy for the coldest possible night in the place and season you will visit; rather, think of a night somewhat below the average. You can make a light bag do very nicely for the occasional chill- ier time, and you won't be carrying needless weight when it's warm.

On summer trips you are unlikely to see many nights below freezing, even in the high country, and in some regions summer nights are in the 50s and above. Even three-season backpacking—spring, summer, and fall—is unlikely to take you much below the 20s. If you have an idea where you will go most often—New England moun- tains, say, or the central Rockies, or the Sierra—you might check trail guidebooks or talk to experienced hikers about the conditions they have found.

How warm-blooded are you? People vary a good deal. Some are obvious cold-sleepers—they shiver in sleeping bags that look like they belong on the Greenland ice. Oth- ers find it unusually easy to keep warm. It depends pretty much on your metabolic rate. This is one of several good reasons for renting sleeping bags before you buy—you learn how cold-proof you actually are, how you compare with the "typical" sleeper that the gear catalogs are always talking about.

There are several different species of bags to choose from. Department stores everywhere sell rectangular bags that look like thick zippered blankets. They have quilted seams and use cheap synthetics for fill. These bags are inexpensive—down to a very few dollars—but they are too cool for most wilderness camping and too heavy and bulky to tote far.

Next up in warmth are the well-made *summer sleeping bags* sold in most gear shops ($50 to $60). These bags, usu- ally filled with good down, are built in the simplest way, with sewn-through seams. The effect is something like so many pillows sewn together at the edges. Such a bag will keep you warm in nights as cool as 40 degrees—maybe down to freezing if you wear all your clothes to bed. That's all you need for the Southeast in the warm half of the year or for the low-lying deserts, except in winter. For such conditions, the light sewn-through bag is not just ade- quate—it is perfect. A shade heavier for the warmth, but less expensive, are summer bags filled with one of the acceptable synthetic insulators (see *What kind of insulation?* below).

Most hikers, though, will be out in a good many nights that are colder than 40 degrees. For this majority the medium-weight *three-season bag* is the necessity. Such bags have no sewn-through seams; there is insulation all around you. No three-season bag needs more than two pounds of fill if the filler is waterfowl down, nor much over three pounds if good synthetic filler is used. A three-season down bag will weigh up to about four pounds total, a synthetic-filled model as much as five and a half pounds. Prices range between $60 and $120, depending chiefly on the material used. As the amount of fill increases, three-season bags grade into *winter* sleeping bags, marvelous constructions intended only for conditions down toward zero, and below.

How can you tell how warm a given bag will keep you? The answer is not so simple as you might expect. How warm you are on a particular night depends on half a dozen things: the padding under you, the wind, humidity, protection from the open sky, how much you ate for dinner, and of course your own warm-bloodedness. Even if we forget all these variations and speak of an "average" sleeper in "ideal" conditions, it can be hard to judge the insulating power of a bag.

You have three things to go by: temperature ratings, weight and kind of fill, and, third and most important, *loft.* Manufacturers and salespeople make predictions for their bags: this one is supposed to be comfortable to freezing, that one perhaps to ten degrees above zero. The better makers are cautious, afraid to claim too much. But there is no agreed-on standard, and other companies, less conscientious, make claims that are way out of line. No guarantee is ever implied.

Every sleeping bag has a fabric tag attached. It tells you the total weight of the bag, the type of filler, and the weight of fill. Now if the same material is used in bags of the same design, more fill means a warmer bag. But seldom is the comparison so simple. More often you are looking at bags of different shapes filled with different substances, or with down of different grades (some insulate twice as well as others). So weight is not the key.

The thing that counts is *loft*. Loft is the height to which a sleeping bag puffs up when it is nicely shaken out. Loft is insulation. Loft is warmth. Loft is what gets between you and the night. And loft is rather easily measured. Manufacturers almost always give loft figures for their bags, so you might think it simple enough to judge and compare warmth.

But even this, the essence of the matter, is not so clear as it might be. When the makers measure loft, they do it in somewhat different ways. Some, for instance, put a slight weight on the bag—most do not. Also, a particular copy of a given model may be plumper or thinner than the average. All this means that you can't just line up official loft figures and know for sure that the seven-inch lofting bag is warmer than the six-inch version.

To cut through the confusion you can measure the loft, in a rough-and-ready fashion, yourself. Here's how to do it. If you've just pulled the bag out of a stuffsack, take hold of it at the head end and shake it gently several times to get air into it. Lay it down for a few minutes; then shake it again. But if the bag has been on display for days, lie down on it first, for several minutes, before you shake it out (display bags may show more loft than you'll ever get in the field).

After the second shaking, stretch the bag out once more. Wait another several minutes; then take an ordinary ruler and read off the height of the top of the bag above the floor. Take the reading about where the sleeper's chest would be. Bags are a little thinner at the edges, so you may have to press a little, indenting the side with the ruler, to get a good result.

This method, frankly, is none too precise. One could wish for a reliable industry standard. But many manufacturers actually get their own loft readings in just this unsophisticated way, and by doing it yourself you can cancel out any differences in their procedures.

Now that you have a measurement, what do you make of it? How do you translate from loft to warmth? Formulas vary—they vary a lot—but a typical scale runs something like this:

- four inches of loft will do at 40 degrees.
- six inches will keep you warm down to about 20.

Table of loft and warmth

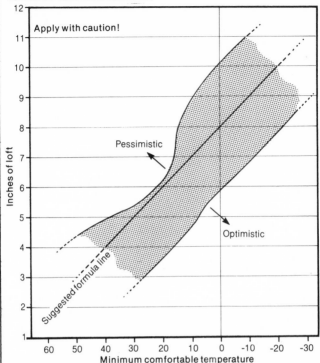

Apply with caution!

Shaded band shows varying estimates of warmth provided by a given amount of loft

- eight inches will do to about zero.
- and ten inches—almost the most you can buy—will carry you down to -20, or even lower.

Such a scale is nothing but an indication. It assumes, among other things, that the sleeper is protected from the wind. And it ignores individual differences. Your comfort is the only accurate measure. Each time you rent a sleeping bag—and you should try several—make a note of its loft and of the temperatures you encounter. When you find out how comfortable you are in a particular bag on a particular night, you will have more than theory to go on. And you can extrapolate: each added inch of loft will give you comfort on a night about ten degrees colder.

Total loft vs. top-half loft. When you lie on a sleeping

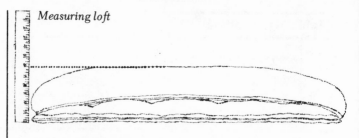

Measuring loft

bag, your weight compresses the part beneath you and destroys much of its insulating power. (You will need a foam pad under you, anyway.) Thus the truest measure of warmth is the loft in just the *upper half* of the sleeping bag—the part between the sleeper and the sky. Why bring up this extra complication? Because this upper loft is not necessarily 50 percent of the total loft. Some bags are built with more than half of the total fill in the upper half of the bag, and they may be warmer than you'd guess from a casual look. A catalog, or a salesperson, can tell you which these are. (Some outfits, incidentally, have begun to provide figures on top-half loft: a good trend.)

What kind of insulation?

What is it that keeps you warm? Your own body heat, of course, trapped by the material around you. Anything that traps dead air will hold warmth in, and the thicker the barrier, the less heat will escape. Thus the importance of insulation thickness: loft. There is no special magic in any particular substance—even steel wool would be fine— except that some materials give you much more loft for much less weight than others.

In fact, there are now just four fillers which are light enough, and lofty enough, to be of use in wilderness sleeping bags. These are *goose down, duck down*, a synthetic fiber called *Polarguard*, and another synthetic called *Hollofil II*.

Down is still clearly the standard. Nothing else gives so much warmth for such little weight. Nothing else compresses into such a tiny volume. Nothing else lasts so long.

Originally, all the best sleeping bags were filled with down from geese, not ducks. But two things have happened to change that. First, the price of goose down has risen hugely. Second, the quality has dropped, and the very best is simply not to be found these days at any price. Thus the down from ducks, once rightly called inferior, becomes competitive. Some manufacturers now use duck down exclusively, and though others still advertise goose down as if it were the magical secret ingredient, it is probably not worth the $10 or $20 extra you will pay. (Three-season goose-down bags are currently selling for $110 and more.)

What counts, of course, is the down's ability to loft. Both goose down and duck down can be good or bad. "Lofting power" can be measured precisely in cubic inches filled by a single ounce of fluffed-up down, but you are not likely to be given these figures, and measurement procedures are regrettably far from standard. (Just for reference, however, 550 cubic inches per ounce is called "good" these days, and anything much over that is premium.) The color of the down doesn't matter. Neither do the high-sounding names that makers sometimes give to the down they use: "AAA prime northern" or what have you.

When we look at the synthetic fillers, the picture is much simpler. These are laboratory products and don't vary. The warmth of a bag depends simply on design and the amount of fill. Unfortunately, even poor-to-fair down is warmer for its weight than the synthetics. It takes nearly twice as much synthetic filler to do the work of a given amount of down. The synthetic bags are not only heavier but also clumsier—they won't compress as well.

They have, however, two strong selling points. First, they are cheaper (though the gap is closing). Second— and this is the telling thing—synthetic bags are safer when it's wet and cold. It would be difficult to overstate how important this can be.

Down—any kind of down—soaks up water and loses nearly all its loft when it gets wet. A waterlogged down bag is not just a nuisance, it is a horror. Anyone who has ever spent a night in a wet snowstorm, two days walk from a roadhead, with $120 worth of wringing-wet goose down, can make the case for a synthetic bag. A synthetic bag loses only a small part of its loft and warmth when it gets wet. You can squeeze it out like a sponge and dry it completely, out in the wind, in half an hour.

So don't reject the synthetic bags too quickly. If you spend a lot of hiking time in rainy country, in soggy snowstorms, or where the air is very humid, the imitations of down, inferior in so many ways, may nonetheless be exactly right for you. In fact, it is not hard to imagine a situation in which a synthetic bag could save your life.

You'll find synthetic fills in many bags, including the rectangular quilted bags that hang in drugstores. But only two of these materials, as yet, are usable in lightweight gear. Dupont makes Hollofil II, masses of short fibers; PolarGuard is a continuous filament spun like cotton candy. Each has advantages, but on balance there seems to be no strong case for preferring one over the other.

Efficiency and total bag weight

There is more than one reason for measuring loft. Even if you don't require the greatest warmth, you can use loft and bag weight to answer another important question about a bag: how *efficient* is it? The more inches of loft you get per pound of total weight, the closer you are to the "ideal" sleeping bag—provided that weight hasn't been saved by the use of flimsy materials.

When is a bag "efficient"? A down-filled bag is adequate if it gives you more than an inch and a half of loft per pound of total weight (counting also the weight of the sack in which the bag is to be stuffed). Three-season bags in the close-fitting mummy style often do much better, giving as much as two inches of loft per pound or even more. Semi-rectangular bags never do quite so well as that and neither do the heavier bags intended for bitter winter conditions. Synthetic bags, of course, take a great deal more to do less: they range between about one inch and an inch and a half of loft per pound of total weight.

The typical three-season down bag weighs something between three and four pounds, lofts to between six and seven inches, and contains less than two pounds of fill. It should be comfortable to 15 or 20 degrees. A well-made synthetic bag in the same range will weigh something between four and a half and five and a half pounds. So the penalty, compared to down, is about one pound, or at the most, two. The difference is real but not backbreaking, and you do save money.

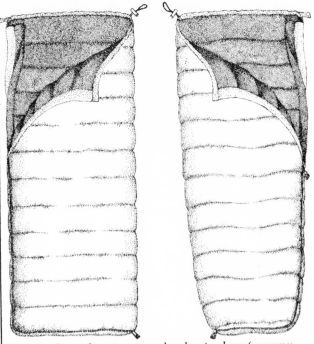

Rectangular and semi-rectangular sleeping bags (mummy-style shown at beginning of chapter)

Design and construction

When you know how much loft you need, and what kind of filler you prefer, you are halfway along toward buying the right bag. What's left to consider is size, shape, design, and the finer points that show that a good job was done.

Shape. The standard is the mummy bag, a close-cut design that is wide at the shoulders but narrows with the body to the toes. The snuggest mummies are more like sleeping garments than portable beds; when you roll, they roll with you. Mummies give the greatest warmth for the least fill. At the head there is typically a hood that can be closed around the face to leave only the tiniest of openings.

Some people find mummies too confining. There are many designs on the market that give you more room: modified mummies with and without hoods; barrel-shaped bags; semi-rectangular and fully rectangular models. In

79

general, it's good to pick the narrowest bag you find comfortable. The wider the bag, the more weight it takes to give the same uniform loft.

There is this to be said, however, for a looser fit: it allows you to take things inside with you. In winter camping water bottles, boots, and cameras may freeze if they're not kept next to your body at night. Also, you can insert a small, inexpensive *inner bag* into a loose outer bag for an occasional trip into really cold country.

Length. Most models come in two sizes: regular, for people up to six feet, and large. When you lie in the bag with the hood (if there is one) tightened over your face, you should be able to stretch your neck and point your toes. When in doubt, it's probably better to take the longer size, despite the penalty in weight. Greater length also gives you more room for boots and such on a cold night.

Shells. The inner and outer shells are usually made of a densely-woven nylon fabric. Since body moisture must be able to evaporate out of the bag, conventional waterproof fabrics are not used; but Gore-Tex, the recently-developed waterproof fabric that "breathes," is now appearing in sleeping bag shells. If the fill is down, the cloth must be woven very densely, or down particles will work their way out between threads. (To check, take a fold of the shell in your fingers and try to blow through it. If you feel your breath on the other side, the fabric is too coarse.) A few bits of down always escape from a new bag, especially at the seams—there's no cause for alarm unless it continues.

Baffles. Synthetic fills come in battings that are sewn firmly in place, but in a down bag the filler is loose. There must be internal walls, called baffles, to keep the down from shifting and opening up cold spots. These walls run horizontally around the bag, leaving the outside seams that give all down bags that familiar segmented look. In *square-box baffling*, now rarely used, the internal walls make right angles with the shell. More often the walls are slanted, and designers prefer this *slant-box* baffling, saying it allows fewer cold spots.

A third design adds more walls and makes small triangular compartments. This *overlapping V-tube* construction is good, because it makes down shift almost impossible, and bad, because of extra weight and expense.

Methods of sleeping bag construction

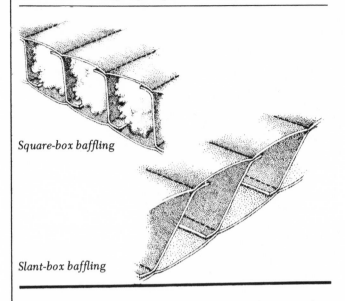

Square-box baffling

Slant-box baffling

In most down bags there is a *channel block*. It runs the length of the bag, on the side opposite the zipper, and prevents down from shifting from the top to the underside of the bag. Some makers leave out the block, and argue that you can shift the down yourself to make the bag warmer or cooler.

The foot end. A good bag won't simply pinch out at the foot. Instead, there's an elaborately constructed bulge, a sort of a box, with room for your toes and a good thickness of insulation beyond.

Zipper. Most bags have them, typically down the sleeper's right side to about the ankle. (Some near-rectangular bags zip to the foot and along the bottom.) The zipper should work in both directions, so that you can open the foot end while leaving the upper end closed. Most zippers are nylon, not metal; it's lighter and doesn't conduct heat away. Before you buy, climb into the bag and work the zipper up and down to see that it doesn't tend to snag. Bags of the same or compatible models can be zipped together to form a single, larger bed (make sure that one of them has its zipper on the *left*).

Sleeping bag structure in cutaway view

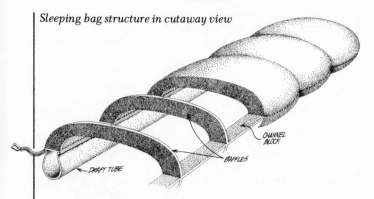

CHANNEL BLOCK

BAFFLES

DRAFT TUBE

Draft tube. The zipper must have an extra flap of insulation inside it, or heat will escape past the zipper. In a three-season or winter bag, check that this draft tube is not attached with a sewn-through seam; it must provide a thickness of insulation without a break. The draft tube should be longer than the zipper, so that no cold gap is left at the lower end.

Workmanship. There are several points worth checking even in a costly sleeping bag. Are the compartments between the baffles—the obvious segments of the bag—equally filled? How good is the stitching? Examine a lot of it, especially where stress comes on the seams: along the zipper and around the hood where the drawstring runs in its sleeve. Double stitching, and of course strong bar-tacking, are important at these places. Check the number of stitches per inch—ten is great, eight okay, five is poor. The best place for the suspicious shopper to hunt for shoddy stitching is inside the foot, the hardest part of the bag to sew. There is, of course, a lot of interior work you can't see, but a bag well-made where you can see it is probably sound clear through.

The vapor barrier idea

As noted, sleeping bags are normally built of permeable fabric, so that moisture can pass away from the skin. This has long been held essential for comfort. Recently, though, a new approach has been tried. People are deliberately surrounding themselves with impermeable layers—"vapor barriers"—in the wilderness bed.

The principle is this. For comfort, the body must maintain a layer of humid air next to the skin. This layer tends to dry out; sweating takes place partly to recharge it with moisture. Along with sweat, some body warmth is lost. Though such cooling doesn't matter when temperatures are moderate, it can be significant in the cold.

But if you go to sleep in some sort of waterproof sack, the layer of air next to the skin rapidly becomes humid and stays that way. You might expect to drown in sweat. Instead, sweating slows down, and the normal loss of body heat diminishes. Its enthusiasts claim that with a vapor barrier you can get much more warmth from the insulation in your sleeping bag without getting unpleasantly wet.

To set up a vapor barrier, you can wrap yourself in a plastic bag or a ground-sheet. The impermeable layer, however, must be next to your skin, not outside the sleeping bag—or the bag will get soaked with body moisture. (One company now markets a three-piece "sleeping system" consisting of a light down bag, a larger outside bag filled with Polarguard, and an impermeable liner.)

Judge for yourself.

Accessories

If you don't use a tent, you will need a groundsheet under you—it's just a rectangle of vinyl or coated nylon plastic, available for something between $2 and $10 in any store that handles sporting goods. The more expensive ones last longer.

Besides the groundsheet, you need a *pad* underneath you. It cushions you from the hardness of the ground, but, much more important, it *insulates.* If your bag is down filled, the part beneath will collapse almost to nothing under your weight. (However, bags with synthetic fills, not so compressible, may be comfortable without pads in summer.)

The typical pad is made of closed-cell polyurethane foam; the commonest brand is "Ensolite." Ensolite sheets, sold in most sporting goods stores, are eighteen to twenty-two inches wide and come in different lengths. Many summer backpackers choose a length of less than four feet. Thickness varies from a quarter inch to three-quarters of an inch; the thinner style will do (for warmth at least) in summer, but winter campers buy the longest and thickest sheets they can find or carry two thin ones. Ensolite and its cousins are waterproof. Depending on dimensions, these pads sell for prices from $3.50 to $10.

Some people carry much thicker pads of light open-cell foam in waterproof nylon covers ($9 to $17, depending on size and thickness). These are both comfortable and bulky. A third possibility is the air mattress. A mattress with just one air valve and interconnected tubes is unreliable. One puncture and you're flat. Such mattresses seem inevitably to fail. Far better is a new type with a tough cloth cover and eight individual air tubes that slide into slots. If one tube fails, you still have the rest, and at home you can replace the flat for a dollar or so; these rigs cost $18 or $28 depending on length. Any mattress, though, has a problem in cold weather: air circulates within it and carries some body heat away.

Very light *hammocks* are sold for wilderness camping—$7 to $10—and might be useful where the ground is very moist. Since wet soil is soft and easily disturbed, you might regard hammock-sleeping as one way of sparing the land. I must admit that I find this hard to take seriously.

What about a *pillow*? Most people use clothing, stuffed perhaps into a cloth bag. Inflatable pillows, favored by some, cost $2.50 or so.

You may possibly want a *bag cover*, a big cloth sack that pulls on over your bag to protect it from dirt (also to add warmth: as much as 10 degrees); these cost around $20. A stronger case can be made for a *sleeping bag liner,* a light sheath which keeps the inside of your bag very much cleaner. This strikes most people as inordinate fussiness, but a liner can add years to the life of an expensive down bag (see below). This accessory may be hard to find; flimsy ones sell at about $3. Wearing clothes to bed helps but not as much as a liner.

You also need two *stuffsacks*. One, which is sold with the bag itself, will be just large enough to hold it tightly stuffed. Between trips the bedding should be stored in a big plastic laundry bag or something similarly roomy.

Storage, cleaning, and care

A down bag should last ten or twelve years, a synthetic

bag perhaps half that long. But all sleeping bags have vulnerable points.

No matter what kind of fill your bag contains, do not store it compressed. Stuffed for weeks or months, down loses part of its springiness and thus its all-important loft. Synthetic fill—and this fact is less well known—collapses even more dramatically. Bags with internal baffles should not be hung by the hood drawstrings; you don't want the fill bearing down on the thin internal walls. Thus the storage in a large, loose sack.

On the trail, too, it's good to leave a bag unstuffed as much as you can. (This may not work out when the air is very humid, as a loose bag will get damp.) If the bag is moist and bedraggled when you put it away in the morning, you can dry it out, weather permitting, at lunch. To pack it, don't roll it; instead stuff it evenly, foot-end first, handful by handful, into its stuffsack. When you pull it out, be gentle.

Do your best to keep the bag both dry and clean. Moisture does no special harm to the synthetics, but down which is constantly damp will slowly disintegrate. It also loses insulating power as it becomes soiled. Thus the advantage of sleeping inside a liner (you'll be surprised just how dirty that liner gets). Air your bag thoroughly after each trip, but don't leave it lying in the sun more than a few hours—sunlight eventually damages the nylon. And of course you have to be extremely careful about sparks around a fire.

Cleaning a down bag is *extremely* tricky. Don't do it any more often than you have to—say once a year with frequent use. No matter how careful you are, there is a penalty: according to one expert estimate, down loses ten percent of its insulating power every time it is washed!

What's the safest way to wash a down bag? Do it yourself in a tub with Ivory flakes or a similarly gentle soap (never use detergent or bleach). The water should be warm, not hot. Knead the bag gently so as not to put strain on the baffles. Don't twist. Don't wring. When the suds have turned dark, drain the tub and start over. Do this as often as you need to until the suds are white. Then rinse again several times, making sure to get all the soap out of the bag. Then, very gently, press the excess water out.

Now comes the crucial move. Lift the wet bag with all the care you can. Cradle the whole soggy thing in your arms. No part should hang unsupported. If you simply grab an end and haul, the wet down will burst the baffles from one end of the bag to the other, and you'll be out your hundred bucks or so.

Don't hang the wet bag on a clothesline. Instead, tumble it in a big laundromat dryer at low heat or no heat at all. Throw some small rubbery object—a laceless tennis shoe is good—in with the load; it will break up the clumps of down that form as drying goes on. When the bag is nearly dry, take it out and leave it in the sun for a day, turning and fluffing it now and again.

Washing a down sleeping bag, clearly, takes a lot of water, a lot of dimes, and quite a bit of time. You can shorten the job somewhat by using a front-loading washing machine (never a machine with an agitator) set on the coolest, gentlest cycle. But most manufacturers urge you to do it by hand.

You can also get the bag cleaned commercially. Some cities have stores which handle only down; these do as safe a job as you could do at home. General dry cleaners are another matter. Some use powerful hydrocarbons which destroy the natural oils in the down. Make sure your cleaner understands the problem and that he uses some extremely mild preparation (Stoddard Fluid is often speci-fied). If you do have your bag dry-cleaned, be sure to air it for several days. If, after that time, you still smell traces of chemical when you close yourself up in the bag, air it some more. These cleaning products are poisons and can linger.

What about bags filled with Polarguard or Fiberfill II? Here the difficulties are much less. Either type can be washed quite safely in a front-loading machine and dried in a large tumble dryer on a low heat. Neither synthetic fill loses loft in washing—Polarguard, as a matter of fact, gains a little insulating power after the second or third cleaning. Several cautions: synthetic bags are never dry-cleaned, period. And you must be extremely cautious with heat. One hundred and forty degrees is the "plasticizing point" of synthetic fills, the point at which the fibers lose their springiness. Wash in water barely warm to the touch.

Sleeping bags and low impact

With sleeping bags as with packs there is just one impact question: what color? A bright-colored sleeping bag is not so obtrusive as a gaudy pack, because it will be stowed away much of the time. Even so, do you want to stand out in the wilderness like a spot of fire wherever you throw down your bag? Or do you choose rather to blend in? In the busy mountains of the later twentieth century, the arguments seem heavy on the side of blending in. The stuffsack, at least, should not be brightly colored.

7:
Shelter

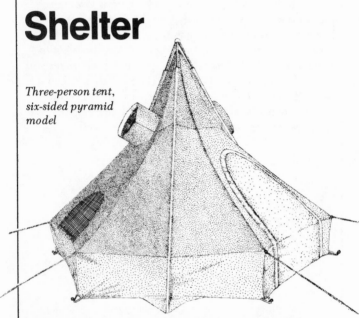

*Three-person tent,
six-sided pyramid
model*

WHEN YOU HEAD INTO THE WILDERNESS—no matter how
fine the weather at the roadhead—you must have some plan
for *shelter*. And that means something carried in your
pack. Don't count on improvising a lean-to, or making a
hut of green boughs (unless it's an extreme emergency).
These methods were elegant when the wilderness was vast
and the population small. Jim Bridger used them, and so
did John Muir, but now it is the wilderness that is tiny, the
human pressure that is great. Don't count on official trailside huts or lean-tos, either; some regions have them, but
they are seldom unoccupied, and when they are empty you
may find them dirty or in disrepair.

What should your shelter be? In the East, in the northern Cascades, and in parts of the northern Rockies, the
case is good for carrying a full-scale tent at any time of
year. In the southwestern part of the United States, however, a regular tent is more shelter than you are likely to
need in the summer. The weather during the southwestern
hiking season is seldom wet for long. Too many expensive

tents weigh down too many packs in such sunny regions as the California Sierra.

Less than a tent: poncho, tarp, and tube

The first necessity, of course, is a roof to shed rain. (It will incidentally keep dew off your sleeping bag and keep you a little warmer. In desert country you may want to rig a sun-roof for a mid-day stop.)

The simplest kind of roof is also an item of clothing: the *poncho*, a rectangular piece of waterproof fabric with neck-hole and hood. While some ponchos are made just large enough to cover the hiker himself, others are long enough in back to cover the pack he is carrying; these, called packboard ponchos, can be pitched as minimal one-hiker shelters. A poncho intended for such use should have several metal grommets along the sides and corners for attaching cords. Some sources seem overly sanguine about what can be done with a poncho—they propose it as both groundcloth and tent (at the same time?). Also, nothing that has been a groundcloth should then be trusted to keep out rain—too much likelihood of punctures. Cheap ponchos are made of rather fragile plastic and are too flimsy to make good shelters; $12.50 is about the minimum for an adequate coated-nylon poncho, and tougher ones cost $20 and over. Dimensions start at about five by nine feet; weight is a pound or a little over.

Next up on the list is the *tarp*. A skillful handler—it takes practice—can make it through a severe rain, at least

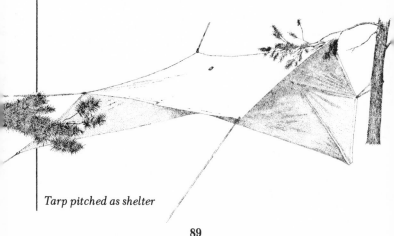

Tarp pitched as shelter

below timberline, under a tarp. Good tarps are made of urethane-coated nylon, tough and grommeted; typical sizes are nine by eleven and ten by twelve. Weights range from two to three pounds depending on size and on the thickness of the fabric. Prices start at $20—some, with many grommets and tabs, are sold for almost $50! A regular tent fly (see below) also makes a splendid tarp when used alone.

As a stopgap, temporary tarp, you can use a polyethylene sheet, in two-mil, three-mil, or four-mil thickness (.002, .003, .004 inch).

These thinner plastic sheets can be bought for a few dollars at hardware stores; tougher ones are sold at gear stores. But except for one type that is criss-crossed with nylon threads and sells for $10 or more, none of these simple plastic sheets are strong enough to stand much wind. Hikers who use them tend to carry several. Rangers in Washington's North Cascades and elsewhere report that discarded, wind-torn plastic tarps have become a major item of litter in those stormy hills. (Don't leave your junk behind you in the wilderness—not even gear that has let you down!)

Another type of minimum shelter—not necessarily better than the tarp—is the *tube tent*: simply an open-ended tube of two-mil or three-mil plastic about nine feet long. Tubes come in several sizes ranging from one to three pounds and varying from three to five feet in diameter (the larger sizes have room for two people). Prices run from $3 to $7 or so depending on size and thickness. More durable

Tube tent

coated-nylon tube tents can be bought for about $15. To pitch a tube tent, you run a line through the tube and pull it tight between two anchors.

Though a tube gives you more side protection than a tarp, it is distinctly a shelter for the forest and for the brief storms of a southwestern summer. The cheap, light-plastic variety won't last through many uses.

In a tube tent, or in any walled tent of waterproof fabric, you have the problem of dealing with the water that is shut in with you. The human body puts out about a pint of moisture in sweat and respiration every night, and that moisture has to go somewhere. What doesn't escape through the ends of the tube will soak your sleeping bag or condense on the waterproof walls and shower you with dew or frost in the morning.

Ponchos, tarps, and tube tents can all, in theory, be pitched with nothing but cord. Actually, it is often useful to have one or two tentpoles and several stakes along; natural anchors don't necessarily come just where you'd like them. For more about pitching and living in various shelters, see Chapter 18.

Between the tarps and tubes on one hand and the true tents on the other, there are some interesting intermediate designs, called *tarp tents*. Most have netting doors to keep the mosquitoes out. Some have floors. Most are pitched with stakes and poles. But all are made mostly of waterproof fabric and share the above-mentioned problems of the simple tube: the more completely they protect you from the wet outside, the more they tend to soak you with trapped condensation. Prices run from $20 to $50, still $15 below the cheapest of the true tents. But it is hard to regard any tarp tent as a bargain. When you get into weather a simple tarp can't handle, it's time to consider a full-scale wilderness tent.

Tents: general

When is waterproof not waterproof?

How can you build a tent that lets body moisture out—as it has to, or you will get very damp—without letting the rain get in?

This is the problem that is partially solved by the standard wilderness tent. These "real" tents come in two parts: an essential main shelter built largely of permeable nylon, not waterproofed, so that moisture can escape and a separate, fully waterproof *rainfly* which is pitched a short distance above the vulnerable structure underneath.

The trade calls this arrangement the "double-walled" tent, which is slightly misleading; you get a picture of two walls in one construction. In most tents the two units are separate, and you can, when appropriate, leave one or the other unused. A rainfly, taken alone, makes a superior tarp, and the main tent alone will keep you dry when the only likely weather is either a sprinkle or the kind of cold snow that won't stick to the fabric and melt. A fly also adds a little warmth, however.

Like boots, like sleeping bags, like backpacks, wilderness tents come in a range of price and sturdiness. Some are for use in fairly undemanding conditions like gentle forest rain, and others are for fierce weather in high and windy places. Oversimplifying by necessity, we can split that range into halves.

1. *Three-season tents: tents for rain, tents to keep insects out.* Three-season tents vary greatly in their ability to stand high winds; some are suitable for use below timberline only.

2. *Winter tents: tents for high winds and heavy snow.* Lighter tents grade into these heavier, more elaborate models. They are stoutly supported, roomy, carefully tailored to shed wind, and, above all, *strong.* A winter tent may have to resist eighty-mile-an-hour gusts or bear a weight of several hundred pounds of wet, clinging snow.

Tents are made in many sizes. The most useful for backpackers are referred to, chauvinistically, as "two-man" and "three-man" models. There is no clear dividing line; a two-man tent will do as an occasional shelter for three hikers; many people, however, carry triple tents for two, enjoying the extra room.

A general backpacking tent need not weigh more than about three pounds per person, all parts included. A two-person model might reasonably go to six pounds and a three-person tent to nine. Prices for a double range from about $50 to $200, with the average well over $100. Triples run $150 to $250. A tent that is to be only a brief refuge can be small, weighing no more than two and a half pounds per person. A tent that you may have to live in for days can't be so cramped. But anything over a total of six and a half pounds is too heavy for a basic backpacking tent.

The standard: two-man rectangular wedge

Tents come in many vociferously competing designs. There is, however, one arrangement that is repeated especially often: the two-man rectangular wedge.

This tent is long and narrow. Its floor is a rectangle or a modified rectangle; its slanting walls converge on a single ridgeline. Dimensions vary but a typical floor is about seven feet long and four and a half feet wide. The roof rises something less than four feet at the highest point.

(Not all "rectangular wedge" tents are in fact perfectly rectangular at the floor. Some add prow-like "alcoves" at one end, or at both. Extending the squared-off floor plan, these give you some extra living room. When you compare the floor areas of different tents, be sure to count in the alcoves. Even the expert equipment-raters sometimes fail to take account of them. In another variation, many tents grow narrower toward the foot.)

There are several ways in which a tent's ridgeline can be supported. Simplest is the *I-pole:* a single, vertical post at each end of the tent. More stable and more convenient is the *A-frame.* In this design a pole is thrust through a fabric sleeve along each side of the triangular tent-end. The poles converge on a gripping device at the top, forming an "A" with no bar. In summer tents it is fairly rare to find a tent with A-frames at both ends. More common is the design with an A-frame at the door and a short I-post at the foot, where it will be less in the way. Whatever combination is chosen, it is common for the roof to slant toward the foot.

A-frame or I-pole, the tent is held erect by the pull of guylines, one from the apex of each end, to solid ground anchors. With its two guys out and the floor staked down, the tent is self-supporting. There are usually several additional lines that attach to the sides of the tent and pull the fabric tight to shed wind and also to recover space that would otherwise be lost in the sag.

All modern backpacking tents are made of nylon, either ripstop or nylon taffeta (a slightly heavier, somewhat stronger material). The tent floor is waterproof (with the urethane-coated side up), and the waterproofing also extends four inches or more up the sides of the walls and up the door or doors. This "tub floor" cannot be built without seams, but the fewer there are the better.

Above the upper edge of the tub floor the walls are made of ordinary permeable nylon, *not* waterproofed. This, of course, is the whole point of a wilderness tent—it allows moisture to escape from the inside. So the tent has a second protective roof above the built-in roof: the waterproof rainfly.

The rainfly stretches between the two apexes of the tent and down over the sides. Supported by the tips of the metal poles at the ends of the tent, the fly never touches the inner, permeable wall. It must overhang the sides enough to prevent slanting, wind-driven rain from reaching uncoated fabric. At the edges, this upper roof is held tautly in place by guylines of its own. These may run to separate stakes in the ground, or (better) to the same stakes which serve the inner tent. In the most convenient arrangement of all, the fly's tensioning lines are simply tied to the guylines which run out from the inner tent, using adjustable grip-slip knots (see Chapter 18).

At one end of the tent (the higher if the ridgeline slants) is the triangular *door*. In the handiest arrangement

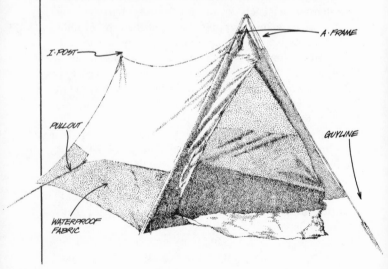

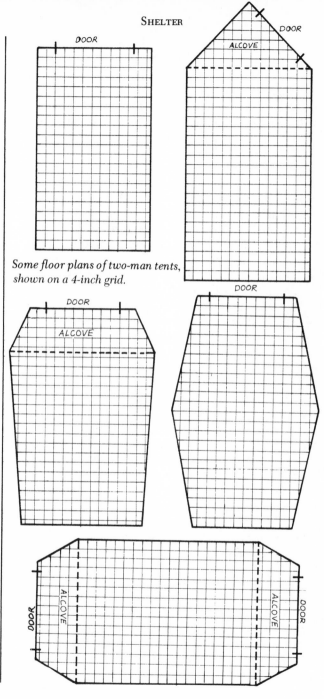

Some floor plans of two-man tents, shown on a 4-inch grid.

the door is attached at the bottom and has zippers running from its apex along each side. The top of the door, protected by the overhanging fly, can be opened for extra ventilation. If the door opens along the bottom, it must zip to a raised, waterproof sill. Summer tents are sometimes built with a door at each end; this gives you a cooling breeze when both are open.

Any tent to be used in warm weather needs *mosquito netting* over every opening and a complete inner door of netting at each entrance. The net door should ideally zip in the same pattern as the solid door. In any case the netting should form a complete seal against insects. There are some specialized "bug tents" made entirely of netting, except for waterproof floor and rainfly; these are ideal where rain and mosquitoes are the problems, but they're obviously not good for dealing with wind and cold.

Ventilation is extremely important in a tent. The permeable fabric of the walls will let some moisture out, but it takes circulating air to keep you comfortably dry. Besides the door there must be at least one vent high up near the ridgeline. Two vents are better. Some manufacturers replace the vents with a single long mesh panel, which is fine too.

Some tents come equipped with *vestibules*. There are several designs, but the object is to give you a rain-sheltered patch of ground just outside the main door—a sort of porch where you can cook or store gear. Some tents protect this working area with an extra-long, low-hanging rainfly; others add an extension to the roof of the main tent. Some vestibules are built in, others add on. (Just to confuse matters, the word "vestibule" is occasionally used to mean *alcove:* but an alcove is of course part of the basic inner chamber of the tent, not a mere extension.)

Other tent designs

The rectangular wedge tent with separate fly is still the most common two-person design on the trails. But no field is evolving more rapidly, or with more debate, than this one. There are various rival designs, each put forward as an improvement on the basic pattern. One maker (he wouldn't touch an A-frame tent with a ten-foot I-pole) dismisses all his competitors in one curt phrase: "They haven't built a tent *yet.*"

Almost all two-man tents, however, retain the more-or-less rectangular floor. It's the canopy that varies. Most of the variants alter the roof by using arc-shaped, hooplike poles rather than straight ones. These are inserted, under tension, into fabric sleeves.

Most like the basic wedge tent is the *tunnel tent*, with a rounded roof held up by several hooplike "rafters" of tensioned poles. Some tunnel tents, like conventional tents, slope downward to the foot. Then there is the *semi-dome*. In this design the poles arch diagonally over the tent, from opposite corners, forming an X. The high point of the tent is at the center, where the poles cross. This design gives good room for the weight, but it is said to be less stable in the wind than equally well-made examples of the rectangular wedge and tunnel tent designs.

Another departure: some tents are made with the fly built in; that is, the waterproof rainfly and the permeable tent-wall are joined by sills with a dead air-air space between them. Instead of having a tent and a rainfly, either of which you may be able to use alone, you have a single tent with a double wall. These everything-in-one tents are warm and are very easy to pitch.

Still another variant, most often found on winter tents, is the *exterior frame*. Instead of running through sleeves of tent fabric, as is usually the case, the supporting poles form a complete, freestanding framework from which the tent is hung by elastic cords.

But one innovation is more fundamental than any of these. Everybody knows that a totally waterproof tent, trapping the moisture the occupants produce, won't work in wilderness camping. Like other things that "everybody knows," however, this rule has been challenged. At least one manufactuer is trying to build a waterproof tent that works. The key is ventilation—putting in plenty of vents and putting them in exactly the right places. Stephenson's of Los Angeles has done well enough with its Warmlite tents to get at least mixed reviews.

Then there is Gore-Tex, a new fabric that sheds rain while allowing transpiration of moisture from within. Gore-Tex is now being used extensively in tenting. Such tents are more expensive than their double-walled

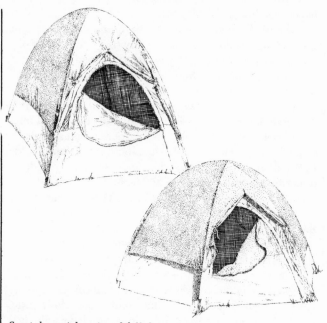

Semi-dome (above) and full-dome tents

counterparts, lighter, and simpler (needing no flies). As with most applications of Gore-Tex, this one is exciting, but new enough to make a judgment difficult.

Larger tents

What's the boundary between large two-man tents and small three-person designs? Any tent that has a floor area much over forty square feet and a volume much over eighty cubic feet is definitely big enough for three. Almost all tents smaller than this have rectangular floors much longer than they are wide; almost all tents above this size have floors that are round, hexagonal, square, or of some other shape.

One common design is the *six-sided pyramid*. The floor is a hexagon. Three poles slide through fabric sleeves to seat in a socketed aluminum block at the peak. Between the supporting poles, guylines pull out the walls to round out the hexagon. This design is roomy and tall enough to kneel in. Somewhat similar but not so convenient is a pyramid-shaped tent with a tall center pole.

Then there is the round-floored *dome tent,* which is supported by several curved poles which arch from side to side, intersecting in patterns that vary from model to model. A recent innovation puts the hoops outside, as an exterior frame, and hangs the tent from this skeleton—it looks something like a geodesic dome.

Beyond the patterns of pyramid and dome, easy to visualize, still larger tents spread into all sorts of geometric combinations. The larger the number of people to be sheltered, the more possibilities the designers find. Though some of these larger tents are good for family use, not many backpackers are in the market for tents of such size and weight.

Tents for wind and winter

Between "three-season" tents and "winter" (or "mountaineering") tents there is no sharp line to be drawn. But there are certain features of construction and design that make a tent suitable for camps in increasingly challenging places.

Very important is *stability in wind.* Most, but not all, highly wind-stable tents are of the rectangular wedge or tunnel design, with either A-frames or curving, hoop-like poles. (The I-pole is almost never used in wind tents.) Three-man pyramidal tents have also been used in extreme conditions, and several tents made specifically for winter have pyramid or dome design.

To be stable in the wind an A-frame tent must have what is called the *catenary cut.* The roofline dips steeply at the middle, in a kind of built-in sag. When the end guylines are tensioned, such a roof pulls beautifully taut, and wind will merely ripple it, not rattle and flap it. (So the theory. Actually, almost any tent is noisy in high wind, but the catenary cut unquestionably helps.) Sometimes the walls are catenary cut as well, bending inward at the sides. Such hourglass designs cut down on headroom and sprawling room, but the security is worth it. The rainfly (not always taken in cold conditions) is cut to hang on a similar plunging curve.

Winter tents tend to be a good deal heavier than three-season models for several reasons. They are often built of thicker material, and very special attention must be paid to reinforcement. Also, they typically have somewhat more room than comparable three-season tents. All this gives winter tents an average weight, per person, of something between four and five pounds, rather than something between three and four.

Many winter tents (and some others) have *cookholes*; these are zippered, semicircular openings in the floor, designed so that in theory you can set up a kitchen on a patch of snow, rather than on the vulnerable tentfloor. The hole is also useful for cleaning a tent; loose granola and what have you can be swept out easily. But some makers refuse to install them, arguing that you should never cook in a tent.

Most winter tents have two entrances. There is usually a round opening opposite the conventional door with an extendable sleeve or *snow-tunnel*. You can burrow out this exit if the zippered entrance gets blocked for some reason.

Some other minor features, useful on any tent, are most common on winter models. A pair of tabs, one at each end of the ridgeline, makes it easy to string a *ridge-seam clothesline* for drying wet gear. Two or more *netting pockets*, hanging from the sidewalls, are great for keeping track of small, losable objects.

A winter tent, even more than a summer tent, *must* be well-ventilated. Usually that means a vent at each end and a door that can be cracked at the top. Vents are set in spe-

Winter tent

cial tubes of fabric that blow with the wind and thus admit less blown snow than a simple window-like opening would. You do take in some powder, regardless, and vents must be closable.

Even if single-walled impermeable tents of new design become popular for summer backpacking, it is hard to imagine using such a tent in winter. In a winter snowstorm you and your gear are likely to get wet no matter how hard you work to keep everything dry; this moisture, added to the body's pint a night and the steam from any cooking that the weather may induce you to do inside, can make the interior of the tent much wetter (although warmer) than the country outside the doors. In the fight against condensation, you need a tent that will "breathe" —standard porous fabric or, arguably, Gore-Tex.

With all these requirements, it's no wonder that winter tents are more expensive than the general-use tent—the average is about $170 for a two-man model, compared with $120 for three-season tents.

There are two further features, found on some winter tents and available for some others, that can be very useful. *Snowflaps* are flanges of extra material projecting around the base of the tent on all sides. By piling snow or rocks on the flaps you make it impossible for wind to get under the floor (one of the dangers in a violent storm); this also makes stakes unnecessary. Flaps add $25 to $30 to tent price and about ten ounces to weight. A *frostliner* looks for all the world like a bedsheet. Made of cotton or a cotton-polyester weave, it hangs on the inside of the tent, tied to special tabs along the ridgeline and on the walls. You get an Arabian Nights effect, but there's a purpose. On a cold winter trip, frost is constantly forming on the inner walls, and with each gust it shakes off: a continual light snowstorm. The frostliner catches the crystals or, at worst, sheds them to the sides of the tent, where it is easier to deal with them. A frostliner can be a real help in wet, cold country, particularly if you are struggling to keep moisture out of vulnerable down gear. The item weighs about twenty ounces and costs about $25.

Shopping for a tent

The decision to buy a tent is a good decision to delay.

Rental tents are easy to find (about $7 a weekend), and
there are questions you need to ask yourself before you
spend a large chunk of money. Do you really need a tent,
or will a poncho, a tarp, a tube tent, or a tarp tent give you
protection enough? If you do need a tent, where will you
use it most often—in rainy, mosquito-ridden woods? On ski
or snowshoe trips? On summer treks above timberline?
How many people should it be able to sleep? How long
will you need to spend in it at a time? And how much can
you afford?

Sort out in your mind what your ideal tent would be
like. Every design has its advantages, but no design has *all*
advantages at once. Every tent is a compromise. The
roomiest tent won't be the lightest, nor the most stable in a
wind. The cheapest tent won't be the most durable, nor the
easiest to pitch. And the harder the tentmaker has worked
to combine different practical advantages in a single
model, the higher his price is likely to be.

Size. You have a choice of one-man, double, triple, and
even larger designs. Two-man tents are the most common.
But within each category there is much variation. If your
tent will be only a now-and-then shelter, it need only be
large enough to stretch out in. But if you expect to spend
days in it, during long rains or snowstorms, with much of
your gear inside, you need a good deal more room.

Height. A related yet separate question. Some tents are
high enough so that you can sit up in them without brushing the roof; lower ones, though, tend to be more stable in
wind. In an A-frame tent equally high at each end (but
with a catenary sag in the middle), two people can sit up
facing each other. In a tent that slopes to the foot there is
only one spot with sitting room.

Ease of pitching. Some tents are easy to put up, some
hard, and the difference can matter. When you consider a
tent, make an inventory of the jobs that have to be done:

●How many stakes must be put in to anchor the floor?
(It will never be less than four unless snowflaps are used.)

●How many poles must be slid into sleeves? And must
they be inserted under tension? (On some tents with arc-
shaped poles, it takes a real effort to get the final pole in
place.)

●How many different guylines must be set before the

tent is roughly self-supporting? (With a dome design, there may be none; most two-man tents take two.)

● How many pullouts—those extra lines that pull the sag out of the walls—must be anchored at the sides?

● What about the rainfly—does it attach to the same anchors, or must it be pitched entirely separately?

● If you expect to use the tent in high places or in winter, be sure to consider how easily it can be thrown together with cold hands, or in the dark.

Durability. An obvious value. Durability comes from heavy materials, lots of reinforcement, and very careful workmanship—see below. It costs you something in weight and something in money.

Light weight. The ultimate good—or is it? Most of the other things you value in a tent mean added weight. Tent innovations are mainly aimed at getting more advantages from fewer pounds, but you can pay a great deal to shed just a handful of ounces.

Wind stability. If you expect to camp in sheltered woods, this may not be worth the extra money it will cost. For typical backpacking, especially in the West, you need a tent that is at least moderately stable.

Things to look for

In buying a tent you have a special problem. You can always get a good look at a boot, or a pack, or a sleeping bag, and see it as it is. But a tent, taken off the shelf, is a shapeless bundle of cloth and hardware. Only when you see it tightly pitched can you guess how windproof it is, how large it is, how well-sewn it is. Catalog specifications may be incomplete or wrong, and some of the very finest tents are sold chiefly by mail.

If you buy a tent you can't look at first, be sure to arrange for a risk-free trial. Most outfits will let you pitch the tent on your rug. Mail-order houses, in particular, are very good about this. A tent that does not please, like a boot that doesn't fit, will be taken back with no hassle.

If you are at all concerned about wind, look carefully at the way the walls hang. Do they form deep wrinkles? Do they sag despite the pullouts? Or is the cloth fairly smooth? (One caution: tents rigged in a store almost always look unnaturally perfect—tents rigged on a rug, where you can't drive stakes, always look sloppier than they really are. Make allowances.)

Look for adequate ventilation. Make sure there is at least one vent, high up.

Check to see that the bottom tip of each tent pole is seated in a grommet on a tab attached to the tent floor—otherwise the poles may sink into damp or soft ground or snow. Tent poles should be smooth, especially at the joints where sections fit together (see below). If the tent has the inexpensive telescoping poles, make sure that the sections slide in and out smoothly.

All seams should be what the industry calls "flat fell." In a flat-fell seam, the two pieces of fabric are folded, each over the other, like hooked fingers of opposite hands; stitching goes through all four layers. The more stitches per inch the better: eight to ten is good, five to seven will do, less is poor. The more places with double and triple rows, the better. There should be no holes without thread in them, no loose, hanging thread-ends, and no "puckered" effect where some stitches, out of line with the others, are taking extra strain. Tentmakers almost always use a *lock-stitch*, so designed that the seam cannot unravel even if the thread is broken. The simpler chainstitch is to be avoided.

There should be plenty of reinforcement. Look for it wherever there is a grommet; a loop where a tent peg will seat; a sewn-on strap; and wherever guylines attach to the tent. At a minimum each stress point should have a heavy, doubled hem. In better tents an extra piece of material may be added, especially at the peg-loops. Grommets and other metal parts should not be steel but rather rust-free aluminum or brass. All points of quality become doubly important in a tent intended for winter.

Poles and stakes

Poles come with tents, but you can also purchase them separately, to replace broken originals or to use with a tarp or tube tent. Most tent poles are of aluminum tubing in three sections, each a foot to eighteen inches long, linked by elastic shock cord running inside. When the pole is set up, the base of each section nests in a socket at the end of the one below. For packing, the sections pull apart, and the pole folds into a manageable bundle. A pair of assembled poles with an A-frame fitting at the top sells for $9 to $10; individual pole sections, fittings, and shock cords can be purchased at something over $1 apiece. When you get replacements, make sure that they fit your tent; poles and parts aren't always interchangeable.

Some cheaper tents use telescoping poles, convenient but not so strong. To put them up, you simply extend them, as you would a standard radio antenna on a car. Stout at the bottom, these poles grow spindly at the top, where the thinnest segments are.

There are many kinds of stakes. The simplest are aluminum skewers with an eye at one end. Steel alloy skewers—heavier but stouter—are used in frozen or rocky ground. "Channeled stakes" are C-shaped in cross-section and will do in normal ground or in snow. For loose soil there are also stout plastic stakes, I-shaped in section. For winter there's the snow stake, a light aluminum angle, V-shaped in section. There are several other variants. Weight is generally about an ounce per stake, and prices run from a dime to fifty cents apiece. If you camp in a variety of places and seasons, you will need a stock of different kinds of stakes to choose from.

When you rig a tent, it is useful to have a way of tightening or loosening the lines without shifting the stakes. Wherever you can make a line loop back on itself, as around the stake or through a grommet, you can use one of several simple grip/slip knots to make adjustments. You can also buy plastic gadgets to do the same thing.

In pitching a tarp or a tube tent without grommets, you can improvise an attachment by wrapping the fabric around a small, smooth stone, and then tightening a noose of cord around the "neck" where the fabric is bunched. There are commercial gimmicks (Visklamps and Versa Ties are brands) that do the same thing with a plastic or rubber "rock" and a plastic or metal "noose." If you care to bother, they cost five or ten cents each.

Handling and care of tents

Tents are much easier to take care of than boots or sleeping bags. In fact, they come close to being care-free.

When you pitch your tent, try to locate a piece of ground without sharp rocks, sticks, or anything else that could puncture or abrade the waterproof floor. Spread out a groundsheet under the tent. If you are lighting a fire, don't pitch the tent too close to it—nylon won't go up in flames, but sparks are likely to melt holes in it.

Cooking inside a tent, or even under its vestibule roof, is a risky business. See more about this in Chapter 19. Any tent in which you cook must have several vents, including one high up and immediately over the stove. Citrus drinks are bad for nylon, and spilled stove fuel can ruin the water-proofing on your floor. Important tools in any tent that gets lived in much are a sponge for wiping up spills and condensation and a whisk broom for brushing out dirt or loose snow.

If you get a minor puncture or a leak during a trip, you can patch it with ordinary adhesive tape or with ripstop repair tape. Apply the patch from the outside, on a dry surface (if you can get one). Wax from a candle, or even lip balm, will stop a leak for a while. Regular adhesive tape is not much good for this purpose. Some people carry a tube of seam sealant to caulk leaking seams.

When you break camp, get everything out of the tent, especially anything sharp or gritty. Take time to rub drop-lets of pitch and bird droppings off the fly and canopy (you can use white gas as solvent on the permeable fabrics only). If the tent is very wet and the weather fine, it makes sense to tie it on the outside of your pack in a loose bundle. Nylon is treated to resist mildew up to a point, but the drier you can keep it the better. When you pack your tent, try to avoid folding it on the same lines each time—this may lead to cracking in waterproof coatings. Some author-ities now suggest *stuffing* a tent into its storage sack, as if it were a sleeping bag.

After a trip, examine the tent for punctures and tears, sponge off any especially dirty spots, and dry it thor-oughly. (Dry cleaning fluid will get rid of pitch and is safe anywhere on the tent.) If the tent is really filthy, you can take a garden hose to it. Experts disagree about whether it is safe to wash a tent in a washing machine. To dry, hang the tent out for several days, supported at points that are built to take strain. The seams will be hardest to get dry.

Wipe the poles clean, too; this is especially important if you have been camping near salt water. Pay special attention to telescoping poles, and to the joints of standard sectioned poles. Finally, store everything in a dry place.

Holes and tears can be repaired. Patching a tent is something like patching an inner tube. Kits are available, with fabric cement and patches of material both waterproof and permeable. An air mattress repair kit will also do. For extra strength it is good to stitch around the edges of the patch, but if you do any new stitching on rainfly or floor be sure to seal the new seam carefully with seam sealant or model airplane glue (several light coats, not one thick one). You can also buy a kit to replace any pulled-out grommets, but the rig is expensive and hardly worth it unless you do a lot of repair work. You can probably find a shoemaker who will do this job cheaply. Many outing goods stores can arrange for repair of the brands they carry, and a few will take anything.

Tents and low impact

The improper pitching of tents is one of the principal causes of damage to wilderness land. *Where* you pitch your tent is even more important than *how*. Even the weight of the tent and its occupants can compact moist ground and do long-term damage to a vulnerable meadow. For much more on impact considerations in camping, see Section 5.

There are, however, several things worth thinking about before you ever get to the wild country: points to consider when you *buy* your tent.

For instance, some tents require more ground-anchors than others. Whenever you pitch a tent in the normal way, with stakes and guylines, you leave a scatter of punctures in the ground. Trivial though this may seem, hundreds of people, passing through a single camping area over the months, can tear up a good deal of soil. Other things being equal, then, you might prefer a tent that requires few anchors. (There is even the self-supporting tent that can be pitched—in theory—with no anchors at all; most of these are domes and semi-domes. But any tent must be staked and guyed when there is wind.) A tarp or tentless rainfly, unlike the typical full tent, can often be pitched without any ground attachments.

It is often possible, instead of driving in stakes, to use natural anchors. This is discussed more fully in Chapter 18.

When you do use stakes, choose the thinnest style the ground condition makes practical.

We must also consider (for the third time in these chapters) the problem of color. Do you make your campsite obvious with a tent in red, orange, or a light, bright shade of blue—or do you blend into the landscape with green or brown? I recommend once more the unobtrusive colors. Nothing makes a mountain landscape seem so populous as a scatter of highly visible tents—a whole seeming village where you would prefer to see no human presence at all.

But two arguments are often raised in favor of "standing out." One is convenience in choosing a camp. If you look up an open valley and see the bright blotches of tents, you know better than to plan your own camp in that place. This argument is valid but—so I believe—inadequate: the virtues of blending in are still the greater. (And what of the hiker who passes these campsites during the day? He isn't yet ready to stop—and meanwhile his pleasure is spoiled by these too-obvious signs of human presence.)

More pressing is the claim of safety—the thought that a visible tent could more easily be spotted by searchers from the air. How much weight you give to this consideration must depend largely on the kind of travel you plan to do. There are places and times in which a bright-colored tent seems not only prudent but also psychologically *right*. On the immense white back of a glacier, or in the middle of a violent cold storm, the orange canopy that shelters you seems somehow in scale. The greater the force and the genuine danger in the environment, the less you need to be concerned about somehow asserting yourself too much.

In summer, though, or below timberline in any season, the same sense of proportion suggests tents in green or brown or dull, dark blue. A good compromise for the climber is a bright-colored tent with a dull-colored rainfly. In the rainy woods, he can blend in; in alpine snow, he can make himself as visible as he chooses.

8:
Clothing

IN CHOOSING CLOTHES for the wilderness, there are two dangers to avoid. First is the danger of going under-equipped. Second (if hardly parallel in seriousness) is the danger of spending more money than you need to. Many backpackers do.

The clothes on your back (and still more important, the reserves in your pack) are a large part of your comfort and safety. They are your daytime protection from cold and from wind; from soaking, chilling rain and snow; from heat and burning ultraviolet rays; from mosquitoes and poison oak and thick, scratching underbrush. An essential item not taken can mean discomfort, even danger, even death.

And yet, if wilderness clothing is all-important, it is also almost surprisingly simple. You can go nearly anywhere, except in snowy winter, with rather ordinary clothes. For a summer trip you may already have everything you need.

There is no such thing as a standard list of clothing for the wilderness. People vary. Every hiker works out the combinations that are right for him. And the wilderness

itself—from hot to cold, from wet to dry, from calm to bat-
tering wind—varies most of all.

To deal with these changes, wilderness hikers have two
sets of clothing. First, there is a simple, almost universal,
fair-weather outfit: boots and socks, cotton pants or hiking
shorts, light cotton shirt, and a few other items. Second,
there is a set of *reserve* clothing, more often in the pack
than on the back, for dealing with cold, wind, rain, and
snow. In spring, summer, and fall hiking, this reserve may
be rather small, but it is always there. In winter travel, the
basic outfit changes from cotton to wool or wool-
substitutes and the reserves are more complete.

The basic outfit: summer

The hiker dressed in just the basic outfit is traveling in
the easiest conditions. He's striding along in the sunlight;
the air is warm, or hot; if there's a breeze, it comes as a
relief. And in much of America's wilderness during the
months when people visit it most, this is the way things
usually are.

Any type of pants will do. Cotton/synthetic and plain
cotton fabrics are cooler and more comfortable than others. Jeans are popular and cheap, and they're fine if you
don't find they chafe you. (Wash them once, if they are
new, to soften the fabric.) Pants should be loose-fitting and
not too close to the point of disintegration. Avoid bell-
bottoms and dirt-catching cuffs. Many women find men's
pants good for the trail. Specially-cut women's pants are
fine, too, but they cost a little more.

Hiking shorts are a nice luxury; in hot, wet places
everybody wears them. You have to watch out for sunburn,
of course; burned legs can make walking painful. You
should always have a pair of long pants along as well.
You'll need them especially for any hiking off the trail, and
wherever irritant plants are a problem. Mosquitoes, too,
can make bare-legged walking unbearable.

There are various pants and shorts made specifically for
hiking. Looser-fitting than the ordinary, they often have
patch-type "cargo pockets." One nice feature, if you happen to find it, is a pocket mounted low enough on the leg
so that you can reach into it when the pack's hip belt is
buckled. Hiking pants cost from $12 to $30; shorts from

$10 to $20, with the higher prices reflecting stronger fabric and better sewing. You can beat those prices in a surplus store.

The outer shirt, in this fair-weather outfit, is usually light cotton. It should have long sleeves and also pockets which button or zip. It shouldn't be too fragile, especially

if you plan to do any bushwhacking. In cooler climates some people use stout "chamois shirts" of a felt-like cotton.

As for underclothes, whatever you wear at home is usually fine for backpacking—but garments should be cotton not clammy, hot nylon. Net undershirts—open work constructions that look like "holes knotted together with string"—are nice but, at $6 to $8, are hardly required. Some hikers take no undershirt at all. The advantage of a net shirt is that it can be either very warm or very cool, as you choose. When your outer shirt is buttoned, the air trapped in the net is a warm, insulating layer. When you open the outer shirt, the gaps let the breeze reach your skin, as if you had no undershirt on at all. If you buy a net shirt, be sure that your model has ordinary close-woven fabric over the shoulders, otherwise the pack straps will drive the netting painfully into the skin. What about spare underclothing? In good weather, it's your choice. Some people take several sets. Some wash them on the trip. Some just don't worry about it. In wet weather, however, it is important to have dry underwear and socks to change into.

Except perhaps in forest walking, you will certainly want a broad-brimmed hat to protect your head from heat, your face and neck from sunburn, and your eyes from glare. In the desert, on snow, and at high altitudes you must have sunglasses. This is so important that you need not just one pair but two, in case you lose or break one of them. The glare from snowfields can actually blind you temporarily.

There are places where mosquitoes are so tormenting that some hikers add to the basic outfit a head-net: a veil of mosquito netting. Most people make do with insect repellent on the trail and netted tents in camp. Bathing suit for swimming? Sure, if modesty requires.

Extra clothing for cold and wind

So much for the balmy day. But now suppose the temperature begins to drop from 70 to 50 to 40 degrees or lower. Clouds move across the sun; a cold air is stirring. Or maybe it has been cool all along. The hiker was warm while he walked, but when he sits down to eat lunch, he feels a chill. So he looks to his stock of clothing.

About the simplest armament you can take against cold is one or two wool sweaters, or a wool shirt and a sweater, or two wool shirts, one large enough to be worn over the other. Shirts should have high collars, long tails, and closable pockets. Prices vary, with $20 to $30 typical. Cheaper ones are made of reprocessed wool, not quite so warm. Polyester fabrics, recently developed, can take the place of wool; they warm like wool but absorb less moisture.

In sweaters you have a choice between the pullover type and the type that zips or buttons down the front. The pullover is simpler, but a front closure lets you cool off without taking off the sweater.

The second essential for warmth is a wool or polyester stocking cap. More than a third of the heat the body loses into the air is radiated from the head. Conserve some of that, and you'll feel warmer all over. Some stocking caps are thick and fuzzy, others thinner and less formidable-looking; either will do fine. For colder places and times, you can buy a longer cap that rolls down to cover the neck, with a gap left for the face, helmet-fashion. Prices run $3 to $6. Hands also radiate a lot of heat; on cold summer evenings in the high country, mittens ($3 to $10) can be nice.

Instead of sweaters (or in addition to them) you may want an insulated jacket or vest. These come in a great range of weights and designs. For most travel, one of the lighter, simpler versions will do.

Some jackets and vests use down fill, others contain Hollofil II, PolarGuard, or Thinsulate. If you do most of your hiking in dry or dry-cold country, down is probably the better choice. But if you expect to be in places both cool and wet, it's not wise to depend on down for warmth: once wet, it loses most of its insulating power. Synthetic jackets weigh a little more for the warmth but don't cost quite as much.

In the cheaper down-filled jackets, sewn-through seams separate the compartments that contain the fill. For most wilderness use—even in winter—this construction is warm enough. Most synthetic-filled jackets use a quilted construction without sewn-through seams. Shell fabrics vary, too. Generally speaking, the lightest alternative—1.9 ounce

113

ripstop nylon—is the best choice; it is quite sturdy enough for normal use. Some jackets have built-in hoods; others, separate hoods that snap on. A hood can be spared in most summer use.

Along with the full-scale jackets, there are various cut-down versions, very light and versatile. Simplest of all is the insulated *vest* or armless jacket, with or without a collar. An extremely light jacket is known as an insulated *shirt*. Take away its front opening, and it becomes an insulated *pullover*.

Down-filled jackets with sewn-through seams sell in the $55 to $75 range, hoods included: synthetic-filled jackets run a few dollars cheaper, warmth for warmth. Down vests have prices between $25 and $50, while synthetic vests average about $25. Insulated "shirts" and "pullovers" cost more than vests, less than full jackets.

It isn't only the temperature of the air that can make you warm or cold. When the wind increases, all at once it seems cooler—much cooler, in fact, than a thermometer would indicate. This is *wind-chill*. Moving air draws heat from your body much faster than still air does. If the air is at 50 degrees, a wind of 20 miles an hour will make it feel like the freezing point. In summer the cooling effect of the wind may be welcome, but in colder places and seasons you must protect yourself from it. The clothes you add for warmth will blunt the wind a little, but they won't block it out.

The simplest wind-shell, adequate for most three-season hiking, is a nylon *wind-shirt* weighing only a few ounces. Department stores sell these for $10 or so, though it can be hard to find them without cotton lining you don't need or want. For some reason, few gear stores stock these light, useful garments. Instead, they carry heavier and more elaborate windgear, mostly suitable for mountaineering and for winter (see below).

Extra clothing for rain and snow

Cold and wind are fairly easy to deal with. They can even be bracing, exhilarating. Rain and wet snow are another matter. They can be pleasant, too, and often beautiful, but there's no denying that they give you problems.

If rain is nothing more than an occasional summer

Basic cold weather outfit, including wool pants

thunderstorm, raingear can be a single, simple garment: a *poncho*. The poncho, discussed earlier, is a big rectangle of urethane-coated nylon with a hole for the neck and a hood. The short-tailed or regular poncho is really just a rather loose, untailored raincoat. More useful is the *packboard poncho*, so long in back that it hangs over the pack and protects the load as well as the porter. Because the pack is inside with you, so to speak, a packboard poncho isn't pinched in around your body by shoulder straps and hip belt. Thus ventilation is reasonably good; sweat gets some chance to evaporate. Packboard ponchos can double as tarps for shelter if the rain is not too serious. Prices start at about $13, but stouter ones run $20 to $30, and the extra dollars may be worth it. Short-tailed ponchos are a few dollars cheaper. Sheet-plastic ponchos, also cheaper, will do as stopgaps only.

When the rain is heavy, and especially if there is wind, no poncho will be protection enough. Rain always works its way in at the sides. When the mist comes down the hills and the sky closes over in a slow-arriving, slow-departing storm, you need a regular raincoat and a separate cover for your pack. City-type rain slickers of rubberized cloth are adequate but heavy. *Rain parkas* are raincoats of urethane-coated nylon, usually with a zipper at the front. An *anorak* is a short, hooded nylon coat that has no front zipper but pulls on over your head. Perhaps the most total rain pro-tection possible is the full-length anorak or *cagoule*, which covers you down to the knees.

All raingear is full cut to leave room for layers of cloth-ing underneath. Hoods are usually built-in but are some-times separate. (Separate rainhats aren't much use because they don't protect the neck very well.) Some coats have drawstrings to tighten them at the waist or around the hem. Raincoat prices run $15 to $40 in gear stores; cagoules are the most expensive.

What about your legs? In warm country some people wear shorts and let their legs get wet. In colder climates you'll need waterproofing all the way down. *Rain chaps* come in literal pairs, a separate tube for each leg, and tie on to the belt at the top. Full *rain pants* protect the crotch and waistline better. Whatever combination of coat and leg protection you work out, make sure there is a generous overlap at the waist. Chaps cost $6 to $10, and rain pants run $9 to $25.

It is never entirely comfortable to hike in traditional waterproof clothing. When moisture can't get in, it can't get out either. Even if the air is cold, you are likely to get hot and sweaty. Designers try to get around this problem by adding generous vents or absorbent liners. The only real answer would be a one-way waterproof fabric: a fabric that would let body moisture escape while keeping the rain outside. The industry has been hunting for years for such a fabric.

The answer may have been found in Gore-Tex, a thin, fragile film with countless minuscule holes. Water vapor from evaporating sweat can pass out through these openings, but water droplets can't get in. To make a strong fabric with Gore-Tex, the film is bonded between layers of ordinary cloth. Such sandwiches are known as Gore-Tex laminates.

And do they work? It depends on who you ask. For many wearers, the laminates seem to perform as promised: to keep the rain completely out, and simultaneously to "breathe," though not so freely as plain porous cloth. Yet other users report continual failures. These complaints, numerous during the first years of Gore-Tex, have lately dwindled; but they have not ceased.

One problem is contamination. If oily substances—body oils, mosquito dope, hair oil—reach central Gore-Tex film, leaks may develop. Soiled Gore-Tex must be washed in soap flakes and warm water. At this writing, you also need to coat the seams of Gore-Tex garments with sealing compound—slow, messy, and effective. It is predicted that sealing will soon be done in the factory.

Great claims are made also for a second fabric: Bukflex, by Peter Storm. Though the manufacturing process is different, Bukflex, like Gore-Tex, contains microscopic pores. The consensus seems to be that Bukflex is nicely waterproof but not so "breathable" as Gore-Tex.

For wet and cold

If it is wet but warm, raingear alone, added to your basic outfit, may be enough to keep you comfortable. In the semi-tropical weather of the Southeast, hikers may shed clothing when the rain starts rather than adding it.

But if it is cold, or even cool, and also wet, your whole costume must change. Cotton, like down, loses its power to insulate when it gets soaked. If anything, it wicks heat away from your skin. A cold wind, rain, and wet cotton clothing add up to real danger. For situations like that, you wear and carry clothes made of wool or polyester pile: materials that warm you even when they get wet.

On your legs go wool or polyester-pile pants. (Ski pants will do but tend to bind at the knee.) Some gear stores sell full-length trousers, but you find these at lower prices in surplus stores and thrift shops. The specialty shops carry knickers, loose-cut wool or polyester pants that stop at the knee; they are worn with special high-top wool knee socks. Climbers and skiers like this rather expensive combination because it allows the leg to bend freely, and also because you can roll down the sock when you're working hard and get some cool air on your calves. Good knickers are made of heavy fabric (lighter versions tear). There should be a double seat and heavy reinforcement along the seam of the crotch. Don't make a mistake and buy knickers made of cotton or nylon for use in winter: they are as cold in the wet as any cotton. Good knickers cost $25 or more, and knee socks run $5 to $10 a pair.

Cotton shirts are also ruled out in wet, cold places. Instead, the wool shirt is the standard. Two thin ones, or a thin one and a thin sweater, will give you more possible combinations to choose from. Jackets should ideally be filled with Dacron, not with down.

Clothing for mountaineering and for winter

This is the basic winter outfit: wool pants, or knickers and knee socks; one or more wool shirts and sweaters; wool cap; mittens; and goggles or sunglasses. Polyester-pile garments can replace some of the wool.

All of the summer garments for wind and cold and wet are useful also in winter. For extremes of cold, extra and specialized clothing is added. For instance, many winter backpackers carry down or polyester jackets with extra fill and without sewn-through seams. These expensive, excellent garments, constructed like fine sleeping bags, weigh two to three pounds and cost $70 and up. Unless you have unusual trouble keeping warm, you should be slow to buy so massive a garment. Even in very cold places many hikers prefer a summer-type sewn-through jacket with several added sweaters.

If the super-thick insulated jacket is of doubtful usefulness short of an expedition, still more questionable is the insulated parka that stuffs filling inside a heavy nylon-cotton windshell. These are among the heaviest and clumsiest of wilderness garments. It's better to do the job with a separate, lighter jacket and a separate, lighter windshell.

What about long underwear? Many people use it in winter, many people don't. It seems to depend on personal warm-bloodedness. Once on, long johns are a chore to get off, and much of the time they will keep you unpleasantly warm. All-wool longies are too prickly for most people. More popular are versions that combine wool with other kinds of fiber. Cotton-polyester fishnet underwear is also much used. Prices run $10 to $25 a set.

Gloves and mittens are essential for winter. People wear different combinations. A typical one in very cold places is a light, fingered wool glove ($2 to $3) inside a heavier wool mitten ($3 to $10) with a nylon mitten-shell on top of that ($2 to $6). Shells are sometimes water-proofed, sometimes not.

Wind-chill, in the winter mountains, can be deadly. If it's blowing hard enough, you can get frostbite when the temperature is barely under the freezing point. In the woods a light summer-style wind-shell may do for winter also, but on exposed ridges more total protection is required: the *wind parka.*

A wind parka is a solidly-made, unpadded coat, generally long enough so that you can sit down on the tail. It has a hood (usually built in) with a drawstring; a good, rugged front zipper, with a flap of fabric behind it and a line of snaps to use if it fails; and usually several enormous pockets. Often there's another drawstring to tighten the coat around the waist.

All wind parkas are built of permeable fabric. That fabric may be thin nylon taffeta or ripstop, heavy English ventile cotton, or a nylon/cotton mix ("60/40" or "65/35" cloth). Both ventile cotton and the compound fabrics are somewhat resistant to water as well as to wind, but neither

is waterproof. While a parka may protect you nicely in a
light sprinkle, or shed cold, dry snowflakes, it won't serve
as your raincoat. It gets wet; so do you; and a wet wind-
parka is cold, clammy, and several times its dry weight.
Parka prices run from $30 to $60.

When it's cold and windy enough to wear a parka, you
will also probably want nylon *wind pants*. These are loose
and pajama-like, with an elastic band at the waist. The
more expensive ones may have full-length zippers up the
legs so that you can zip yourself in and out without taking
off (for example) your skis. Prices run $10 to $20. Rain
pants can be used in a pinch, but, again, your legs will be
hot and sticky with trapped sweat.

Another winter essential is a pair of gaiters. These
tough nylon sheaths fasten around the ankle, closing off
the gap at the top of the boot, where snow would otherwise get in. Some gaiters, for wading occasional snowbanks, are simple and collar-like. For real snow travel you
need the fitted or "spat" type that covers the upper half of
the boot and rises well up the leg. Most gaiters have zippers, either in back or in front—front is easier to reach—
and usually a line of snaps as well. A cord or buckle, running under the boot, keeps the gaiter from creeping up out
of place. Gaiters may be waterproof or not, or waterproof
only in the lower part; some wearers find the coated ones
hot and clammy. Prices range from about $6 to $25.

Adjustability: why less is sometimes more

When you hike, whether summer or winter, you burn a
lot of fuel and produce a lot of heat. At the same time,
you're losing that heat, mostly to the air. To stay comfortable, you have to maintain a rough balance between the
heat you generate and the heat you give away. Retain too
much, and you'll be miserably hot; lose too much, and
you'll be miserably cold. Not too far beyond misery, in
either direction, is danger. The diseases of overheating are
known as *heat stroke* and *heat exhaustion;* the disease of
serious chilling is called *hypothermia* (see Chapter 27 for
more about these and other problems).

Every moment you spend on the trail, something happens to shift the heat balance a little. Maybe at first you
are walking along a flat, shaded valley, feeling comfort-

able. Then the trail climbs a ridgeline in the sun, and you are hot and sweating. Later, a chill takes you as you reach the windy height above. Wind, sunlight, temperature, terrain, your own metabolism—everything is constantly changing.

The body has certain built-in ways of managing heat, but the adjustments it can make are limited. Beyond that narrow range, you have to adjust your clothing. The adjustment may be as simple as rolling your sleeves up or down or as complex as putting on a jacket and a wind-shell; the purpose is always the same.

And the easier it is to make these adjustments, the more comfortable you will be. In choosing clothes for the wilderness, you look for the garments that allow you to change your protection exactly as required when the heat balance shifts from too much to too little and back again.

For this reason, most hikers (not all) prefer several thin garments to one thicker layer. If you have two light shirts along, you can wear neither, or one, or both, for three degrees of warmth. If you have only a single, heavier shirt, it's either on you or in your pack; you've lost an intermediate choice.

In the same way, backpackers tend to favor pieces of clothing that do a single job to those that try to serve several purposes at once. If you have both a light insulated jacket and a wind-shell, you can wear the jacket alone when it is cold and still; the wind-shell alone when it is warmer but blowing; both together when you need the greatest protection. But if you bought the monstrous down-stuffed parka that is shell and jacket in one, you have no choice. You either wear the thing or you don't.

A third principle: if each piece of clothing is adjustable in itself, you have an extra advantage. Thus most people prefer an open-front raincoat or sweater to a pullover style. If the pullover gets too hot for you, you can simply suffer. Or you can stop, take off your pack, take off the pullover, put it away, hoist your pack again, and go. By that time you may be chilled again anyway. But with a front closure, you can let a cooling breeze in any time.

All of this matters, in typical summer weather, only to a degree. It is in really bad weather, and especially in winter, that ease of adjustment can make the most striking difference. When you are hiking in a bitterly cold wind, you don't want to work up too much of a sweat; it will chill you the moment you stop. The world you are in, wonderful though it may be, is also hostile. You have to keep the balance to survive.

Putting it together

How, then, do you choose the clothes for a particular trip? Whether you're heading for a 12,000-foot peak in December or for the local woodland in June, the questions are the same. Start with the basic outfit appropriate to the season, and then ask yourself: what else, if anything, do I need to add for *cold*? What should I add for *wind*? What should I add for *wet*?

There are three or four typical climates that back-packers encounter and three or four typical lists of clothing that result.

First, there's the comfortable weather of the Southwest hiking season. In the wilderness lands of California and the mountain states to the east, temperatures may either be hot or cool in summer, depending on month and elevation, but the air will seldom be wet for long. Humidity is almost always low and rain comes, if at all, in brief, torrential thundershowers. Under these circumstances, the hiker is likely to wear and carry, besides his boots and socks and underclothing:

- hiking shorts
- jeans
- light cotton shirt
- sunglasses and spares (depending)
- hat
- bandanna
- one or two light sweaters or light insulated jacket
- light wind-shell
- poncho
- stocking cap

At lower elevations, and in places almost totally free of summer rain, this short list can be shortened still further.

Less hospitable, in some ways, is the moister, cooler summer landscape of Maine or western Washington or Minnesota. Really hot days are not common; storms can blow in at any time and last for several days; the temperature can drop quickly and far. Under such conditions the hiker may well start out in cotton clothes, but he will carry wool or polyester-pile.

- hiking shorts
- jeans
- light cotton shirt
- sunglasses and spares (depending)
- hat
- bandanna

- sweaters or light polyester-filled jacket
- light wind-shell
- raincoat
- wool pants (or knickers and knee socks)
- stocking cap
- pack cover

Different again are the regions where it is both humid and, in the normal hiking season, either warm or hot, with perhaps the relief of cool nights at higher altitudes. Here the usual hiking uniform is boots and shorts and as little else as possible. The clothing packlist grows shorter, here, because there is little need to carry wool. If wet cotton is cool, so much the better.

- hiking shorts
- jeans
- light cotton shirt
- hat

- bandanna
- sweater or wool shirt
- raincoat
- pack cover

In wet lowlands many hikers choose the army's ventilated tropical combat boot instead of regular leather boots (see Chapter 4).

These lists could be varied—there are a thousand personal preferences, and legitimate arguments for adding this, deleting that—but I hope they make the point: trail clothing, for most wilderness conditions, need not be complex. It is only in winter (or in places that are always wintry) that the whole range of wilderness clothing may have to be drawn on at once. One typical winter packlist looks like this:

- knickers with knee socks (or wool pants)
- two wool shirts
- rain pants
- wind pants
- insulated jacket with hood
- wind-shell or wind parka
- rain coat or cagoule

- wool cap
- regular hat
- goggles and spares
- gaiters
- wool gloves
- wool mittens
- nylon overmitts
- long johns (possibly)

9:
Stove and Kitchen

Too many backpackers, in sunny regions at least, carry tents they may not need. But too few backpackers anywhere have yet formed the habit of carrying stoves. The stove, in the modern wilderness, is a necessity treated, too often, as an option or a luxury.

There is no denying the pleasures (or the uses) of the old-fashioned campfire. An evening fire is a presence; almost, strangely, a pet or a companion. It gives pleasant light, pleasant heat, pleasant noises. It is an event, an entertainment. It draws a group together around it. For many, it is a symbol of camping, a symbol of the wilderness even—a return to a far older, far simpler way of doing things.

And yet the fire, in the wilderness today, is slowly falling out of favor. There are simply too many of us now and too little pristine land for old habits to hold. Fires near timberline, where wood is scarce and the growing season short, are not now defensible. Nor is there much case to be made for the building of new fire-rings where none have been before. In the more populous wilderness landscapes, firespots mark the ground like so many black sores, and these, more quickly than anything else we leave to mark our presence, make the land look used and overused.

Thus the managers of wilderness have found it increasingly necessary to close large areas to fire. And there are times and places where no rule intervenes, but where you nonetheless feel reluctant to make a mark. Perhaps you are setting up camp on a ridgeline miles from the nearest traveled trail, a place so remote and changeless that you could imagine yourself the first human being to walk there. There is no one to object to one small fire-scar. There may not even be a compelling "ecological" argument against leaving one. And yet you recoil. It seems important (perhaps beyond reason) that you not leave that place diminished in any way.

The case against fire should not be overstated. There are times and places where a fire cannot, by the longest reach of conscience, be accused of doing harm: a sea beach tangled with drifted logs for fuel; a sandbar or a gravelly river bank (below the winter high-water line); an old firering in a moist forest littered with down wood. And even in a pristine landscape there are ways of handling a fire so that nothing visible is left behind.

But this is the point: if you have a stove, you simply don't have to worry about the propriety of the kitchen site you have chosen. You are self-sufficient. You take nothing from the land and leave nothing behind. No ashes. No rings. No blackened stones to clean or conceal. You are much more free to camp where you will.

There are other practical advantages as well. Simplicity is the main one. The next few pages will inevitably make stoves sound like complicated, rather tricky gadgets. But once you have the stove and have grown used to it, you'll find its operation quick and easy. You'll be boiling water while the wood-burner is still gathering kindling. And you'll be working with a steady, controllable flame. No question about it: pleasant associations aside, stove cooking has campfire cooking beat all hollow.

And whether you choose a stove for conscience or convenience, you may in time discover something more. You may find that the stove brings with it pleasures of its own, equal, perhaps, to the pleasures of a fire. A stove, too, becomes a kind of companion. It has its own rituals. It burns with a comfortable, reassuring roar. It calls to your mind, each time you light it, the other places you have used it: other camps, other journeys, other times.

But most important is that curious moment, after dark, when at last you turn the valve-key and bring the stove to instant silence. There are no embers, of course, to sit by and watch fade. What happens instead is rather hard to explain. The wilderness, kept at a certain distance for a while by your noisy and lighted kitchen, appears all at once around you. The night sky comes into being over you as if its black and its brilliance had just then been invented. The colors of the night, the movements, the slight noises, become instantly present. Against all these things the wood-burning fire is a lively defense—but a defense (you may come to feel) no more to be desired than it is needed.

On some trips in some regions you can have it both ways. If you carry a stove and fuel, you can leave them in the pack when conditions are right for a fire. Maybe your first night will be spent in the rain in a low-lying forest, where wood is plentiful, a fire a real comfort. But the next night you are at timberline in a no-fire zone. Or maybe, arriving at a place where you planned to build a fire, you find there is no dead, down wood within scavenging range. Far better to carry the stove and leave it unused than to carry none and find yourself forced to choose between eating cold food and lighting a fire where no fire should be.

Stoves suitable for backpacking are small and light. They come in many different models—forty or so—but in just three essentially different popular designs. There is the old wilderness standard, the *white gas stove*. There is the fussier but safer *kerosene stove*. Finally, there is the butane- or propane-burning *cartridge stove*, which uses prefilled, pressurized fuel cannisters.

White gas stoves

What is "white gas"? It comes in two forms. The cheaper type, available at a very few service stations, is generally like automobile fuel. (You couldn't use it in your car, though, because it is free of *any* chemical additives, and all auto gas, including the unleaded kind, contains extra substances which gum up stoves. Leaded gas is dangerous in a stove. White gas of the service-station type must be burned within a couple of months of purchase—it deteriorates quickly.

The second substance known as "white gas" is somewhat different and about twice as expensive. You see it in sporting goods and hardware stores as "Coleman fuel," "camp fuel," and the like, for about $2 a gallon. It is specially refined and contains additives, different from those in auto fuel, to fight rust and make for easy lighting. This fuel burns very cleanly and leaves no residue. It can be stored for at least several years.

A gallon of white gas, wherever you bought it, will cook 30 meals or more for two or three hikers.

White gas stoves are simple. There is a *fuel tank*, holding between half a cup and a cup and a half of fuel (larger models, not much used by small groups in summer backpacking, hold much more). A *wick* draws fuel out of the tank into a *vaporizing tube*, from which it passes through a controlling *valve* to the *burner*. In the burner, the stream of vapor strikes against a *burner plate* where it mixes with air and ignites. When the stove is burning, its own heat

Working parts of a white gas stove

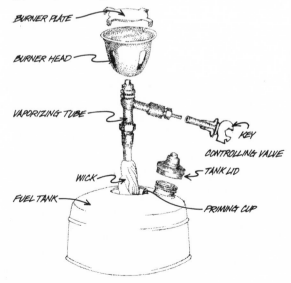

BURNER PLATE

BURNER HEAD

VAPORIZING TUBE

KEY

CONTROLLING VALVE

TANK LID

WICK

FUEL TANK

PRIMING CUP

keeps the fuel flowing; the tank grows warm, and vapor pressure inside it drives fuel up along the wick. The vaporizing tube, grown very hot, transforms the liquid instantly into a gas. To get the operation started, though, you have to heat both the tank and the vaporizing tube by burning a little fuel in a special *priming cup.* The height of the flame is controlled by a *key* (or knob) that opens and closes the valve in the fuel line.

There are two main layouts in white gas stoves. In the *upright style* (Svea 123, for instance), the burner sits right on top of the fuel tank, and the priming cup is nothing but an indentation in the roof of the tank. In the *separate-tank style* (Optimus 8-R), the fuel tank is set a short distance away from the burner and to one side, behind a metal heat-shield; the whole unit sits in a squarish metal box.

All gas stoves have a *pressure-release valve* set into the tank cap. This is a safety device. It won't happen if the stove is run with normal care but if the fuel in the tank should ever become extremely hot, vapor pressure inside would build to dangerous levels. If this were to go on indefinitely, the tank would split, and you'd have a nasty

Svea 123

Optimus 90

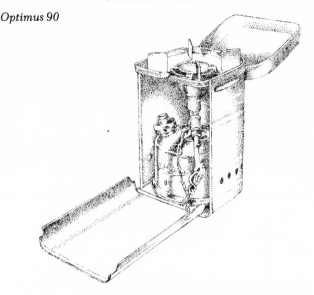

explosion on your hands. Instead, when the pressure hits a certain very abnormal level, it springs open the valve in the tank cap and spits a stream of gas into the air. If this happens, it is a dangerous moment: the escaping gas, catching fire from the burner, will be a powerful jet of flame. But there won't be an explosion. Cases in which the release valve lets go are rare but not so rare as they should be, due mainly to mistakes the operators make. See Chapter 19 for some notes on the proper handling of stoves.

The weight of a stove depends on many things: size and ruggedness, carrying case, capacity of fuel tank, and more. Separate-tank stoves run a little heavier than upright models (the compensating advantage is stability). Some stoves are sold with specially fitted *windscreens* (see *Accessories* below). Prices for the small stoves used in summer lie between $20 and $40. The cost of fuel averages ten cents per cooking hour. Weights without fuel run from eighteen ounces (Svea 123) to 29 ounces (Phoebus 725).

When you look for a small white gas stove, there are just a few brands and models to consider. The classic and very popular Svea 123 is an upright model. You can get it with or without a round carrying case that serves also as windscreen. The identical stove is sold in a square box as the *Optimus 90,* and with a set of pots as the *Optimus 88-N.* Another familiar model is the *Optimus 8-R,* which has a separate fuel tank and a heatshield, and rides in a side-hinged steel box. The *Optimus 99* is the same stove in an aluminum box with a separate windscreen. The *Phoebus 725,* a squat, heavy, sturdy upright model, is one of the few small stoves not built by the A. B. Optimus Company. The *Baby Enders 263,* a separate-tank stove by Hy-score, is the only light stove with a built-in pump. (Add-on pumps, to be discussed later, can be purchased for Svea and Optimus models.)

White gas stoves continued: mountaineering stoves

There are a number of much heavier stoves to be had, both in the upright design and in the separate-tank style. Most of these are chiefly useful to large parties, or to smaller parties in winter, when snow must be melted in large quantities for water. Fuel tanks are larger, holding almost a pint (10 ounces) or more. In addition, all of these stoves have a feature not generally found on lighter units: a *pump.*

The simpler stoves discussed above use their own heat to drive the fuel up to the flame; they are *self-pressurizing.* But self-pressured stoves can be hard to start and run in the severe cold of winter. Thus the value of a hand-operated push-pump—air is forced inside the fuel tank and drives the fuel directly to the burner. The temperature in the tank doesn't matter. Priming is also much easier, though it is still necessary; the vaporizing tube must be hot before the stove will run on its own. After starting a pump stove, you give the pump a couple of strokes every few minutes (say every time you stir the soup) to keep the flame hot and bright.

There are just a handful of mountaineering stoves. There's the massive *Optimus 111-B,* a separate-tank, metal-box model resembling an expanded Optimus 8-R. There's the *Phoebus 625,* a solid upright model. The *Coleman 502 Sportster* looks much like the Phoebus. The *Coleman 576* is a new upright model intended for the general backpacking market; you can regard it either as a very heavy basic stove or as a very light mountaineering type. Coleman claims that its stoves can be started without

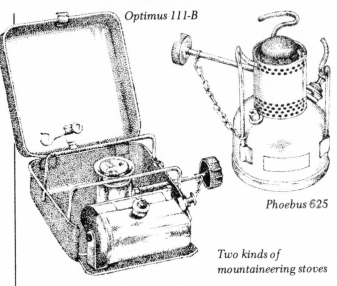

Optimus 111-B

Phoebus 625

*Two kinds of
mountaineering stoves*

priming, at least under good conditions. For these various stoves, weights without fuel run from two pounds to three pounds five ounces, and prices range from $23 to $60.

I have so far deliberately ignored the nonconformist among high-output mountaineering stoves: the *Mountain Safety Research Model 9-A*. This extraordinary gadget is light enough to be a summer stove—it weighs only eleven ounces without fuel!—yet its heat output and its price, near $50, place it among the mountaineering stoves. In the Model 9-A, there is no built-in fuel tank. Rather, the stove draws its fuel, through a tube, from an ordinary Sigg storage bottle (see below), the kind in which you typically carry your extra gasoline. You don't put fuel *in* this stove— rather you plug the stove into the fuel. There is, of course, a pump. The MSR, a somewhat complex and delicate machine, burns its fuel more quickly than any other, but gives you a correspondingly greater amount of heat.

One more point. There are two distinct styles of burners in mountaineering stoves. Two stoves—the MSR and the Optimus 111-B—have the simple, traditional *burner plate*. The fuel jet, striking the plate, eddies and mixes with air. This mixing, without which there can be no flame, does not happen unless the jet is strong. Thus stoves with burner

131

plates don't throttle down to simmering level very well. The other style, common to the Coleman stoves and the Phoebus 625, is the *ported burner*. Here, the flame is divided and burns out of numerous vents; even a small flow of fuel mixes easily with oxygen—you can simmer readily with such a stove. If you like to do slow, home-style cooking on the trail, this can be a convenience.

Kerosene stoves

Kerosene-burning stoves look much like white gas stoves. Yet there are differences—special features are necessary because of the nature of the fuel.

Kerosene is a far less volatile fuel than gasoline. It is slower to evaporate and slower to ignite. This makes it a bit more difficult to work with than white gas. Kerosene also has a greasy feel, makes long-lasting stains, and has a tendency to burn with smoke and soot.

With these disadvantages, why consider kerosene? Because it has a selling point that no other powerful fuel can match: *it is very safe to use*. Once lit, it burns brightly—kerosene actually yields more heat per volume of fuel than white gas does—but it must be almost persuaded to ignite. This means that spilled fuel won't flare up in a flash fire, as can happen with spilled white gas. Nor is a kerosene stove at all liable to dangerous overheating. No stove can be guaranteed safe if you abuse it, but with kerosene it is much harder to provoke an accident. Partly because of the safety angle, large groups (say ten people or more) almost always favor kerosene stoves.

All kerosene stoves have pumps. The fuel won't evaporate readily enough to build up vapor pressure in a warm tank, so it must be forced up to the burner by air pumped in from outside. The vaporizing tube must be *very* hot before the fluid will turn to gas; so these stoves must be primed with care. They are slower to take off, and are likely to smoke annoyingly if you hurry matters. Nor is kerosene itself the fuel to prime with. Hard to light, it burns with soot and a gummy residue. Most people use alcohol, a clean, quick-lighting fuel, to prime their kerosene stoves. Solid fuel can also be used.

The classic among kerosene stoves is the upright *Optimus 00*, the lightweight standby of organized groups.

The 00 has no valve to control the height of the flame. Rather, you raise the flame by pumping and lower it by letting pressure out of a manual valve in the tank cap. This is *not* an automatic safety valve like those found on white gas stoves; with a single exception, noted below, white gas must never be used in a kerosene stove.

All other kerosene stoves do have controls to adjust the height of the flame in addition to the pump and the bleeder valve in the tank cap. The *Optimus 45* is generally like the Optimus 00, but larger. The *Optimus 111* is a heavy separate-tank stove, a kerosene version of the gasoline-burning 111-B. The *Mountain Safety Research Multi-Fuel Stove* is an adaptation of the MSR-9A; alone among kerosene stoves, it can also burn white gas, and several other fuels as well.

The Optimus 00 presently sells for about $35. The other kerosene burners, more expensive, range to $60.

Kerosene is found at a few gas stations and in hardware and sporting goods stores. Though raw kerosene has an odor unpleasant to some, most kerosene now sold is nearly odorless. Its cost is equivalent to that of white gas—about $2 a gallon in the stores—and it weighs just slightly more, but it is consumed somewhat more slowly. Overseas, kerosene is sold as "paraffin" or "petroleum" and may be the only available fuel (regular gas is "benzin," while "gas" or "gaz" refers to propane or butane).

Cartridge stoves

Compared to the small but real complexities of kerosene and white gas stoves, cartridge stoves are attractively simple. That's why they now outsell all other types. Their fuel, usually butane, is sold in prefilled cartridges. The butane, which ordinarily would be a gas at room temperature, is kept liquid, under great pressure, in its solid-walled container. Open the valve, and the butane instantly streams out as vapor, ready to burn. The stove needs no priming cup, no wick; it is composed of a *stem* that plugs into the fuel cartridge, a *valve* that controls the rate of flow, and a *burner*. All cartridge stoves have ported burners and burn well at low flame. The flame is silent.

The basic parts—cartridge, stem, and burner—can be arranged in different ways. Often the cartridge sits upright

133

and supports the burner on top as in the popular Bleuet S-200. On other models the cartridge may form one leg of a tripod supporting the burner. It can sit under a self-supporting stove top, plug in from the side, or have a separate burner and cartridge linked by a flexible hose. One model even has two burners. But the working parts are always much the same.

The cartridges differ too. With certain exceptions they cannot be interchanged from stove to stove. Some must be left attached to the stove once a seal is broken; others can be removed between uses. And some cartridges contain a wick to help the fuel flow in the cold.

There's no monkey business about lighting a cartridge stove under good conditions; it's like touching a match to a burner on a kitchen range. That's what makes the design so very popular. But despite such advantages, cartridge stoves have limitations that may prevent them from expanding their present share of the market.

First, and most important, it appears that cartridge stoves are somewhat more dangerous than their competitors. Cartridges have been known to leak, to spray their highly inflammable fuel, and even to explode in use. While such accidents are surely very rare, considering the number of stoves being used, they are disconcerting because they are so random; no amount of care will prevent a faulty unit from misbehaving.

Second, cartridge stoves simply don't put out as much heat as gas and kerosene types; in fact, you're lucky to get half the heating power. This makes cartridges more suitable for summer than for winter use. Cooking times are longer.

Third, though cartridge stoves run a few dollars cheaper than gas and kerosene types, butane cartridges are much more expensive than white gas or kerosene. Since the used containers must be discarded, they are also wasteful of natural resources. And an astonishing number of people are still unconcernedly discarding their newly-emptied cartridges on the spot—in the wilderness! Needless to say, *don't*.

Fourth, and crucial, is the low-pressure problem. In most (not all) butane stoves, the gas streams out simply because the pressure inside is greater than the atmospheric

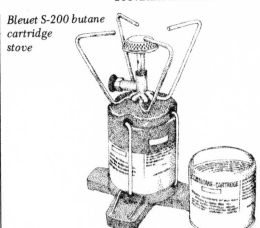

Bleuet S-200 butane cartridge stove

pressure outside. But the more fuel is used, the less the inside pressure. After about the halfway point, the flame begins to weaken. It may take twice as long to boil water with a fading cartridge as with a fresh one.

And that's when the cartridge is warm. The problem becomes much worse in cold places. When the pressurized butane gets chilled, it presses outward less strongly. When it's cold enough, the stove will simply refuse to work. At sea level the failing point is about 32 degrees—freezing. (Oddly enough, butane stoves do better at high altitudes. Because the atmosphere is thinner up there, there's less competing pressure from outside to block the exit of fuel from the cartridge. At 10,000 feet, a butane stove will work down to 12 degrees; at the altitudes encountered on Asian expeditions, the crucial point falls below zero.)

There are several ways of getting around the chill/ pressure problem. You can make a stove work, no matter how cold the air, by keeping the cartridge itself very warm. Carry the fuel next to your body; wrap it in ensolite; take it into your sleeping bag—there are many possibilities. You can set up a foil reflector to bounce the stove's own heat back to the cartridge. In addition, you will need to apply heat to the stem between cartridge and burner.

Not all cartridges and stoves are equally vulnerable to cold. You may eventually be able to buy a special variety of the fuel, called *iso-butane,* which is much more volatile than normal butane; at sea level, it will keep flowing at 15

135

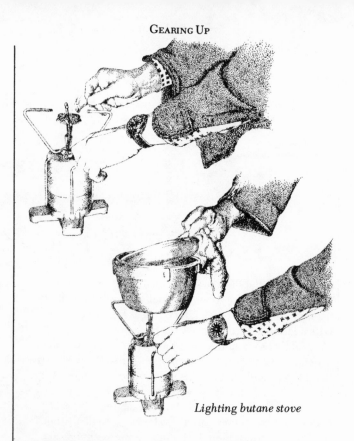

Lighting butane stove

degrees. But iso-butane is presently used in few if any cartridges.

It's more practical to turn to a *liquid-feed* butane stove. Originally, all butane stoves used *vapor-feed:* that is, they depended purely on internal pressure to drive the fuel to the burner. Most still do. But the new liquid-feed stoves use special cartridges with built-in wicks. It takes very little internal pressure to send fuel creeping along the wick. Liquid-feed stoves function down to the freezing point of butane, which, at sea level, is 15 degrees. Liquid-feed cartridges also burn somewhat more brightly than the traditional vapor-feed type and don't suffer the same annoying fall-off in heating power. On the minus side, wicked cartridges don't last as long as vapor-feed, and they tend to flare and fade erratically on lighting, especially in the cold.

Two well-known liquid-feed stoves are the *EFI Mini-Mark II* and the *Optimus Mousetrap.* Among vapor-feed stoves are Bleuet, Globetrotter, Instaflam, Primus Ranger, Prolite, and the Rich-Moor stoves. Models by ALP will accept cartridges of either sort.

There is still a third option for cold weather. *Propane stoves* work exactly like butane models, but propane, much more volatile, keeps flowing in bitter cold. Unfortunately, propane cartridges must be very heavy to contain the energetic gas and thus are little used in ordinary backpacking.

Cartridge stoves run from about $10 to $30, with an average near $18. Their weights vary widely, too, from as little as five ounces (without cartridge) to as much as thirty ounces; the average lies somewhere under a pound. Most very light cartridge stoves don't put out much heat and are mainly of use to the single, weight-minded hiker who does little cooking. Butane cartridges typically weigh about ten ounces and contain six to seven ounces of fuel, with a burning time in the neighborhood of ninety minutes (liquid-feed) or three hours (vapor-feed). They cost about $1.50 each. Propane cartridges, on the other hand, typically weigh thirty ounces, of which fifteen ounces is metal; they burn three to six hours.

Other kinds of stoves

While kerosene, cartridge, and white gas stoves command the backpacking market, there are nonetheless other possibilities.

Liquid alcohol stoves are of several kinds. In the simpler ones the fuel burns in a cup under a housing that is both windscreen and pot support. The *REI* alcohol stove is the neat minimum and costs about $3. The *Optimus 77-A* is a combination stove and cookset with a round base, alcohol cup, and two pots: $18. The larger *Optimus 45-A* is a modified version of the kerosene-burning 45; by weight and price, at least, it is a mountaineering stove. Alcohol is easy to work with, but it isn't cheap ($4 or more a gallon in hardware stores) and it gives less heat than other liquid fuels; thus more must be carried.

Then there are *solid fuel stoves.* These are mostly just housings over a can of Sterno (jellied alcohol) or a fuel pellet. The stoves are cheap and simple but are too weak to be of much use in wilderness cooking. Sterno is found most readily in hardware stores, and pellet fuel (Hexamine, Esbit, Heat Tabs) is available in sporting goods stores. Then there's the curious *Zip* solid fuel stove; priced like a butane model, it burns charcoal briquets, or just about anything else, with the help of a battery-operated fan.

Buying a stove

What stove is best for you? The choice is broad enough to be a bit confusing. Start by asking yourself when, where, and for whom you will be cooking. Summer? Winter? High elevations or low? Large or small parties? Then consider these points.

Kerosene, white gas, or butane? Let's summarize. *Kerosene* is the safest and least convenient of all the fuels; kerosene stoves are most often used by large groups. The safety advantage is especially great if you expect to cook frequently inside a tent or have small children underfoot. *White gas* is safe enough, used carefully, but gives you less margin for error. It is slightly easier to use than kerosene, less so than butane. *Butane,* the convenience fuel (under ideal conditions), is perhaps best suited to short trips in summer. It puts out less heat, costs much more, and may be harder to locate away from home.

How powerful a stove? There are three grades. *Superlight* models—EFI Mini-Mark II, Prolite, and others—are mainly suited for use by one or two hikers who do only the simplest cooking and go out mainly in good weather. Solid fuel stoves and most liquid alcohol stoves are also in this group. No white gas or kerosene stoves are in this category.

Then there are what might be called *basic* stoves—the more substantial butane models and white gas and kerosene stoves weighing less than a couple of pounds with fuel. They will do admirably for summer use by small groups, and some are very usable in winter as well.

Finally, there are *mountaineering* stoves with pumps. All burn gas or kerosene. If you plan to do a lot of winter camping, a powerful pump stove will be best for the endless job of melting snow (some smaller stoves, good in summer, can only with difficulty be coaxed into boiling water

138

in the winter). But "mountaineering" stoves can also be useful if you do a lot of cooking for groups of more than three or four, "mountaineers" or no.

Vapor-feed or liquid-feed butane? You can avoid some of the problems of butane by using liquid-feed stoves, especially in cold weather.

Boiling time? How long does it take the stove to boil a quart of water from room temperature? Under good conditions at sea level, average boiling times range from under four minutes (MSR Multi-fuel stove) to more than sixteen (Prolite Pocket Stove). However, the same stove will turn in widely varying performances at different times. Most stoves boil more slowly in the cold and still more slowly in wind. *Backpacker* magazine, in a recent study, found only five stoves that could boil water in a cold breeze, all of them white gas or kerosene stoves by Optimus or MSR. In bad weather, a fast boil is all-important.

Simmering ability? There are many stoves which, while they don't burn very hot, maintain a low, controllable flame. This is fine if you travel in good weather and like to cook dishes that need simmering. All white gas and kerosene stoves tend to be quick boilers; all butane stoves tend to be good simmerers, but there's much variation within each type. Stoves with ported burners simmer better, and heavier stoves often have a more controllable flame.

Weight and price of fuel? How much fuel will your stove use in the course of a typical trip? A light, cheap stove that gulps fuel may not turn out to be the best bargain. Butane stoves are economical for short trips, but when you start packing extra cartridges the weight adds up quickly. And cartridges cost between five and ten times as much as white gas, per hour of burning.

Time between refills? The smaller your fuel tank or cartridge and the faster fuel is consumed, the more time you will have to spend fiddling with fuel. Most stoves burn between one hour and four.

Stability? Some stoves give very good support to the pot on the burner and have low centers of gravity. But the majority are quite tippy. Look at each model and ask yourself how easy it might be to lose a pot of goulash.

Workmanship? Take a look at the fuel line from tank or cartridge to burner. Does it have rough, unfinished-looking

welds? Do any screw connections tend to loosen? Generally speaking, the simpler the arrangement, the better. The
best materials in stoves are stainless steel and brass.

The package? Some stoves come more or less bare, others in cunning packages. You may also find cooksets and
windscreens designed to fit one particular stove or another
(consider these accessories when you judge stability).
There's no need to buy the package deals, but you should
consider how neatly your stove will pack, how well it will
fit your pots, and how it will be screened from the wind.

For information on specific stoves, there are two
sources very much worth consulting. One is the pamphlet
Stoves for Mountaineering, published in 1976 by *Off Belay*
magazine ($1.00). The second is *Backpacker* magazine's
Issue #16, Summer 1976, which contains detailed com-
parative ratings of stoves. See addresses in *Resources.*

Care of a stove

A stove is not a difficult item to care for. Given proper
use, it will almost take care of itself for long periods. For
occasional maintenance you'll get, with your stove, something in the way of instructions and perhaps a tiny wrench.
Many gear stores will do repairs on stoves they have sold
you.

When you first buy a kerosene or gasoline stove, take
the time to flush out the tank with a little fuel. Make sure
that the burner plate (if there is one) is firmly attached
(you'll see metal tabs that can be crimped to hold the plate
more tightly to the burner head). Be sure to test the stove
at home well in advance of your first trip with it (this job
should be done outdoors). Burn at least a full tank or a full
cartridge of butane to get an idea of how the stove
behaves. How long will it burn? In the case of vapor-feed
butane cartridges, when does the fall-off in heating power
begin? How much does it tend to flare on ignition? (For
more on starting and running a stove, see Chapter 19.)

When stoves do break down, it's often because of
deposits of solids in the fuel line. Do what you can to prevent them. When you fill your tank, pour the gas through a
funnel with a strainer. Don't leave the tank full of fuel
between trips. Over hours of burning, carbon builds up at
the burner nipple where the fuel jet issues. This has to be

cleaned out frequently. On some stoves you use a special tool, a needle mounted on a handle; others, called *self-cleaning* stoves, have a built-in cleaning needle that works by turning the valve key. It does no harm to use the needle with every meal, and this may prevent trouble later. Every few years, though, you will probably need to take the stove apart and clean the works (or have it done in a shop). Stove anatomy is not complex, but takes a little time to learn.

If you drop a stove, check it for bent connections and possible leaks. On separate-tank stoves with heatshields, make sure that the shield stands well away from the fuel tank, and keep it shiny and reflective.

The majority of white gas stoves are made by a single company, A. B. Optimus (Optimus, Svea, and Primus are its brands). Parts in this line are broadly interchangeable, and most gear stores have them for sale. If not, the larger mail-order gear houses stock them. Most items are under a dollar, but tank caps cost $3 to $4 and vaporizing tubes $5 to $6. Perhaps the two most important parts to carry are a spare burner plate (they do sometimes get lost) and a spare tank cap. If, for some reason, you do get your fuel tank so hot that the pressure-release valve blows, the valve is supposed to reclose itself neatly. But it's reported that some caps don't. Either way, it's a good idea to replace the cap after a blowout, and indeed it should be switched every couple of years, accident or no.

Fuel and accessories

Optimus also markets a special *Mini-Pump* that can be used to start its self-pressurizing stoves in cold weather ($5). This gadget doesn't convert a small stove into a mountaineering type, but it helps adapt a summer stove to winter use. Though it fits any Optimus or Svea, it is most convenient with a separate-tank model.

How much fuel you need depends of course on your stove, your cooking style, and your trip. It also depends on altitude; cooking times increase as the air pressure drops. Generally speaking (for a closer look see Chapter 12), a quart of gas or kerosene is a generous supply for two hikers for a summer week. Unless a stove is used lavishly, a quarter cup of fuel per person per day is a good figure to reckon on; in winter, double the amount. The number of butane cartridges you need for the same summer week depends on the burning time and the heating power of each, and can be as few as two or as many as six; liquid-feed cartridges burn out faster.

White gas and kerosene are sold in cans much too large for trail use. You must transfer the fuel you need to smaller, lighter metal cans. Most used is the cylindrical Sigg bottle of aluminum, with its single, gasketed, screw-on cap. Sigg also makes this bottle with a red anodized coating which is good when you want your fuel to be plainly distinguishable from other fluids. Bottles come in liter and half-liter sizes, weigh four and five ounces, and cost $3 to $6. If you lose the cap, you can get a replacement for 50¢ or so. Incidentally, Siggs are the only type of bottle you can plug into MSR stoves.

While Sigg bottles are popular, you can also get square-cornered cans of tin-coated steel. These have two openings: a broad spout with a built-in strainer, and a narrow projecting snout for easy pouring. It's a handy setup, but the two small caps are easy to lose. The cans come in quart and pint sizes and in different shapes—tall and thin, short and squat. They cost about $5 and weigh five to seven ounces. If the tin coating is broken, they will rust.

You will need a small plastic or metal funnel for filling a fuel tank with kerosene or gas; these cost under 50¢ plain, but a dollar or more if there's a built-in strainer, and the protection is worth the price. Some have replaceable filters. Sigg makes an alternate cap for its bottles, a pouring cap with a built-in spigot—you switch caps to pour ($1.50). With white gas stoves lacking pumps, you may also want an eyedropper to use in priming.

You will almost certainly need a windscreen. Several models come with specially fitted screens of their own, and some are so made that the sturdy screen also supports the pot. Others are commonly sold with cooksets which include windscreens. If your stove has no screen when you buy it, several kinds of separate screens are sold. The Ski Hut carries a three-sided folding windscreen that fits most small, low stoves ($5). Mountain Safety Research makes a two-piece screen of aluminum foil—ugly but highly effective—that can be trimmed and restapled for use with stoves other than MSR's ($4). Smilie Company markets an unusual windscreen developed by the Sierra Club, an aluminum cylinder supported by short metal legs; while letting in plenty of air at the base of the flame, it channels the rising heat efficiently around the pot ($10). Some separate-tank stoves, like the Optimus 8-R, have no screen but the lid of the box they are seated in; though a salesperson may tell you otherwise, the lid alone is not enough to block out a capricious breeze.

Windscreens

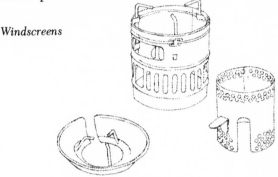

Whenever you improvise a windscreen, you must take care to allow plenty of ventilation around the fuel tank. The tank on self-pressurizing stoves needs to be warm, but it should not be painfully hot to the touch. Make sure the flame doesn't tend to blow *toward* the tank. You can also improve the performance of some stoves, in the wind, by bending the pliable pot-support wires to bring the pot closer to the flame. However, there's a penalty: a flame that licks against the pot puts out more carbon monoxide, a problem if the stove is to be used in a confined place.

If you are camping on snow, you will need a couple of extra items: a small piece of ensolite or other closed-cell foam, about six inches square or round, and an extra pot lid or other piece of light metal. The stove sits on the metal and the ensolite. Without the insulation, the hot stove will sink out of sight in the snow—or at least be chilled too badly to function well. Without the metal, the stove may melt a hole in the ensolite.

Most people who use kerosene stoves bring a separate squirt bottle of alcohol to prime with. (This should be the denatured solvent form of alcohol, not rubbing alcohol, which has high water content and burns poorly.) Or you can use one of several solid fuels. Whatever you use, take plenty of it, especially at first. Beginners often have trouble persuading their kerosene stoves to catch, and may have to prime several times.

Fire-starters

Carry several sets of matches. Put them in your kitchen gear, in your first aid or emergency kit, and in at least one other place—perhaps tucked in with some emergency food. Some stoves have built-in flint sparkers; they're nice when they work, but not cause to leave your matches home.

There are several sorts of matches to choose from. Cheapest, of course, are ordinary folder matches. They have to be dry to work, and must be struck on their own sandpapery striker pad. Then there are wooden kitchen matches, which will ignite on any dry, rough surface. Third are waterproof matches, very good to have in wet weather. Some brands can be struck on any rough surface; others require a special striker. But both match and striking surface can, in theory at least, be soaking wet. (You can also waterproof ordinary kitchen matches by dipping them in wax.) Finally, there are waterproof/windproof matches. These burn like sparklers and cannot be blown out. At about 2¢ per match, they are worth the price in stormy camping.

In dry summer climates it scarcely matters what sort of matches you take. Many people favor the strike-anywhere kitchen type, or a mixture of strike-anywheres and waterproofs. But even in summer you want your matches, and especially your backup supply, protected from damp. You can use doubled plastic bags, foil envelopes, or (for wooden matches) a plastic or metal *matchsafe*. You needn't spend more than a couple of dollars for a matchsafe, though they go to $5. Some have built-in strikers. Safest for wet-weather camping are those with rubber gaskets under the lid. Don't forget to carry several striker pads for matches that require them.

If you plan to camp in rainy country or on snow, your matches should certainly be waterproof, and you should have perhaps a handful of the more expensive windproof ones as well. Take pains to keep them dry, despite the manufacturers' claims. Regard waterproofness as insurance, not as a substitute for normal care. Experience suggests that windproof matches are *less* resistant to water than the merely waterproof type.

In very wet weather, it takes more than matches to start a wood fire. (Even stove-users, in an emergency, may need to light one.) Stove fuel, poured over rain-soaked wood, will not persuade it to burn. You can, however, soak a piece of porous wood in a pool of gas or kerosene, letting it absorb the fluid: this makes a good, long-burning fire-starter. You can also search the forest for pitchy wood in a decomposing log. Then there are various fire-starters you can bring from home. Some people take a candle-stub or two and nothing more. Others make little "logs" of wax-soaked newspaper.

Fire ribbon is a sort of inflammable toothpaste.

Heat Tabs, Hexamine, and *Esbit* are brands of solid fuel in tablet form. Anything that burns, of course, can also be used for priming a stove.

Cookware

A single hiker can get along with a single small pot (or none, if he chooses to eat cold food). In a small group you need a couple of cooking vessels. It's hard to do much with a pot of less than quart capacity, and a pair, say one of three pints and one of five, will serve most purposes. Backpacking pots are aluminum or stainless steel and should weigh no more than twelve ounces in a two-quart size; some weigh much less. Prices range from $2 to almost $10 a pot. Cheaper ones, though less durable, may also be much lighter.

Many people buy their pots in elegant sets. The best known cookware package is the *Sigg Tourist* ($18); it gives you a pair of pots and a stout supporting base that doubles as a windscreen for a small upright stove like the Svea 123. But there are other lines, some designed for specific stoves, some usable with any. You can also buy cheap aluminum pots in a department store and cut off the handles, leaving only stubs.

Some pots are wide, some deep and cylindrical. The tall, narrow pots are inefficient for cooking on most stoves. But there is this to consider: if you are using a separate-tank white gas stove, like the Optimus 8-R, you do not want your pot completely overhanging the fuel tank. Reflecting heat back onto the tank, a very wide pot can raise the fuel temperature enough to provoke a safety-valve blowout. As for support, some have strip or wire bails, others short handles; still others have neither, and while these "naked" pots are bad for campfire cooking, they work fine on a stove. Lids are important to shorten cooking time.

You'll need, in any case, a potlifter ($1), a leather glove, or (for pots with cutoff handles) needlenose pliers. A bandanna will do in a pinch. When it's very cold, a pair of light cloth gloves will take some of the sting out of the touch of freezing metal or spilled fuel.

What about other cooking tools? Some people like bacon and eggs enough to carry frying pans (some pots come with lids that are made to double as frypans). Separate pans weigh twelve to fifteen ounces in steel or teflon-coated aluminum and cost $4 and up. With a pan, you need an appropriate spatula. Certain other gear is strictly for campfire cooking. Lightweight backpackers' grills cost $7 to $10 (but cheap cake racks are reportedly also good). Campfire gourmets may take reflector ovens, just under three pounds; these run $13 to $15.

As you gain in altitude, cooking takes longer. For one thing, most stoves become less efficient in thinner air; for another, the boiling point of water declines. At 10,000 feet, the boiling point is about 192 degrees Fahrenheit, 20 degrees below the normal 212, and it takes more than six minutes to cook a "three-minute" egg. Instant and just-add-water foods, of course, are affected less.

One way of speeding up mountain cooking is to use a pressure cooker. A four-quart cooker weighs three pounds and costs about $25. But in normal backpacking you needn't consider such a thing; cookers are mainly taken to very high altitudes or on trips so long that the saving in fuel makes up for the weight of the cooker many times over.

For the simple cooking that most backpackers do, about the only other essential utensil is a ladle or serving spoon.

Your personal messkit can be minimal. Most people carry nothing more than a plastic or metal cup and a spoon; others like plastic or aluminum plates, or bowls, or both.

For dishwashing you need a wire or teflon pot scrubber, and biodegradable soap (either ordinary cake soap or liquid). Detergents, of course, are never used, and washwater must be dumped well away from any lake or stream. No small party has any need for a washbasin, at least not for doing dishes. Dishcloth? A clean bandanna will do.

Containers for food and liquids

Aluminum Sigg bottles, the kind used for fuel, can also be used for other liquids, but not for acids (like fruit juices) or for alcohol. Your fuel cans should be plainly distinguishable from drinkables.

Other bottles are made of plastics like polyethylene, polyvinylchloride, and polypropylene. Polyethylene tends to pick up flavors and hold them; the other plastics don't so much. There are narrow-mouthed types for liquids and large-mouthed types for liquids and bulk solids. Some are round, some squarish. Prices range to $2.50, depending on size and material, and weights run to four ounces. Bottles set up as canteens cost a bit more.

There are also large collapsible water carriers of several types. These can be useful around camp, and also whenever water is carried a long way from the last source to a camp you will occupy for more than a night. Such carriers hold from one to five gallons; prices run about $3.

Most solid food goes into plastic bags. You need both small, flimsy bags and larger, tougher ones, sold for a few cents apiece in some gear stores. There are also square plastic boxes with snap-on tops; flat, round screw-top butter dishes; plastic egg carriers; and much else. Squeeze tubes, with a back you can open for filling, are handy for things like peanut butter so long as the weather stays warm. Cheap two-part shakers are commonly taken for pepper and salt. If you have cans to open, you can use a minuscule GI-style can opener or simply a knife blade. Multi-bladed knives usually include a serviceable can opener.

The bear bag

In some American wilderness areas you have to protect

Containers for fuel and other liquids

your food from scavenging bears. This means hoisting it into a tree at night, and whenever you leave an established camp unoccupied. So your kitchen gear must include, along with plenty of cord, a stout container for the hoisting. Sometimes an empty pack can be used, or a tarp gathered into a sack shape. Otherwise you need a laundry bag or something similar. A hammock also makes a good daytime bear bag.

10:
The Rest of the Load

Sleeping gear; shelter; clothing; cooking gear. With these we have covered the bulk of what goes in the pack (for food, see Chapter 12). What remains, though, is important: medical and emergency supplies, personal items, and some tools so essential and so useful that they demand a category of their own.

Health and Safety I: the first aid kit

Most summer backpackers need carry only a rather basic medical kit. (Some don't even carry *that*, but should.) Let's face it: today's wilderness is small and growing smaller; most trips are quite short; rescue is often almost literally around the corner. It's true that climbers (especially winter climbers), and inveterate solo travelers, and hikers in such true wilderness lands as are found in Alaska, must be prepared to do more than give first aid; this book has little to tell them. But first aid, in the busy mountains of a temperate-zone American summer, is as far as you are likely ever to have to go.

First aid kit

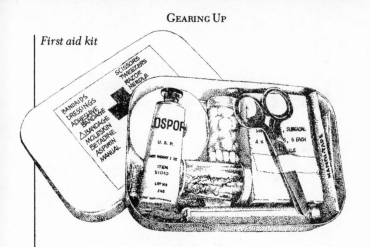

Every member of the party should have a personal first aid kit and with it (perhaps in the same container) survival items for an unexpected night out. These he should keep with him at all times—on side trips and day hikes most especially. In the typical two-hiker, three-hiker, or four-hiker backpacking party, there is no group kit; larger parties in difficult country may carry more sophisticated medical supplies.

What about prepacked, commercial first aid kits? There are several on the market; prices range from $4 on up. Large suppliers also sell individual kit items and containers. But the prepacked kits have disadvantages. For one thing, their choice of items is never quite the choice you would make; second, and more important, there's nothing like putting a kit together from scratch to teach you exactly what you've got in it.

Let's run down some of the common and not-so-common components of wilderness medical kits. Items marked with an asterisk are of special importance.

°1. *The container.* It's a good idea to have a rigid box; otherwise the items in the kit can get mangled. A fairly generous kit should fit in a box of about 50 cubic inches—say two inches by four by six, though almost any shape will do.

°2. *First aid manual.* Especially for people who haven't taken first aid courses, a mechanical, step-by-step routine for dealing with emergencies can be highly useful. There are various portable manuals, from densely-printed cram cards published by the Red Cross to James A. Wilkerson's hefty *Medicine for Mountaineering*, published by the Seattle Mountaineers. One good pamphlet is Fred T. Darvill's *Mountaineering Medicine,* which you can get for a dollar from the Skagit Mountain Rescue Unit (see *Resources*) if your gear store doesn't have it.

°3. *Band-Aids.* Several sizes. Three or more of each.

°4. *Gauze pads.* Three or four pads, three or four inches square, in sterile envelopes.

*5. *Gauze bandage.* One inch wide. Need not be sterile. Take not less than ten feet.

*6. *Adhesive tape.* Also one inch wide and plentiful. Should be of porous, not waterproof, cloth (try REI). To save bulk, pry the ends off the roll on which the tape is wound and stamp on it to flatten the core.

°7. *Moleskin or molefoam.* Stick-on pads to cushion feet where blisters show signs of developing. Moleskin is thin, molefoam thicker. Found at drugstores in three by four inch pads. Take two or more sheets, depending on how easily you blister. Some people find adhesive tape works just as well.

°8. *Triangular bandage.* An item with many uses; the classic arm-sling. Bulky (about 11 square feet) and often missing from the small kits.

9. *Elastic bandage.* Can be useful if you *must* walk on a wrenched ankle or knee.

°10. *Soap in some form.* Liquid in tube; powder in film can; or a fragment.

11. *Antiseptic.* This item, often taken, is not really required. If you do carry it, remember that few preparations are considered gentle enough to use directly *on* or *in* a wound. Aqueous solution of Zepharin is one of them.

12. *Antibiotic burn ointment.* Neosporin is often recommended.

13. *Cotton swabs.* Various possible uses.

°14. *Needle.* For draining blisters.

°15. *Tweezers.* Mainly for splinters. May be on knife (below).

°16. *Scissors.* Mainly for cutting dressings, moleskin, repair tape. May be on knife.

°17. *Safety pins.* Like needles, you think of these as sew/repair items, but they have uses in first aid too, as for fastening arm slings and bandages.

°18. *Razor blade.* Various uses. Can substitute for scissors. Also used to shave skin before applying tape, or the suction cup of a snake bite kit.

°19. *Snake bite kit.* An item you're most unlikely ever to need, even in prime "snake country." There is a lively debate among doctors as to whether or not backpackers should be encouraged to carry kits; for more on this, see Chapter 26. The familiar snake bite kit is Cutter's, neatly packaged in a rubber cylinder ($4); Johnson & Johnson and Becton & Dickson make similar kits at lower prices. All contain a constricting band, a sharp blade, antiseptic, a suction device, and directions.

°20. *Aspirin.* A dozen tablets for pain and fever.

21. *Painkiller.* Many hikers carry half a dozen 30-milligram tablets of codeine/empirin, or some other prescription painkiller. Discard and get a new prescription about every year.

22. *Salt tablets.* Another debatable item. Some people rely on them, especially on the first strenuous trip of the season, to prevent cramps. See also Chapter 12.

23. *Antacid tablets.* For indigestion. Some researchers suggest that they may be of help against altitude sickness.

°24. *Personal medicines.* Anything you know you need. Toothache drops . . . laxatives . . . prescription drugs . . . antihistamines. If you have a medical problem, consult your doctor before you head into wild country.

25. *Other drugs.* Many are possible, but few are needed for ordinary travel. Doctors hesitate to prescribe except for immediate need. However, on long trips it may make sense to carry a broad-spectrum antibiotic, like tetracycline. Drugs should be replaced every twelve months.

26. *Poison oak/ivy/sumac lotion.* Can be carried for off-trail travel where these irritant plants grow thick. Unless you're really wading through the stuff, though, you can save yourself by scrubbing exposed skin with soap and water immediately after exposure.

27. *Sting-kill ampules.* Some hikers carry these where mosquitoes and stinging flies are a major problem.

28. *Water purifier.* Though hardly a first aid item, this

can conveniently be stored in the kit. In more and more
wilderness areas, hikers must purify the water they find on
the land. Boiling will do it, but chemical tablets are often
more convenient. The most widely available product,
Halazone, releases chlorine. Halazone, however, loses its
potency quickly. Most sources now recommend Globaline
or Potable-Aqua tablets, which release iodine. If you can't
buy these locally, you can order them by mail (see
Resources). Even iodine purifiers lose their strength in
time, so you should probably replace them at least every
other year. Since exposure to air speeds up deterioration,
keep tablets in a tightly-closed container. Price: about
$2.50 for a hundred tablets.

Health and Safety II: skin protection

These items, often listed with the first aid kit, will be
used too often to be packed away.

Insect repellent. At certain times of the year, in certain
places, this will seem more like a survival item than a mere
convenience. The most effective preparations are those
that contain the chemical N,N-Diethyl-meta-toluamide.
Concentrations vary from 25 percent to 75 percent; the
stronger the brew, the better. In surplus stores you can find
the army's "jungle juice," which is the same stuff. Prices
range from 50¢ an ounce to almost $2. Buy liquid repel-
lent, not the bulkier and more expensive aerosol or foam.

Suncream/sunblocker. At low elevations any suntan
cream will do (and in the woods even that can be spared).
But above 8,000 feet or so, and on light-colored rock or
snow or near open water, most people need more protection. There are many sunblocker creams intended to prevent *any* of the sun's ultraviolet rays from reaching your
skin. You won't get much of a tan, but you won't burn
badly, either. Various compounds are used in these creams.
At present manufacturers seem to be favoring the substance PABA (Para-amino-benzoic acid). Prices vary, with
the top at about $3 an ounce.

Lip balm. Most hikers need this to prevent cracked,
burned lips. Any brand will do.

Other protective creams. There are creams designed
specifically to keep you warmer (by blocking the flow of
heat from the skin), to keep your skin moist (in the wind),

and to protect you against poison oak and the like (applied before exposure). None of these are very commonly used.

Health and Safety III: emergency and survival

In this third group are some special items you would want to have with you if you were lost, if you had to spend an unexpected night out without normal equipment, or if you hoped to attract the attention of rescuers. There are prefabricated emergency kits ($2 to $3) which contain some of the most essential items.

Whistle. A traditional item but of questionable useful-ness. The theory is that you blow it, should you get lost, to summon help (three signals of any kind indicate distress, two indicate response). However, rescue workers report few cases where a whistle has actually helped much. The noise just doesn't carry far, though it *is* better than shout-ing. Whistles may help in keeping a large party together, and parents often give them to their kids when on long outings.

Mirror. Also recommended as a rescue signal. Does this one work any better? It seems doubtful. It is hard indeed to flash a spot of light to exactly the place where it will be seen even if you have bright sun to work with.

Signal cloth. Perhaps more to the point is a piece of bright-colored cloth—an item of clothing, a groundsheet, whatever—which you can spread out to attract the atten-tion of aerial searchers.

Dimes. For an emergency phone call if you must hike out to a road for assistance.

Waterproof-windproof matches. A special supply in your first aid kit or emergency kit, so that you will never be caught without.

Candle stubs or other fire-starters. Also essential. Fire ribbon (a paste) or fuel tablets can be used.

Emergency shelter. There are several possibilities, but the idea is simply to have something to wrap up in on a cold, wet night. Some carry reflective "space blankets"; fragile, one-use models sell for $2 or so and somewhat stouter ones go for $7 to $9. Another type of shelter is essentially a large, tough plastic bag. If you have a hooded waterproof raincoat of some sort, a shorter plastic bag, into which you thrust your legs, will serve. This is one function of the long raincoat called the *cagoule* (Chapter 8). You can pull your legs up inside it, tighten the drawstring at the hem, and make yourself almost weatherproof. A night in such a waterproof sack will not be comfortable, but it will probably be tolerably warm.

Snares, fishhooks, and such. Sometimes packaged with commercial survival kits, these are scarcely necessary in most travel. Food, if you're lost for a short time in wild country, is by no means the main problem: warmth and water are primary. Still, it can be entertaining to learn a few skills for living off the land: how to build a "figure 4" snare or a noose of thread or hair, how to recognize edible and poisonous wild plants, and so on. A number of books now on the market give instruction in these skills.

Manual. Prepackaged kits may contain manuals on how to stay alive. Useful, maybe, but probably not worth looking for; common sense is the key. Handbook or no you should plan in advance just how you would conduct yourself if, separated from your party and your pack, you had to ride out a night, or several nights, with less than the usual gear.

Essential tools

Map and compass. As a rule, each member of a party should carry both. See Chapter 16, *Finding the Way*.

Knife. You don't need a big bowie knife. Any folding pocket knife will serve. Multiple blades are nice *if* the extra tools are things you need. The standard knife, not

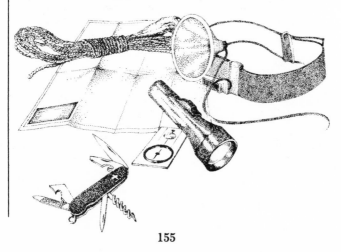

cheap, is the Swiss Army Knife, familiar with its bright red handle and imprinted cross. These come with as few as three and as many as fourteen different blades. Perhaps the two most useful items of all (besides the main blade) are *scissors* and *tweezers:* the latter slide into a socket in the handle. Other blades—can opener, Phillips head screw-driver, fish-scaler—may be useful to some hikers, useless to others. You can probably do without saws, magnifiers, plastic scrapers, and metal files. Prices run $7 to $30.

Flashlight or headlamp. It's no easy thing to find a flashlight that works, all the time and without persuasion, when you need it most. So you might as well buy a cheap one. One popular model is the flat, pocketable Mallory Compact Light, which takes two AA cells. Conventional metal C-cell flashlights are also much used. Prices run $2 to $3 without batteries. (Some claim that Kel-Lite flashlights, costing $12 to $14 in the C-cell size, are unusually durable and trouble-free.)

Along with the original batteries, take a couple of extras and a spare bulb. There are several types of batteries to choose from. AA batteries of the ordinary zinc-carbon type last three hours or more, while C cells should run at least six hours. Batteries labeled "heavy-duty" do a little better. The new alkaline power cells last several times as long as zinc-carbon batteries. Finally there are lithium cells, the most powerful and the longest-lasting now on the market. A single lithium battery, backed up by a space-filling dummy, can replace two ordinary batteries in any of the larger flashlights. Alkaline and lithium batteries both work relatively well in the cold. Only lithium cells can be stored for long periods without deteriorating. Battery prices run from 50¢ for a pair of the cheapest zinc-carbon cells to $8 or more for a lithium D size.

Be sure to reverse one battery in your flashlight when it is not in use. You don't want it turning itself on in your pack. Alternatively, tape the switch to keep it in the off position.

Climbers, night hikers, and perfectionists should consider spending extra for a battery-powered *headlamp.* (Fuel-burning *carbide lamps,* much used in mines and spelunking, don't work well in wind or in cold weather.) The battery of a headlamp rides in a separate case kept at the belt or in a shirt pocket; a cord runs to the lamp itself, which straps to the forehead and shines wherever you are looking. Best of all, your hands are free. One headlamp often seen is the Wonder Light, which uses its own special battery; this battery, however, tends to give trouble in the cold. You can get an adaptor which allows you to use the headlamp with ordinary C cells, and Mountain Safety Research sells another modified version using a single lithium battery. Headlamp prices run from $7 to $15 without batteries.

Inside a tent (or snow cave or igloo) a candle can give you good light. Or you can spend $10 for a candle-lantern which protects the flame from drafts. Although mainly a luxury item, this is genuinely useful under some conditions.

Cord. One of the real necessities, anywhere at all. Carry not less than 50 feet. Take more if you will use cord to pitch a tarp or tube tent or to haul your food into a tree at night (in bear country). Cord is also a repair item. It needn't be enormously strong; typical 1/8-inch parachute cord, 550 pound test, is fine (two or three cents a foot).

Axe, hatchet, shovel, trowel, saw. Not ordinarily needed, or even desirable. However, a large group may need a light shovel for digging latrines. A trowel is sometimes suggested for digging a sanitary "cat-hole," but most of the time a stick will do as well. Please note this, however: the U.S. Forest Service, in some regions, requires every party to carry a small shovel or trowel if fires are to be built. Fire safety is the thought behind this little-regarded rule. If you plan a trip to one of the National Forests, inquire about local regulations.

Notebook and pencil. For notes concerning route, gear problems, natural history, whatever. Also useful in emergencies to leave word for possible rescuers or for other hikers.

Essential tools: repair kit

This will vary greatly with the trip and with your gear. But these seem to be basic items:

Sewing materials. Stout thread. A couple of needles with large eyes for easy threading. A couple of buttons. A few safety pins. Larger groups may carry sewing awls for mending boots and pack straps.

Repair tape. You can buy nylon tape for making emergency patches on tents, sleeping bags, jackets. But adhesive tape from your first aid kit will work just as well.

Wire. A foot or more. Stout enough to be strong, pliable enough to bend around corners. A dozen uses in repair. Very important if you are traveling on snowshoes.

Pack fittings. Packbags are commonly held to frames by clevis pins and lock-rings. Rings can break (especially if the pack is heavy and travel rough and jolting) and clevis pins occasionally get lost. Though you can usually substitute wire, some people take a spare pin and a ring or two.

Stove tools and parts. Depending on the stove you may need one or more of these: stove wrench, spare burner plate, spare tank cap, orifice cleaning tool.

Mattress patchkit. If you use an air mattress; will also work on a tent.

Other tools. Less often taken. Screwdriver and screws, for repairing pulled-out ski bindings; for anchoring loose boot-soles. Pliers, for various uses.

Personal items

These can be few or many. Most people take a *toothbrush,* some toothpaste, and floss. Don't forget a generous supply of *toilet paper.* About the only other items *all* hikers take are a *comb,* a sliver or tube of *soap,* and several *bandannas,* one of which serves as a washrag. Some like a towel. Some like a light pocket mirror. Some take handkerchiefs. Some take moistened, packaged paper washcloths. You know what you need.

Winter and technical gear

There are various items which you'll need only in snowy winter: snowshoes or skis, waxes and ski accessories, avalanche cord, perhaps snow shovel and snow saw for building igloos or snow caves. Then there's the endless range of more technical gear for mountaineers: ropes, ice axes, crampons, hard hats, protective anchors of various sorts, avalanche probes, and so on. For more about certain of these extras, see Chapters 22 and 23.

Luxuries and specialties

A list of these would be endless. While none can be

called essential, there are many items that add comfort or pleasure to a trip, if you're willing to put up with the weight. Some luxuries frequently taken: camp shoes to put on when the boots come off; cameras (and all the paraphernalia that goes with them); natural history guides; tree and flower keys; geologic maps; binoculars; magnifying glasses; walking sticks; fishing gear; barometers; altimeters; thermometers; books and games; cards; chess sets; even elaborate board games.

You name it, somebody has probably loaded it into a pack, somewhere, sometime. And everyone has a short list of personal "luxuries" that seem as necessary as boots and cooking gear.

Preparing the Trip

Then find in the horizon-round
One spot, and hunger to be there.

—Gerard Manley Hopkins

11:
Designing the Trip

THE EASIEST WAY to take your first longer trip is to sign on with an organized party (see Chapter 2). But it's when you start setting your own targets and making your own plans that the real adventure begins. The whole ritual of preparation—the packing, the planning, the study of the maps that build a landscape in your mind—is not just the dull means to the pleasant end: it is the first part of the journey itself.

Experienced packers—some of them, at least—can throw a trip together quickly. On a few hours notice they are packed and gone, needing little time to prepack, prepackage, preplan. But at the beginning, at least, you will need to be a little more methodical.

First step: pick a place and a time

Most trips seem to start with gossip: "They say it's nice at Stonecup Basin . . . the Big Craggies . . . Silver Falls." But if you're not tied in yet to a grapevine, you may need to do some research.

If you live in the West, or on the eastern seaboard, there is probably wild country within 200 miles of you. If you don't know where, there are several ways of finding out quickly. You can ask at gear stores. You can consult some of the numerous area guidebooks now in print. Or you can start by writing the regional offices of the U.S. Forest Service, the National Park Service, the U.S. Fish and Wildlife Service, and the Bureau of Land Management. Some state-owned lands, especially in California, Michigan, Maine, and New York, are also wild. Federal and state agencies publish maps showing roads, trails, and the boundaries of zones in which wilderness is explicitly protected. (See *Resources* for these addresses.) The answers you get from agency offices in your state or region will help you focus your interest on particular parks, National Forests, National Wildlife Refuges, and so on, and give you the local addresses you need. Then you can write those local offices for more specific help.

These sources will lead you first to the well-known, well-used landscapes. That may be just what you want at the beginning—or perhaps much longer, if you don't mind a certain amount of company. It does appear, though, that many backpackers *are* disturbed by company. You can avoid it in several ways.

You can, for instance, plan trips at odd times. Weekends in the wild are always busier than weekdays; holiday and August weekends are busiest of all. In larger or less publicized areas, and in wild places more remote from the cities, the weekends are not quite so crowded.

Outside the southwestern deserts, most wild areas get their biggest crowds in August. It is often hard to see why. Over much of the United States, autumn is a more pleasant hiking season than midsummer. In many regions, September is drier than August; and often in wooded places you get the wonderful bonus of fall color. Spring, too, is lovely and not very populous. But it should be noted that the soils in many areas are waterlogged in the spring, and easily damaged by human traffic. Managing agencies are moving to restrict spring hiking in some of these fragile landscapes.

In regions where winter brings snow, that clean, white surface, covering the fragile meadows and the mountain roads, creates a wilderness at once more spacious, starker,

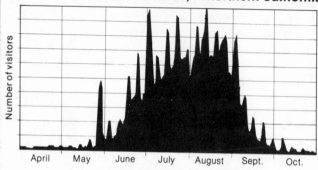

Use of Desolation Wilderness, in northern California

Number of visitors

April   May   June   July   August   Sept.   Oct.

and less vulnerable to our abuse.

But even in summer, and even in the best-known regions, people flock to a few favorite lakes, a few peaks, a few trails. The accompanying map shows where a recent study found people going in the Spanish Peaks Primitive Area of Montana. Trooping along a couple of main thoroughfares, hikers left large sections almost unused. This is by no means a bad thing. You wouldn't want all parts of an area to be used equally. But the hiker who is slightly more adventurous, or simply better-informed, can take advantage of the unequal distribution and go where others do not.

As a rule, you can be more alone on the middle-elevation trails that do not lead straight to picture-postcard alpine climaxes. (Westerners, especially, tend to be narrow-minded about scenery. They love their peaks and lakes and glaciers—as who would not?—but often overlook the beauty of their deep coniferous forests.) Write the managing agency and *ask* where use is light. Both the Park Service and the Forest Service have lately begun publishing maps that show the zones of crowding in certain wilderness areas.

Then there is cross-country travel; it's more adventurous, more solitary, and more of an exploration. But this takes skill, preparation, and caution (see Chapter 22).

Informal wilderness

Now we speak of a special kind of country. In the Far

Concentration of trail traffic in the Spanish Peaks area of Montana

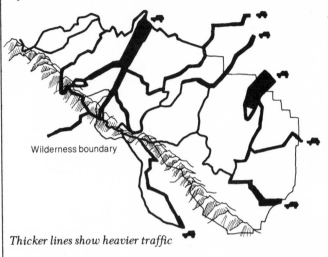

Wilderness boundary

Thicker lines show heavier traffic

West, especially, there are vast areas of what is called *de facto wilderness:* lands that are perfectly wild but which do not have official labels or official recognition. They have no legal status as National Parks, Primitive Areas, or Wildernesses by federal law; little stands between them and exploitation. They are simply *there.* These unacknowledged wild places—the closest thing we have today to blank spots on the map—lie chiefly on lands controlled by the U.S. Forest Service and by the Bureau of Land Management. Some are used by hikers almost as much as their protected counterparts, but most are much less used, and some are all but unknown. And many are superb. You never know what you may discover in one of these out-of-the-way landscapes: an unmapped desert cavern; a cool moist canyon among arid mountains; an exciting peak that few before you have thought to climb; an untouched lowland forest of fir and hemlock, yew and spruce and cedar; or perhaps a rare and vivid flower.

Some argue that these hidden lands should be left hidden. Are they not, in their obscurity, the truest wilderness we have? And if there were some reason to believe that de facto wilderness lands could, in the absence of public use

165

and public interest, remain wild, that argument might be telling. But the facts are otherwise. These lands, for all their obscurity, are not truly hidden: not hidden from those who would alter and destroy them. Wherever there is a piece of wild country, there is already someone who is making plans to log it, to mine it, to build roads across it, to dam its streams—to change it in some fashion, for reasons plausible or not, from what it is. And where there is the will to exploit, there is, very often, the power. So the fragments of unprotected wilderness in America shrink year by year.

This does not mean that they cannot be defended, for they can. But protection must be formal, legal, definite. And such protection never comes—at least it comes only seldom—without a test of political strength. None of our most loved and celebrated landscapes—not the Grand Canyon, not the Smokies, not the Everglades, not Yosemite itself—was saved without a fight. If our unprotected wilderness areas are to have a chance of surviving, they must have strength on their side. They must be known by many, admired by many. They must be valued. And to be valued they must first be seen.

If you visit an unlabeled wilderness area, take a few minutes, when you get back home, to write a letter in defense of what is there. You will be doing an important service to the country you enjoyed (see Chapter 30).

How do you learn where these places—by nature underpublicized—are found? The usual source is the grapevine, but a call to the nearest office of the Sierra Club may yield some information. In California, a group called the California Wilderness Coalition has published an invaluable map showing the location of *all* wild areas in the state, both protected and unprotected (see *Resources*). While such maps are not available for other states at this writing, they may soon be prepared.

In 1974, the U.S. Forest Service published a set of maps showing the remaining wild lands in the western National Forests. These maps, prepared by the various regional offices, show which areas are now protected, which will be studied for possible protection, and which, given no special status, will most likely be turned to other uses, their wildness destroyed. Unfortunately, these maps are out of print, though you can see them at regional offices. No such surveys have yet been done for the eastern states. In 1976, Congress instructed the Bureau of Land Management, which controls even more land than the Forest Service, to start work on its own inventory of wild places.

A caution: these unprotected areas are not, generally, the best destinations for your very first trips. Some of them, fascinating though they are, lack that instantly recognizable, photogenic charm that is always the first quality to be preserved. And you will need to check with the local offices of the Forest Service or the BLM about the condition of roads and trails. Maps are often out of date, and trail systems may have gone unmaintained for years. On the plus side, you can forget about wilderness permits and quotas, and chances are you can forget about crowds.

Second step: get the detailed information

There is a pleasure in going off to the woods with no very firm idea of where you'll wind up. But this is not a pleasure for the beginner. As a rule, planning makes a better trip. Besides, it's fun.

Your basic tool is always the topographic map or "topo sheet" published by the U.S. Geological Survey. These can be ordered by mail from Denver and Washington, D.C. (see *Resources*) and cover every corner of the United States. They are webbed with thin brown lines that show elevation in feet above sea level. A further grid of horizontal and vertical lines divides the mapped territory into Sections, each one mile on a side. For more about these maps and how to use them, see Chapter 16.

In addition, the agencies publish maps for each State Park, National Park, National Forest, National Wildlife Refuge, or Bureau of Land Management district. These maps are small scale, show little detail, and generally lack contour lines, but they are fairly up to date about roads and trails. Of special value are the "recreation maps" published by the Forest Service for its extensive holdings. In exploring de facto wilderness especially, you will find the agency maps indispensable.

Even if you have the maps already, you will probably need to get in touch with the local office of the agency, for several reasons. First of all, there's the matter of wilderness

Two kinds of maps for laying out a trip

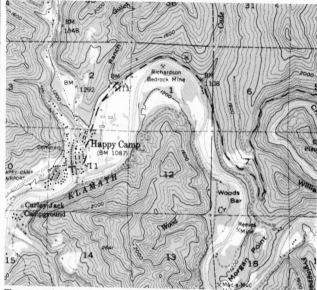

Topographical map

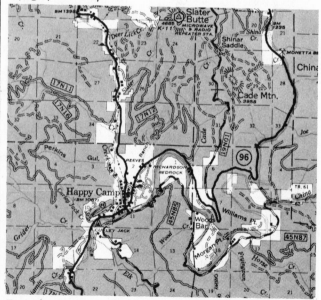

Forest Service recreational map

permits (more below). Second, you may need information about weather, trail and road conditions, and—not least—about the agency's own regulations. The less well known and populous the area you will visit, the more you need to learn in advance.

Third step: map the trip

Now comes the pleasant job of laying out your trip in detail. You know how many days you have to spend—how many of those days would you like to spend resting, or on side trips out of a fixed camp? How many will you have left to use on moving forward, onward, deeper in? And how far can you walk in that time?

It all depends on the land. A fairly standard rule of thumb makes ten miles an average day on easy terrain with pack. Some people routinely do much less, others much more. Another formula runs like this: allow two hours for every three miles of trail, plus an extra hour for every 1,000 feet you climb. This may sound slow—you may indeed find it slow in the field—but it's a good figure to start with. So you might allow eight hours of hiking to cover nine miles of easy trail with 2,000 feet of elevation gain—a longish day. Soon, of course, you'll know better than any book what you actually can do and want to do.

Now study the map for likely routes that take you to the places you want to see. One thing is obvious: you can enjoy a lot more country if you don't repeat yourself. Look for trails that loop back on your starting point or that bring you out to another roadhead. Sometimes a loop can be made by crossing a short gap between trails, but read the map carefully—are you going over a precipice? If you will exit at a different roadhead, you can set up a shuttle by parking a car at each end of the route; by hitchhiking between roadheads; or, in some well-provided regions, by taking the bus. Most hikers, unfortunately, go in and out on the same track.

How long is the line you have just traced? A guidebook may tell you and so may an agency's response to your request for information. If not, you can fall back on this estimating trick, unscientific but surprisingly helpful: simply add one mile to your tally every time your trail crosses one of the ruled boundaries of square-mile sections. Throw in another mile for each particularly circuitous stretch, as when the route is working up a slope with many switch-backs. This gimmick works best on trails over five miles long, because the inevitable errors tend to cancel out. When you get to the trailhead you may find mileage signs there; these are sometimes very accurate, sometimes not.

Try "walking" your entire route on the map. A skilled map-reader can get a good mental picture of the place to be visited—here there is a sharp drop, there a gentle for-ested valley; here an easy stretch, there a sustained ascent; here a long view over the plain, here a closed-in canyon.

Give some thought also to your camps. If you plan to build wood fires, you may find yourself limited to estab-lished sites, to particular, designated locales, or to lands below a certain elevation. (Why not carry a stove and avoid the problem?) If your trip is in the desert away from a perennial stream, or along a high ridge without lakes, springs, or snowbanks, you will have to take note of water points and plan your stops with these in mind. In desert travel it is common to plant water caches in advance.

In such eastern ranges as the Catskills, wilderness sometimes lies in narrow, mountainous strips between low-land valleys. Often the long ridgetop trail will send short spurs down to roads on either side. This makes trip plan-ning somewhat simpler, because you can make a quick exit to a road and perhaps a bus stop if the weather turns nasty, or if you get blisters, or if you simply run out of time. But in larger wildlands, you can seldom "bail out" except by going back.

If your trip will take you to high altitudes, try to allow time for adjustment to the thinner air. At a minimum, schedule a night's sleep at a high roadhead.

Wilderness permits and such

If you are going into a National Park; into a designated wilderness zone in a National Forest; or into certain state parks, chances are good that you will need a wilderness permit. In many cases you can obtain your permit by mail, if you write the appropriate agency office far enough in advance. (If you don't know where to write, contact regional headquarters.) Otherwise, you will need to stop at a field office—seldom too many miles from the roadhead—

before you start your trip.

Why permits? Their first purpose is simply to gather information. As wilderness use increases and impact problems grow, managers have a clear need to know more about hikers, their preferences, and their habits of travel. At certain trailheads permits are further used to limit use: only a given number of people are passed through each day. If, on some August weekend, you arrive at the local office and find the limit already filled for the day, you will be asked to take another route or to stay overnight and be the first party on the trail next morning.

When you get your permit in some National Parks, you will be asked to list the general areas in which you plan to camp. A very few parks insist that you reserve a specific camping *spot* for each night, but the trend seems to be to dispense with this extra, indeed chilling, bit of regulation.

The Boy Scouts are issuing a series of regional guides called *Wilderness Digests.* Each gives the latest word on permit requirements and other regulations in designated wilderness areas, together with a lot of sound general advice. You can buy these at gear stores or from the Boy Scouts' High Adventure Program (see *Resources*). In 1979 there were two *Digests:* one for California (with the Grand Canyon thrown in) and one for the Pacific Northwest including the northern Rockies.

The wilderness permit scene is a rapidly changing one, so much so that it would be hopeless to sketch the differing procedures now common in different parts of the country. But there is an unmistakable movement toward uniform methods across the agencies and across the regions. With any luck the matter of permits should become somewhat simpler, not more complex, as time goes on.

12
Planning Food and Fuel

LIKE MANY THINGS IN backpacking, the matter of food and cooking is often made to sound more complicated than it is. Elaborate, time-consuming planning is not ordinarily required, and you can stock up for any trip of normal length at the local supermarket, with help, if you like, from a health food store. Specialized freeze-dried foods are convenient and, for very long trips, essential, but they are appallingly expensive. Most of the time you can do fine without them.

Nutrition

The main thing you require of backpacking food is that there be enough of it. That means, simply, calories to keep your body running under fairly heavy work.

Even when you are getting very little exercise, your body burns about fifteen calories a day per pound of body weight. So a 170-pound man with a desk job might expend some 2,550 calories a day just living. On the trail, that goes up to twenty calories per pound; a really strenuous hike can push the rate to twenty-five calories or even higher. (Cold weather, too, adds to your needs.) An "average" man, then, might need 3,500 calories a day for "average" hiking and an "average" woman about 2,500; teenagers are likely to require up to twice as much.

Few people bother to compute these things precisely. It's useful to bear in mind, though, that pure sugars and starches provide about 100 calories to the ounce. Proteins are about the same, and pure fats run 250 calories to the ounce. Most foods are mixtures of these elements and fall somewhere in between. Surprisingly enough, most breads and crackers, and candies made mainly of sugar, provide relatively little energy, no more, per ounce, than dehydrated fruits and vegetables. Fattier foods like chocolate, nuts, bacon, and dried eggs cluster near 150 calories per ounce. Margarine and oils are over 200. (If you care to know more, the U.S. Department of Agriculture publishes a book giving calories and nutritional values for just about every imaginable substance: see *Resources*.)

If you analyzed a typical trail menu, you'd find something like half carbohydrates (sugars and starches), about one-third proteins, and about one-sixth fats. The carbohydrates are basic running fuel; they don't stick with you, but they keep the muscles working. Fats are energy in concentrated form and burn more slowly. In winter, and on sustained, difficult trips, backpackers carry more fatty foods. Proteins deliver about the same energy value as carbohydrates, only more gradually. Note, however, that because of something called "specific dynamic action," proteins do more to keep you warm when you are *not* exercising.

So how much food, in pounds, do you need to carry? Two pounds a day of typical lightweight foods should give you 4,000 to 5,000 calories, more than enough for most people most of the time. Children and light eaters may be happy with less than that; in winter, everyone needs more. If you carry almost exclusively freeze-dried foods, a pound and a half per person per day is an adequate daily ration.

While appetites go up in the wilderness, you may actually find the increase less than you expected. At dinner, for instance, two or three cups of a meaty stew will satisfy most hikers, even large and hungry hikers. Most people tend to carry too much food the first few times out, though that's much better than carrying too little. There is of course a great deal of individual variation. You'll learn from experience exactly what you need.

What about the finer points of nutrition: vitamins, minerals, balanced proteins, and such? By and large, on the trail, you can set such questions aside. You have license—strictly temporary, of course—to eat exactly what you want. Important though a well-constructed diet is over months and years, it matters little over the length of any ordinary wilderness excursion.

There are nonetheless a couple of matters to consider.

First, many people find that they function better in the mountains if their wilderness diet is not too different from what they eat at home. Sudden changes can upset the system and lead to diarrhea or, more commonly, to constipation. Foods with roughage are valuable in the trail diet. Some people carry laxatives as well.

Second is the problem of replacing substances lost in sweat. One of these is sodium salt—ordinary table salt—but there are others, including, notably, potassium. These chemicals, known as electrolytes, are very necessary to the body, and on a strenuous trip they can become depleted. Cramping is one possible result. So your diet must restore what has been lost. The salt you add to dinner (and be generous about it) will supply one of these chemical needs. Meats, dried bananas and apricots, raisins, nuts, and eggs are good sources for other necessary salts.

Recently much has been made of special powdered drink mixes, formulated to replace the needed substances lost in sweat. These are available in gear stores and cost about twice as much as ordinary fruit drink powders. One widely-distributed brand is Gookinaid ERG. Many hikers claim that they have a lot more energy on the trail if they continually drink this stuff. So here's another experiment worth trying.

You rarely need to take salt, or anything else, in tablet form. If you do take tablets, be sure to drink plenty of water when you swallow them.

The wilderness meals

At breakfast some people like to fire up a stove and enjoy a full-scale meal with cooked cereal and bacon and eggs or pancakes. Others limit themselves to just-add-water foods such as instant cereals, drinks, and concoctions like Instant Breakfast. Still others prefer cold foods like granola, crackers, cheese, and sausage. There is absolutely nothing wrong with cold cuts, at breakfast or at any other meal, but to some people they just don't seem like food.

Lunch, these days, is very seldom cooked. In fact, there may never be a formal lunch stop. Instead, the hiker nibbles all day long as the appetite takes him. Some travelers make no distinction between breakfast and lunch—they just keep munching. But other parties still prefer to light a stove at midday for hot drinks, soup, even for real cooking. On an exceedingly strenuous trip you may need a definite lunch stop just to make sure you take in the proper amount of fuel; nibbling isn't enough. Common lunch foods are breads with or without spreads (not dairy butter—it doesn't keep); dried fruit; sausage; nuts; cheese; candy; and of course cold drinks made from powdered mixes.

At higher elevations—say above 8,000 feet—many hikers find it best to avoid nuts, meats, and cheeses during the day. They find these fats and proteins hard to digest without a long rest after eating and don't want to risk exaggerating any queasiness brought on by unaccustomed altitude. If you don't like to pour sugar into your mouth all day long, eat starches. They give you energy almost as quickly.

Dinner is almost always hot and is the largest meal. Commonly it begins with soup, goes on through a solid, one-pot main course, and ends with hot drinks, or dessert, or both. Often there are cold cuts on the side. You'll often see noodles and cheese, vegetable stew with beef, instant rice with meat or fish or cheese, instant puddings, and such prefabricated main courses as beef stroganoff and chicken tetrazinni. On short trips some people take fresh vegetables and salad.

But the fact is that there are no rules. So long as they are not scanty, your meals can be plain or fancy, slow or fast to prepare, meaty or vegetarian, "organic" or supermarket standard. The possibilities are endless, and most of them are good. And you're likely to find the simplest and most familiar foods tasting better, on the trail, than they ever did before.

Planning food

Who plans the meals? In a party of more than three or four members, it's customary to split into smaller cooking groups, each of which works out its own menu and carries its own stove. Only on large organization trips are you likely to find a central commissary.

Dinner, if hot, almost has to be a group project. (You can, however, find individual just-add-water dinners if you're willing to pay high prices.) The other meals are often handled individually. Each packs his own breakfasts and lunches, plus a dinner for the whole group on one or several nights. For example, if four hikers are going out for four days, each can bring one dinner to feed four, plus four breakfasts and four lunches for himself. If you do it this way, you may want to make sure that you don't wind up eating macaroni and cheese every night; aside from that, little consultation is required.

Whether you're planning for one or for ten, the first step is to work out a *menu*. Some people think they skip this step, but in truth they don't; they write the menu in their heads even as they push a cart down supermarket aisles. Most of us have to be a little more methodical, at least at the beginning. You may find it useful to check books on backpack cookery—there are many good ones—for recipes and sample menus. Soon your own preferences and your own experience will take over.

When you plan a meal with several courses, it's very easy to bring a little too much of each element. Result: you eat more than you want—or have to throw food away. Try to avoid this.

Given a menu, it's no trick to figure the quantities of groceries you need.

Choice of foods

You need foods that are *light in weight*—tolerably light for normal trips, super-light for very long trips. Cans, as a rule, are out (except for certain compact and popular foods like sardines). Fresh foods—vegetables, oranges—are practical only on short trips or as occasional luxuries on longer ones. You need food that will *keep*—except that perishables are fine for the first day or in cold weather. You need food that is *easy to cook*—unless you find cooking a positive pleasure. And of course you need food that you will enjoy eating.

You have three types of stores to work from. Sporting

goods stores stock mainly freeze-dried meals and ingredients. Health and organic food stores carry some useful staples that you may not find elsewhere: fruit-flour biscuits, roasted soybeans, various uncommon dried fruits, nuts, and seeds. But the supermarket, in truth, can give you most or all of what you need. There is no reason in the world to pay premium prices for such products as macaroni, granola, other cereals, dried milk, instant rice, or hard biscuits. For warm-weather trips you avoid foods that will need refrigeration; but note that firm-textured cheese, despite what it says on the label, lasts perfectly well in a warm pack. (Cheese does "sweat," yielding a sticky oil. It's best to carry it wrapped in butcher paper, rather than in the original plastic.)

If you use freeze-dried foods, there are several options. The easiest but most expensive method is to buy the elaborate, prepackaged multi-course meals, package within package, that are wholesaled to gear stores by such suppliers as Rich-Moor and Mountain House. Or you can buy concentrated bulk ingredients, like dried eggs, dried peas, and meat bars, to use in your own recipes. A middle course is to choose freeze-dried, premixed main courses—chop suey, beans and franks, stroganoff, whatever—and round them out with cheaper foods.

Recently there have been two further innovations in freeze-dried foods. One is the just-add-boiling-water meal introduced by Mountain House/Teakettle. These foods, packed in individual or group servings, can be very convenient when cooking is difficult; it is hard to think of a normal wilderness situation in which the time and fuel saved are worth the price. The second new development is food not only freeze-dried but also compressed into small, flat wafers, reduced in bulk as much as in weight.

Whether you are buying food at the supermarket or at the gear store, be wary of the printed claim that such-and-such a package serves three, four, or six. With luck, a "serves four" package from the local market will serve two. While gear-store meals are more generous, hearty eaters will also find these somewhat scant. An eight-ounce serving of a main course is a reasonably large one (this is, of course, reconstituted weight, not dry weight). If you will be using the main course as the bulk of a meal, with little

177

else on the side, you need to make a still further allowance.

At the other extreme from these highly processed foods, there is a new interest these days in foods you assemble yourself to eat on the trail. People are baking journey-cakes and nutritional fudges, drying their own jerky, compounding their own pemmicans and granolas. The Sierra Club book *Simple Foods for the Pack* contains many such recipes.

How much should food cost per day? This can vary hugely. $3 a day per person shows decent economy; $3.50 to $4.50 is not unreasonable; more than that is getting out of line.

Packing food

There are several ways of packing food and the ingredients of meals. One traditional method is quite elaborate: each individual meal is premeasured, pre-arranged, and packed in its individual, labeled plastic bag. Everything you need for that particular job of cooking will be there. Such packing can take a good deal of time at home, especially if meals are cooked from many bulk ingredients. It does save time on the trail, makes it almost impossible to run out of food on the last day, and eliminates any need for a menu.

A simpler method is to pack all the ingredients that will be used in dinners, throughout the trip, together in one large plastic bag. Needed directions, of course, go in the same bag, and probably a menu. Similarly, you can pack lunch and breakfast foods in large bags of their own. Each morning before leaving camp, you pull the day's lunch out of the bag and stow it where you can easily reach it.

Or again, you can sort foods simply by day: a bag for Monday, a bag for Tuesday.

However you arrange things, you will probably have to do some weighing and packaging. Get rid of cardboard packages (but not the directions printed on them) and excess wrapping. (Exception: crackers keep better in the original packages.) Most foods can be stored in pint and quart freezer bags, the kind found in any supermarket. Oily items and powders should be double bagged. Either wire twists or rubber bands are fine for closures. (Be careful not to litter with these!) You can also make some use of rigid plastic boxes and bottles; a few compact foods—meats and fish—are carried in their original cans. Larger, tougher polyethylene bags, sold in gear stores, are good for keeping related items together. Bags will last many uses, so wash and reuse them whenever you can. If you do a lot of weighing of bulk ingredients, you will need two scales: a postage scale for small amounts, a diet scale for larger quantities.

For very long trips you may need to plant caches of food, or water, or both, at accessible points along the route you plan to hike. For food caches you need large, light, metal boxes or cans to protect supplies from animals. Somewhat hard to find, these can best be obtained through gear stores.

Emergency supply

After a few trips you will be making increasingly accurate estimates of the amount of food you actually need. But if you err, it is better to be generous and come home with unused food. While some people claim that nothing is healthier than a good hard workout during a fast, the long march to the car is not the place to make the experiment. (Many people, to the contrary, are acutely reminded when they hike that food is *fuel*.)

If it's your ambition to meter your food exactly, taking nothing not required, it's a good idea to make up a special compact package of concentrated food for an emergency; it can be largely candy, pemmican, jerky—anything that will keep a long time. Wrap it tightly in a couple of plastic bags (you might seal them shut with a hot iron), stick it in the bottom of your pack, and forget it. Ten to one you won't need it on any given trip. But if you are a serious hiker, the chances are that someday, sooner or later, you will. Once a year go ahead and eat such items as pemmican and dried meats, and replace them; they don't last forever.

Planning fuel

How much fuel do you need to cook the meals you have outlined?

That depends on your stove (some are thirstier than

179

others) and on your cooking habits.

Let's say you plan fast-cooking meals, and light up the stove only briefly, if at all, at breakfast. Then you can reasonably expect to get by on about one-quarter cup per person per day of white gas, burned in a typical small stove. That's twenty or thirty minutes of burning time per person per day. The same amount of kerosene, burned in the Optimus 00, will last a little longer. Most of the large mountaineering stoves are markedly less economical.

What about butane stoves? It takes about an ounce of butane, in a vapor-feed cartridge, to run such a stove for twenty to thirty minutes. With a liquid-feed cartridge, two ounces are consumed in the same period. The typical cartridge contains about six ounces.

If you do a lot of simmering, with perhaps substantial cooked breakfasts, your fuel needs will increase, even double. It is slow cooking that consumes the most impressive amounts of fuel. Moreover, foods that must be simmered to become fully cooked will take far longer to prepare at high altitudes. And remember to double your fuel supply on a winter trip where you will be melting snow.

Nothing can replace your own experience. Take somewhat more fuel than you think you need, and form your own impressions.

Water

On most trips water is taken for granted; there's no need to plan for it if it's plentiful along the way. But sometimes it is not so easily found. When a supply must be carried, it's important not to underestimate how much you need.

Even a person who is exercising only slightly needs two quarts of water a day, part of it in liquids, part of it from solid food. A hard-working hiker loses much larger amounts in his sweat and his breath. On a strenuous trip you require *a full gallon a day* or even more.

Don't wait for thirst to warn you that you aren't taking in enough water. When you're working extremely hard, as in very fast hiking or in winter travel, the mechanism of thirst seems to grow sluggish. Dehydration can set in without your knowing it, robbing your energy, and clouding your judgment. It is wise to drink more, and more often, than you actually want to. That's another good reason for carrying flavored fruit drink mixes, along with tea and chocolate and such: they keep you interested.

If you're headed for heavily-used or semi-civilized hiking areas, or to the desert, be sure to have a means of purifying water. For the options, see Chapter 20.

13:
Common Sense in Packing

You've got your gear. It's lying in great, disorganized piles all over the living room.

You've got your trip. You're leaving tomorrow morning.

How do you get all that junk into your pack without utter confusion? How will you know where things are when you need them? How can you make sure of leaving nothing essential behind, and of taking not an ounce more than you need to take?

These are problems (if "problems" they can be called) which every backpacker must deal with. Every backpacker finds his own solutions, his own organizations, his own shortcuts and odd arrangements. What follows here is a set and rather fussy procedure to make use of, if you care to, the first few times you put a packload together.

Step one: make a list

If you are more than usually efficient, you may in time be able to pack a good pack without a list. But it's best not to skip this step at the start. When you make your first list of objects to be taken, divide it by category. List all items connected with food and cooking in one section, all items

connected with shelter and bed in another, and so on.
Think carefully about the places you are going. In such a
month in such a spot do you reasonably need to take a
snakebite kit? Sunblocker cream? A spare pair of dark
glasses? Clothing of cotton, or of wool? Imagine the situations you may be facing. As a starting point, you may find
it useful to consult the accompanying skeleton list.

When you're done packing, don't throw your new list
away. File it. Later, when you walk the trails, you can be
making notes—mental or written, conscious or unconscious—as you go along: "Flashlight should be in outer
pocket . . . ." "Did not need down jacket this trip . . . ."
"Could have used another pot . . . ." and so forth. Remember which items you had but didn't need, and which you
needed but didn't have. Then, when you get home, you can
correct and rearrange your original list to make it a better
guide next time you head into similar country at a similar
time of year.

Who hasn't heard the slogan, "When in doubt, leave it
out"? And it's a good one. But it needs qualification. It
applies properly to luxuries only. For other items—possible
necessities and emergency items you may never need at all
but could want desperately—the rule had better be:
"When in doubt, leave it in." If you aren't sure just when
you'll finish the trip, take food for the longest possible
period. If you aren't sure how cold it will be, put in the
extra sweater.

Step two: assemble and check the gear

Here's one way. Get a big box. Locate the items on
your list one by one, place them in the box, and check
them off the list. If you haven't done this already, examine
each item as you go for needed maintenance. (This is the
point at which you find that none of your flashlights are
working.) Actually, the best time to check your gear for
major problems is immediately on your return from each
trip, or at least while there's plenty of time to do whatever
needs to be done.

Step three: combine the objects in groups

A typical pack may contain as many as 150 separate
items, many of them small and loseable. If you just dump

Skeleton List

This is meant as a starting point for a precise packing list of your own. Ask yourself: Do I need...? *and then:* Do I have...?

Bed and shelter
Sleeping bag
Foam pad or mattress
Groundcloth
Weather shelter (poncho...tarp...tube tent...rainfly...full tent)

Kitchen
Stove
Cookware
Method of handling pots
Spare fuel as needed
Funnel or pouring cap (liquid fuels)
Priming items (eyedropper or special fuel)
Matches
Firestarters
Personal eating tools
Provision for dishwashing

Tools
Maps
Compass
Knife
Cord
Notebook/pencils
Repair kit
Flashlight or headlamp
Spare batteries and bulb

Personal
Toothbrush
Toilet paper
Other as needed or desired

Skin protection
Bug dope
Suncream (tanning lotion or blocker)
Lip balm

Clothing
Boots and socks
Spare socks and underwear as desired
Clothing for cold and wind
Clothing for rain and snow
Hat
Glasses or goggles
Bandannas

Emergency
Signals (whistle, mirror, bright cloth)
Emergency shelter provision
Matches/firestarters
Medical kit Snakebite kit

Haulage
Stuffbags
Plastic bags and closures
Water containers
Daypack (where appropriate)

them in, your confusion will be hopeless. Instead, handle them in groups. Keep all the kitchen items together, the medical kit together, the repair tools together. Or forget superficial logic and work out convenient groupings of your own. Build a pattern that enables you to find what you need when you need it. Avoid leaving tiny objects loose.

A typical frame pack, with its multiple compartments, suggests an organization. Almost everyone seems to use the lower compartment of a two-level packbag for clothing, for instance. In a pack with fewer built-in divisions, as in most soft backpacks, many hikers rely on cloth stuffbags to organize their gear. If you use many of these bags, you'll find yourself leaving much of your gear packed in them, even between trips; this shortcut can make the final packing fairly quick and easy.

Step four: pack it in

This hardly needs explanation, yet there are certain things to consider as you start the pleasant job of loading the pack, the big cloth cupboard from which, in the next few days, everything you need for life must come.

Consider the order in which you will want to get at things

Try to cut down on the number of times each day you will have to burrow deep into your pack. Thus, there needs to be an accessible slot for the food you will eat for lunch each day. A water bottle should be reachable. Camera and accessories, if you carry such, should certainly not be buried, and neither should the first aid kit. (Know exactly where to find that vital item!) Likewise sunglasses, hat, bandanna, bug dope, suncream, and whatever else you are likely to want as you go. This will never work out perfectly, and on a leisurely trip it doesn't matter, but it's nice not to have to rummage all the time. In the typical frame pack the least accessible region is the large upper compartment, under the storm flap; here you store the things you will not need till evening, like tent, dinner food, and possibly your stove (but see below).

Consider the distribution of weight

For ordinary trail walking, you want the heaviest objects *high* and *close to your back*. This will place most of

the weight on the hip belt and prevent the pack from dragging back on the shoulder straps. This is why the sleeping
bag, very light for its bulk, is so typically strapped at the
bottom of the load. (If you are climbing, skiing, or scrambling cross-country, you deliberately place the weight low
so that the pack won't swing back and forth so much on
your back.) The weight should also be evenly divided
between the two sides of the pack. You don't, for instance,
want two quarts of water and fuel in one side pocket and
nothing but a sweater in the opposite one.

Consider special problems

Some objects shouldn't be packed together. Fuel and
water should, when reasonable, be packed outside rather
than in the main compartments of a pack; gasoline and
food should never be together. Leaks can happen. Then
there are a few fragile items. Some stoves, for instance,
won't take much mashing. Sharp objects like tent poles
shouldn't be so packed that they could poke holes in a
jacket, a food bag, or in the pack itself.

Make sure you know how you will manage objects that
will only occasionally be carried on your back, like skis or
snowshoes for winter travel. If there is likelihood of rain,
consider how you will protect pack and contents. If you
have a number of items strapped on to the outside of your
pack, will your packcover or poncho fit over them? If not,
how will you strap them on outside the waterproof cover?
It's easier to plan such things ahead of time than with
water running down your neck.

When your pack isn't quite large enough for the load,
you can make more hauling room by adding a frame extension and tie-on patches, as discussed in Chapter 5. Shock
cords and straps with buckles are always likely to be useful
and can be tightened better than simple cord.

...Followers of trails and of seasons, breakers of camp in the little dawn wind, seekers of watercourses over the wrinkled rind of the world, o seekers, o finders of reasons to be up and be gone...

Saint-John Perse

14:
To the Trailhead

A SIZABLE PART OF EVERY backpacking trip is spent, not on the trail at all, but on the road. And while getting to the trailhead is by no means half the fun, the drive to the edge of wilderness is certainly a pleasure in itself. On the road you are in between, anticipating, imagining, watching the land unfold around you. The work is done, the decisions made. You're both excited and relaxed. You're on your way.

I have said already: "the *drive* to the wilderness." And indeed there is no other way to travel the remote and rugged roads which so often mark the borders of the wild. Yet there are some wild areas which begin at the shoulders of major paved highways, and some of these you can reach quite easily by bus or—a bit less plausibly—by hitchhiking.

There is regular bus service, for instance, over McKenzie Pass in the Oregon Cascades and Snoqualmie Pass in Washington's part of that range; along Interstate 80, which runs next to interesting roadless areas in the California Sierra and elsewhere; and on other major western mountain roads. There are services to some national parks: Yosemite and Grand Canyon, Yellowstone and Glacier, Point Reyes National Seashore and the adjacent Golden

Gate National Recreation Area.

Generally, though, the car-less backpacker has better luck in the East, where public transportation is more developed. Bus lines thread the Adirondacks and the Catskills, run through Cumberland Gap and across the Great Smoky Mountains, and intersect the Appalachian Trail at many points. In the White Mountains of New Hampshire, too, wildland trails begin at the side of main paved roads where buses run.

If you need to pick up a wilderness permit, perhaps at an office miles away from your trailhead, this can complicate matters. All the same, the possibilities of public transportation are worth looking into.

Even if you arrive by car, a local bus service can be useful in another way; it can be your shuttle from the end-point of your trip back to your original roadhead. Some National Parks provide just such shuttle buses in the heavy use season. And in eastern ranges such as the Catskills, where the major wild ridges lie between bus routes on the valley roads, you can walk the whole length of such a lofty trail, and then ride back to your car.

How far should you drive?

Backpackers sometimes feel virtuous (even smugly virtuous) compared to those other users of the land: the people who do their "hiking" on motorcycles and their water travel in motorboats. There are various reasons, some of them sound, for this professional snobbery. One common argument, in these days of energy shortage, is that the mechanized recreationist burns up a lot more gasoline than the self-powered walker of the trails.

But that is only true if the backpacker has driven a merely moderate distance to his trailhead. If you live, say, in Cleveland, and drive to British Columbia for your wilderness vacations, you may be using more gas than even the bikers and boaters can burn.

So you might consider this balancing rule of thumb: *try to drive no more than one hundred miles (one way) for each day on the trail.* By this formula day-trips would take you to places less than 100 miles away; a weekend trip would lie within a range of 200 or 300 miles; the week-long trip within 700.

Leaving word

Especially if you are planning a long or a challenging trip, be certain to leave some vital information at home with a friend or relative. Note where you are going, your route, so far as you know it, names and addresses of people in your party, and when you expect to return. Give also the phone number of the National Park, National Forest office, or local police station to be contacted if you should fail to come out of the wilderness on time.

What about that date of return? Most hikers, in telling their friends when they plan to return, ask that the alarm not be sounded unless they are *well* overdue, say twenty-four or forty-eight hours. They hate the feeling that people will begin worrying immediately if they switch to a longer route or take an extra day at an irresistible campsite. However, if you give yourself this margin, be sure to pack food and fuel for the extra time.

Permits and information

You may need to stop at a local agency office before you hit the trail, for any of several reasons. If a wilderness permit is required, you may not have been able to obtain it by mail. (In some areas all hikers must pick up permits in person.) Some National Parks have registration booths at the parking lots where major trails begin, but in other parks and in most National Forest areas, the responsible office is some miles away. You'll have to check in during business hours, which can pretty well scotch plans for an early start on the trail. Incidentally, even if you are headed for an area that doesn't require wilderness permits, you may be expected to pick up a fire permit at the local office. Not even stove-users are exempt from such requirements.

Permits aside, you may want to stop at a ranger station to ask some last-minute questions, or to double-check information you got in advance. What is the latest local weather forecast? How about the chances of flash-flooding in a desert canyon you plan to travel? How are snow conditions? Are key roads in good condition? And so forth. These questions are particularly important for unprotected de facto wilderness areas. The less you learned beforehand by phone or correspondence, the greater the need to talk to the local managers. There's a safety aspect, too: if a permit isn't required, it's a good idea to leave word of your projected route and schedule.

One more point. Many wilderness roadheads lie at the end of long, rough logging roads, far from the nearest service station. You may have some trouble tracing the maze of branching roads to your destination. And rough roads eat up gasoline. Don't head into the hills without a full tank of gas.

The trailhead

It always seems as if you could just park the car at the trailhead and start walking. Seldom does it work out that way. Unless you have done more planning, conferring, and prepacking than most hikers find time for, you will need to do some last-minute rearrangement. Most important, you will probably have to redivide community gear—shelter, stove and pots, food, fuel—to everyone's satisfaction. (A family group, of course, has a better opportunity to sort out such details at home.) Hikers with sensitive feet sometimes apply moleskin before the stresses of the trail begin.

If freezing temperatures are likely, be sure to leave the parking brake off (a frozen brake immobilizes the car). Nor should you set the brake if you have recently driven through water; the problem here is rust.

What about keys and wallets? Some prefer to take both on the trail; others leave wallets in the car and hide keys in the woods nearby. But at some of the most popular trailheads, there is an increasing problem with theft. It's best not to leave your car unlocked, even on the night of your arrival, when you may be lying asleep right next to the vehicle. There's a whole new guild of roadhead thieves that steal gear from under the owners' noses.

One more thing as you set out: pause to sign in at the trailhead register if one is provided. Even though you may have filled out a wilderness permit already, or left word with the office, the register is still the final record of where you are going and who you are.

15:
Walking with Pack

DOES ANYONE SERIOUSLY NEED INSTRUCTION in how to walk a trail? Probably not. Complicated though the art of back-packing sometimes seems, the *act* of backpacking—the moving-along-with-a-load—is almost too simple to describe. There are, nonetheless, some points worth mentioning.

When the last stray object is stuffed into the last pocket, when the car is locked and the maps folded, when the boots are tightly laced, comes the Moment. You've done it before: just grab the pack by the shoulder straps (or, better, by the upper crossbar), haul it up your back, and wriggle your arms, first one, then the other, under the shoulder straps. Or you can hoist the load first to your knee, or have a friend hold the pack in position for you, or lean it against a tree and sit down to shrug it on.

As you walk, you will occasionally want to adjust the way the pack rides on your back. You might wish to tighten the hip belt, since most rigs tend to loosen, if only slightly; or perhaps loosen the belt deliberately now and then to carry more of the load on your shoulders (just for variety). If you come to a section where you have to scramble over stones or plow through bushes, you will want to take more weight on your shoulders; the pack is less inclined to lurch from side to side that way. In a risky situation, like fording a deep, rushing stream, it's a good idea to unbuckle the waistbelt entirely—you might conceivably need to jettison the pack in a hurry.

The first time you carry a pack—and almost any time you carry an excessively heavy load—your hips and shoulders will get sore. Aside from the slight discomfort, this does no harm, and will happen less as time goes on.

The long stride and the rest step

The most comfortable trail pace for most people is not fast—at least the legs are not pumping rapidly—but it is very steady. Swing each leg as far forward as seems natural to you; three long strides take less energy than four or five short ones. (Long-legged hikers do seem to have some advantage.)

A hiker in good condition can go up a fairly steep and sustained hill without either gasping for breath or slowing down to a crawl. If the rise is severe, he may switch to the *rest step.* In the rest step you simply pause briefly every time you begin a new step, at that moment when the forward foot is planted but has not received any weight. Each leg thus gets a series of tiny rests. On a steep slope heavily loaded packers may break stride in this manner for a second or more with each step. While most experienced hikers find this tactic effective, others prefer to climb in a series of short rushes, pausing in between to let energy come back.

Party pace and stops

Usually the members of a group hike at different rates—some go faster, some slower. Should the slower hikers puff and strain, or should the faster ones slow down? It's important to have some agreement, not necessarily explicit, among companions. It can be miserable to be the one slow member of a group that is moving at racing speed: the only one who can't take the time to look around and enjoy. So sort these things out in advance. It's important that fellow-hikers be able to tell each other what they want and need. Someone who suffers in silence is likely to make a chilly companion.

Take stops, of course, whenever you like. It's not a marathon unless you happen to want to make it one. There's always a picture to be taken, a snack to be eaten, or just something worth looking at.

Physiologically, several short rests serve better than one long one. As your muscles work, they build up a waste called lactic acid. When you rest, you can get rid of about thirty percent of this waste in five to seven minutes. But fifteen more minutes of rest will eliminate only another five percent. Some people find long "flop-down" rests actually demoralizing: it can be hard to get started again, especially if tired legs have stiffened up. (But it's also true that a nap can be marvelously refreshing.)

Regulating warmth

We've already talked (in Chapter 8) about the *layer system:* the trick of staying comfortable by varying the thickness of the clothing you wear. You may start out on a chilly morning with long pants, a heavy shirt, a stocking cap, even a down jacket, but be down to boots, socks, and hiking shorts by afternoon. You learn quickly that it makes sense to start cold; however chilly the air at breakfast, you'll warm up fast on the trail. If you start hiking in the clothes that are comfortable for puttering around camp, you will be hot and sweaty in a few hundred yards.

There are two competing principles here. One is: *keep comfortable.* The second is: *don't spend all your time fiddling with clothes.* With garments that you can adjust while you wear them, like shirts and sweaters with buttons in front, you can have it both ways.

Eating

There's no "right" way of eating on the trail. Some people subsist on granola and raisins all day long. Some like to stop and eat a solid midday meal. In normal hiking your appetite will tell you what you need. Be sure to drink plenty of water, either straight or in flavored drinks. (Incidentally, if you ever find yourself short of water, there is no good physiological reason for rationing yourself; you might as well drink it as thirst suggests and postpone the beginning of dehydration.)

Fighting blisters

The best way to handle blisters is not to get them. Make sure your boots fit properly and that they are nicely broken in before you set out with them (Chapter 4). Do enough preliminary hiking to toughen your feet somewhat. If you aren't sure you're ready, or if you know you blister easily, you will want to cover the danger points with moleskin or adhesive tape before you leave the trailhead. Pay attention to the heel, the outside of the big toe, and the sides of the foot at the base of the toes.

If you feel a spot of irritation forming as you walk—a "hot spot"—don't wait. Sit down, pull off the boot, and find out what's going on. Put on moleskin or tape; if you have some on already, make sure that it hasn't developed wrinkles (they can cause extra irritation) and add another layer. Make sure that your boots are very snugly laced, particularly in the upper part of the lacing pattern, and that your heel is not rising too far inside the rear of the boot as you stride. If the fit seems loose, try adding another pair of inner socks.

Some people find that an extremely thin pair of inner socks, about the thickness of dress socks, inside the other pairs, will help head off blisters. The thin socks slide inside the other layers—so the theory—rather than passing fric-

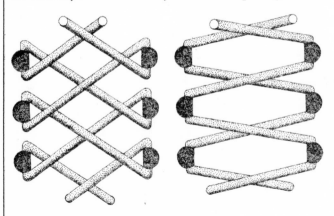

Loop pattern (left) vs. normal lacing

tion on to the skin. It's an experiment worth trying if you have consistent trouble.

Many hikers adjust the lacing of their boots depending on the slope of the hill. At the start of a climb, they loosen the toe and tighten the heel, which tends to shift and chafe in uphill travel. On the downslope they loosen the heel and tighten the toe. Again, only your experience will tell you whether you need to bother. This kind of adjustment is most easily done on boots that lace around hooks, rather than through D-rings or eyelets. The trick: run the laces around each hook in a loop. Laces set up this way won't slip around the hooks; they stay tight where you want them tight and loose where you want to ease the pressure on your foot.

On a warm day, it's good to cool your feet in a stream at lunchtime—or at any rate to pull off boots and socks for a while. Don't soak your feet for very long, though, as this can make them tender. Wet feet in wet socks blister easily. If you wade a stream with your boots on, you may want to change to dry socks on the other side. (Dry the wet ones on the outside of your pack if it's sunny.) Some people find it necessary to switch socks, or at least to change the inner pair, several times a day.

If the worst happens, and you do get a blister, you aren't by any means crippled. If the blister is well swollen, you may need to let the fluid out. First, wash the spot carefully with soap and water. Sterilize a needle by passing it through a flame, and puncture the swollen area at one edge. When the skin is dry cover the blister with a thin sterile pad from your first aid kit. Some people like to apply antibiotic ointment for more protection. Then put on a layer or two of moleskin or adhesive. Walking a long distance with such a patch is slightly uncomfortable, but it is by no means agonizing. Waiting around doesn't help much; it takes several days for a blister to heal. Though blisters very seldom lead to any further trouble, it's important to watch for signs of infection.

Trail ethics: manners and low impact

Everybody knows it but it bears repeating: if you're hiking a trail, *stay on it*. Cutting corners, taking shortcuts, walking outside the trace—all these break down trail edges and cause erosion and gullying. There is even some risk, on slopes, of dislodging rocks that can strike hikers below. (If this happens, yell at the top of your lungs: *Rock!*)

Not all trails are well-designed, and rather few are actually well-maintained. Some are laid out so badly that it is hard indeed to avoid doing some damage; these trails push straight through boggy meadows or head directly up erosive slopes. In such places people tend to move to one side or the other to avoid the mud or the rocky footing of a gully. This is one of the main causes of *multiple trailing,* in which five or six parallel tracks scar open slopes and mead-ows. This is not, strictly speaking, the hikers' fault—blame it rather on bad trail layout and poor maintenance—but the hiker can best help by gritting his teeth and keeping to the original line. Always walk single file, not side by side, on a trail. (In cross-country travel, where you wish to avoid establishing any visible track, the principle is precisely the opposite: always walk abreast, each hiker in his own line.)

There is another cause of multiple trailing. In snow country spring hikers may encounter a melting snowbank across their trail. Often they detour around the retreating margin of the snow, not wanting to wade in slush. By the following weekend the snowbank has shrunk; new parties come through and detour along a different arc, and then a third, until a whole fan of tracks is worn in the moist earth. This problem is so acute in some places that managers are closing routes to public access during the thaw. If you encounter such a snowbank, don't detour, but put on your gaiters and wade through.

Whether on a trail or on a cross-country route, you should restrain any impulse to build ducks (small rock cairns used as route markers) or, should you have the tools, to blaze trees. Let the next traveler find his way as you did. Chances are he wants it that way. (However, there is one possible exception: the mapped, special trail which is faint from lack of maintenance. Here you may be doing a serv-ice by building an occasional duck. It's wise to find out first whether such a trail is meant to be abandoned for some good reason—this is occasionally the case.) If a trail is clearly blocked—if for instance a log has been carefully laid across it—respect the block. If you meet stock on the trail, stand quietly aside and let the animals pass.

Side trips and party-splitting

There's no great harm in splitting your party—if you do it carefully, making sure that each splinter group has map, compass, and other essentials, and that everyone is clear about a place and time for coming back together.

When a party gets split by accident, problems can result. This is one danger in spreading out too far along the trail. Sometimes the people at the end of the line won't know what the leaders plan to do and take the wrong turn at an intersection. Make sure that everyone knows what's going on. A person who simply follows, blind to the choices and landmarks of the route, runs the risk of losing himself.

You may want to vary a trip by taking side trips with nothing but a daypack. If you take such an excursion, you must be certain to have some essential items with you. Always plan for an unexpected night away from your main camp. The classic list of "Ten Essentials," first formulated by the Seattle Mountaineers, goes like this:

Extra clothing. This may be as little as a sweater or as much as a jacket, parka, rainpants, and cagoule. Just as you do when you're packing the main pack at home, think of clothes to keep you *warm* and clothes to keep you *dry*.

Extra food. Perhaps nothing more than a generous lunch; perhaps an emergency packet of high-energy food. It's true that a person can survive for days, even weeks, without food, and take no permanent harm, but in an emergency you need energy to work with and, still more important, to think with.

Sunglasses. Essential above timberline, in the desert, and, most of all, on snow. Snow blindness is no joke. Wherever glasses are truly essential, take a spare set as well.

Knife.

Matches. Waterproof/windproof matches are good for this purpose.

Firestarter.

First aid kit.

Flashlight or headlamp.

Topo map and perhaps others.

Compass.

To these traditional ten you may want to add some of your own. Here are some other items you may not want to risk doing without:

Provision for emergency shelter. If you don't carry a plastic sheet, footsack, reflective blanket, or the like, at least have some kind of shelter in mind.

Suncream. A probable essential wherever sunglasses are important.

Signal. Whistle? Mirror? Bright-colored item of clothing?

Toilet paper. Not a survival item but . . . take it.

Insect repellent. Important, sometimes, for sanity.

Notebook and pencil. You may want to leave a note somewhere.

Weather

The weather that hikers dread most is extended rain. Even rain, though, is troublesome only when it comes time to set up camp; walking in the rain, with the proper gear, can be a very special pleasure. If you have good waterproofs for yourself and your pack, you will be relatively comfortable (though it is hard to keep water out of your boots).

There is real danger for the unprepared in wet, cool, windy weather. If you don't have the gear to stay dry and warm, you run the risk of losing so much body heat that you suffer the spectacular collapse called *hypothermia.* Common sense and proper clothing, however, are all that's required to prevent such situations. For more on hypothermia, see Chapter 27.

In brief, western-style thunderstorms, you may be able to wait out a swiftly-passing shower under the shelter of a tree. But make very sure it's the right tree. In thunderstorm country you have to give thought to lightning. Lightning is a definite hazard in the American wilderness, much more to be feared than, for example, the rattlesnake. Yet, like most hazards, it's easy to avoid.

Lightning doesn't strike just anywhere. It is drawn to prominent objects: the highest outcrop on a stony peak, the sharp brink of a cliff, a tall, isolated tree. When the bolt strikes, the charge spreads out through the ground, and can shock you badly many feet away from the original strike. The current tends to move along cracks in rock and down small, shallow watercourses, especially when water is running in them. (Knowledgeable readers will notice oversimplification here; the most dangerous type of lightning does not strike down from the clouds at all, but *up* from the ground. In practical terms, though, it doesn't matter.)

When you hear a thunderstorm working its way through the sky, stop for a moment and count the number of seconds that pass between a flash and the resulting thunderclap. Each five seconds that passes indicates a mile between you and the flash. If you are in a high or exposed place, don't wait till the last minute to start your retreat; thunderstorms typically move a mile every two or three minutes.

What are unsafe positions? A peak, of course, or a hilltop. A flat meadow or plain or rocky plateau where you yourself are a prominent object. The shelter of a tall, isolated tree. The top of a cliff but also the *base* of a cliff. A shallow cave on a slope. You are much less vulnerable at the bottom of a valley; in timber with trees of fairly uniform height; or in a deep, dry cave.

If you're trapped on a mountain top or out in the open, with no time to retreat, at least get back from the highest points and from cliff edges. Among boulders, you can crouch between rocks of similar size and low profile. Members of a party should spread apart, keeping thirty feet or more between them.

Get rid of your pack, your pocket knife, your belt, your camera, and anything else that might have metal in it. If you can, try to get some insulation between you and the ground. A rope, if you are carrying one, is good; a foam sleeping pad will help some. Crouch or kneel on the insulation. Don't lie flat. If you are inside a tent pitched in a vulnerable spot (bad planning!), do the same. If you feel a tingle, hear a buzzing from metal objects, or see, on metal, the weird flame of St. Elmo's fire, you have very little time.

If a companion has been struck by lightning, your quick action may save his life: see Chapter 25.

Stream crossing

On most well-traveled trails, at least in the regular

hiking season, you will find simple bridges across large streams. More primitive routes, however, don't have bridges. Lacking convenient stones, you wade.

Some people stride through such fords and keep walking, letting feet and socks and boots dry as they go. Others change socks on the far bank. Still others put on tennis shoes to cross, or take off their socks, putting their boots back on, over bare feet, to wade. Don't try to cross a stony streambed barefoot. It's bad news for a backpacker to cut a foot or stub a toe. Don't try to throw boots across a broad stretch of water.

Most fords are very innocent. But there can be genuine danger in crossing a high-volume, swift-running stream such as you may encounter at the spring thaw or in cross-country travel. Crossing a wild stream can be quite an undertaking, with rules and techniques adapted from mountain climbing. You may have to spend some time looking for a good crossing point. Often it is better to turn back, even if it means abandoning a destination or going the long way around. Ask yourself what will happen if you are swept off your feet. An astonishing number of people have been carried over the terrible verges of Yosemite's thousand-foot cataracts after they tried to cross the harmless-looking mountain streams above. Unless you know exactly what you are doing, it is not wise to tie in to a rope at a dubious crossing: the seeming protection can do more harm than good.

These dangerous situations, however, will not be encountered in ordinary backpacking.

16:
Finding the Way

LET'S FACE IT. Few corners of the American wilderness are now so vast, so trackless, or so primitive, that they afford us much excuse for getting lost. Not truly lost, not lost without a clue, not North Woods lost. Nor are the techniques that brought the trappers in northern Canada back to their caches of more than casual use to the hiker of well-marked trails. Navigation these days is more often a simple thing, a matter of keeping track of where you are, how fast you are progressing, what landmarks you are passing. It's a matter of awareness: common sense.

Yet people do get lost, and even in serious trouble, in the most populous of wild areas. And it is a rare hiker who has not had moments of disorientation along the way. Did I miss the trail junction? When did we cross into the Horse Creek watershed? What are those cliffs up there? What happened to the trail?

Even for the hiker who never moves on anything but the plainest of our paths, navigation can be fun, not so much to tell him where he *is* as to identify for him what he *sees*.

The topographic map

The basic tool of navigation is the topographic or contour map. Add to it a compass and a little thought, and you can answer almost any question about your place in the land.

These invaluable maps—many thousands of sheets in all—are published by the U.S. Geological Survey and cover the whole area of the United States. Maps for the western U.S. are ordered from Denver, eastern maps from Arlington, Virginia. Similar maps for Canada can be ordered from the Department of Energy, Mines, and Resources in Ottawa (see Appendix). The topo maps suitable for backpacking come in two scales. "Fifteen-minute" quadrangles represent a mile of land by an inch of map and cover named areas of about thirteen by seventeen miles. "Seven-and-a-half-minute" sheets, four to each fifteen-minute sheet, cover smaller areas more minutely. ("Minute" here is a unit of space not of time.) Both types cost $1.25. The fifteen-minute style is actually more useful to the hiker, more compact (fewer sheets are carried) and yet quite sufficiently detailed. Unfortunately, this series is being phased out. For some areas only seven-and-a-half-minute maps can now be obtained. At the other extreme there are a few sections of the Intermountain West which have yet to be mapped at all on a scale useful to the backpacker.

Recently, the U.S.G.S. has begun publishing a series of "orthophoto maps," really aerial photographs of tremendous accuracy. Orthophoto maps correspond to conventional seven-and-a-half-minute sheets. They lack contours and other symbols, but so fine is the detail that even trails can often be picked out.

There are several kinds of information on a regular topo map. Most important are the thin, brown lines called "contour lines" or just "contours." These are labeled to show elevation above sea level. If you imagine the map as a three-dimensional model that could be flooded with water, the rising surface would first touch the 1,200-foot contour wherever it appears, then the 1,400-foot, and so on.

On fifteen-minute maps the interval between contour lines is eighty feet. Every fifth line is heavier and darker and marks a gain of four-hundred feet from the last such emphatic line. On seven-and-a-half-minute maps the basic

Topographical map, 7.5 minute scale

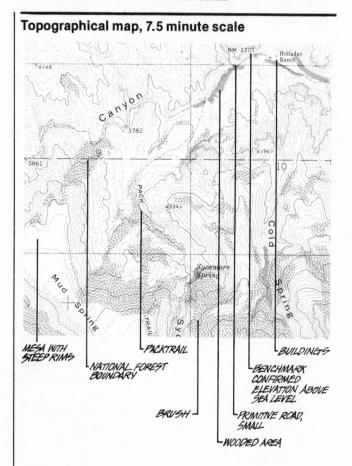

interval is forty feet, and two hundred feet separate the heavier lines. Occasionally you will find an older fifteen-minute map on which the contours are not eighty but fifty or one-hundred feet apart; don't take the interval for granted.

Topo sheets ordinarily have a pale green shading to show forested areas. Green stippling indicates brush; uncolored areas are grassy or barren. Most sheets are ruled with squares a mile on a side (each with a number) called *Sections*. These are the fundamental units of the national land survey (see *More about maps*, below).

In 15 minute scale

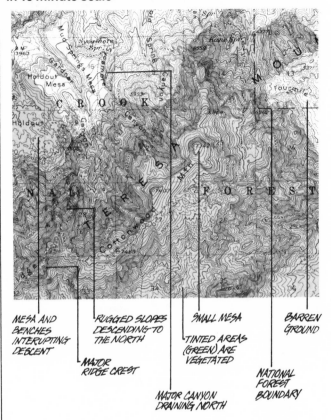

MESA AND BENCHES INTERRUPTING DESCENT

RUGGED SLOPES DESCENDING TO THE NORTH

MAJOR RIDGE CREST

SMALL MESA

TINTED AREAS (GREEN) ARE VEGETATED

MAJOR CANYON DRAINING NORTH

BARREN GROUND

NATIONAL FOREST BOUNDARY

Topo maps are highly accurate; you will find few minor and hardly any major errors, at least in the portrayal of the land itself. Manmade features, though, do change, and some of these maps were last updated in the early 1950s. Check the date in the legend. Many trails shown on these older maps have been abandoned or rerouted, and the road systems in the rugged mountains of the Far West have expanded almost beyond comprehension in the last quarter century. Looking at 1950s topo maps, you get the impression that, even so late in our history, the mountainous parts of the West were dominantly wilderness. But that has changed in most of our mountains, and changed beyond recall.

The Geological Survey, by the way, has no current plans to go metric. But a kilometer is about 0.6 miles; a mile contains 1.6 kilometers; and a twenty-kilometer day does sound more impressive than a hike of just twelve miles.

If you do a lot of hiking in rain or snow, it's worthwhile to cover your topo maps with clear adhesive plastic, the kind sold in ten-cent stores. A wet map quickly becomes an unreadable mess.

Map reading

The basic skill is the ability to build, from the map, a picture of the land—to translate swiftly, automatically, from map to land and back again. You can practice this skill most easily by buying the topographic sheet for a familiar landscape near home. Soon you'll know without thinking what a particular shape of land looks like in contour lines; that an outward eddy of lines along a slope indicates a spur ridge; that an indentation means a gully or a streamcourse; that one valley is broad and shallow, a second precipitous and deep. You will know a short steep hill from a long gradual one, and a plateau from a knife-edge ridgeline. It is a fascinating study. The map begins as a dead graphic, a mere representation, but it comes alive as you learn it and instructs you endlessly. The map *becomes* the country.

The perfect tool for navigation (too perfect: may it never be invented!) would be a topo map with a built-in spot of light showing your own position—a little dot that would shift as you moved. Lacking such a gimmick, you reproduce it in your mind. Navigation, in its essence, is not a set of techniques but a habit of thought; a custom of awareness; of knowing where you are, and what the land is doing. In typical wilderness landscapes, unlike those of the city, there is seldom anything really inexplicable or arbitrary; there are broad, discernible patterns—drainages running one way and another; major and minor systems of ridges; plateaus and deep-carved canyons. If you keep alive this sense of pattern, it is rather hard to become entirely lost, whether you have a trail to follow or are striking out cross-country on a route of your own.

Some landscapes, of course, are easier than others to get lost in. Most confusing are areas that are level, rather patternless, or chaotically jumbled, and places where timber or topography cut off your long-distance views. Fog or low overcast can complicate matters, and every winter hiker knows (and somewhat fears) that brilliant-white, opaque, and snowy mist called "white-out." But these are special cases. For more information on advanced cross-country routefinding, see Chapter 22.

More about maps

While topo maps are important, they are not necessarily the only guides you will need. Usually you also want the maps put out by the agency that controls the land you are hiking on—Park Service, Forest Service, Fish and Wildlife Service, Bureau of Land Management, or state agency. These agency maps, though mostly less detailed than topos, do reflect more recent changes in roads and trails. When you are traveling wilderness areas that have no formal protection, like so many Forest Service and BLM lands, this information is vital. Roads may be advancing, trails vanishing every year.

Almost all maps share with the topos a basic organization. All the area of the United States (outside the original Colonies) is divided into squares, normally six miles on a side, called *townships*. Each contains thirty-six *Sections* of one square mile, and these are numbered within the township in an unvarying back-and-forth pattern:

6	5	4	3	2	1
7	8	9	10	11	12
18	17	16	15	14	13
19	20	21	22	23	24
30	29	28	27	26	25
31	32	33	34	35	36

Hikers and other people who work with the land soon become familiar with this pattern and use it to identify points on the map: "Looks like that must be a real cliff in Section 17!"

In the woods you will sometimes come across yellow metal plates nailed to trees. Each is stamped with the thirty-six section pattern shown above. A nail through the plate tells you where you are: highly convenient when prominent landmarks are few.

How do maps distinguish one township from another? Townships are stacked in vertical and horizontal rows. The horizontal rows called "extended townships," or (rather confusingly) just "townships." The vertical rows are called "ranges." Each extended township and each range has a number of its own marking its position in the broader land survey. Using these numbers, it's possible to describe any point on the map exactly, as a location in the land survey grid. But this is not especially a hiker's game.

The compass and how to read it

With the map, the compass is the second fundamental aid in wilderness navigation. Its function is to help you place the map in the right position, so that the map's north and the world's north are exactly the same. Then the compass helps you to read the land, from the map, with precision.

Nothing is simpler, in practice, than using a compass. Nothing is more difficult than to describe this simple act without giving an altogether spurious impression of complexity. I suggest that, after reading the next few pages, you locate a compass and review them with compass in hand. Only thus will the seeming complications disappear.

The circle of directions

Before we talk about the compass itself, we have to deal with an essential concept: the idea of the *circle of directions*.

Imagine yourself standing on a peak from which you can see a hundred miles in every direction. Imagine yourself turning slowly in one spot—facing north, then east, then south, then west, then north again.

How do you name the directions you have been facing? The cardinal points—north, east, south, west—are easy. For the directions in between, you can combine and say: northeast, southwest; then north-northeast, south-southwest; then north-by-north-northeast; and so on. But obviously you can only go so far with this. To simplify matters, we supplement the names with numbers. The circle of directions is divided into 360 units called *degrees*. Zero is north; 45, northeast; 90, east; 180, south; 270, west; 350, just a little west of north; and 360, north again (zero and 360, in the circle, are names for the same point).

It may seem odd at first, this use of numbers for directions, but it is indispensable for any careful navigation. It allows you to define a direction simply and quickly—using words, it might not be possible to pin it down at all.

The compass

The key part of the compass is the magnetized *needle*. The needle points to that location on the earth's surface called the *Magnetic North Pole*. (I am oversimplifying, but it will do.) This point has nothing whatever to do with the true North Pole, the end-point of the axis on which the earth spins, and the "north" of every map. For our purposes it is to be regarded as sheer accident that the Magnetic North Pole is located just 1,400 miles from the true North Pole, on an island called Bathurst, in the Canadian Arctic Archipelago. It is not even a lucky accident. The two points are far enough apart to make a profound difference in navigation but close enough together so that many people, including many hikers, fail to distinguish between them.

There are many kinds of compasses. The type most used in backpacking is the *orienteering compass*. The needle rides on a pivot inside a round, fluid-filled plastic chamber. One end of the needle—the end that points

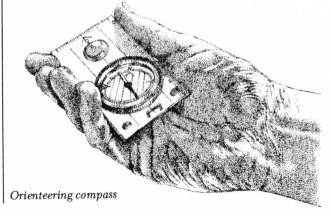

Orienteering compass

toward magnetic north—is specially marked, often with red paint. The lower surface of the chamber is a *dial* marked with 360 degrees running clockwise—the circle of directions. While no small compass has room for a separate mark for each of the degrees, the better models mark every five degrees, or even every two.

The needle-and-dial assembly sits on a rectangular *base plate* of clear plastic and can be rotated upon it. The bigger the base plate, the better for close navigation—five inches is good. The plate is marked with a big lengthwise *directional arrow;* this extends partway under the dial and can be seen through it. On many compasses the base plate is also marked with several *scales* to use in reading maps: inch, millimeter, and other intervals shown because, on maps of different standard scales, they represent miles.

Good orienteering compasses without superfluous extras cost between $10 and $15. Almost all are made by two Swedish companies, Silva and Suunto. Very simple compasses, with small dials and no base plates, can be found much more cheaply and may in fact be sufficient for your needs. If you plan to depart from the main traveled thoroughfares of the wilderness trail system, you need a tool of greater precision. When you buy a compass, compare it with others in the store to make sure that the needle points in exactly the same direction. It is possible for a needle to be misaligned or to stick in a false position.

Compasses are confused by metal. You won't get an accurate reading from a compass held near a camera or other metallic object.

Compass step one: knowing the declination

The compass needle points to a place conveniently known as magnetic north. Depending on just where you are hiking, magnetic north can in fact be *any* direction from you: northeast, northwest, even due east or west. And if you were standing on the true North Pole, magnetic north would be south of you!

Since magnetic north is located north of the Great Plains, most American hikers find their compass needles pointing either just east or just west of true north. To make use of your compass, you have to know how much east or west. Every topographic map has, in the lower margin, a

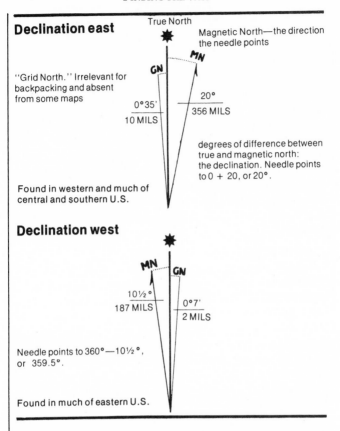

Declination east

True North

Magnetic North—the direction
the needle points

MN

GN

"Grid North." Irrelevant for
backpacking and absent
from some maps

20°

$\dfrac{0°35'}{10\,\text{MILS}}$

$\dfrac{20°}{356\,\text{MILS}}$

degrees of difference between
true and magnetic north:
the declination. Needle points
to 0 + 20, or 20°.

Found in western and much of
central and southern U.S.

Declination west

MN   **GN**

$\dfrac{10\frac{1}{2}°}{187\,\text{MILS}}$

$\dfrac{0°7'}{2\,\text{MILS}}$

Needle points to 360°—10½°,
or 359.5°.

Found in much of eastern U.S.

diagram that gives this information. The vertical line with
the star represents true north; the slanted line labeled
"MN" indicates magnetic north. The angle between them
is defined by a number. This is called the *declination,* and
tells you how many degrees you go east or west of true
north to find magnetic north. The same diagram also shows
a second angle which you can ignore; it has to do with
technicalities of mapping.

Compass step two: orienting the dial

Suppose the declination is 19 degrees east: the "MN"
line is 19 degrees to the east, or right of, the true north
line. When you are in the area represented by that particular map, your compass needle will point in the direction
represented by 19 degrees—about north-northeast. To ori-

ent your compass for that region, then, you rotate the dial until the number 19 comes into position at the tip of the needle. With your compass dial thus oriented, it has become an accurate guide to direction. Following this adjustment, true north on the compass matches true north on the land; southeast on the compass is southeast in the outside world; and so on.

In the eastern United States, compass needles lean west from true north. Say the declination is 10 degrees west—the "MN" line is 10 degrees to the left of the true north line. Rotate the dial so that the needle rests at a point 10 degrees to the west of north. This point bears the number 350: 360 (north)–10 (declination west) = 350. (To go west from north, counterclockwise around the dial, you have to subtract.)

Compass step three: orienting the map

Once you know how to orient the compass, it's no trick to do the same for the map. First, rotate the compass dial until the directional arrow on the base-plate is seen to pass through the "North" mark. Then place the compass on the map, with the arrow in line with north on the map. Now rotate both map and compass until the compass is properly oriented, with the needle pointed to the declination. The map is now oriented as well—it parallels the land.

Compass step four: taking a bearing

Now that both map and compass are oriented, you can use them together to give you many kinds of information. Often a simple procedure will do. If you already know within a mile or so where you are on the map, it is easy to read the identities of prominent points. The big massif just east can only be General Steele's Backbone; the forested valley can only be the drainage of Horsethief Creek; what is glinting in the socket below can only be Hungry Packer Lake.

But sometimes you will need to read the land more precisely. Perhaps you don't know at all where you are; perhaps the topography is downright confusing; perhaps you must make a difficult choice of route. All these problems are reasons for taking *bearings*.

How is it done?

The idea is to find the precise direction from you to a

Using bearings on distant points to find position

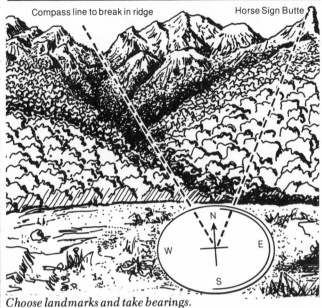

Compass line to break in ridge

Horse Sign Butte

Choose landmarks and take bearings.

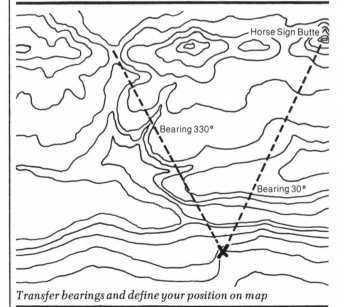

Horse Sign Butte

Bearing 330°

Bearing 30°

Transfer bearings and define your position on map

particular object, say a prominent peak. Raise the compass
to just below eye level. Make sure it is correctly oriented.
Now, keeping the dial in that same correct position, turn
the base plate underneath it so that the arrow on the plate
is pointing exactly toward the object you want the bearing
on. Now look down through the transparent dial. You will
see that the directional arrow is visible and cuts the circle
of degrees at a particular point. Read the number at that
point. This is your bearing.

This information has many uses.

*You know where you are and want to know what you're
looking at.* Take a bearing on the point you want to identify. Note your own position on the map. Place the compass on the map with the center of its dial at your position.
Say the bearing on your landmark was 120, or about southeast. Simply draw (or imagine) a line running from your
position to the number 120 on the dial and on across the
map. The first height it crosses that seems of proper size
and distance is the one.

*You know what you're looking at and want to know
where you are.* Take bearings on two known peaks (or any
other prominent features). The farther apart they are, the
more accurate your fix will be. Placing the compass on the
map as before, draw (or imagine) lines running from those
landmarks at the proper angles. Where these lines intersect, you have your exact position. To double-check, you
can sight on additional points.

Or perhaps you already know that you are on a certain
line in the landscape: a major stream, a trail, a ridgeline, a
road. This simplifies matters. Just one bearing, just one
additional line on the map, may be enough to show you
the single place where you can reasonably be standing.

*You have the whole picture but want to find this place
again.* Say you've discovered something interesting a little
way off the trail: an old cabin not shown on the map, a
good shortcut, a pleasant meadow. You want to come back
next year. But there's no obvious landmark along the trail
to tell you where to leave it next time you come along. A
bearing on a more distant landmark will do just as well.
Write yourself a note: "Next time walk east along the
Kangaroo Trail until Sawtooth Mountain is on a bearing of
315; then cut down the ravine to the left." You can further

describe your cross-country route as a compass direction or *azimuth*: "then head downslope on a line of 125 degrees."

Simple uses of the compass

All this is compass work at its most precise. Most of the time you will be using this tool in a simpler, more casual way. (This is one item you don't want far out of reach!) Just a glance at the dial, now and again, can guide you when you are uncertain or keep you from drifting off an ill-marked route. If you know, from the map, that you are supposed to be heading essentially north, then something is plainly wrong if the compass shows you moving steadily east.

Substitutes for the compass

There are no very good substitutes for the combination of topographic map and compass in finding your way. It is worth mentioning some rough-and-ready methods of determining direction, all the same.

"Sense of direction"

Do human beings have a built-in "homing instinct" or sense of the proper way? Say the experts: absolutely not. This is simply not our gift. People who try to walk straight lines without constant correction veer in circles.

Signs in the land

In the northern hemisphere, the north and northeast sides of objects are heated less by sunlight each day than the south and southwest sides. Other things being equal, then, moss *does* tend to be thicker on the northern side of trees; timber tends to grow lusher on north- and east-facing slopes; snow and ice linger longest on the northern sides of ridges. In rare cases you may also be able to guess direction from the effects of a strong prevailing wind: lopsided trees, sand patterns, and so on. But all of these signs should be used with caution. Local conditions complicate them, and, at best, they are crude.

The sun

It's well to be aware of the arc the sun follows in the sky at a given time of year. At the equinoxes, mid-March and mid-September, the sun rises and sets very close to due east and due west. In mid-June it rises northeast and sets

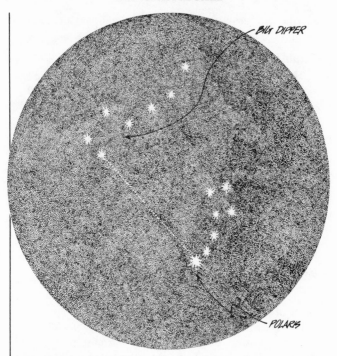

Using the Big Dipper to find Polaris

northwest; in mid-December, it rises southeast and sets southwest.

Then there's the old watch trick. (It presupposes that you carry a watch and keep it running accurately.) First, set the watch to standard time (turn it one hour back if it's on daylight-saving time). Second, hold the dial level and point the hour hand toward the sun (that is, toward the ground point that would appear to be directly below the sun). North will be a point on the watchface halfway between the hour hand and 12. Before noon, you must read backwards around the dial to find this middle point; after noon, you read clockwise. (If it's 7 A.M. standard time, north will be at about 3:30 on the dial; if it's 4 P.M., at about 8:00 on the dial. At 12 noon, north lies opposite the hour hand.) This method is none too accurate, but it's good in a pinch.

Lacking a watch, you can read directions, roughly,

from the shadow thrown by a straight stick. There are different versions of the technique. In the quickest procedure you plant your stick in the ground, not straight up, but slanted toward the sun, so that no shadow is thrown. Then wait until a shadow appears. This shadow will mark an approximate east-west line. The reading can be taken at any time of day and does not require a long wait.

Polaris

Our "polestar" isn't always at true north, but it's close enough for emergency purposes. To locate it in a clear night sky, first find the Big Dipper. The two stars which form the end of the Dipper's "bucket," opposite the "handle," point straight toward Polaris.

Following a trail

Ordinarily, there's no skill to following a trail. It's there, unmistakable, and you just plod. But even obvious trails grow faint at times and can be confused by game traces. And we have in this country a huge network of what might be called "ghost trails"; these were built in the 1930s, under the New Deal, and have never been maintained since. (As fast as the American hiking public is growing, our trail system seems to be shrinking still faster.)

Faint trails, especially above timberline, may be marked with small stacks of stones called "ducks" or "cairns" or "birds." Occasionally these piles are high, but most are just large enough to be clearly artificial. Often a single stone, placed at one side of the main stack, indicates the direction of the continuing trail.

In wooded country the guiding marks are *blazes:* deep, clean axe cuts which have chipped out whole sections of bark and underlying wood. Usually, these are placed at about chest height. Often they are stacked in groups of two or three; this stacking may or may not indicate a turn. Blazes ordinarily face along the continuing line of the trail, so if you see one facing sharply off to the right, it probably marks a bend in the route. However, blazes cut by different workers at different times aren't necessarily standard.

Recently, plastic tags, metal disks, and paint spots have been much used instead of classic blazes, perhaps to avoid injuring trees. In the East marks of different colors are used to distinguish trails.

When the trail is clear, of course, you don't have to be too much concerned with these guides. But if it starts going hazy on you—if it disappears under patches of snow, if it threatens to dissolve in a maze of deer trails—or if the brush starts closing it over, begin watching the blazes meticulously. Don't go on for long without locating one. Stop and hunt if you must. Few of us can trust instinct, and a surprisingly official-looking trail can be made by deer and bear. Be aware, too, that natural marks can counterfeit blazes—occasionally a rock bounding down from a cliff gouges a good imitation. Yet another caution: lines of blazes are sometimes used to mark the boundaries of land-survey squares, or Sections, away from any trail.

When the ducks and blazes fail you, there are other signs you can look for. Have the branches of trees or shrubs been cut or clipped? Is there a terrace effect where the path was cut into a hillside? In a place where brush has obscured a route, the treadway itself may be free of new stems; plants are slow to root again on compacted ground.

If such detective work is required for long, though, you are probably no longer just bridging a difficult section of an otherwise plain path. Rather, you have to count the trail as defunct and regard the trip as a problem in cross-country routefinding. Bear in mind that the original trail-builders may have taken the most logical line through the landscape; it may be worthwhile continuing on that line even if the trail refuses to reappear.

What if you do get lost?

What *is* getting lost, anyway?

If you lose the trail in the undergrowth; if you hesitate at a junction; if you see a landmark you don't recognize; then you aren't lost. You're disoriented merely, and though disorientation can be the beginning of "lost," it is not the thing itself.

You are lost when you do not know how to retrace your steps to a place where you feel sure of your bearings. But perhaps even more than a situation, being lost is a state of mind: panic.

If you find yourself disoriented, whether you are "lost" yet or not, sit down. Get out map and compass. Think back on where you have been in the last hour. Think back to the last point at which you were sure of your position. Scan the landscape for features you can reason from. Consider the lay of the land—are you, for instance, in a valley that drains in a certain direction? If you find yourself initially too worried to think, start by making this a rest stop. Eat something, have some lemonade, take a picture.

Most of the time you should be able to reconstruct where you are, or at least how to get back to known ground. After all, a pedestrian moves only so fast. You won't be two counties away.

And if you can't reconstruct? Sometimes, especially on flat terrain, it is appropriate to walk a *search pattern,* a sort of rectilinear spiral spreading from your starting point. This can be useful if you are looking for something—say a trail—that is probably nearby. One caution, though: never lay down your pack or daypack while you search. You might not find it again, and this could turn a minor problem into a major one.

If you get lost on a side trip, away from your party, try to make contact with the rest of your group. Shout, blow your whistle, flash your mirror. Three signals of any kind is a distress signal; two signals of any kind indicates response—"We read you." Or you can light a smoky fire. (Distress or not, be careful where and how you light it.)

If none of this works, about all you can do is make yourself comfortable, keep signaling from time to time, and stay put until searchers turn up. Eventually your friends will report you missing, or an alarm will be sounded when you fail to return at an appointed time.

The first priority is *warmth and shelter.* If you are on a exposed, windy ridge in chilly country, you may have to get off it. Leave something there, though, to attract attention, like a bright cloth or a circle of stones. And don't just blunder away from the starting point. You can't afford to get still further lost. Rather, move away on a definite compass bearing. If you are hiking alone, you may have a whole packful of equipment on your back, in which case you can make yourself cozy. If you are on a side trip, you should at least have your ten essentials. If you need to cut boughs for shelter, this is justifiable in a genuine emergency.

The second priority (under some circumstances the

first) is *water*. Food can wait.

As time passes, keep thinking about the land and your position in it. You may sort it out yet. But don't shift position unless you are quite sure of what you are doing. (If you do move, leave a note.) Be cautious in following such traditional advice as "Follow water downhill." It all depends on what water and what hill. Sometimes, as in the Southwest, a downhill grade leads not out of wilderness but deeper into it.

Continue signaling. Nothing attracts the interest of the authorities so quickly as smoke. Don't try to send up puffs in threes: just make sure the smoke is plentiful. (This is one situation in which there is an excuse for putting green wood or foliage on a fire.)

To repeat, however: in summer backpacking, and in our modern wilderness areas, so small and so well mapped, nothing should be easier than staying out of this kind of trouble. And in fact it is fairly rare for well-equipped backpackers, traversing the deep backcountry, to lose their way. The casual hiker, wandering away from his car without a map, is much more at risk. If you know what you are doing, and walk with a mind aware, the land should have no unpleasant surprises for you.

Making and Managing the Camp

It is legitimate to hope that there may be left...the special kind of human mark, the special record of human passage, that distinguishes man from all other species. It is rare enough among men, impossible to any other form of life. It is simply the deliberate and chosen refusal to make any marks at all.

—Wallace Stegner

17:
Making Camp

A FRIEND OF MINE, an instructor in a wilderness education program, once brought back a disturbing story. "We ruined a meadow," he told me. Quite innocently, casually, unintentionally, he and his students had started the destruction of a vulnerable piece of wilderness—a destruction that can now be reversed only with difficulty, if at all.

What did they do that was so damaging?

They camped—for one night only—on an irresistible green expanse of grass and flowers, at the edge of an aspen grove in a Colorado wilderness—a picture-postcard spot where few or none had ever camped before.

That was all.

They knew better than to dig ditches, cut limbs, or build new fire-rings. They left no litter, no blackened stones. They were careful, even sensitive, as hikers go. But they bedded down on the meadow, and then went on their way.

Ordinarily, the wilderness traveler doesn't see the results of his own presence. My friend, though, had a special vantage point. He stayed in those mountains all summer, working with successive groups of students. And a few weeks later he was back at that same meadow. What he saw appalled him.

Where there had been the faultless, textured green, there was now a cluster of pockmarks—pads of bare and flattened ground, sterile, stark, as if no grass had ever grown there. Exactly what had happened he could not tell. Had that single earlier night of use, that minimal trampling of grass, that brief compaction of moist earth, been enough by itself to blight the ground? Or had other parties, attracted to a site that was now just discernibly *used*, added their own, more serious impacts to the first? No matter. The result was the same. After that summer the meadow would be a marked place. Inevitably, it would continue to draw campers where no campers should be. Inevitably, the scars would grow. A piece of wilderness had become a casualty.

Low-impact travel means many things. But among them, one is paramount: the proper making, managing, and breaking of the wilderness camp.

It is hardly surprising that the agencies responsible for our wilderness are particularly concerned with camping habits. In fact, of the guidelines they set, most have to do with campsites and camping practices. That's something of a pity. You'd prefer not to have the feeling of someone looking over your shoulder, in thought at least, when you stop for the night. But until wilderness travelers reeducate themselves to the needs of a new time, the rules can hardly be spared. When you're confronted with them, examine them; ask questions and learn from them.

Regulations are not uniform across the country. Different regions have different problems; different experts have different ideas to propose. Sometimes the managers seek to concentrate use in a few areas, leaving the rest untouched; sometimes the plan is to disperse campers widely, and this viewpoint seems to be gaining. In many areas there is a double standard. While campers who build fires must stay at designated sites, those with stoves face no such restrictions. Sometimes particular areas may be closed, not only to fires, but to any camping, all the time or at given times of year, for various good reasons (wildfire danger is one;

the welfare of wildlife is another). Details of local provisions are generally printed on the back of wilderness permits.

In what follows I speak as if these regulations did not exist, as if nothing affected your choice of site but sensitive common sense. This does not mean, of course, that official advice is to be ignored; on the contrary, I hope and assume that you will follow it. Don't be put off by the way the rules change from place to place. The agency people, like the conscientious hikers, are feeling their way in a complex and many-sided matter.

Choosing the low-impact camp

Where then *should* you camp? What standards can you go by—not only for low impact on the land, but for comfort and convenience as well?

We need to begin with an important distinction. There are two very different sorts of camping spots in the wilderness. First is the pristine site: the random piece of unmarked ground which, for a certain time, you make your own. If you camp in such a place, you take onto yourself a considerable responsibility. It is your job to leave that land exactly as you found it: still unscarred, still unfrayed, recognizable to no one as a place that has been used. Some sites, like that Colorado meadow, are much more vulnerable to scarring than others, and these the low-impact camper must be at pains to avoid.

In contrast, campsites of the second type are clearly marked as areas of use. They have worn paths, fire-rings, bare ground, perhaps even terraced tentpads cut from a hill. Logs and stones may have been shifted to make tables and seats. Such camps, if you find them vacant, can be both convenient and charming. And from the point of view of low impact, they have a telling advantage: they are already barren. It is relatively hard to injure them further. The price has already been paid.

It might seem that you could make very sure of doing no harm to the land by restricting yourself to sites already marked. Actually, that's only true if the developed site is in the proper place to begin with. In many open alpine landscapes you find many more firespots and tentpads than anyone needs; the same may be true along popular forest trails. Many of these excess sites, built at random by the uninformed, could not have been worse chosen if the makers had drawn up a plan for maximum impact, maximum ugliness, maximum disturbance to wildlife and land. These scars should be allowed to heal. The low-impact camper will avoid them and choose, from established campsites, the ones that are best justified upon the land.

Now the criteria:

Flatness

Surely this is the first requirement of all. A fairly level site is important, and not for comfort only; steep ground, if it is anything but solid rock, is easily disturbed and easily eroded. In steep, forested mountains, almost the only viable campsites may be artificial flats scooped from the unbroken slopes.

Surface

This is *highly* important. The best kind of ground to camp on is forest duff without vegetation; the second best is bare ground: sand, gravel, rock, rocky soil, or an area already worn bare by human traffic. Avoid damp ground and don't camp on vegetation when it can possibly be helped.

Look at almost any catalog of backpacking equipment. Chances are you'll see bright tents and sleeping bags spread out on backgrounds of green glossy meadow and windswept alpine tundra. You can't blame the photographers for composing these elegant scenes, but you can blame the equipment dealers for exploiting them. Beginning backpackers take the implied advice and camp where they should not. Meadows and tundra are the places, above all others, where camps must *not* be sited.

Plants at timberline and above live at the edge of survival. A few inches of stem and leaf may take a decade to form; a trampled heath may keep the scars for a lifetime. If you camp among the treeless peaks, find barren ground or snow. Otherwise, make your place in the woodlands below, where life has a little more margin.

Moist grasslands, especially those at higher elevations, are especially vulnerable. Trampling, the pounding in of stakes, even the weight of a sleeper (because it compacts the water-saturated soil) do them harm. Moreover, such meadows as campsites are anything but ideal. They are cooler than the surrounding uplands, mosquito-ridden, damp, lacking in privacy. Grassy ground is not even particularly soft!

The drier grasslands of high western ranges—"shorthair meadows"—are somewhat less sensitive. They can take a fair amount of pounding before damage begins to show. Unfortunately, these meadows are among the slowest plant communities to recover once damage is done.

Water supply

Few people find much charm in a camp without nearby water. (It isn't absolutely essential, however; you can fill your containers at a handy stream in the afternoon; then make your evening stop with no need for a local supply.)

Dispersal

If you are going to be camping at a pristine site, however, it is best to choose a spot that is both some distance from the waterside and some distance from the trail. One writer on eastern wilderness has estimated that ninety percent of all camps in New Hampshire's White Mountains are made within one hundred feet of the intersection of a stream and a trail! When this happens, scarring is inevitable, and so is crowding. Both are to be avoided.

In fact, land management agencies are commonly making it a requirement that you move some distance away from stream and trail to camp. Two hundred feet is often specified. This is doubly important in the desert, where the isolated springs are absolutely vital to wild animals—you can disrupt a whole web of natural patterns by settling down near the local waterhole. But there are also wilderness areas so steep and rugged that you have little choice but to camp near water, because that's where you find level ground.

In the lake basins of western mountains, look for sites behind low trees on the hillsides, some distance back from the water. Often you will find little terraces of twiggy soil, just the right size for a small party.

Ecotones

Ecotone is the ecologist's word for a place where two

environments come together: the line where forest adjoins meadow, or where meadow comes down to water, or even a juncture of low brush and tall timber. These border zones are of special importance to wildlife. In them you find the species of each of the two habitats and still other species native to the ecotone itself. So a camper who wants to disturb the natural order as little as possible will do his best to avoid such sites as the forest edge, the streambank, the lakeshore. This may take some self-restraint for ecotones, by their nature, are pretty places.

Privacy

Consider your own and others'. Researchers find that many backpackers prefer an uncomfortable but solitary camp to an ideal spot with neighbors. Even if you don't feel that way yourself, it's courteous to assume that others will. (Backpacking parties that meet in camp or on the trail tend to greet each other cordially, chat a moment, and then, as soon as politely possible, withdraw.) Try to stay out of earshot of the next camp. Remember, sound carries readily across lakes and meadows, less so through trees.

Safety

Be aware of possible hazards: snags or branches that might break in the wind, cliffs from which stones might fall, and, in the winter, avalanche paths. In the desert, during the thunderstorm season, be careful not to camp in dry washes; arid though they seem, a flash flood can turn them into rivers deeper than your tent is high. In bear country (and that means above all on wooded trails in the National Parks) you should look for a proper tree to hang your food from at night. It's just as well not to drop your gear in the middle of a game trail—why draw the attention of the bears and other animal raiders?

Local climate

Cool air settles at night in basins; night breezes move downslope along ravines. A hillside flat or the top of a knoll may be as much as fifteen degrees warmer than lower ground. Whether you want more warmth or less, you can take advantage of these variations. Consider also the wind; you may want to escape it or use it to blow away mosquitoes. If you are hoping for an early start, a site with an eastern exposure, bringing early sun, will help.

Luxuries

If you are planning to stay in one place for several nights, you'll be somewhat choosier about the site. Now you consider the overwhelming view, the nearby swimming hole, the peaks to climb, the valleys to explore. But it is also important that you find a specially impact-free site for such an extended stay; vulnerable areas, if they must be used, should not be used long at a stretch.

Setting up the low-impact camp

When to make camp is a matter of taste—and of haste. In good weather there is nothing specially unpleasant about making camp at dusk or later, but when conditions are bad, flashlight camping may be highly uncomfortable. And an early stop gives you time for good cooking, for relaxation, perhaps for a side trip or a few minutes with a camera or a natural history guide.

If you carry a stove and water, and merely need a spot to pass the night before you press on, you can throw down your gear nearly anywhere that darkness finds you. (These brief, utilitarian camps, while perhaps not very memorable, are pleasant for their simplicity, and they impact the land very little.) If you depend on wood fires, nearby water, or both, your choice of site will be narrower. If there is some distance between suitable camps, you may have to stop somewhat earlier—or later—than you might like.

There are four essential elements to even the simplest camp. There is the *kitchen*, perhaps nothing more than a stove sitting on a boulder. There is the *water source*. There is the *sleeping area*. And there is the *toilet area* or latrine.

A small group, especially at a little-used camp, needn't specify a toilet area, so long as everyone resolves to go well away from camp, trail, and water, and uses normal care. But in a large group, it is well to select an area in advance, choosing ground that no later party is likely to pick for kitchen or bed sites. If a latrine is to be dug, it should be set up first thing, not as an afterthought.

Normally, kitchen and bed are fairly close together. but campers in the northern Rockies, and in Alaska and Canada, learn to set up their food department at some remove from the rest of their gear. The reason is the magnificent but sometimes unpredictable grizzly bear. If a bear raids a somewhat isolated kitchen spot, it may not occur to him to rummage through the rest of the camp as well.

When you camp at a well-marked site, you try to make most use of the ground that is already bare, already stamped by human presence; a little more traffic won't alter it further. When paths and pads are there, use them. But avoid doing anything to extend the barren area. If you are at a pristine site, most especially if there is vegetation underfoot, the strategy changes. You try to avoid repeated traffic over any one piece of ground. In moving between kitchen and spring, or tent and toilet area, take a slightly different route each time, and try to walk on duff, rocks, and mineral soils. Try not to mill around too much in one place, as at the entrance of the tent or in the cooking area. If you go barefoot, or in soft camp shoes, your tread will compact the ground less. Compaction, breaking down the loose texture of the soil, stops the natural passages for air and water; the effect is almost as if the earth had been made sterile.

Engineering has no place in the design of your camp. The perfect site is found, not made. Spend your time finding the right piece of ground, not reshaping the wrong one. Don't clear brush, drive nails, build cupboards, or move any more logs and stones than is absolutely necessary. However hard you try, it is never possible to restore such objects so perfectly that the natural effect is completely regained.

What happens first when you get into camp? In the rain, or late in the day, raising shelter has to be the first job. Otherwise, cooking often takes first place. The weather, the time of day, the number of people, the site, and personal preference decide. A large group may have to organize itself to get things done; in a smaller party, there's nothing so formal about it.

The pleasure of wilderness camping

Of necessity this chapter has contained a lot of "don'ts." Because good wilderness practices so often go against the pull of habit, it may take a little conscious effort to adopt them.

But soon enough new methods, like the old, are automatic. And the camper is free to enjoy the place he has found for himself—the smells and sounds of it, the views (short or long), the quality of its light, the taste of its water. Every campsite, when you come onto it, seems strange and even a little unwelcoming (why just here and not a mile farther on?). Every campsite, once you have eaten and slept there, becomes a known place and a comfortable one. Your camps, after all, are the spots in the wilderness of which you have special knowledge; it is your campsites that you particularly remember.

The low-impact game has added, to the pleasure of wilderness camping, a new, keen edge. To blunder through a landscape, never guessing that you could damage it, or that you have done so, is one thing. It is quite something else to know that you might have harmed a place and that you did not; to know that your skill and knowledge were great enough to let you use the wilderness without consuming it.

18:
Shelter and Bed

Setting up beds is exceedingly simple if the weather is
fair and likely to remain so, and if the mosquitoes permit
you to stay outside. Sleeping roofless, under the big,
brilliant dark, is a real wilderness luxury. Without a shelter, party members can scatter, each to his own spot of
level ground; this tends to lessen impact. If you're uncertain about weather, you always have the option of setting
up shelter but starting the night in a bed outside.

As for the campsite in general, so for the bed: high
ground is warmer. Cold air sinks and gathers in chilly
pools. Watch out for draws and hollows that might gather
water in a sudden rain. If there is considerable humidity, a
bed under the open sky will be coated in the morning with
frost or dew; condensation will be less under the trees. A
sheltered site will also be somewhat warmer.

The most comfortable sleeping surface is fine forest
duff; sand is also good, if you smooth and shape it in
advance. Grassy ground is rather hard. A bedsite should be

flat, but not necessarily table flat—lie down on it first and judge for yourself. Then smooth and police the ground, removing sticks and stones; the less leveling you have to do, the better. If you find a place with a natural hollow for your hip, or if you can scoop one in sand or duff, that's fine. The digging of hip-holes in hard ground is no longer recommended. Spread your groundsheet—dirty side down—and mattress or pad.

Should you unpack your sleeping bag immediately, or leave it in the stuffbag? If the air is not humid, it's good to let the bag expand as long as possible. Down, particularly, takes quite a while to regain its full loft. But on a cool, damp evening, the bag may start getting clammy as soon as you expose it to the air; in this case, you're better off leaving it stuffed until you can get inside it. When you unpack a down bag, shake it out gently to fluff the fill.

Pitching shelter

If you are pitching shelter, you may need to take some time locating the right spot: bare ground, as level as possible, and, of course, well-drained. With a tarp or a flimsy tent, you may have to seek a wind-sheltered spot; with a good tent, level ground is more important than natural wind protection. But if there is a chance of a considerable breeze, make sure you have room to pitch the tent parallel to it, rather than crosswise.

Consider anchors. With a tube tent, you ideally need a pair of straight trees about fifteen feet apart. For a regular tent you want ground firm enough to hold any stakes you use but soft enough to drive them into. Look also for rocks, trunks, and sound snags to which you can tie guylines. A boulder or big log may serve as one wall for a shelter made with a tarp. A walking stick, if you use one, can also be useful as a supporting pole.

Don't engineer the site, beyond removing rocks and sticks, unless you are working with something loose like leaf mold, snow, or sand. Don't dig ditches in solid ground to carry off water; you don't need them, and they make all-but-permanent scars. If you are pitching a tent on stony or twiggy ground, you can save wear and tear on the water-proof tentfloor by spreading a groundsheet under it.

Tents are different from one another, but pitching

methods don't vary that much. You almost always begin by staking down the principal corners of the floor. (It doesn't matter which way the entrance faces relative to wind; if the ground slopes, you probably want your head uphill.) With some designs the staking of the floor is not essential, but it is hard to finish the job cleanly if the floor is not taut and neat, and the corners must invariably be staked in wind. You may on occasion be able to replace stakes with short lengths of cord tied to stones. Winter tents often have snowflaps around the base on which stones or snow can be placed for the solidest possible mooring.

The second step, with most tents, is to insert sectioned aluminum poles into sleeves sewn to the tent canopy. Some models will stand up by themselves after this is done. With others—including the familiar rectangular two-man models—there follows a third step. Pulling firmly on the guylines attached to each end of the tent, you attach these firmly to stakes or other anchors. (It takes two people to do this right.) The final action is to extend additional guylines called pullouts. These are not part of the basic support, but they draw the walls out tautly, help the tent shed wind, and make it roomier inside.

When you can, it is better to use anchors other than stakes. However, no method is entirely free of impact on the land. In Rocky Mountain National Park the managers now *urge* campers to use stakes; so many cords have been tied around timberline trees that trees are being killed by girdling! Here, not for the last time, we see how hard it is to set firm rules for the low-impact camp. What spares the land in one place may harm it in another.

Guylines tend to grow slack after they have been set. It's useful to set them up to be adjusted without moving the anchors. To do this, pass the line through the loop or grommet where it joins the tent; then double it back and tie it to itself, using one of several knots that will grip under tension but slide when you loosen the strands. The commonest are the *clove hitch* and the *tautline hitch.* Adjustable loops can also be tied where the lines attach to their ground anchors, but often there is too much friction at the anchor end. Commercial gripping devices are sold to do the same job.

The tentfly, pitched over the basic tent and supported

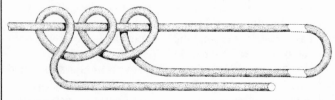

Clove hitch

Tautline hitch

by the same poles, has guylines of its own. These are commonly tied either to the tent's anchors or to the tent's guylines a little above the anchors, using sliding knots for easy adjustment.

Below timberline you may be able to pitch a tent without poles, using overhead lines to hold it up and more or less in the intended shape. But if you are in an area where this is possible, you may not need a full tent anyway but only a tarp or tentless rainfly.

Pitching a tarp is both simpler and more tricky than setting up a tent because there are so many possible variations. You can arrange the tarp like a typical A-frame, with a long ridgeline and sloping sides; like a lean-to, with one side high and one close to the ground; or even like a pagoda, with the center raised. Your choice depends most of all on the natural anchor points you find. Most tarps come with stout grommets built in at several points along the sides. Some have tie-on cords as well. If you need an attachment where none is provided—like the middle of the

234

sheet—you can make one by wrapping a small, round pebble in the fabric and tying it off with a noose of cord. There are also commercial devices for this purpose. If your tarp is a light one (especially if it's a plastic sheet), you'd do well not to put too much stress on any one part. For instance, run a line under the entire ridgeline rather than attaching a short line at each end and letting the sheet pull taut between them.

A tube tent would seem to offer the easiest pitching job of all: just run a line through the plastic tunnel and string it between two trees. Actually, there are not all that many perfect pairs of trees with flat, open ground between them. You may have to improvise. For instance, you can tie one end of your ridge cord not to a tree but to a second line strung crosswise between two less accessible anchors. With a tube tent you take clothespins to hold the plastic firmly on the line (otherwise it tends to bunch) and also to close one or both ends of the tent against rain. Do this reluctantly, however; your own output of water, a pint a night in sweat and breath, will make it clammy inside a shut-up tube.

Tube tents are hard to pitch above timberline, and most are too fragile for conditions up there.

Line attachment with pebble and noose

A good night's sleep

Nothing should be more automatic than a restful night in the wilderness. The harder you have worked during the day, the more luxurious the warmth and softness of the sleeping bag become; the colder it is in the world outside, the lovelier the contrast feels.

If you've been accustomed to soft beds, however, you may find it odd and even uncomfortable at first to sleep on a thin foam pad. This is one excellent reason for beginning with an air mattress, despite the extra weight and a certain loss of warmth. Rolled up clothing will generally do for a pillow.

If you don't use a sleeping bag liner, it's a good idea to

wear a layer of clothing to bed. Body oils gum up the fluffy
down, even if you keep fastidiously clean; the cure, washing the bag, destroys some of the all-important resiliency
of down. Wear a stocking cap, or put a shirt under your
head, to protect the bag from oils in your hair. (Bags filled
with PolarGuard or Hollofil II, however, aren't damaged
either by dirt or by washing.) It's handy to leave your boots
by your head, with such small objects in them as you'll
want during the night or first thing in the morning. It's best
to turn them sideways if you're sleeping outdoors in
the dew.

Cold and other problems

If you've planned well, you shouldn't find yourself in a
sleeping bag too cool for the region you are visiting. But
maybe you're testing the limits of a summer bag in winter,
spring, or fall. If you do find yourself getting chilly at
night, there are various things you can do about it; some
have been mentioned already.

● Move under cover. Lying in the open, you radiate
extra heat to the sky. Even the branches of a tree will cut
that loss somewhat. And protect yourself from any chilling
breeze; for instance, you can put your head downwind so
that cold air won't enter the open end of your bag. A tent,
protecting you in several ways, can add ten or fifteen
degrees of warmth.

● Speed up your own metabolism. Take a brisk walk or
get some other exercise before you crawl in. (Some people
do isometrics in the bag.) If you feel warm when you lie
down, your body will heat the bag quickly and give you a
good start. Don't linger outside getting chilled. When
you're cold, it's good to eat something last thing at night,
preferably protein (the best fuel for warmth when you
aren't exercising).

● But the main thing to do against cold is more
obvious: wear more clothes to bed. The single most useful
item is a woolen head-cap; the head loses more heat than
any other part of the body. Dry socks are also important.
Then come pants, shirt, sweater, mittens, possibly a
jacket—even, if required, your raingear—until your whole
wardrobe is on. Or, instead of wearing it all, you can stuff
some items into your sleeping bag, especially at your feet,

to stop air motion and add insulation.

• It may also help to add to the insulation beneath you. A wind parka, a rope, the emptied pack itself—almost anything will help.

• If you get seriously cold, you can try sticking your hands and feet in waterproof bags: moisture won't escape, but neither will the considerable warmth that is carried off with it.

If none of these ideas work, you are probably badly underequipped for the trip you're taking. If it's any comfort, you can lay plans for next time: perhaps a longer, thicker foam pad, or a second pad . . . more clothing . . . even a pair of down or polyester-filled booties for your feet. You can also have more filler added to a down sleeping bag, though manufacturers sometimes don't recommend this. Synthetic bags can't be so modified.

Whenever the wilderness world is both cold and wet—in winter camping especially—keeping dry is an important part of keeping warm. Sleeping gear always gets damp at night. While synthetic bags will keep on warming you, no matter how wet they get, down bags will not, so you have to fight any buildup of moisture. If the weather allows, you can dry a bag by hanging it on a ski, a snow-free branch, or over your pack as you walk. Where moisture is a problem, it's best not to try to dry damp clothing by taking it into the sleeping bag with you.

If you should ever feel that you are dangerously chilled, don't hesitate to say so. There is a quick remedy: strip and get into a warm sleeping bag with a companion. (People can survive in desperate situations by pooling body heat.) Hot drinks also help; alcohol, when you're cold, only does harm. If you recognize in yourself the symptoms of what is called *hypothermia*, it's a true emergency (see Chapter 27).

But a wilderness night need not be cold to be uncomfortable. There's also the balmy night with mosquitoes; it's so warm that you can't escape them by shutting yourself up in your sleeping bag. To stop mosquitoes, you need a netted tent, or a separate piece of netting to put over your head. Repellent can prevent most of the bites, but it won't spare you the sense of being under siege. In desperation, lacking a net, you can breathe through a sweater.

19:
Fire and Food

COOKING ON A PORTABLE STOVE is, at its easiest, almost like cooking on a range at home. Yet the use of stoves, like the use of open fires, is not entirely without its problems, even its risks. Statistically slight and easily avoidable, these risks are real nonetheless. The use of a stove requires no less care and common sense than the building of a fire.

Let's start with the procedures used with white gas stoves; then turn to the somewhat different drills for kerosene and butane models. (For more about the kinds of stoves and their anatomy, see Chapter 9.)

Running a white gas stove

In operating a white gas stove there are two possible hazards to understand and avoid.

First, white gas must not be spilled near flame. White gas ignites easily and burns fiercely. Probably three-quarters of all stove accidents result from spillage of fuel.

Second, the fuel tank must not be allowed to overheat. For the stove to run properly, the fuel tank must be warm, even moderately hot, but if it grows too hot to touch, vapor pressure inside will build to dangerous levels. Should the pressure become extreme, it will force open a spring-loaded safety valve in the tank lid and send a stream of vapor into the air. This stream is more than likely to catch fire from the burner, turning your stove into something like a blowtorch. (So why do they call it a "safety valve"? Because, without it, the stove could eventually explode; a blowtorch is much easier to handle than a bomb.)

Let me repeat that normal and careful use is enough to prevent such problems. The instructions given here are cautious in the extreme and should just about remove the chance of trouble.

First, pick your site: a level wind-sheltered spot out of the line of traffic (so that nothing gets knocked over). Just set the stove on the spot. Never dig a hole for it, or bury it, or build up a hearth of stones around it—all these things will trap too much heat around the fuel tank. The stove should be some distance from any other flame, from the rest of your gear, and from burnable underbrush. The cap of the tank, with its safety release valve, should be pointed away from flammable objects. If your stove is the type that has a separate tank mounted behind a heat shield, make sure that the shield is clean and shiny, and that is has not been knocked out of alignment (there should be an air-space between shield and tank). Consider wind shelter: a really good windscreen will protect the flame in any rea-sonable breeze, but not all screens do the job as well as they might. If you are camping on snow, you'll need to place the stove on a scrap of foam pad or wood, with a pan-lid or a piece of light metal between the stove and the insulation.

Second, before each use of the stove, fill the tank. Don't overdo it; a small air space should remain. In moving the gas from storage bottle to tank, use a funnel or a pouring cap. If you spill fuel, wipe it up and let the residue evapo-rate (it will do so quickly). If your spill has soaked into the ground beneath the stove, better shift the operation.

This is a good point in the routine to clean the orifice where the fuel jet issues. Some stoves come with separate cleaning needles which you insert by hand; on others you operate a built-in needle by turning the fuel-flow valve control to "clean" and back again.

The third step is *priming*. When a stove is running, its own heat vaporizes the liquid fuel as it rises from the tank—a self-sustaining process. But in order to get the stove started, you have to apply heat to the vaporizing tube beneath the burner. You simply burn something—anything—in a little priming cup which is built in around the base of the vaporizing tube.

What fuel do you use? How to get it into the priming cup? There are various answers; indeed a whole Minor Arcanum has grown up around the simple operation of priming.

It's traditional to make the stove cough up some of its own fuel into the priming cup. One method: open the fuel-flow valve; then warm the tank with your hands and your breath until the warmed, expanding fuel rises into the priming cup. Another method: leave the stove in the hot sun till the fuel expands; then open the valve and let it flow. There are other variations. On stoves with pumps there's no need to warm the tank. You build up pressure inside it with a few strokes of the plunger.

It's not so traditional, but often convenient, to put the priming fuel into the cup yourself. In that case you use any burnable substance you like: white gas, drawn from the stove tank (or a fuel bottle) with an eyedropper; alcohol from a squeeze bottle; bits of mashed solid fuel pellet; or toilet paper.

How much priming fire do you need? Under good conditions a single eyedropperful of white gas, or the equivalent, may do it. But any amount is okay as long as you don't overflow the cup with liquid fuel (if you do, wipe up the spill). Some bizarre stove accidents have occurred when people drenched their stoves with several cups of fuel. They were surprised that the tanks overheated enough, in the resulting bonfires, to blow the safety valves!

Before you put a match to the priming fuel, make sure that the tank cap is screwed on firmly; that the fuel flow valve is shut off; and that all containers of liquid fuel are capped and set well away from the stove.

Then light. If you have primed generously with white gas, the flame may rise quite high before it fades; this is normal. By the time your priming dose has been consumed, the vaporizing tube should be hot enough to do its job, and the fuel tank should be warm enough so that vapor pressure within will keep fuel flowing upward toward the flame.

The fourth step is the real ignition. Just as the priming flame fades, open the valve to admit fuel from the tank; it should catch smoothly, powerfully, and without any flare. (Sometimes, however, especially in cold, windy weather, you may have to prime more than once.) Many stoves have metal valve keys; these must be removed from the valve while the stove is running, or they will grow too hot to touch.

Stay with the stove as the meal cooks, just as you would stay by a campfire. With pump stoves you'll need to push the plunger a few times every now and then. If there is wind, make sure that the flame is not blowing around the fuel tank. And keep an eye on the temperature of the tank. If you find it getting too hot to touch, better shut down the stove and see what you can do to increase ventilation. Pay special attention to this problem if you have an improvised windscreen that encloses the tank or if a broad pot or frying pan is overhanging it.

If you run out of fuel in the middle of a meal, don't refill without first letting the burner grow cool enough to touch. Fuel spilled on red-hot metal can ignite. However, even the smallest tank will last through one meal, perhaps two, except in a winter camp where quantities of snow must be melted. Do not, of course, remove the tank cap while the stove is running, to check the fuel level.

If your stove should spit and sputter when first lit, that's no cause for alarm. If it keeps acting oddly, however, turn it off and check it over. Has the tank gotten hot? Are there any fuel leaks in the line between tank and burner? If the stove continues to give you trouble after you relight it, it's prudent to switch to a campfire or eat cold. Most stoves are harder to operate in the wind. A good screen can make all the difference. Keep lids on your pots, too.

If, improbably enough, your stove should overheat and suffer a tank blowout, try to shut down the fuel flow to the burner and direct the spout of flame away from anything burnable. Then all you can do is wait for the fireworks to stop (they will as the pressure is discharged). The valve in the tank cap should close itself automatically, but reportedly valves sometimes fail to reseal perfectly; it's good to replace the cap with a spare from your repair kit.

After this catalog of possible problems, one more thing should be said. Most of the time white gas stoves, and stoves in general, work simply, swiftly, and very well indeed.

Kerosene stoves

Much of what has been said applies to kerosene-burning stoves as well as to white gas models. Some kerosene stoves lack a valve to control the flow of fuel; instead, you increase flow by pumping up pressure in the tank and reduce it by releasing pressure through a manual vent in the tank cap.

Kerosene stoves, like white gas stoves, must be primed. Most people prefer not to use kerosene as the priming fuel—it burns sluggishly and somewhat messily—and instead burn white gas, alcohol, or solid fuel. Just before the priming flame begins to fail, pump a small amount of air into the closed fuel tank. This sends gaseous fuel rising through the hot vaporizing tube to the burner, where it should ignite. Then, when the priming flame dies out, pump vigorously. Now you should be in business. If you get a yellow, smoky flame, you need to prime a second time. Kerosene is a much less volatile fuel than gasoline, and though some care must still be used with it, it is unlikely to flash into flame when you spill it. A tank blowout is not a potential hazard with kerosene.

Butane cartridge stoves

In warm summer weather butane stoves are utterly simple to light; there's no priming or pumping, just the touch of a match.

Great care is needed, though, when you refuel. There's no liquid fuel to fuss with; instead, you remove a spent cartridge and install a full one. Follow directions scrupulously. Some cartridges must be held carefully upright. Some can be removed between uses; others, once attached, must be left until empty. Some stoves use cartridges that screw on; others plug in. With screw-on cartridges, be careful not to strip threads. Especially with the screw types, a little fuel may spray out at the moment of connection. If you hear a continuing hiss when you're done, check the fuel line for a loose connection and the cartridge for a possible leak; even the tiniest leak will make the surface feel frosty. If you can't stop the hiss, try another cartridge. Manufacturing defects are not unknown. All in all, refueling is a good operation to handle away from tent and gear.

To light a butane stove, hold a match to the burner; then, and only then, open the valve to let the gas stream out. Cartridges which do not contain wicks—vapor-feed models—yield a smoother flow at first and light more readily than the liquid-feed types with wicks. All butane cartridges have a tendency to flare and fade erratically when first lit; the colder it is, the worse the problem. Liquid-feed cartridges, though they work at much lower temperatures than the vapor-feed type, flare badly at the lower end of their range.

In cold weather you may have to warm your cartridge before you light the stove; one method is to take it into your sleeping bag or hold it under your jacket. A cartridge should never be shaken.

Butane, like white gas, is a volatile, highly flammable fuel. Cartridges, like the tanks of gas stoves, must not be allowed to overheat. They don't have reclosable safety valves but some are equipped with wax plugs that melt out at a certain temperature. The effect, if the plug lets go, is the same as with gasoline: a spray of vapor that is likely to catch fire. A cartridge should always remain cool enough to hold in your hand. Some stoves link burner and cartridge with a flexible hose; watch that neither hose nor cartridge rests too close to the flame. And never pile rocks around a cartridge, as for instance to steady a pot on the burner.

Some hikers report that partially used cartridges can leak in the pack; they suggest putting tape across the orifice. Don't discard a cartridge until you have burned it dry; even then, never toss it into a fire (enough gas may be left to cause a sharp explosion). Needless to say, you pack your empties out of the wilderness with you.

Cooking in a tent

Cooking inside a tent is never free of risk. There are

times, especially in winter storms, when you may not have much choice, but you shouldn't do it by preference. (If you have to do it a lot, consider a kerosene stove.)

When you light a stove in a tent, make sure the burner isn't too close to a tent wall. Tent fabrics don't exactly burn, but they do melt. If you prime with liquid fuel, watch out for any high flare of the priming flame (a pan-lid will stop an alarming surge). If fuel spills, wipe it up, let it evaporate, and air the tent before you strike your next match. All fuels are bad for the waterproofing compounds on tent floors, by the way.

Stoves put out carbon monoxide, a poison. Make sure that ventilation is good. Leave your vents open, and unzip the upper part of your door. Symptoms of monoxide poisoning are dizziness, nausea, and headache. It would be hard to get a dangerous dose in a tent at low altitudes, but in the high country the chemistry of respiration alters, and the peril becomes very real—doubly so since altitude sickness may be blamed when the symptoms appear.

Fire

Campfires these days are not popular with wilderness conservationists, nor with wilderness managers. The impact of fires on the land—so many people have come to feel—is simply too great. Fires can sterilize fertile ground for decades, leave ugly scars, and consume down wood that should be left to rot and replenish the soil. But in this, as in so many of these questions, common sense must be the guide. A fire in an old ring of stones in a middle-elevation forest littered with down logs can't possibly be called an attack on the land. A similar fire built (illegally) of green wood on a peak in the crowded Catskills, or built (illegally) against a granite boulder in an unscarred alpine meadow, is an atrocity.

What makes a fire acceptable?

An abundance of available wood.

An existing fire-site in a good location.

And very great care.

I would urge once more that no party set out for the wilderness without a stove so that no party will be forced, or even strongly tempted, to build a fire in the wrong place at the wrong time.

Campfire or cookfire?

If the cooking fire is in disfavor, still more, in some circles, is the pleasure fire: the comfortable blaze you sit
around after the meal is done. The logic is easily seen: why
use wood without the excuse of cooking? Yet, if fire has a
legitimate use in the wilderness, it is not, in truth, for fixing
food (stove cooking is simpler) but for fun. For fun and for
something a little more than fun: for relaxation . . . for
sociability . . . for the odd beauty of flames . . . as a special
focus (*focus:* Latin *hearth*) of a place and time you enjoy.
It may well be argued that the occasional small pleasure
fire, lit as a deliberate luxury, makes more sense than a succession of cooking fires lit for a dubious utility.

Fires not built for cooking can ordinarily be set up
without stone hearths, and this is a considerable advantage
if a previously untouched site is to be used—see below.

Siting a fire

The fact that you find a fire-ring does not necessarily
mean that you should use it. Not long ago the National
Park Service reported counting 300 fire rings in a single
lake basin in Yosemite National Park; many of them, sited
on grass at the lakeshore, should not have been built and
should now, if possible, be destroyed.

Keep your fires, like your camps, on bare ground well
back from water. Further, there is no case to be made for
fires near timberline and above it, even if they are still permitted there. Vegetation is too fragile and wood too hard
to find. (A possible rare exception is a fire built with wood
you have packed up from below, and in such a way that no
new scar is made.)

Why so many fire-rings? Partly, no doubt, because
many people still put value on the *creation* of a camp, the
carving-out of a home in the wild world. But there's
another reason. Established rings are often left dirty,
unpleasant, full of cans, tinfoil, and organic garbage half
rotted and half charred. You'll be doing a service if you
choose one of these ruined rings, clean it up, use it, and
leave it clean.

Make sure that your fire is not too close to the rest of
your gear. Sparks burn holes in nylon tents and sleeping
bags. Make sure there are no low branches overhead and

no dry brush close by. If you have a choice of rings in otherwise acceptable places, you can afford to consider such
things as sun (nice for cooking in the morning, sometimes
too hot for cooking in the afternoon), and the direction of
the wind (typically upslope during the day, downslope
after dark).

Now, fuel. If you have settled on a well-used site, the
chances are good that the woods within, say, 300 feet will
be pretty well picked over. Yet it is astonishing how much
fuel you will find just outside that narrow circle. Wood-
hunters have been lazy.

Remember when you gather wood that it must be both
dead and *down* to be eligible. Rooted, rotten snags are not
firewood: they are habitat and hunting territory for owls,
woodpeckers, and a whole community of animals small
and large. Don't use wood you can't break. Axe and
hatchet are no part of the wilderness tool kit today.

Does the burning of wood—even dead, down wood—
withdraw enough material from the nutrient cycle to
impoverish the forest soil? Research into this question has
only begun, but early results are somewhat reassuring.
Except in the harsh world of timberline (where wood
should not in any case be gathered), this does not appear to
be a significant problem. The balance of life in the forest is
not so delicate as might be feared.

Operating a fire

Get together a reasonable supply of wood, in all sizes,
before you begin. Then take a final look at the weather and
the site (Has the day turned windy? Will sparks get into
dry underbrush?). The risk of starting a brush- or forest-fire
is not one you want to take.

If yours will be a cooking fire, you may want to rearrange stones and place a grate or perhaps a "dingle stick"
(a sort of jib, braced at one end by stones, resting on a fire-
side rock or log, and protruding over the fire). From this
you can hang your largest pot. (If you do much campfire
cooking, you may find it convenient to rig pots with bales
of thin wire attached at *three* points around the rim, so that
they do not tip when hung.) Don't cut a green branch for
a dingle stick, or a marshmallow stick, or for any other use.

Starting a fire is both straightforward and slightly tricky;

skills that were automatic to a generation of woodsmen may be less familiar in the age of stoves. Your starting
point can be paper or knife-whittled, paper-thin shavings;
fuzz sticks, sometimes useful, are shaved sticks with the
shavings still attached. Some firemakers always lay the
whole fire, small to large, before they touch a match to it;
others start with the tiniest sticks, get them burning, and
then add larger bits and pieces gradually and carefully. If
you lay the fire in advance, don't pack the wood in over-
tightly; fire needs air. Don't put on fragments of wood
larger than you can reasonably expect to burn completely
to ash.

Starting a fire in the rain is no fun, but it certainly can
be done. Woodsmen look for pitchy wood, which you can find
as unrotted streaks in the decayed trunks of fallen conifers. This stuff burns delightfully. Firestarters of some
sort—fire ribbon, fuel pellets, wax-soaked "logs" of rolled
newspaper, candles—can also be helpful when the wood is
wet. A fragment of porous wood, left to soak in a pool of
gasoline, is another firestarter. Many people simply drench
wet kindling with white gas; more often than not, though,
the fuel flares off, leaving the stubborn wood uncharred. If
it hasn't been raining long, you may be able to whittle the
damp exterior of a fragment and find dry wood at the center. But when the wood is truly sodden, as in rain-forest
country, only the experts seem to get very far. Once the
fire is burning brightly, of course, it will dry and burn even
the most sodden logs.

Whenever conditions are drier, fire is a beast that has
to be watched with the greatest care. Never leave one
burning or even smouldering (though a low fire may be left
to consume its embers on a windless night with sleepers
close by). When you break camp, of course, the fire must
be absolutely and unmistakably cold, drowned and
drowned again with water.

Fire at an unmarked site

There is rarely either reason or excuse these days for
building a fire where none has been before. This is true
without exception throughout the crowded wilderness
lands of the East and in well-used areas of the Far West. In
remote and little-visited sections, though, even this prin-

ciple may be slightly bent.

Should you ever build a fire on a pristine site, you want all traces to disappear. I don't, frankly, recommend the experiment, but the techniques that make it possible are worth discussing.

First, of course, there are certain sites to avoid. Never build a fire in deep, woody forest duff, on peat, or on humus. Never build one next to a log or tree, next to a clean standing rock, or on vegetation.

Instead, find mineral soil of some sort. The ideal sites are sandy or gravelly spots where any mark that is made can be simply erased. Sea-beaches and river-shingles, washed periodically by tide or flood, are best of all. Given any kind of loose mineral surface, you can dig a small trench for the fire; then smooth over the site with clean material. If you're building the fire on a hard surface—like rocky soil or a stone slab—you can bring sand or gravel from another place and lay a raised base for the coals. When the fire is out, you can then sweep up both ashes and sand, leaving little trace.

What about a fire on grass? If, for some reason, you must make one, never light it on the living surface of the ground. Rather, cut out a square of sod and set it aside. In the hole you have created, light the fire, preferably without a lining of stones. Then, when the fire is dead out, replace the sod. The same technique will work in soft ground without sod. Dig a pit. Light the fire. Let it burn dead out. Drown it. Refill the trench with the original soil. Stamp it down. Ruffle and smooth the surface. Replace natural litter.

If a fire must be made beside a standing rock, put a smaller flat rock between the fire and the boulder to take the mark. Then the flake can be put back where you found it, blackened side down.

Obviously, these techniques—you might call them slash-and-patch methods—can only work where few parties travel. Little of this sort of thing can be done, even with extreme care, before an area begins to seem subtly scuffed and scarred. Signs of use attract more use. In some places it is already hard to find a stone not darkened by a smear of soot. Long before this point is reached, it's time to switch to stove cooking, limiting fires to definite, suitable sites.

Perhaps the greatest selfish advantage of cooking with a stove is that you need spend no time wondering just what stage has been reached in the place you choose for your camp. You know that your kitchen impinges on the landscape not at all. It's not a sacrifice you're making. Rather, you are making it easy for yourself: sparing yourself a worry, cancelling out a possible cause for concern.

Garbage

All the old rules about garbage have given way to a simple, single principle: *pack it out.* The only exception, and then only if you build a fire, is material that can be readily, totally burned: paper and also plastic bags, which combust cleanly if they are fed, a little at a time, into a very hot fire. (Allow them to smoulder, though, and you get smoke, dark, rancid, and probably poisonous.) Tinfoil won't burn: it only breaks up in fire. Watch out for packages that have a foil lining inside paper. Cans, if you have any, should be flattened; then washed or seared, and carried out.

Rarely is it proper to bury anything. (Researchers have found that an alarming percentage of today's wilderness travelers still regard it as good practice to bury garbage; it isn't.) In many mountain areas soils are shallow; animals, water, and frost-heaving expose the waste; or the ground may settle, leaving an unsightly pit. Moreover, the soil in alpine areas may never get warm enough to allow much decomposition. Whenever you find yourself with a piece of litter—even a piece as small as a gum wrapper—it goes into your pocket, a plastic junk-bag, or the fire.

What if you find yourself with a lot of organic garbage to get rid of—uneaten food, or refuse left by ignorant earlier campers? Some parties still scatter food, in small amounts, for animals to take care of. In remote areas this is probably harmless, but the land agencies have begun to advise against it. On well-traveled routes it is plainly a bad idea; you are training raccoons, bears and other animals to scavenge and make camp nuisances of themselves. Orange peels dry to a kind of leather and last a long time; they should never be scattered.

It isn't generally practical to dry out extra food on the fire, and then feed it to the flames; too much fuel is required. The best answer is simply to avoid over-cooking. The second best, when the excess is large, is to bury the food in an out-of-the-way location.

Dishwashing

All washing should be done well away from any spring, creek, or lake. If you use soap, make sure it is non-detergent and biodegradable. Individual dishwashing can be very simple. To clean a pan, for instance, just add a cup of hot water, and scrub; a second cup, and scrub; a third cup, and rinse. In larger groups where dishes are washed commonly you do need to use soap, and to scald the dishes in boiling water, to prevent any sharing of illnesses. Wash-water should be dumped out of the way, among brush or stones.

Protecting your food

Depending on just where you are, you may have to take precautions, more or less elaborate, to protect your food from piracy by wild animals.

On snow, in winter (in regions where winter is cold), and above timberline, these problems are generally less. Even in low-elevation forests off the beaten track you may need no special care. Few animals in remote areas have yet learned to scavenge human supplies.

It's always a good idea to keep your camp clean so there's no food scattered around for the taking. Where small rodents are common, you can protect open packages by putting them under pots or in pots with the lids wired on. There are reports that porcupines and other rodents will gnaw at boots and sweat-soaked packstraps; you might inquire whether this is a problem in the area you plan to visit. Deer also like salty things.

Shelters attract animals. (Some hikers in the East report that they never have problems except in such developed campsites.) If you camp at a site that has food lockers, better take advantage of them.

It is, oddly enough, in the most used, populous, and "civilized" of our wilderness areas that wild animals, most especially bears, become a major problem. In such well-used regions as the High Sierra and the Blue Ridge, and in most of our National Parks, precautions have to be elaborate.

Your pack smells of food and may be a target even if nothing is in it. (Keep it as clean as you can.) At night, or whenever you leave camp, make sure your empty pack is unzipped. A bear may come along, investigage every pocket, find nothing, and depart. But if the animal can't get into the pack easily, it may simply tear its way in.

Where there are interested bears, hang all your food in a tree at night. Nothing short of that makes any sense. (Don't just leave your loaded pack by your bed, in your tent, or under a stack of pots as bear-alarms; the modern National Park bear is not so easily deterred.) To hang your food, take a good length of stout cord, tie a rock to one end, and lob it over a high, horizontal branch. Then place your food in a large, tough bag, and tie it to the end of the line where the stone was. Some people tie pans to the bag to work as an alarm. Then haul the load into position.

In the old days you finished the job by simply tying the free end of the line around a tree. But the National Park bear has learned that the food comes down when he gnaws the accessible cord. For more protection, use the counterbalance method. Instead of tying off, haul on the free end to raise the load up close to the branch. Now tie to the line—as high as you can reach—a weight equal to the foodstack. Wrap the remaining free line around this "counterbalance" so that nothing dangles. Finally, use a long stick to nudge the counterbalance as high as you can. Counterbalance and food sack should finally be dangling side by side, fifteen feet or more above the ground, ten feet away from the nearest trunk and five feet below the supporting branch. To get your food back, you must push the counterbalance still higher, thus lowering the goods to within reach. Figure out how to do this in advance.

In other areas, where the problem is not so great, you will have to decide for yourself each night whether the effort of bagging is worth the security. Consider the state of your supplies. If you're two days away from the end of your trip, the loss of your food might be merely an annoyance. But if your supplies must last for another week, you don't want to take chances. In such a case it makes sense to split your larder into several bags and string them up some distance apart.

What do you do if you actually find a bear investigating your suspended cache, or, worse, heading down the trail with your food-bag in his jaws? If it's a grizzly, as in the northern Rockies, you'd better simply let him have it. The brown and black bears encountered elsewhere in the contiguous United States are typically more docile; shouts, flashing lights, banging pans, and whistle blasts may make such a beast retreat or drop what he has taken. If not, you're probably dealing with a professional robber; don't argue. Never try to take food away from the creature. The more accustomed the bear has become to human beings, the less manageable it will be. And keep this in mind: a sow bear with cubs, no matter the species, is a touchy and dangerous animal.

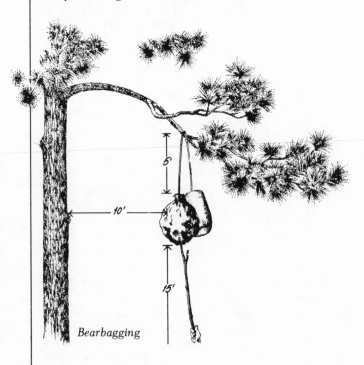

Bearbagging

20:
Sanitation and Clean Water

TIME WAS WHEN NOBODY DREAMED OF A WILDERNESS being anything other than *clean,* clean beyond the measure of any city or town. One writer observed happily that wilderness dirt was "perfectly sanitary, being rendered so by oxygen and remoteness from human habitation." Then there was the notion that running water purified itself every two hundred feet.

And it is undeniable that wilderness waters are still, in general and in most places, about the cleanest we have. But as early as 1960 you began to hear reports of unpleasant exceptions to the rule. Waters along the John Muir Trail in California began to be called *polluted.* In backpacking areas all over the country—in Idaho, in Colorado, in the White Mountains of New Hampshire—researchers began to find unexpectedly high counts of the bacterium *E. Coli,* a harmless organism, but one that indicates contamination by the feces of warm-blooded animals.

Just how much of this contamination comes from human beings is not clear. But you need only spend a few days in a popular hiking area to know that many people are careless. Feces left on the surface of the ground, especially anywhere near water, can pollute an astonishingly large area. Even when the amounts of waste are very small, there is risk that diseases can be transmitted. It is no longer unheard of for mountain hikers in this country to suffer punishing bouts of diarrhea or, much more serious, to come home with hepatitis.

Precautions

What can backpackers do about this? Two things. First, each must begin to use a certain amount of caution in choosing wilderness water for drinking and personal use. Second, and absolutely vital, is this: each of us must be absolutely scrupulous in the disposal of body waste.

At heavily-used campsites you may find chemical or pit toilets, installed by the managing agency. These will probably become rarer, however. Many managers now hold that a site where an outhouse is needed is a site that is getting unacceptable amounts of use. And parties may increasingly be discouraged from digging their own latrines.

Still, if you are traveling in a group of unusual size, say ten people or more, and if you plan to use one spot for several days, a latrine is probably the best solution. Site it well away from trails and water. The rules often say 200 feet; there is no good reason not to go twice as far. And be sure not to dig the pit in a place that might appeal to another party as a bed or kitchen spot.

If you know you will need a latrine (and if regulations permit one), dig it first thing. Dig it narrow and shallow. In no case should it be more than about 17 inches deep and a foot wide. If you need more capacity, make it longer, not deeper; go farther down, and you will get below the biologically rich "disposer" layer of the soil. It is in this layer that microorganisms convert waste to fertile humus. Only excrement and toilet paper go into a latrine; garbage must be handled otherwise, and tampons, sanitary napkins, and disposable diapers must be packed out with you. Throw in fresh soil after every use; you don't want flies circulating between kitchen and pit.

Lacking a latrine, the hiker turns to what is rather

comically labeled the "individual cat method." Dig a small hole, never deeper than about six inches. When you finish, fill it in carefully with the soil you scooped out and restore the surface as neatly as you can. If it is safe to do so, touch a match to your toilet paper; burning it speeds decomposition. In the desert and in the high, cold country, where natural processes are slow, this is highly advisable. But *never* burn toilet paper when your cathole is in dry forest duff, or anywhere else where fire might spread.

With catholes as with latrines, siting is all-important. For instance, a sandy, diggable place is probably a seasonal streambed and should be avoided. The rule is to disperse. Members of a party should go in different directions to dig their holes. If you find it practical, it's good to take care of these needs during the day, when the party is between campsites; this prevents the buildup of waste in popular areas. Around some camps, late in the season, you may find so many catholes that it is hard to locate fresh ground. This is a sign of too much use, but also indicates a certain laziness; go far enough from camp and you won't have this trouble.

When you're traveling on snow you probably won't be able to reach the soil. You can only dig your hole in snow, and, when the thaw comes, that's no hole at all. This is a troubling problem. As winter backpacking becomes more popular, the chances of serious pollution are real. There are only two things the hiker can do. First, he can go still farther away from water than he would in summer. Second, he can take special care to burn his toilet paper. (When you come back in August to look at the place you camped in in March, you'll see the point of this. Toilet paper lasts much better than you'd think, and just a few flags of tissue are enough to make a landscape look unclean.) Further, if you can't get the paper to burn, consider packing it away in a special plastic pouch to be disposed of later. In the cold there won't be an odor.

It isn't necessary to be so fastidious about urination. The care you take here is mainly a matter of courtesy. In the one way that matters, urine is surprisingly clean; that is, it contains few or none of the organisms that can transmit diseases. Remember, the chief reason for attention to these matters is not exaggerated prissiness; it's health.

Water, water

The pollution problem in the wilderness has gotten a lot of publicity. It should. If the huge new generation of back-packers acquires the wrong habits, it could become a very serious problem indeed.

And yet there is no need—at least not yet—to forego the very special pleasure of drinking wilderness water straight from the land, flat on your belly, sucking it up from a stream, or getting its tang across the cool rolled lip of a metal cup. Just be somewhat cautious about where you take your water. Don't drink downstream from a heavily used camp or trail crossing; rather, go upstream, or find a side stream flowing from a pristine watershed. Avoid warm, shallow, stagnant waters. Avoid streams that have their sources outside wilderness, in civilized country; this is not an uncommon situation, especially in the Southwest. And here is a surprising conclusion of some recent research at Yosemite: it is better to drink from the *outflow*, rather than from the *inflow*, of a large lake. The water at the center of sizable lakes appears to be about the cleanest in the mountains.

What about pollution from animals? The amount caused by deer, bear, and other wilderness creatures is gen-erally low enough to disregard; there aren't all that many of them, they don't congregate much, and rather few of their diseases threaten us. Cattle and sheep, though, can't be so safely ignored. Outside the protected boundaries of parks, you may find otherwise wild landscapes that are not only grazed by livestock, but overgrazed and indeed grossly spoiled. If you find a water source fouled and trampled, better treat the water. Even a few cows scat-tered around the landscape, especially upstream, are a cer-tain cause for concern.

There are several ways of treating dubious water. The best is the old way: boil it vigorously for at least ten minutes (up to twenty at high altitude). The second best method is to purify it with iodine in one of several forms.

Tincture of iodine. The normal dose is five drops to two percent tincture per quart of water.

Iodine/water solution. From a drugstore, get about four grams of iodine crystals in a small, tightly-capped bottle. Add about an ounce of water. About a tablespoon of this solution will purify a quart of drinking water. As you use up the solution and add more water to it, more crystals dissolve and its concentration remains the same.

Iodine tablets (Potable Aqua). The normal dose is one tablet per quart. Since tablets lose potency on exposure to moisture and air, keep them in a tightly sealed container.

Procedure is similar for all iodine treatments. After adding the chemical (give tablets three minutes to dissolve), shake the water bottle with lid slightly loose, so that the threads are moistened. Then let it stand for fifteen minutes. When water is very dirty, double both the dose of purifier and the treatment time. Very cloudy water can be strained through cloth or let to stand for several hours.

If you think water is polluted, you should also treat the supply you use for dishwashing and brushing your teeth.

Two final cautions. First, iodine in large doses is a poison—don't use more than called for. Second, water that already contains poisonous minerals won't be made drinkable by sterilizing treatment. (Suspect a spring without insects or signs of use by animals.) This circumstance, though, is very rare.

Washing

When you wash yourself or your clothes, use biodegradable soap (never detergent), and do the washing well away from any lake or stream. Don't go swimming to get rid of a lather of suds; carry water and rinse ashore. And too many backpackers who should know better are still brushing their teeth at the water's edge.

21:
Breaking Camp

SOME CAMPERS, VERY CAREFUL when they choose their campsite and organize their brief life there, are rather casual and careless when they depart. Yet it is in breaking camp that you have a special responsibility and a special opportunity to score points in the low impact game.

Suppose you have camped at an established site. It is, inevitably, a beaten-down, impacted place. That is its great advantage. Even here you can look around and ask yourself: how much have we added to the problems of this place? How much can we undo?

There is little point in getting rid of a properly located fire-ring that the next party may want to use. But if you see a ring where no ring should be—at the lake's edge on grass, for example—it can be a good service to remove the stones and disguise, as much as you can, the scar. Make sure that the ring you used yourself is completely clean, ready, and inviting. Otherwise you may be encouraging the next comers to start a fresh one.

Your fire must, of course, be unmistakably dead. Stop adding wood to the flames well before you are ready to leave, so that coals will burn into ashes. Never bury the fire with dirt; this may fail to kill it properly and also spoils the ring. Instead, douse fire with quantities of water. Comb through the ashes with your fingers to make sure they are cold clear through. Be certain to pull out any unburnable fragments like tinfoil. If, in spite of all care, you do have sizable chunks of wood left over, it's okay to leave them in the ring.

There is a gracious woodcraft tradition that calls for leaving a stack of wood for the next traveler. Though this may seem somewhat at variance with the current creed of "leaving no trace," it is still a nice gesture to leave wood at an obvious campsite in a forested place where fuel is plentiful.

Gather up all litter—your own and as much as you can carry of what may have been there before.

If your camp has been in a place not obviously used before, there is more to do. Your traces must be made to vanish. Some instructors in wilderness programs like Outward Bound have made a game of it. They ask their students to imagine themselves fugitives, with hostile trackers behind them examining every yard of ground for signs of their presence.

If you have used a stove, your job will be simple; with a fire, it is much more complex (see *Fire at an unmarked site* in Chapter 19). It is very important in this situation that *all* charred wood be consumed to ash. Ashes pass quickly back into the soil, but charcoal lasts so long that archaeologists count on it for dating ruins. Try not to wind up with a big, half-burned log; there is no good way of disposing of such an object.

Should fire remnants be scattered or buried? It makes sense to scatter cold ashes, if it can be done inconspicuously—the best way of getting nutrients back to the soil. Black extinguished coals should probably be buried when you restore the ground surface at the fire site. Exception: where wildfire has left obvious traces in the scene, it probably does no harm to scatter dead embers. Sooty stones, if you have any, should be returned to the landscape, blackened side down. This does not mean scattering them about. Rocks should be reseated where you found them. Better yet, they should never be moved in the first place.

The bed site needs policing too. Restore rocks you've removed. Ruffle the smooth surface. Scatter twigs, leaves, or gravel to replace the natural litter you swept away. You won't succeed in eliminating *every* trace, but you should be able to restore the natural scene well enough to fool any casual eye. Weather, in a little time, will do the rest.

Variations

F

At the same time that we are earnest to explore and learn all things, we require that all things be mysterious and unexplorable, that land and sea be infinitely wild, unsurveyed and unfathomed by us because unfathomable.

—Henry David Thoreau

22:
Cross-Country Travel and Other Variants

OF ALL THE MILES THAT BACKPACKERS travel each year, ninety percent are probably hiked in summer. And of that ninety percent, ninety percent are hiked by trail. Sometimes we speak of wilderness as "crowded," but for those who are ready to take a further step into wildness—to leave behind the busy channels of the summer trails—the wild country still has room to spare.

Not that you could call these remoter lands "underused." Wilderness serves purposes beyond recreation; the lands where the hiker seldom comes may be the best preserved of all for watershed, for wildlife, for scientific study. None of the back country is wasted. Wilderness itself should have within it a deeper wilderness—wilderness, so to speak, to the second power.

Cross-country hikers are not numerous. And here's a paradox: should they ever become truly numerous, the experience they seek would vanish before them. Whenever a cross-country route begins to carry more than a handful of people a week, informal paths start to appear, and then to erode and deepen. When this point is reached, the land-managing agency has several choices: to restrict use . . . to build a formal trail . . . or (as happens too often) simply to let the land take scar upon scar. A well-built trail is not a convenience merely, but also a way of accommodating use without excessive damage to the land.

Meanwhile, the trail-less outback is still there. And for a certain number of hikers, it is the only wilderness that really counts; the one experience that has the full reward.

Travel off the trail

It's hard to make rules for hiking cross-country, because "country" itself is endlessly diverse. A *trail* along a talus slope may not be so very different from a trail in a rainforest, or a trail through a thicket of wild lilac. But leave the path and you deal with the land in every shape and texture it has. Here you may struggle at half a mile an hour through an enormous, fragrant field of rhododendron; here you slip and slide on scree or the abominable sliding stuff called "rock-mulch"; here you jump from stone to stone in the bed of a rushing stream; here you scramble up a steep rock scarp; here you clamber over and around the trunks of fallen trees.

Cross-country travel is typically slow. If three miles an hour is a lively pace with a pack on a level trail, one mile an hour is good progress through woods and brush. And yet not even this is a rule. There are open, parklike forests as well as thick and tangled ones. And on the smooth granite plateaus of certain western ranges, it may be scarcely harder to move off-trail than on. In the desert, too, marked trails are rare and scarcely required.

To hike off-trail you need a genuine backpacking boot, weighing four pounds or more, the pair, in an average man's size, and with a good high top; lighter boots, so comfortable on easy ground, protect the ankle too little for rugged travel. Make sure you have an elastic bandage in your kit. Should you wrench a knee or sprain an ankle, the support of the firmly-wound bandage can keep you mobile enough to retreat.

For travel in rough country, you will be happiest with a soft pack that rides close to the back. Frame packs, with their tendency to lurch and swing, can be harder to manage. If you have a frame already, though, it will serve. Just try to lower the center of gravity of the load. Put your heaviest objects at the bottom, reversing the usual order, and mount the sleeping bag on top rather than underneath. On some models, you can shift the entire packbag lower on the frame. Before you wade into vegetation, make sure that zippers are shut tight, and try to get rid of any trailing loops or protrusions where bushes and branches could catch hold. Stow away any objects that are hanging on the outside of your pack, or at your belt.

For scree and loose ground, as well as for crossing snowpatches, you can borrow an item from winter camping: gaiters. These zip-on cuffs fit tightly over the gap at the top of the boot, preventing loose rocks and the like from bouncing in.

Two animal problems, common in many regions, become slightly more troublesome when you leave the trail. Ticks, which are thick in the brush especially in the spring, are hard to avoid. Gaiters may help here, and so do dabs of insect repellent at neck, wrists, and ankles, but about the only sure defense is to strip each evening and get rid of the creatures before they get deeply attached.

Second, snakes—rattlesnakes and, in the East, copperheads and cottonmouths—are somewhat more of a hazard off the trail. Snakes can't function either in heat or in cold and are most active on warm nights and in the morning and the evening of hot days. Thus you are often warned to watch for them at those times. But in the heat of midday there is another danger; a snake, lying low, may be too torpid to move out of the way of a descending boot. Watch where you put your feet and hands. Don't step down on the far side of a rock or log without first getting a look at the ground there.

On the plus side, the bears of remote areas, unaccustomed to human traffic, are typically quite timid.

Routefinding and navigation

Routefinding—picking your detailed line through the landscape—is perhaps the greatest (and most fascinating) of cross-country skills. What is the easiest way through this brushfield? Which of several gullies will get us through this band of steep rock? Can we get around the head of this valley without losing too much elevation? Where is the safest spot to ford the stream? Will the going be easier up the creekbed or on the ridge to the side? Shall we pass to the left or the right of that sharp horn? Decisions are made every minute. The cross-country hiker is constantly looking both near and far; the route that looks easiest in the short run may lead you into problems later on.

It is always good, in the wilderness, to travel with a mind aware, conscious of the shapes of the land, their correspondence to the map, and your own progress among them. Even on the trail you need this skill, but don't even consider leaving the beaten path until it is automatic to you. Nobody in a cross-country group should be a passive follower. Every member must understand what's going on. It's important, among other things, to look behind you now and then, fixing landmarks in your mind, in case you must retrace your course.

In trail travel it is rather hard to get seriously lost, even if you should, at times, lose track of your exact position on the map. You know, after all, that you are on a certain *line*, or at worst (if you think you have overlooked a junction) that you're on one of several lines. Either way, you have only half a problem to solve.

Even off-trail, you may at times be following a prominent line—a major stream, a ridgeline without confusing branches, an ocean beach. But much of the time you have no such lifeline to hold to.

In broken, mountainous country, topography—the lay of the land—is your most important guide. Your problems start when you can't see to read the land—due to fog, or clouds, or winter "whiteout"—or when what you *can* see is uninstructive. Some landscapes are like that, flattish and jumbled, or flattish and forested, with no particular pattern to go by. In featureless country, as in blind weather, navigation has to go beyond the obvious. Here are a few of the tricks that professionals rely on.

Trick #1: Walking a straight line

Sometimes, with nothing else to go by, you need to walk with compass in hand, following a selected direction or azimuth. Even with a compass, it's hard enough to keep straight. At one point you circle left around a thicket or a

Plotting a course around an obstacle

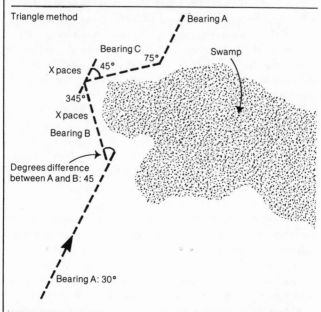

Triangle method

Bearing A

Bearing C

75°

Swamp

X paces

45°

345°

X paces

Bearing B

Degrees difference
between A and B: 45

Bearing A: 30°

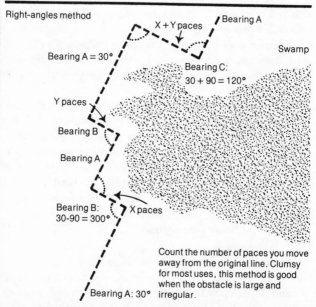

Right-angles method

X + Y paces

Bearing A

Swamp

Bearing A = 30°

Bearing C:
30 + 90 = 120°

Y paces

Bearing B

Bearing A

Bearing B:
30 – 90 = 300°

X paces

Count the number of paces you move
away from the original line. Clumsy
for most uses, this method is good
when the obstacle is large and
irregular.

Bearing A: 30°

266

massive log; at another you turn right along a stream, looking for stones to cross on; you zig and zag simply in moving among close trees.

In general you try to zig about as often as you zag. But if you have to move off course for more than a few yards, don't do it blind. Instead, plot yourself a whole new course around the obstacle. Suppose, for example, you have to turn left around a large marshy area. Simply note the bearing of your new line. As you go, count your strides. When you clear the obstacle, turn back toward the original line at the same angle you used in leaving it, and walk an equal number of paces. Then return to the old bearing. When you've done all this, you should be more or less back on track.

Trick #2: Aiming for a line of destination

Nobody, no matter how careful he is, can walk a perfectly straight course by compass. If you try to follow a bearing to a particular point—a campsite, a car, a water cache on a sagebrush steppe—you are almost certain to miss it. You may drift left, you may drift right, but you won't be precisely on target.

What's the answer? This: you give yourself an easier assignment. You don't try to reach one particular point; instead, you aim for a recognizable *line* on which the point is to be found. It may be a stream, a lakeshore, a ridge, a road, a trail—even (if you have long views) a compass direction to a prominent landmark (when Big Marvine Peak is at 210 degrees, you're on the intended line).

Once you're on the destination line, the problem is only half way solved. Assuming you have no further landmarks to work from, how do you know which way to turn along the line to find whatever it is you're heading for: the car on the road, the camp on the stream, the cache on the compass line? There are two main ways of making sure you know: *deliberate error* and *bracketing*.

Trick #3: Deliberate error

Though the idea takes some getting used to, this is the simplest way of protecting yourself from confusion. Instead of heading straight toward your destination point, you consciously veer to one side or the other, making *an error you know about.* Let's say you're hoping to reach a

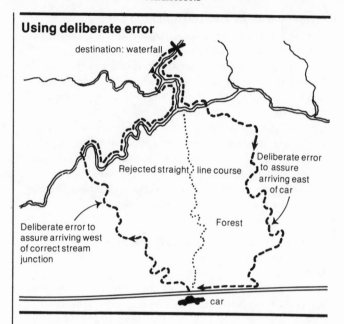

Using deliberate error

destination: waterfall

Rejected straight line course

Deliberate error to assure arriving east of car

Deliberate error to assure arriving west of correct stream junction

Forest

car

car parked on a road. Angle deliberately left or right from the course that would take you to it. Don't err blindly, but use a compass azimuth, and make your error large enough so that your smaller, uncontrolled deviations won't matter. Say you've angled, consciously, to the right. You'll know, then, when you reach the road, that the car can *only* be somewhere to your left.

Here's another application. Say you are following a faint trail down a ridge toward a stream. The trace disappears in the underbrush, but you want to locate the exact point at which the old route crosses the water, in hopes of picking up a plainer trail on the other side. Now, if you try to follow the mapped line of the trail, you won't know, when you reach the water, whether you should search upstream or downstream. Unless, by unusual good luck, you're right on target, your error may have led you either way. All you can do, lacking landmarks, is wander back and forth, searching alternately in each direction.

But if, coming down the hill, you had *deliberately* angled upstream, then you'd have known to search downstream, possibly saving an hour or more of time.

Trick #4: Bracketing

Remember the problem: how do you find your destination once you've reached the destination *line*? Besides deliberate error, there's a second answer: bracketing. You establish two landmarks—two things to look for—on the destination line, one on each side of the point you are planning to reach and far enough apart so that you're sure to come out somewhere between them.

There are several kinds of brackets and several ways of "establishing" them. Sometimes you can set up your own artificial landmarks in advance. Say you've parked your car on a road through featureless woods and have to make sure of getting back to it. Then you can simply tie rags, or leave some other markers, a mile or so away from the car in either direction. More often, though, brackets must be natural features, predicted from study of the topo map. Maybe you are trying to reach a given point on a stream; the map tells you that your destination lies between a waterfall upstream and the junction of a major tributary downstream. Or, to take a third case, brackets can be compass bearings to a landmark visible in the distance (but not

Bracketing

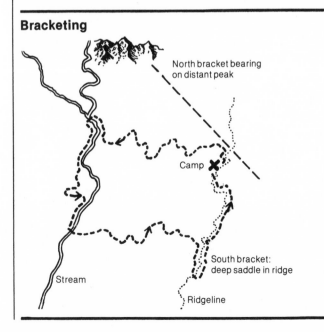

North bracket bearing on distant peak

Camp ✖

South bracket: deep saddle in ridge

Stream

Ridgeline

visible from the destination point; otherwise there wouldn't be a problem).

It doesn't matter what your brackets are, or how you establish them. When you encounter your destination line, between the brackets, no harm is done if you guess wrong at first and head in the wrong direction. You'll soon run into one of your brackets and be turned back to the center.

On the edge of climbing

This is not a book about mountain climbing. But if you begin taking trips away from the trail, you may sooner or later want to learn at least the simplest of the climber's methods. With a rope and the skill to use it, you can deal with unexpected obstacles; more important, perhaps, you can plan trips in country where obstacles *are* to be expected. A rope-carrying party isn't balked if, hiking down some desert canyon, it comes to the brink of a steep, dry waterfall; or if, in some north-facing mountain gully, it has to cross lingering, slick-surfaced snow. Peaks that are out of reach to most hikers, because of a little steep rock at the top, are open to the party with a rope. Even on easy ground a rope can be a comfort, if a careless stumble could pitch someone over a dangerous edge.

The great point of the rope between climbers is this: it allows one partner, braced in a strong position, to protect a second, who is moving on hazardous ground. As the moving climber advances, the stationary partner—the *belayer*—feeds out rope. If the climber slips, the belayer can stop his fall. Belaying, then, in all its elements, is the first and greatest skill to be learned.

There's another technique that can be of use in cross-country travel, and that is the *rappel*, a way of sliding, slowly and safely, down a doubled rope. This is sometimes the only way to get down a scarp without leaving the rope behind you. Running the line around a tree or knob of stone, with both ends dangling, you slide down it, and then recover the rope by pulling on one of the strands.

This isn't the place to describe these methods further, or to discuss the various knots, body stances, signals, and safety considerations that go into their use. These basics are much too important to be learned from a thumbnail

Belaying

sketch. Consult instead the specialized climbing texts, look
for instruction (formal or informal), and practice again and
again.

If your trips will take you onto steep snowslopes—and
that can happen, in some regions, at any time of year—you
will need to carry another tool, an *ice axe*. This is a stout
metal or wooden shaft fitted to a head with two blades, one
narrow (the pick) and one wide (the adze). For this kind of
occasional use, a light, medium-length axe is best; with the
end of the shaft on the ground, you should just be able to
rest your hand on the blade. The axe has several uses, but
one is especially important in cross-country travel on
snow: *self-arrest.*

When you slip on snow, you can save yourself from a
long, dangerous slide by throwing yourself face down on
the snow, with the shaft of the ice axe pinned beneath your
chest. If the axe is gripped as it should be, the pick will cut
into the snow beside you, causing so much friction that
your slide will stop. Done properly, this self-arrest will

271

stop you even on a steep, slick snowchute. But this is another skill that must be specifically, carefully learned.

There are competing models in ice axes, but for casual use the differences don't much matter. Prices start at about $40, and the weight of a typical medium-shafted axe is near two pounds. Longer axes, more convenient as walking sticks, are clumsier in self-arrest.

Stream-crossing

One of the most difficult wilderness obstacles is the major, rushing stream. There is a whole craft of stream-crossing and plenty of debate and disagreement about how to do it.

A slow, deep river is not a particular problem; it's usually safe enough to swim such a stream, floating your pack in front of you on an air mattress. (Note this special point in favor of the mattress—you can't float anything on a thin foam pad.)

A fast, shallow stream can be tricky if the current is fierce enough. Instinct tells you to cross slowly and cautiously, but some expert travelers prefer to hurry over, almost at a run, giving the current no chance to knock them off their feet.

But the really daunting problem is the swollen mountain stream, thigh-deep or hip-deep, fast-moving and murky—just such a stream as you may encounter at the thaw. The first question to ask when you reach such a barrier is: shall we attempt it at all? For there is real danger here. It may be better to retreat or change your route. Steep, violent torrents—especially the ones that are accelerating toward dangerous rapids or falls—should be left alone.

If you decide to cross, consider both place and time. Streams fed by snowmelt will be lowest in the cool of the morning. Generally speaking, it is better to cross where the course is straight (rather than at a curve). It may also be easier to cross at a shingle, where the water is broken but shallow, than at a deeper, calmer spot. Above all, consider what would happen if you were swept off your feet. Are there dangerous spots downstream into which you might be carried? Would it be easy, downstream, to clamber to the shore? Are there shelving banks or steep, difficult slopes?

Unbuckle the waistbelt of your pack (so that, if you must, you can shed it). Stand sideways to the current, facing just slightly downstream. Set your feet wide apart and take short steps, moving one foot at a time and keeping the same foot always forward. Test each new footing before you shift your weight. A long-handled iceaxe, a staff, or a pole will help you keep your balance against the tug and haul of the flow.

Several hikers, crossing together, can give each other extra support in a circle of three, with linked arms; in a line, each gripping the belt of another, facing upstream but moving sideways; or abreast, with arms linked and wrapped around a long pole, facing across the stream. In this "line-abreast" method, all move forward at once; otherwise, only one person moves at a time.

Should a river-crosser, like a climber, tie himself on to a rope and get a belay? You might well think so. Strangely enough, however, a rope can actually add to the crosser's danger. If he's swept off his feet, the force of the stream, dragging his weight against the rope's resistance, can press him down into the streambed until he drowns. If the water's that fast, the person on the bank will have trouble pulling the victim to safety. There are various ways, all more or less involved, of using a rope with lessened danger. In general, though, these are specialized climbers' methods.

In a large group it makes unquestionable sense to string a rope across the water for the middle members to use as a rail or "handline"; only the first crosser and the last will then be unprotected.

These hazardous crossings are often made in winter and spring when deep, rushing streams are also bitterly cold. Wool clothes, which you should be wearing anyway at that time of year, will continue to insulate even when they're soaked, but you'll probably want to change socks and underwear, at least, once you're across. If someone gets dangerously chilled, you may have to strip him, dry him, and get him into a sleeping bag, following the drill for hypothermia. A fire may also help. Lacking a hypothermia crisis, though, the best thing to do is to eat starch and sugar and start hiking, fast and hard, to produce a lot of body heat. Wet clothes dry out fast when you hike at full speed.

Low impact off the trail

Rules change when you leave the trails. On established paths, you deliberately confine your impact to places impacted already. On the trail you walk single-file. In camp you build fires (if at all) at old sites. You concentrate your impact in the smallest possible area.

But in off-trail travel, exactly the opposite applies. To avoid leaving traces, you disperse. A party, walking through the woods, or on any surface where a mark could be left, should always walk abreast, each hiker in his own line, so far as the land allows. A little impact, spread over a lot of land, will simply vanish.

Don't build cairns or ducks; don't blaze trees or break branches. Don't spoil the experience of others by remind-ing them, oppressively, that Kilroy has already been here. Though he may know better, the walker on the trackless ridge or in the empty forest would like to think that no one else has been in that place, at least this year. Don't kill the illusion for those who come after.

What kinds of land are most easily damaged by cross-country hiking and camping? The types are familiar: tim-berline vegetation of all kinds . . . wet meadows and bogs . . . erosive slopes. While subalpine meadows are known for their fragility, woody shrubs and heathers at the same high elevations are in fact more vulnerable still. Dry mountain grasslands, though slow to repair themselves, are also rather slow to scar. The rich, moist forest floors of lower-elevation wilderness may seem fragile as your boot punches down among moss and ferns, but this living fabric restores itself very well.

There's an interesting pattern in all this. Lands which are truly rich—where living things have an easy time—are somewhat resistant to abuse. And so are lands which are truly harsh: the barren peaks, the ice, the volcanic wastes of cinder and lava flow. But in between there is another class of lands, places where a seeming richness is main-tained in a harsh world. Here damage is easily done but only over many years repaired, if at all.

Take the High Peaks of the Adirondacks, 4,000 and 5,000 feet high. In that region 4,000 feet is already sub-alpine. Yet these summits are not barren but are green with a thick fur (unlikely though it seems) of sphagnum moss—

274

"inverted bogs," one writer has called them. Many of these peaks are trail-less, and most people seem to want them that way. But so often are they ascended by cross-country hikers that their sides are striped with steep, eroding scars. These are trails in all but name, and the mossy tundras on the narrow crests are being trampled away.

What can be done in cases like this? Except where roads can be closed, reducing access, the answers seem to come down to two: either the authorities must put some sort of limit on the number of people permitted to make these climbs, or they must build formal trails and over-looks, protecting the fragile summit vegetation with railing and with signs: "Keep off the moss." Neither answer is appealing. But where there is little wilderness and many who would use it, we come to such uncomfortable choices again and again.

For the extreme case, consider Switzerland. The Swiss have set aside a single National Park of about 40,000 acres—a magnificent landscape, by all accounts, but, as wild preserves are counted in America, almost untenably small. In this Swiss park the hiker cannot camp, nor can he set foot off the elaborately maintained trails. It would be, to our temperament, hard to take, but it's a way.

The more wilderness we manage to preserve, the less often we will be driven to such difficult choices.

Desert

There are many kinds and degrees of desert in America and many kinds of desert travel. They have in common the dominant problem of *water.*

The desert is not, of course, truly waterless, but you have to be very sure of your information before you rely on local sources. Many springs and waterholes shown on topographic maps don't seem to exist. Often desert waters must be purified, and a few sources contain arsenic or other poisons (beware of springs that have no signs of life in and around them: no hoofprints or droppings of burros and bighorn sheep, no drowned insects).

Always your water must be measured not in quarts but in gallons—not less than one and a half gallons a day, in food and drink, and sometimes much more. One experienced Death Valley hiker adds one quart to this minimum for each five miles of hiking—this in the cool of winter. If you had to carry all that water in your pack, two days supply at two gallons a day would already weigh thirty-two pounds. Of course, when you're hauling fluid anyhow, there is little advantage to carrying dehydrated foods. You might as well get some of your liquid from oranges, fresh vegetables, or, for that matter, from canned beans.

Often, on desert trips of any length, water caches must be placed in advance. If you will be hiking out and back on the same line, carry water to plant a cache a few miles up the trail. Always leave a generous supply in your car. Use gallon plastic water bottles (bleach bottles, thoroughly cleaned, are good) with screw tops, taped shut. Bury them eighteen inches underground, or under a stout cairn, and mark the spot both on the ground and on your maps. Though it's hard to believe, desert veterans have learned by dangerous experience that they must place their caches *unobserved.* It is by no means unknown for vandals to steal or destroy these supplies, risking what could amount to manslaughter. Caches shouldn't be placed so far apart that you would be unable to reach the next if you found the first one gone. Always plan your trips with a considerable margin for error.

Desert navigation is typically easy. Hiking down some deep-cut canyon, your world is only a few yards wide; the way is scarcely losable. Even on the open desert, views are long, weather mostly clear, and the structure of the land quite unmistakable. (The chief problem seems to be that distances look shorter than they are.) But intermountain flats can be very featureless, and you can't afford to make major mistakes when today's destination contains tomorrow's entire water supply. It's good to place such caches in places easily recognized—areas with "character"—and on some clear "destination line," like the bank of a deep wash (but not down in the streamcourse) or near a road. To further identify the spot, take three bearings on prominent landmarks.

We speak of "desert hiking," but there are really three quite separate sorts of hiking to be done in the dry places. On one kind of trip—perhaps the most popular—hikers follow watercourses, keeping to the deep-cut canyons of

276

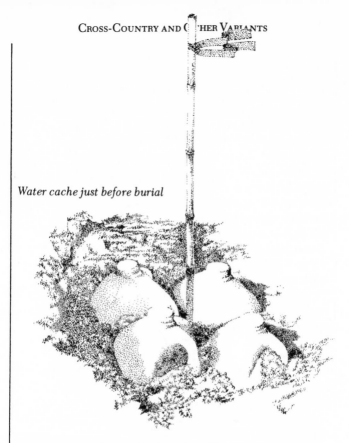

Water cache just before burial

major streams. Canyon backpacking has its peculiarities. Consider the odd fact that your trip, more often than not, begins *above* your destination; from the roadhead you hike not up but down. Some canyons are wet, with perennial rushing streams and borders of bright vegetation—in the desert but not of it. Others have less reliable streams, or none at all, except in their brief periods of flood.

Flash floods are a major danger in canyon travel. Thunderstorms are common in the Southwest throughout the summer and fall, reaching a climax in August. Even if the air is perfectly dry where you are, floods can be sent down by downpours in mountains miles away. Never camp in a streamcourse, especially in the narrows of a deep-carved gorge.

Besides the flash-flood danger, canyons can hold other problems. There's quicksand, for instance, in some places;

experienced hikers know how to *swim* the shifting sand if there's no other way to pass. Then there are "dryfalls," sheer drops in bone-dry canyons that become cataracts three or four times a year when the floods tear through. In many of these gorges it's good to carry a rope; in some, there's no progressing without one.

A second type of desert trip is the high-mountain back-pack where you climb into ranges lofty enough so that true desert gives way to something cooler, wetter, and a little easier to deal with. Some desert ranges aren't arid at all but green, with rushing streams, considerable timber, and even, in some places, lakes.

Finally, there is what you might call extreme desert travel, the desert taken without compromise. If you choose to head out across a plain of sagebrush or creosote bush or saguaros, or head up into the summits of a truly arid range—one of those highlands that rise, one after another, from the edges of certain western highways like handsome, gloomy piles of bone—the adventure grows more serious. Extreme desert, like deeply subzero winter, like the high-est of mountains, is both lovely and severe.

Only light equipment is required for most desert hiking in the warmer nine months of the year. No tent, certainly; poncho or tarp will do. You don't need heavy clothing or a massive sleeping bag (though nights can be distinctly cool). In hot weather, light-colored clothing and gear will keep you more comfortable. Hikers in extreme desert may carry tentpoles to use in pitching a canopy for the midday stop, and air mattresses for insulation from hot ground.

Many desert hikers prefer boots with flat composition soles for hiking in gravel and sand. In wet canyons, tennis shoes are often the best footgear; leather boots aren't com-fortable for continual wading, and leather doesn't hold up well under repeated wetting and drying out. For cooking, a stove is essential, unless you eat cold food.

Desert travel, clearly, takes special planning and spe-cial care. It's vital to get information on local water, local weather, local dangers, before you set out. You may have to convince some skeptical ranger that you know what you're doing; extreme desert trips, in particular, may be flatly discouraged. Try, by all means, to take your first few trips in the company of experienced hands.

Low impact on the desert

Easily scarred, slow to recover, America's desert lands are in trouble. Desert hikers, never numerous, are not among the major causes of that trouble. Rather the problem is overgrazing, only a little less cruel than the worst the West has seen; the problem is random, destructive mining, with its open pits and endless bulldozed roads; the problem is the off-road vehicle: jeeps and motorcycles growling across the accessible parts of the desert in ever-growing, unmanageable herds. Very little of the wild desert has much protection against these things.

The conscientious hiker, though, will want to use care here as elsewhere.

Maybe the most important single point is this: don't compete with wildlife for water. If you draw water from an isolated waterhole or a short section of perennial stream, don't camp beside it, but move a good distance away. This is especially crucial in desert mountains where bighorn sheep are found. These magnificent creatures, already suffering from the competition of feral horses and burros and domestic stock, simply won't remain where people are.

In the desert, as at timberline, fires have no place. You won't find much burnable material anyway; what you do find belongs on the land. Plants that appear dead are often only dormant.

The barren desert soil might seem, in its sterility, to be invulnerable to any disturbance as tiny as a hiker's footfall. But that is not true for all kinds of ground. Some desert lands—especially the slopes of alluvial fans—are covered with a sort of cobbling of darkened stones. It doesn't take too much traffic to discolor this "desert pavement" and leave a long-lasting, visible track. Moreover, repeated passage over a track packs the soil and breaks down the protective stony shell. This "impressment" leaves a strip that is easily eroded by wind and rain.

At the moment managers are mostly worried about off-road vehicles, which can scar "desert pavement" for decades or longer with a single passage. But desert hikers, if they should ever get numerous enough, might eventually add to the problem.

Caches should be buried in soft soil, where the smallest

possible mark will be left behind.

Very long trips

This is another variation on the "normal" backpack: the trip measured not in days but in weeks. The longer the trip, the more elaborate the planning has to be. Unless you plant food caches or come out to reprovision, your food will have to be of the lightest, most compact kind. Your appetite will grow as time goes on; experienced long-distance trekkers add about half a pound per person per day to the normal ration of one and a half to two pounds. Balance in the diet—scarcely a consideration on the shorter jaunt—becomes important on a long trip.

There are various ways of placing supply caches. You can leave food on the ground in tightly sealed metal boxes (available at some gear stores) or hang it from trees in boxes or in waterproof bags (as for bear-bagging). If your route passes close enough to towns, you can mail your supplies ahead (Special Handling, Insured). You can also lay in groceries at such places. The Appalachian Trail passes quite close to many settlements, and the Pacific Crest Trail approaches a few. Along with food, you may need to replace first aid supplies and some of your minor gear as the weeks go on.

Hiking alone

"Nobody should ever hike alone."

If the land agencies had their way, if the rescue workers had their way, that's the sentence that would stand at this spot. The authorities don't welcome anything that might encourage people to undertake adventures. And you can't blame them for that. They're too accustomed to retrieving—at great effort and expense—the overambitious, the overconfident, and the underprepared.

You may even hear that no party is safe with less than four people. There's a logic to this. If someone is injured, there should be one companion to stay with him and two (since no one should hike alone) to go together for help. When a single hiker gets in trouble, it may be quite a while before anyone knows about it, and the problems and dangers increase.

Okay, there is risk in hiking alone.

There is double risk whenever the solo hiker leaves the beaten paths—when he ventures into cross-country travel, or into the desert, or into the world of snow and winter storms.

And yet there are people who do all these things, matter-of-factly and without mishap, year after year. And they have their reasons. Some of the sharpest and most memorable statements of the wilderness idea—the formulations of a Muir, a Thoreau, an Aldo Leopold—have been made by the solo travelers. Whatever it is that wilderness gives you, you come back with a double dose of it when you go out alone. And then there are the practical advantages. "The man who travels alone," Thoreau observes, "can start today; but he who travels with another must wait till that other is ready, and it may be a long time before they get off."

So if you feel like taking up solo hiking, by all means do it. Do it, though, with preparation, with understanding, and even (the word is not too strong) with healthy *fear*. Things *can* happen out there. You may want to start your solo travel on frequented trails where you will meet many parties a day; later, you might find yourself drawn to remoter country, perhaps even to off-trail and off-season adventures. But take it slow. Don't overrate yourself. Don't underrate the wilderness. The wilderness is bigger.

If you do head out alone, take special care to leave a precise itinerary, both at home and with the local office of the managing agency. Take extra food and fuel (also water, if that's a consideration). For other gear the solo traveler's rule can only be: *when in doubt, leave it in.* You'll have nobody else along this time to loan you the item you forgot, the thing you decided to do without.

23:
The Winter
Wilderness

IN SNOW THE WILDERNESS grows and is wilder.

Except in the South, in the deserts, and in the foothills of the Far West, most of our wild country is snowed in during winter. The new, white surface covers scars, smooths old mistakes, shelters the fragile ground. It covers the trampled campgrounds, the beaten trails of summer. And, most of all, it closes roads. In winter the California Sierra becomes once more the huge mystery that John Muir explored. Yellowstone, clean of cars and noise, is once again an amazement. In forested mountains the labyrinth of logging roads becomes a land of flat, white corridors— still artificial but no longer ugly and (except by snow- mobiles) no longer driveable. Peaks that were an hour away by summer trails become the reward of a three days' march.

Once the snowy hills were pretty much empty of trav- elers. Even now winter is, by comparison, the empty, spacious season. But the winter wilderness is tracked by two species of travelers, specially equipped, and moving with the extra vigor that seems natural in cold places.

There are, first of all, the cross-country skiers. Moving swiftly on narrow, elegant wooden or fiber glass skis, they don't often push very far into the wilderness. Most are daytrippers, lightly burdened, skiing a fast in-and-out.

But besides the daytrippers there are those more committed travelers, the winter backpackers. Though their numbers are increasing, they are still rather few. Compared to the crowds of summer they may always be few. Some shuffle along on snowshoes; some slide along on skis of heavier make than those of the daytime skiers they meet on the first miles of trail. Some are climbers heading for remote winter summits. Some are downhill skiers, weary of busy commercial slopes, come to shuffle up steep peaks for the giddy, controlled ride down. Some are simply backpackers, moving, camping, enjoying, dealing with the white, crisp world. But these travelers have in common a shared problem and a fairly similar set of solutions to it.

The problem: how do you stay comfortable—and more important, safe—in the beautiful, strange, and unforgiving country of the cold?

Getting into winter

Winter is another world. So different are its rules, so special its demands, that it would take a separate book to deal with them thoroughly. Winter gear, in particular, is full of complexities of its own.

The great reality, in snow, is *cold*. Never underestimate it. On a typical winter trip you will be cozily warm while you travel, and cozily warm once you're lying in your sleeping bag, drinking soup. But the times in between are rarely perfectly comfortable. Fingers get cold and disobedient. Bare metal can be so frigid that it stings bare flesh. Flashlights balk, cameras jam, water freezes solid in canteens. Everything you do takes longer—and there is more to do: more gear to deal with, more fixing, more finding, more figuring, more rigging to be gotten through. And to add to it all there is less daylight to work with.

Then why camp in the snow? Because the world of the snow is endlessly, cleanly beautiful. Because experiences in it—the good and the bad alike—seem to happen with double intensity. Because the land is emptier, lonelier, wilder. Because you have, more than you have in any summer travel, the sense of being on a frontier.

Some backpackers value these things so much that they turn the year upside down, like downhill skiers or Australians; it is November that sets them to scanning the maps and checking out their gear, not May. Even if you don't go that far, the taste for winter camping gives you a twelve-month hiking season. You can simply go when you have the time, without concern for the calendar.

It's a real jump, the move into winter camping—almost like learning to backpack all over again. Most people will want to break into it gradually, starting with day trips, and then short overnight jaunts not far from the road. Test all your gear where the retreat is easy. If your summer stove is going to balk in the cold, you want to know about it before you're absolutely depending on the thing. Don't take on too many problems at first; there are so many. It helps to travel, the first few times, with more experienced companions. Some outings clubs offer valuable courses.

Winter gear

For winter travel you will have to make some changes in your gear—some substitutions, even more additions. The most obvious new requirement is a pair of skis or snowshoes—for more on the possibilities, see below.

Your summer hiking boots may or may not do for winter. Fairly heavy backpacking boots can generally be made to serve, with extra waterproofing; lighter boots, especially those made of "split-grain" leather, will not. ("Split-grain" leathers are the middle layer of the animal's skin; "top-grain" leathers include the outer surface, the toughest, most waterproof part.) The more massive the boot, and the thicker it is in the sole, the warmer you will find it.

There are several ways of increasing the warmth of a chilly boot. You can, of course, add socks—but don't overdo it (if you find the arrangement uncomfortably tight, it may be cutting off circulation to your feet, with resulting danger of frostbite). Dry socks are important in winter; take plenty of spares. You can also add foam inner soles. (They'll insulate better if you wrap them in plastic.) Some people like to put plastic bags on their feet, inside the socks; this keeps heat in but also perspiration (wet feet are somewhat more likely to blister).

In really extreme winter conditions, overboots ($30 to $40) can help. These are tough fabric shells that cover the boot, adding insulation, and rise up the calf. Some cover the sole of the boot, others leave it free.

In the West, most people seem to wear lug-soled hiking boots in winter as in summer. Not so in the East and the Midwest. In these regions, hikers in mud and snow often prefer the high rubber boots known loosely as "shoepacs." There are various designs. All cover most of the foot with a single piece of vulcanized rubber, so that waterproofing is total. The rest of the upper—ankle and calf—may be of leather. Heights vary. There may be detachable foam liners. The Maine Hunting Shoe by L. L. Bean is a familiar standard among shoepacs. The Army's Korean boot, known also as the Mickey Mouse, packs insulation between two layers of rubber, and is exceedingly warm. Shoepacs are not for use on rough snow-free ground. They cost some-what less than leather-and-Vibram hiking boots.

Of course you need more clothes in winter, clothes of a special kind. Cotton is out (except in underwear); wool is in. Down-filled jackets and sleeping bags are good in dry-cold climates, but dubious in wet cold; synthetic fills are safer, because, like wool, they will continue to warm you when it's wet.

Even more than in summer, it's important to choose clothes that allow easy adjustment. You don't want to let yourself get either cold or hot—excessive sweating will chill you by evaporation later on. Front zippers or buttons, and adjustable closures at the wrists, are good. You need both wind protection (a parka or thin windproof shell) and protection against rain and wet snow (raincoat or cagoule and rainpants or chaps). In high places you may need sepa-rate windpants as well. (If you own Gore-Tex garments, and find they work for you, you will be able to combine raingear and wind protection and leave duplicate clothing at home.) The more pockets you have on your outer cloth-ing, the handier.

Some people wear long johns in winter; others dislike them. Many find string underwear more comfortable in the wet than other types.

It's important to have a stocking cap that pulls down over the neck, leaving a gap for the face. For colder places and above timberline, you may need a cap with a built-in facemask. For warmer days in bright sun, an ordinary hat is a good idea.

You must have dark glasses or goggles—two pairs, in fact, in case you lose the first. For the fierce, bright lands above timberline, you need glasses that protect the sides of the eyes as well as the front. Though glass lenses block more burning ultraviolet light, plastic glasses are easier to find, and they will do for altitudes to 14,000 feet.

"Soft" backpacks with internal supports are much used in winter, especially by skiers who find standard frames awkward. Whichever kind you have, make sure you can fit all your needed gear into it, or onto it, tied to the outside. Attach pull-loops of cord to zipper tabs; these make it easier to work stubborn zippers with cold hands. (Such tiny comforts and conveniences have real meaning in the snow.)

True winter sleeping bags are, of course, heavier than summer types. As always, the key factor is not mere poundage but insulating thickness or loft. A bag with seven or eight inches of loft, in a mummy style, takes most sleepers down to about zero in comfort. "Three-season" bags, a little lighter, can be made to serve, especially within the protection of a tent. You do need more ground insulation than in summer. A closed-cell foam pad for winter should be half an inch thick and long enough to protect the legs and feet. (You may even want two such pads.) Though some use air mattresses in winter, these are less efficient because air circulation inside them takes some heat away.

For shelter you'll need a tent that can carry heavy snow weights and stand up in strong winds. Where snow is deep, you can build your own shelter—igloo, snow trench, or cave. You'll need a folding snow shovel ($10 to $15) for this work; some igloo-builders also carry light snow-saws ($7 to $10).

Doesn't all this add up to a heavier load in your pack? You bet it does. It is difficult, in winter, to trim your pack-weight much below forty pounds on an overnight trip. Winter mountaineers, adding ropes and other paraphernalia, seldom carry loads of less than sixty pounds. This is one of the prices you pay.

Travel in the snow

Especially on your first trips, don't commit yourself to covering too much ground too fast. Two miles an hour is a good pace on snowshoes in open country; four miles an hour is decent progress on skis. Often you will do much less. A ten-mile day on snowshoes, when you carry a pack, is an extremely long one, as is a twenty-mile day on skis. In some situations skis may be no faster than snowshoes.

Take into account the shortness of winter days. At the winter solstice near the Canadian border, daylight lasts no more than eight hours. If you allow two hours after dawn for breaking camp and one, at dusk, for getting settled in, that leaves only five hours for travel.

You can simplify matters by hiking in to established shelters. It's unwise, though, to count on finding the less elaborate shelters free of snow, while those that are open will sometimes be crowded. And it is dangerous to head out so underequipped that you would be in deep trouble if

Wind-chill chart: effective temperature

	Thermometer reading, degrees fahrenheit								
	50	**40**	**30**	**20**	**10**	**0**	**-10**	**-20**	**-30**
calm	50	40	30	20	10	0	-10	-20	-30
5	48	37	27	16	6	-5	-15	-26	-36
10	40	28	16	4	-9	-21	-33	-46	-58
15	36	22	9	-5	-18	-36	-45	-58	-72
20	32	18	4	-10	-25	-39	-53	-67	-82
25	30	16	0	-15	-24	-44	-59	-74	-88
30	28	13	-2	-18	-33	-48	-63	-79	-94
35	27	11	-4	-20	-35	-49	-67	-82	-98
40	26	10	-6	-21	-37	-53	-69	-85	-100

Wind speed

To the right of line travel becomes increasingly dangerous; unprotected flesh is liable to freeze.

you didn't make it all the way in to a distant refuge.

Whether you're on skis or snowshoes, the first problem of snow travel is keeping warm (but not hot) and, so far as possible, dry. Don't delay any changes in your armor of clothing that will keep the balance of heat-production and heat loss. Allow all the ventilation you can. If there's snow in the air, you need to be wearing smooth-surfaced fabrics from which the flakes will slide; brush them off when they accumulate. Knock snow from branches *before* you pass under them.

The thermometer doesn't tell you everything about cold. What chills you is the loss of heat from the skin (as well as from the lungs), and warm but windy air will remove warmth as quickly as colder air that is still. Humid air seems colder than dry air, and if you are wet, evaporation in the wind will still further increase your loss of heat. If your body keeps on losing more heat than it can make, you will enter the dangerous and even deadly condition called hypothermia, described at length in Chapter 27.

Nibble starchy or sugary foods as you walk, and drink plenty of water, more than you think you want. If it's so cold that water freezes during the day, insulate the containers. For instance, you can pull a thick wool sock over the bottle. Pack canteens upside down, so that plugs of ice won't form in the necks. Water freezes more slowly when it's mixed with something; lemonade stays liquid longer than straight water.

There are certain dangers in traveling on snow. Snowshoers, in particular, need to watch out for "tree-wells." Tree-trunks, warmer than the surrounding snow, melt deep pits, embarrassing to fall into. There's a much more serious danger in crossing snowbridges over flowing streams. A collapsing bridge can dump a backpacker into bitterly cold, rushing water. If you must cross, look for the thickest bridge you can find, and take your party across one member at a time, probing carefully in front with an ice axe or ski pole. Sometimes it's worth unpacking a rope and giving the crosser a belay.

Avalanches

Nothing in the wilderness is quite so terrifying—quite

so massive, quite so deadly, quite so inexorable—as the avalanche. In the last quarter-century, about 150 people in this country have died in avalanches. There is a whole science of avalanche safety, and every winter traveler should know at least the rudiments.

Avalanches, or snowslides, are of several kinds. The most dangerous is the *slab avalanche,* the great mass of snow that breaks, all at once, from a mountainside and plunges into the valley. Slab avalanches are likeliest during, and just after, heavy winter storms. The more new snow that comes down in a storm—and the faster it comes down—the greater the risk. It's cause for concern if more than a foot is added, especially if it piles up at the rate of an inch an hour or more. High wind adds to the danger. Remember that it may be snowing and blowing much harder up the ridge you must cross tomorrow than it is at tonight's campsite in the valley.

Once snow has fallen, it immediately begins to change and consolidate, growing much more stable. If the air is warm, this will happen quite rapidly, and the risk of massive slides may vanish within hours. In very cold weather, however, the snow changes slowly, and danger can last for many days. Watch for tiny "sluffs," harmless slides of loose, powdery snow; they indicate that the snow is settling nicely.

Slab avalanches can also form without fresh snow if it's cold and windy enough. Winds over twenty-five miles an hour can build up dangerous hard drifts on the lee sides of ridges. These "hard slab" avalanches of wind-packed snow are especially important as a danger in clear but windy periods following storms.

Up to a certain point warm temperatures mean lesser risk. There is, however, such a thing as a *wet snow avalanche.* Such snowslides occur when snow becomes water-

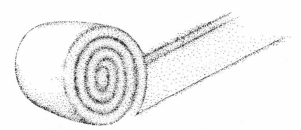

Sunball

289

logged and loses its grip on the surface below. This can
happen whenever temperatures rise. If it's suspiciously
warm, watch for "sunballs," curious wheels of snow
that run down the slope, rolling up the surface layer of the
snowpack in a sort of scroll. Small sunballs don't indicate
much danger, but very large ones, several feet thick, suggest danger of wet avalanche. Wet-snow avalanches don't
kill as many people as the slab type, but they are dangerous enough and very prevalent in the mountains of the
Pacific Coast.

Avoiding avalanches

Before you head into the wilderness, inquire at the
local agency office about current avalanche conditions;
you can also phone the National Ski Patrol.

Whatever the type of avalanche, the danger is greatest
on treeless slopes of middle steepness, between about
thirty and forty-five degrees. Gullies and open swathes in
forested landscapes are especially risky. Dense timber provides some reassurance, but a few trees on an open slope
don't prove a lack of avalanches there. Avoid the lee sides
of steep, high ridges. Above all, keep out from under *cor-*

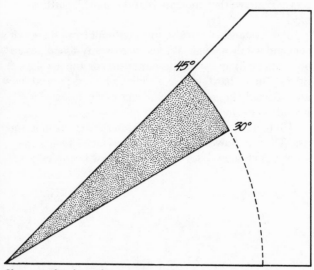

*Slopes with relatively greater and less avalanche hazard
(zone of greatest danger shaded)*

nices, the solid waves of snow and ice that hang over the crests of windy ridges like paralyzed ocean breakers.

If an indicated avalanche path lies across your course, it's best simply to go around it. The safest method is to circle it at the top; the second best, often more practical, is to bypass the swath on gentler ground at the bottom. Ridges are safer ground than steep valleys and draws.

If you find no way around an ominous path, try to judge the risk. Is it "avalanche weather"—has it been snowing or blowing a lot? Consider also what might happen if you were caught in a slide. A short avalanche path that widens at the bottom is not quite so perilous as a long chute that funnels in. Are there rocks and trees at the bottom of the slope against which a victim would be crushed, or a cliff over which he would be carried? In some cases, by far the best choice is to turn back.

If you are to cross a wide avalanche path, you may be able to take advantage of natural shelters: clumps of trees and patches of bare rock. Go across one at a time. Every member of the party should keep his eyes on the crosser; the last to go is in no less danger than the first.

If the crosser is on skis, he should undo the wrist loops of his ski poles and the safety straps of his skis and set his ski bindings for easy release. The snowshoer should undo the wrist strap of his ice axe or pole. The waiststrap of the pack, too, should be undone. Stiff encumbrances, tumbling with the victim in the snow, can drag him down. They also impede his freedom to use his arms—a very important thing. Make your shell of clothing as smooth and perfect as you can: zip zippers, button buttons, raise your parka hood, put on stocking cap and mittens.

One useful item in avalanche country is the *avalanche cord,* a 100-foot length of brightly-colored cord marked with arrows ($2 to $4). You attach one end—the end to which the arrows point—to your belt and trail the cord behind you. It will help companions recover you quickly if you are buried.

As you cross the danger area, watch the behavior of the snow. If you hear cracking and grumbling noises, or see cracks shooting out in front of your skis, you'll do well to retreat; these are signs of an imminent break. Most victims themselves trigger the avalanches that overwhelm them.

Avalanche survival

If you're caught in an avalanche, things will happen terribly fast. By all accounts it's a little like being caught in a flash flood, but a flood at the same time fluid and solid. Immediately shed your ski poles or ice axe, your pack, and your skis (there's not much you can do about snowshoes). Make the motions of a swimmer; try to keep on the surface of the tumbling snow, and to work over to one "bank" of the flow. If in spite of all this you feel yourself going under, cover your face with your arms to preserve a cavity of air. When you stop moving, make an attempt to dig yourself out before the snow hardens around you. (You may have to spit to make sure which way is up; some avalanche victims have lost their orientation so totally that they started by digging *down*.) Don't bother to shout; sound carries very poorly out of snow. If you can't dig, there's really nothing to be done but discipline yourself to calmness, and wait.

If you, the person spared, see a companion carried off in an avalanche, follow these steps.

1. Mark the point where you last saw the victim. Make a quick search down the apparent main line of the avalanche. Mark the location of any pieces of gear you find. Look carefully behind trees, on ledges and benches, and wherever any obstacle might have slowed or diverted the rushing snow.

2. Next comes the careful search. Probe systematically with skis, ski poles, ice axes, or (if by any chance you should have them) with special sectioned avalanche probes. Reexamine the likely "traps" where the victim might have been stopped; then spread out to cover the whole surface of the avalanche.

3. When you find the victim, you may have to give him artificial respiration. Get the snow out of his clothing and place him in a sleeping bag, head downhill. Treat, as needed, for shock and for hypothermia (see Chapters 25 and 27).

What about sending for help? *It is almost never worth the loss of time.* Half of all buried avalanche victims die within thirty minutes. Unless you're right next to a ski resort, every member of your party should stay and search. Keep searching for six to eight hours. While very few victims last beyond the second hour, there have been astonishing exceptions.

Navigation on snow

In some areas trails are as useful in winter as they are in summer. A trail may be the only tenable line through tangled woods or over a hazardous slope. Abandoned roads, healed over into simple paths, make especially good and obvious routes for snow travel in rugged country. Following a less pronounced trail can be difficult when the trace is under snow; you have to pay special attention to blazes and clipped branches, or to such signs as ducks or cairns, if they protrude above the cover.

Most of the time, though, trails simply cease to matter in the winter, except as landmarks, guides to where you are. The snow is a whole new country which you cross. One route through the trees may be as good as another. Navigation in winter is generally like cross-country navigation in summer but with special problems added.

Your views of distant landmarks will almost certainly disappear in any overcast. But much more serious are low, thick fog and the opaque misty snowstorms called "whiteouts." In a whiteout you see only a few yards. Shapes are strange, unrecognizable. You can lose all sense of place and direction. When you are thus blinded, it's terribly easy to go wrong; here as nowhere else the compass becomes your lifeline. You need to know, not only how to walk a compass course, but also how to plan a whole trek as a succession of compass lines, or azimuths as they are called—so many paces on azimuth A, so many paces on azimuth B. Keep close track of where you are on the map, so that you can plan a retreat by compass if whiteout settles in. Be sure you understand the tricks of navigation without good landmarks described in Chapter 16. Trails, even if you don't follow them, can be fine helps in navigation; you can use a line of trail blazes as a "destination line." In winter travel, as in cross-country hiking, no one can afford to be a passive follower; each person in a group must be aware.

Your detailed route over snow depends largely on the skis or snowshoes you are wearing. Skis and snowshoes, and different models of each, handle differently; some are

more, some less able to cross icy slopes, to float in deep,
soft powder, or to climb steep hills. Often the snowshoers
in a party will head directly up a soft slope, while skiers
will circle around, climbing in a series of switchbacks.

Camping in the snow

Let's be honest about it: no winter camp is entirely
without discomfort. The snow camp can be, on balance,
very pleasant or pretty miserable. It depends partly on
things you can't control (like the weather), but mostly it
depends on your gear, your skill, and your intelligence.

You generally have a wide choice of campsites in winter. You scarcely have to consider "low impact" when the
vulnerable earth is yards beneath your feet. It is polite,
though, not to set up your tent right beside the route down
which other travelers will come.

If you don't find a level place, you can make one in
deep snow with a little engineering. (The winter camp, of
course, *can* be engineered without harm. Build a whole
city, if you like—it will last, at latest, to the thaw.) Just
make sure that you are out from under dead limbs and
standing snags, and, of course, away from avalanche paths.

If there is water to be found near camp, count it as a
special luxury; you won't have to spend so much time and
fuel melting snow. You can lower water bottles to a stream,
rushing in a trench of snow, or perhaps carve steps down
to waterline. And if you dig a deep enough well, you can
get water from under the ice of any sizable lake.

But the first camp job is to pitch your tent. Without
taking off skis or snowshoes, stamp out a level site. To
anchor guylines in snow, you need special, broad, aluminum *snow stakes*, or you can use *deadmen*, small chunks of
dead wood which are stamped into the snow and buried.
Not even dead branches should be broken for deadmen,
however, in popular hiking areas, or anywhere near timberline. And if you use them, make one set last the whole
trip. Stakes and deadmen will quickly freeze into place,
and you may well have to dig and chop to free them when
you take the tent down.

You may or may not need to pitch a rainfly. If you are
in Yellowstone in February for instance, you can all but
count on cold, dry snow that will slide right off the per-

meable surface of the inner tent. But if you are in the Cascades or the Appalachians, you can expect a wetter, more clinging snow, and you'll need all the protection you can get. A fly does add some warmth. On long trips in foul weather, and especially if you are riding out a storm, you will be drier in a tent with a *frostliner,* a fitted sheetlike inner liner that catches and sheds the frost that forms perpetually on the inner surfaces of tents in winter.

If you have good weather and daylight, you can dig out a luxurious kitchen in the snow. Start with a natural depression, like a tree-well. Straighten the vertical wall, and then dig out a waist-high "counter" for your stove and cooking gear. But when conditions are less pleasant, hikers cook and eat lying down, setting up the stove just outside the door of a tent. In truly awful weather you may be forced to cook entirely inside, but watch out for any flareup when you prime your stove, and keep ventilation generous. Most summer-type stoves are somewhat balky in cold and wind. Larger stoves with hand-operated pumps work better; Optimus's optional add-on pump, sold for about $5, makes the various stoves in the Svea/Optimus line more useful in bitter weather.

Winter dinners tend to be simple. Nobody wants to deal with six-course menus in the cold. Except in the leisurely, fair-weather camp, the standard is the meaty one-pot meal, with hot drinks, possibly soup, and cold snacks on the side. (In winter as in summer, it's perfectly possible and even luxurious to forget cooking and eat a well-planned selection of cold food, but when you have to fire up the stove anyway, to melt snow for water, it's natural to cook as well.)

Melting water takes time, and it's tempting to stop after a quart or two. Don't. Make sure that each person is getting at least a full gallon of water, in food and drink, each day. As you melt snow, keep drinking; have more tea, more fruit juice, more chocolate. If you wake up with a violent thirst toward morning, it's a good sign that you've been shorting yourself.

Don't drink up the last of your old supply before you begin to melt more water. You need a few spoonfuls, at least, to moisten the bottom of the melting pot. Snow, especially dry, powdery snow, absorbs quite a bit of heat before it liquefies, and the metal of the pan may actually scorch before there's enough water to carry the heat away. (The old joke about "burning the snow" isn't just a joke.) Add small amounts of snow to your starter pool, then gradually more.

The ultimate luxury in winter is a warm, comfortable bed. Nights are long; you spend a lot of time there. If your sleeping bag isn't really intended for winter, you may wind up wearing most of your clothing to bed. Very wet clothes, though, will only chill you. It's particularly important to put on dry socks and, if you have them, insulated booties.

Certain objects need to be brought inside your sleeping bag at night: your boots (in a plastic bag, or in your sleeping bag's stuffbag—turned inside out); your flashlight or headlamp; and, if it's very cold, your camera, in several layers of plastic. If the temperature is much below freezing, water bottles will have to be brought inside or at the least tucked alongside your bag, away from the tent wall. Make sure the caps are on tight!

The battle against damp

Bitter-cold weather, even with wind, is not what the winter camper fears. Given the right gear, he will enjoy it. But when the sky closes in, the temperature rises, and a warm, sloppy snow begins falling, he curses. Most especially if you are using down gear, you will have to keep things dry, and that can be hard work when everything around you is wet.

Avoid bringing snow into your tent with you. Keep a whisk broom and a sponge just inside the tent door. Brush yourself off as you crawl in; take your boots off at the entrance and make sure the snow is out of the laces and the spaces between lugs.

Keep air flowing through the tent. Give the humid air inside every possible chance to escape. Be quick to mop up spills. If you can cook outside the tent door, you won't have the steam to contend with.

Don't take wet clothing to bed in an attempt to dry it. The moisture doesn't vanish; it just goes into the filler of your bag. Clothes hung from a line run along the peak of the tent, inside, may dry out at least partway. While it's unpleasant to put on wet and frozen clothes in the morning, it's not as unpleasant as a wet sleeping bag. Even if it's very cold, don't cover your nose and mouth with the bag; your breath shouldn't be trapped inside.

Precautions like these are always advisable. If you are depending on a down sleeping bag, they are absolutely vital.

Shelters made of snow

Though many never bother, every winter camper really ought to get some experience in building a shelter in the snow. These skills can be invaluable in an emergency, when there's no tent to be had, and a growing number of travelers use snow shelters all the time, saving a certain amount of weight. (Typical two-person winter tent: eight pounds; shovel and snow-saw for building a snow shelter: under two pounds.)

The simplest and quickest snow shelter is the trench. It's just what it sounds like, a moat, three or four feet deep, six or seven feet long, and wide enough for two or three sleepers (wider trenches are hard to cover). In the old days you would make a roof of interwoven conifer boughs. That won't do now, of course, unless a life is at stake; instead you use a tent fly, a tarp, or some such, laid on beams made of ski poles, axes, or whatever you have (down branches, should you find them, make good supports). For insulation, cover the roof with snow. Snowtrenches, in their simplicity, are perhaps the best of emergency winter shelters.

More elaborate is the snow cave. To build one, you need soft to medium snow—the kind that holds its shape when cut—and a good thick snowbank. Creekbanks are good places to find suitable drifts.

There are at least two ways of digging a snow cave. The traditional method is simple to describe but difficult to carry out. You burrow into the snowbank, making an entry tunnel. About four feet in, you angle the tunnel upwards; then excavate a chamber with its floor raised well above the tunnel so that warmth will be retained. The job takes three or four hours, even with a snow shovel, and the excavators get soaking wet.

There's a new, shortcut method, as easy to use as it is hard to describe. The trick, essentially, is to dig the snow-cave with one whole side open to the air, so that shoveling is easy; then you reclose this temporary gap with snow blocks, so that only an entry tunnel remains clear.

First, you dig an *entrance slot,* about eighteen inches wide and open to the sky. Push it about three feet into the snowbank, or until the snow is six feet deep. You will stand in this slot to work.

Second, you excavate a horizontal *shelf,* about four feet wide, at the end of the slot, as if you were putting a bar on a T. Make the floor of the shelf level with your belt; leave a ceiling of snow about eighteen inches above that. This is the beginning of the waisthigh platform which will be the floor of the cave itself.

Now, start expanding this shelf, extending it backward into the snow. Don't, however, make the initial open-air gap any bigger: just hollow out behind it, inwards, sideways, and upwards. Don't dig down—the floor should run back on a level.

When you've dug out all the snow you can get at from your first position, deepen the entry slot about twelve inches and push it another two feet into the snowbank. This extension of the slot will be a trench, cutting partway across the floor of the roofed chamber inside, and giving you room to stand up there.

Now finish out the cave. Make it as large as you like: a typical plan is more or less the shape and size of a tent, seven feet long, five feet wide, and three to four feet high. Make the ceiling a smoothly-rounded dome.

What you have now is a snow-cave with one side open to the air, a sort of cutaway model. It remains to close off the open side. You do this by cutting several big snow-blocks and placing them in the unwanted "window." One of these blocks will bridge your original slot, turning it into a short tunnel—your permanent entry. Fill in cracks and gaps with more snow.

Complex as it sounds, this method eliminates most of the misery of building a snow cave, and you don't get very wet (though it still does no harm to put on waterproofs). Practiced cave-makers can do the job this way in an hour or so.

After the shelter is essentially done—by whatever method—you "furnish" it. Cover the raised floor with a groundsheet, and cut niches and shelves for a candle, your

Snow cave construction

(Method worked out by Dick Mitchell)

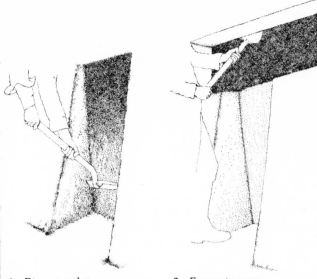

1. Dig entry slot

2. Excavate cave

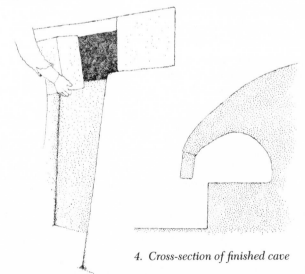

4. Cross-section of finished cave

3. Close off space above entry slot

stove, and odds and ends. Punch a ventilating shaft up through the high point of the dome and a second above the stove. Narrow to start with, these shafts will widen as heat rises through them.

An igloo is something like a snow cave above ground. To build one, you need snow firm enough to hold its shape in blocks cut with shovel (or shovel and saw). If loose snow is all you have, you can trample it down with skis or snow-

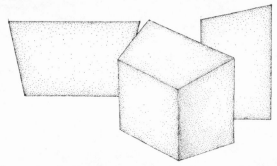

shoes, then let it set for twenty minutes or so. The bigger the blocks you work with, the faster the job gets done: eighteen inches by ten inches by fifteen inches is typical. Because you're building a dome, the blocks must be beveled, with top and end surfaces sloping inward.

To guide yourself, outline the base of the igloo (round or oval—an eight to ten foot diameter). Then choose the location of your entry. The best position is downhill and crosswise to the prevailing wind. Dig a trench from the center of your circle to the entry and several feet beyond. Remove the snow from this trench in usable blocks.

Trench dug, you begin laying blocks around the circle. (One of them will bridge the trench.) When you finish the first circuit, trim the first couple of blocks you placed to make a gradual ramp, and take the second course right on up over them, starting a spiral. Then just keep going.

Typically, one of the snow-masons works outside, cutting blocks, while the second stands inside to take them, place them, and finish the shaping. Five or six courses will be required. Because of the shape of the blocks, the walls will lean increasingly inward. If the blocks are regular enough and carefully beveled, they'll support themselves clear to the final large keystone block which closes the top.

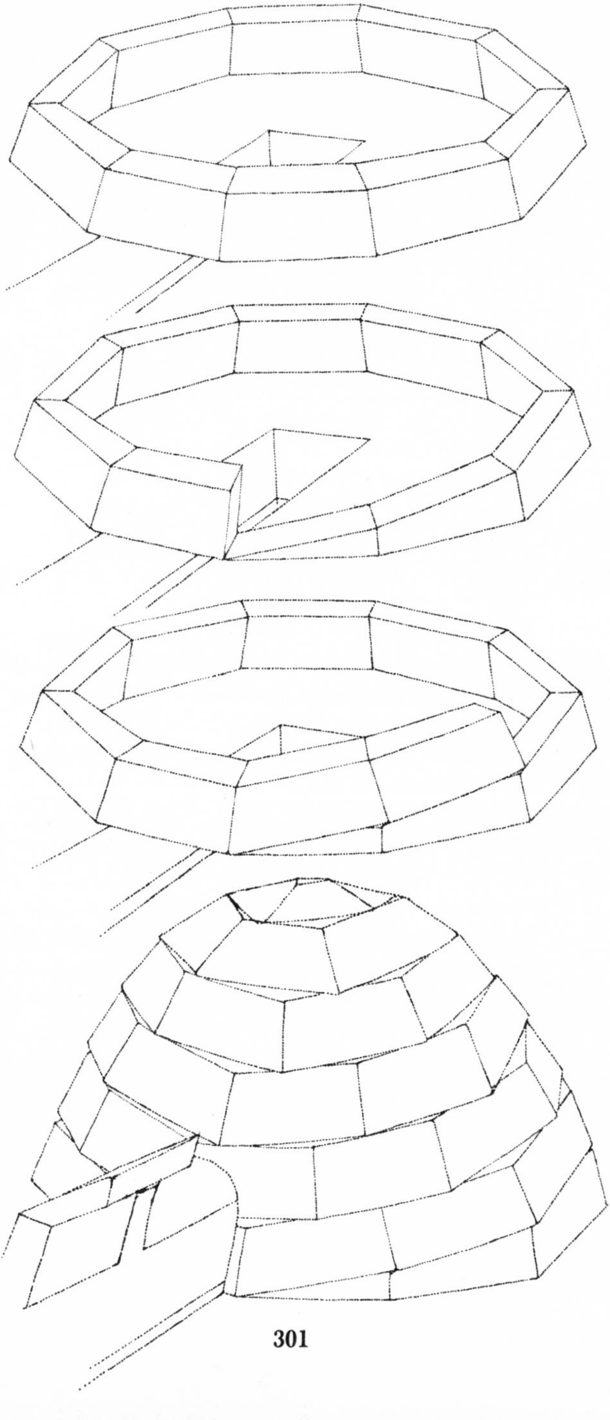

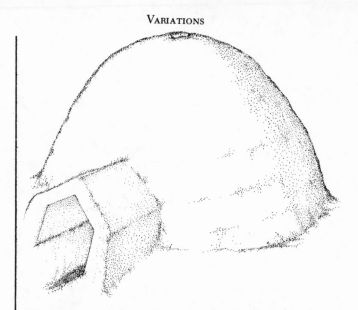

When it becomes convenient, cut an arched lintel into the block that spans the trench, making a door.

At this point you have your basic igloo. For extra protection you can add a raised roof of blocks over the trench outside the wall, making a covered entryway. Then coat the outside of the igloo with loose snow. You should be able to move inside, and out of the wind, in less than an hour. The structure will knit together quickly as it warms up inside. As with a snow cave, you finish the interior for convenience, punching or cutting a generous air vent at the peak.

Igloos and snow caves are quite astonishing places; they're dead silent, warm, comfortable, sheltered. No blizzard outside can touch you—can scarcely make itself heard. The snow admits daylight, a curious light, colorless, dim, yet very clear.

There are things to be aware of in any snow house. Just as in a tent, you have to make sure your ventilation is good. Don't block the air shafts or your entryway. See that the entry doesn't get sealed by drifted snow; a low, outlying shield-wall of two or three blocks may trap a drift where it does no harm. Then there's the moisture problem. When stoves are running, the snowy roof will drip. Since drops collect on projections, the smoother you've made the roof, the less problem there will be. Both caves and igloos are very strong, if their roofs are properly thick.

Skis and snowshoes

For the person who wants to take up winter back-packing (as opposed to unburdened cross-country skiing) the snowshoe is the simplest tool of travel. Snowshoes aren't hard to use, they are still relatively cheap, and, unlike skis, they are practical when you carry a frame pack.

As you gain experience, you may want to switch to skis, or at least to substitute skis part of the time. It depends partly on personal taste (how much does speed matter to you?) and partly on the kind of country you visit. In lands that are largely flat and rolling, or steep but not densely timbered, nothing moves like a pair of skis. Yet in rugged, timbered, tangled mountains such as the Appalachians, skis can be clumsy; the more maneuverable snowshoes may actually serve you better. In deep, fresh powder, too, skis may lose much of their advantage. Don't be over-awed by skiers who dismiss the snowshoe as a beginner's tool.

The snowshoe

The snowshoe is a piece of basketwork: webbing of rawhide, neoprene, or other materials, stretched tightly across a wooden or metal frame. Wearing snowshoes, you walk much as you would on bare ground without them. At first you will step on yourself a few times and take some comical falls, but the skill teaches itself.

Snowshoes come in many styles and designs. The smaller ones are mostly of the *bearpaw* design: typically eight to twelve inches wide and some thirty inches long, with a rounded toe, swept slightly upward, and a rounded tail. Bearpaw-like shoes that extend to a narrow point in the back (a more durable construction) are called *beaver-tails*. Then there's the so-called *Yukon* style, longer than others—some models as long as sixty inches—but narrow, with a sharply upswept toe for breaking trail in powder.

The bearpaw may be the most widely useful style. Bearpaws are good for working among trees and in brush, and for kicking steps up steep slopes. They are also easy to

303

strap onto the back of a pack when you don't need them. They edge pretty well on hillsides and grip well on hard crust. However, typical bearpaws, with rather small bearing surfaces, will sink deeply in powder under heavy loads. Beavertails are like bearpaws in many ways, though they track somewhat better because of the dragging "rudder" of the pointed heel.

Yukon snowshoes, the long ones, are harder to handle in closed-in places. They don't seem to climb hills quite so well (though the difference is small), nor are they easy to carry on a pack. In their place, though, they are unbeatable: in open country, over yards of soft powder snow, at the head of the line. Even breaking trail, and even with a 250-pound load of hiker and pack, they float high and clean in the snow.

Within the styles there's a great deal of variation. Some shoes are as wide as fourteen inches, but ten inches is about the widest most people find manageable. (Narrow shoes are much better for crossing steep slopes.) The weights of snowshoes vary widely, from less than three pounds to almost six pounds the pair. Since "a pound on the feet is like five on the back," there's an obvious advantage to lighter weight. Weight, however, generally goes with increased surface area, and a heavy (or heavily loaded) person needs a sizable bearing surface when he walks on

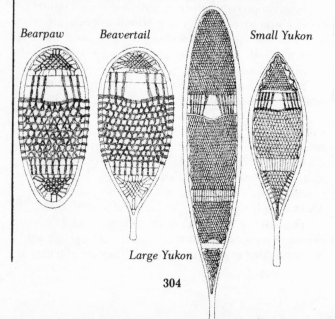

Bearpaw   *Beavertail*   *Small Yukon*

Large Yukon

304

powder. Also helpful in powder is a pronounced upturn in the toe of the shoe; the tip won't bury itself in the snow. But short, flat tips are better for kicking steps. You can't find one snowshoe for every purpose.

Construction. The traditional snowshoe is built of blond ashwood and stretched rawhide; it is probably the single most exquisite object used in wilderness camping. In recent years, though, other constructions have come to dominate the market. Cording now may be of nylon, neoprene, even metal, and frames are often metal. These alternates have different advantages; some are more durable than rawhide-and-ash. If you're determined to find the perfect shoe, the best plan, as always, is to rent various types. One material to avoid, though, is solid, molded plastic. One-piece plastic snowshoes aren't stout enough for backpacking.

Climbing gimmicks. When the snow is soft, you can climb at remarkable angles in snowshoes by stamping the shoes firmly into the slope. On a hard or icy slope, though, you'll slip. Some shoes come with built-in gripping devices, blades or rough surfaces mounted on the bottom to grip the snow. Similar gimmicks, called "snowshoe crampons," can be purchased separately ($6 to $15). They can also be made, much more cheaply, out of surplus U.S. Army crampon sets. Or you can simply shed the snowshoes when the snow gets hard and walk up in boots.

Snowshoe prices vary all the way from $20 to $90, with prices clustering around $50.

Boots and bindings

When you wear a snowshoe, your boot rests on webbing attached near the toe to a stout crossbar of some sort. With each step your heel rises clear off the snowshoe, and your toe dips into an opening in the basketwork, cutting briefly into the snow below. On some models this opening lies very far forward on the snowshoe; on others it is closer to the center. A forward opening is better for climbing hills, worse for descending, and worse for wading through powder.

There are many different rigs for binding the boot to the snowshoe. A few models have very secure bindings built into the shoe. Otherwise you purchase bindings separately ($7 to $15). If you are wearing a standard hard-leather hiking boot, and if you do *not* use snowshoe crampons for hill-climbing, the likeliest choice is the "H binding." The "H" has narrow straps which must be cinched up very tight (and thus should be worn over a hard boot). It does not cover the toe of the boot. Thus it allows the lugs of the boot-sole to cut into the snow with every step. Lacking snowshoe crampons, you need this extra traction.

If your boots are soft shoepacs, you need a binding that grips your foot more gently over a larger area. One such is the "Howe binding." It does cover the entire toe with a flap of material; thus you need snowshoe crampons for climbing steep slopes with this arrangement.

Most beginning snowshoers have at least some trouble with bindings. Different models have different weaknesses, but most of them seem to work their way loose in one fashion or another. All you can do is keep on working with the harness until, as it will, it stops misbehaving.

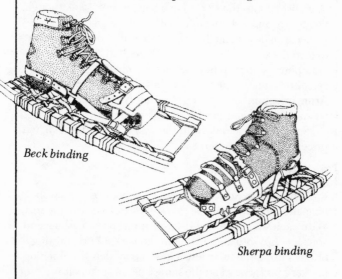

Beck binding

Sherpa binding

With a snowshoe you need support for your arms (it's easy to fall over without it). A ski pole will do in easy terrain. If you cross steep, icy snow on snowshoes, you definitely need, instead of a pole, a long-shafted ice axe fitted out with a detachable ski basket ($8 to $10).

Rawhide snowshoes must be coated, now and again,

with spar varnish or an equivalent (available at gear stores and nautical supply stores). If you travel mostly in deep powder, you may only need to recoat once a year, but trips on hard and abrasive snow, or on very wet snow, wear off the protective coating much more rapidly. Snowshoes of other construction may have to be coated with other materials, but some models require almost no maintenance at all.

Skis

Skis might seem to be simple objects. They are, after all, more or less of one shape with no free-form variations as there are with snowshoes. But in truth the world of skis is the more complex one, changing constantly, and with constant commercial fanfare.

Skis are built in a range of weights, from superlight "racing skis" used on packed, level courses up to heavy mountaineering skis and, heaviest of all, the conventional downhill ski models. For backpacking you need a ski of at least medium weight, neither too light nor too narrow, in the class often referred to as "general touring" models. About the lightest skis suitable for backpacking weigh four and a half pounds the pair and are not less than 52 millimeters wide under the foot. If you hope to do rugged backpacking, or to do much downhill-style skiing in the wilderness, chances are you will need skis a good deal heavier than this minimum.

Most wilderness skis used to be built, handsomely, of laminated wood. Many still are, but a new material, fiberglass, seems to be gaining the advantage. (Unfortunately, the flashy colors of downhill skis are being adopted, too.) Whole or partial metal edges, like those on downhill skis, are valuable to the skiing backpacker in hill country; they help in crossing icy slopes and making turns on downhill runs.

But the most important choice after weight is whether to wax or not to wax.

In skiing cross-country you fall into a steady, gliding gait called the *diagonal stride,* which looks (and sometimes feels) perfectly effortless. For this technique to work, your skis must grip the snow at certain moments and glide freely forward at others. Different models work this magic in different ways.

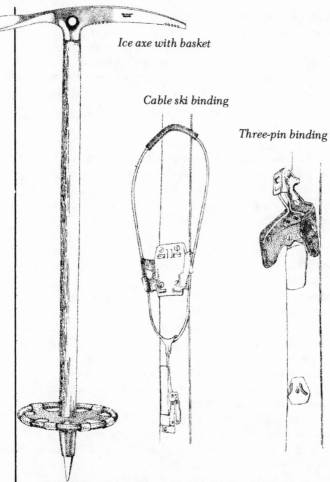

Ice axe with basket

Cable ski binding

Three-pin binding

Traditional skis have a smooth wood or plastic under-surface (or "base"). These surfaces you coat with a cun-ningly-formulated wax. When the ski is stationary, snow crystals press into this coating and grip the ski. When you push forward, the projecting granules melt and let the ski glide. When the stride is finished the surface refreezes and the bond is restored, giving you a firm base for the next for-ward push. One wax won't do for all conditions and types of snow, however. In fact, there are several dozen waxes for the most varied conditions, and you need five or six on almost any trip. Good waxers can do marvelous things with this selection, gliding up very substantial slopes with little trouble. (Recently, several companies have produced "broad-spectrum" waxes, supposedly good for wider ranges of snow conditions. Relying on these you would need to carry only two or three different containers. These new waxes seem to work reasonably well, especially on moderate terrain.)

To many people the skill of choosing and applying the right combination of waxes—a fascinating business—is the center of the skiing experience. And a perfectly waxed pair of skis is the perfect way to travel on snow. But there's a period of learning in which you may have trouble choosing the right goop, and even practiced waxers must stop and do the job anew several times a day, as conditions change. Also, there are accessories that have to be carried: scraper, cork, some wax-removing solvent and rags or a butane-fired torch and maybe some hand-cleaning lotion. Total cost of the kit can be as little as $12 or as much as $35, depending largely on whether or not you buy a $17 torch.

For the matter-of-fact, the lazy, and people who regard their skis as mere transportation, the industry has produced several different kinds of no-wax skis. These models have bases modified so that they can slide forward but not back-wards. Some do it with plastic fish-scales, some with little sloping steps, some with strips of synthetic hair (the hairs all pointing backwards). These no-wax skis never perform quite as well as perfectly-waxed conventional skis, but they do move. And because the no-wax skier has less stop-ping to do, he may after all get into camp about the same time as his friend with the wax-kit.

With a heavy pack on your back you can't expect to get the full joy of skiing *as skiing*. A laden skier still uses the diagonal stride, but it is a subdued, slower stride; at times he will simply trudge. A frame pack is awkward when you're on skis, and further hampers the free motion you want; soft packs are much more practical, especially when you pick up speed on downhill slopes.

Boots, bindings, and accessories

With skis as with snowshoes, the question of bindings is a separate and complex subject in itself. There are three current possibilities. First and simplest are the *three-pin*

Cross-country ski boots

bindings. These consist of three short pegs mounted on the ski, a toe clamp, and a heelplate. You need a special ski boot with three small pits in the sole, matching the pegs. To get into such a binding, you press the toe of the boot into position, fit the pegs to the holes, and close down a securing clamp. You can get into such a binding quickly and easily, and the foot has a lot of freedom to flex. How-ever, the special boot is thin, low-cut, and light; thus very cool. It's ideal when you're in motion, but it's not a good boot to wear when you're pitching a tent, digging a snow cave, or cooking a meal in an outside kitchen. Thus you will need to carry a pair of ordinary boots or soft shoepacs for wear around camp. (You can, however, find insulated *ski-overboots,* which, worn outside the ski boots them-selves, have holes for the pegs to penetrate. Heavy socks, worn *over* the boots, also help.)

While every combination is being tried these days, the three-pin/special boot arrangement is more popular among daytripping skiers than it is among committed, load-carrying winter backpackers.

Second there are the various *cable bindings*. These are like old-fashioned downhill ski bindings, except that the heel of the boot can be left free to lift. From a toe clamp a cable runs around the back of the boot, resting in the welt (joint between sole and upper). This harness will work with any ordinary boot that has a pronounced welt. Though experts can ski almost any slope with almost any arrange-ment, cable bindings give better control on downhill runs.

Finally, there are several newer types of bindings, all of which, like the cable, allow you to use your regular leather boots on your skis. These lack cables and usually give you safety releases at both toe and heel—pleasant insurance in case of a nasty fall.

You need ski poles, of course, of bamboo or aluminum (aluminum is somewhat stronger but still vulnerable to breakage). Short downhill ski poles won't serve very well. Cross-country poles are longer and have tips swept sharply back for poling in the diagonal stride. Get a shop's advice in picking the right length.

Ski prices vary prodigiously; most now run $50 to $100 in the types backpackers are most likely to use. The true cost to you, of course, includes essential accessories as well. Three-pin bindings cost around $10, but with them you must have special boots at $35 to $50. Cable bindings also start near $10, but the heavier and more elaborate ones may exceed $50, as do the new ski mountaineering bindings. On the other hand, no special boot is required. Bamboo poles sell for about $10, aluminum poles cost somewhat more. No matter how you choose these components, the total outlay for skis will certainly be over $100. Special package deals, frequently offered in stores, may save you a few dollars.

In buying skis and the paraphernalia that goes with them, be sure to get plenty of advice before you spend. Today's state-of-the-art will be out of date tomorrow. While all kinds of backpacking gear are evolving, no other object is changing quite so rapidly as the ski.

Repair kit

Skis and snowshoes—even the new models built of tough synthetic materials—do sometimes get broken on the trail. So you need a repair kit. For snowshoes, especially wood-and-rawhide types, you should have plenty of adhesive tape, wire, and cord. For skis, you need a handful of screws, a bit longer than the original ones, to use in case a binding pulls out of the ski. Add to that a screwdriver with the proper sort of blade (regular, Phillips head or pozidrive). A pair of pliers is likely to be useful. You should always carry a spare ski tip: an emergency substitute, metal or plastic, which you can slide over the stump of your ski if you should break the point (around $3). A ski without an upturned leading edge just won't travel. If you use cable bindings, it's wise to carry a spare cable (another $3).

24:
Hiking and Camping with Kids

THREE-QUARTERS OF ALL WILDERNESS TRAVELERS—so say the studies—are married, and most of them have children. (Interestingly enough, married couples who do *not* have children are underrepresented in the wild places.) For more and more people backpacking has become what, in earlier years, it was for few: a family sport. And more and more often, the kids, even the very young ones, are coming along.

It's perfectly practical to backpack, not only with middle-sized children, but also with babies. In fact, people who have done it—who have raised their children half in the wilderness, half at home—seem to find the process delightful.

True, you may not be able to go very far or very fast; true, you may have to carry a certain amount of extra gear and do a few extra chores on the trail and in camp. But a slower pace can be a pleasant change. And the child who has among his earliest memories the woods, the streams, the far-off mountains, may well have gained an advantage that will last him all his life. Even the youngest child, too, seems to value the sense of being part of the enterprise his parents are carrying out. Something important, pleasant, and adult is going on, and he is part of it, not excluded. To older children, the actual responsibilities of the trail—even scaled down to their size—are a firm link with the parents, and a kind of preview of growing up.

Parents who backpack with their children, and enjoy it greatly, warn that you mustn't expect the wrong things. A trip with kids is quite another experience than a trip with adults; it's another style of travel. It is—it has to be—more leisurely. You have to give yourself more leeway, more margin, than you would on an ordinary trip. It isn't just that children have shorter legs than their parents; they also have different attitudes. Up to a certain (and quite vari- able) age, kids just don't look at the wilderness the way their parents do. They enjoy it for different reasons, value different things.

Most kids are tougher, physically, than we give them credit for. They'll make out just as well in the wilderness as out of it—maybe better. They won't be as clean as they might be at home, but you quickly learn not to bother much about *that*. Otherwise, common sense is enough to keep them healthy. It's true, of course, that you're far away from the doctor. If you've put off learning first aid on your own behalf, it's a good idea to take it up when you begin traveling with children.

When you're starting a backpacker small, you want to start him slow—partly for his sake, even more for yours. All those special items, all those plans for traveling with children need shaking down. It's best to start with day- hikes, very short at first, then longer. Here's where you find out about temperaments and problems. How happy is the two-year-old in the baby-carrier? How much walking does the five-year-old feel up to? Before you move on to overnight camping, you may want to test your methods on safe ground. Try cooking meals on day-trips; try a risk-free "camp" on the back lawn or at an auto campground.

It's best to begin with trips in familiar territory. Make plans that don't put your group under pressure, and try excursions you'll enjoy whether or not you make it all the way in to such-and-such a peak or such-and-such a water- fall. Most people who hike with young children don't fight bad weather when it catches up with them; they just go home. Don't let a youngster get the feeling that misery and wilderness belong together. The great principle is simply to take things easy.

For backpacking purposes you can say that children come in three sizes. There are the very small ones, the *portable* ones, who aren't able to walk much yet. There are the older ones, five years and above, who (if not exactly hikers at first) are more or less *hikable*. And in between are the youngsters of two and three and four—kids who want to do things for themselves but can't very well. Backpacking parents find it most challenging to travel with children of this age. But they do it, and the young and the old seem both to enjoy it.

Portable kids

How soon do you start taking an infant into the wild country? As soon as you like. Some families backpack with babies only a month old; most wait till about six months. In some ways these youngest children are very easy to manage. You will, of course, be slowed down somewhat by feeding and diaper-changing, and most of the family's gear will have to ride in a single pack. On the other hand, the baby will go happily as fast and far as you feel able to take him.

Not all destinations are suitable, though. Because babies won't stand for wearing sunglasses, they can't very well be taken onto snowfields or to high elevations above timberline. (Sunburn, incidentally, can be quite serious in a very young child.) Also note that until the end of the first year of life, the body doesn't have the ability to adjust to altitude.

What do you carry your passenger in? The choice is wide. (The old leather papoose-carrier, lined with sphagnum moss as an absorbent diaper, was elegant, but the materials are hard to find these days.) You can buy various contraptions in backpacking stores and also in department stores and through mail-order catalogs. For very young children, you can use soft slings. These hold the baby against your chest, or on your back, or at either side, depending on the model. The Japanese use a simple wide band of cotton, swathed around carrier and child, called a *kumori*. Typical slings cost $5 to $6.

Most people start using a backpack-style carrier as soon as the child (at six months or so) can hold himself upright. These have seats of nylon or canvas, slung inside a metal frame. Some models have the rider facing forwards, some backwards. The forward-facing design—so most people find—is easier to carry. The child should be held quite close to the back. A carrier, like any other pack, should have padded hip and shoulder belts and room to strap a sleeping bag on below; the more incidental storage room there is, the better. A restraining belt, for safety, is also a good idea. Carriers run about $20.

Most babies, delighted by the motion, ride well in their perches. A familiar toy, tied to the frame, makes a good diversion. Not until a youngster has begun to walk does it occur to him that the ride is confining and dull.

When you have a passenger on your shoulders, you obviously have to watch out for low branches and avoid leaning over (especially if there's no restraining belt). Though some babies seem amazingly warm-blooded, you have to assume that the rider should be dressed more warmly than you are; he isn't doing any work. If it's at all chilly, you need to pay special attention to keeping him dry. Make sure also that eyes and skin are protected from bright sun.

The same baby clothes used at home will do on the trail. Elastic one-piece garments, lighter or heavier or doubled-up according to the season, are good. Whatever clothing you bring, carry a *lot* of changes: you can hardly bring too many. Raingear? Wilderness-quality waterproofs are hard to buy in small sizes. Some people make their own child-size parkas or cagoules. (There's a monstrous-looking, two-headed parka—one head for the porter, one for the baby in the carrier—that you sometimes see on the trails. It's very practical, reportedly.)

The various items you take to care for a baby don't add up to much, in bulk or in weight, yet it's easy to get off without some essential object. It's important, here again, to make a list.

In camp the very young child isn't likely to crawl or toddle clear away into the forest. But he's quite likely to head for the attractive flames of a fire (stove cooking is a little safer). Some people carry a tent (where they ordinarily would not) to use as a playpen. You can also make a pen out of a tarp, hung low at the middle, raised around the edges. Some parents even use a leash and a harness.

As for feeding, make it as simple as possible. Breast-feeding is of course the easiest all around. If you use bottles, make sure they're made of plastic, not of glass. Baby foods should be in cans, not jars. Quite a few freeze-dried foods are purée-like, anyway, and you can always mash solid food to make a usable paste. Kids who are just learning to feed themselves need a deep, generous cup with a big graspable handle: no Sierra Club cup, this. Also bring the usual plastic cereal bowl, bib, and washcloth. Whatever the child has been eating at home should be continued; this is no time to make big changes.

For diapering you have the choice of plain cloth diapers or "disposable" ones. Most people continue whatever routine they use at home. Do avoid, however, those disposable diapers that are made in one piece with an absorbent liner and plastic shell: this makes one of the most unredeemable pieces of garbage the human race has yet invented. Stools, of course, should be carefully buried, but not even the liners of disposable diapers should go into the cathole—they're durable. Not many people wash diapers on the trail. If you must, keep the operation well away from natural water, use a special basin, and pour the wash-water into a hole (fill it in later). Even if you do laundry, you'll of course need a strong, leak-proof plastic bag (or several, one inside the other) for carrying soiled diapers. Take plenty—more than you expect to need—along with all the incidentals.

At night a baby can be tucked (cautiously) into a parent's sleeping bag or wrapped up and placed in a stuff-sack—a comical but very sensible bed. A jacket makes a "sleeping bag" of about the right size. It's obviously better not to use down gear as bedding for young children—you'll no doubt have to launder it repeatedly, and down is damaged by washing. A plastic sheet will help.

In-between kids

It's not the infant—the object to be carried—that parents find most difficult to take to the wilderness with them.

Rather, it's the two-, three-, and four-year-old who is neither a mere passenger nor quite a self-operating human
being. Too heavy and restless to carry for long, he can't
walk fast or far. A four-mile day, with such a companion, is
about the most you can plan on. At this stage quite a few
people sign up with organized groups for aid and comfort
and take mostly easy trips to accessible basecamps.

In the earlier part of this period, youngsters are of
course still mastering the basic skills of being alive: learning to walk with confidence, to talk, to feed themselves, to
use the toilet. Wilderness toilet methods, in particular, can
sometimes upset a child who has just learned that virtue is
the porcelain flush toilet. Now he's asked to squat over a
hole in the ground. It may seem not only odd but also
downright sinful. Some youngsters have more than a little
trouble with this. It's up to the parent to stay with the
child and reassure him. Some people bring along light plastic toilet seats. (Make sure the child knows to wash his
hands in a basin, not in a lake or stream.)

This is the time when kids are exploring, handling
things around them, getting into things. There are plenty
of dangerous objects around a camp that have to be
watched. But there's also a lot of gear, soft, harmless, and
fascinating, for a child to play with.

Clothing gets simpler at this stage. You still need generous spares but not quite so many. For sleeping some people
give their middle-sized kids adult bags and let them floun-
der; there are also the short "bivouac sacks" used by climbers in combination with thick jackets. Polyester bags are
best, especially for the occasional bedwetter. Though kids
need some insulation under them, they're generally happy
without the soft padding that many adults require.

Hikable kids

Once youngsters are able to walk at a fair clip, the
problems change; some of them disappear. Older kids will
wear what anybody wears on the trail, with a few
differences. Boots, for instance. There just aren't any real
backpacking boots in children's sizes. On easy trails in
summer, high-topped tennis shoes are fine. Inexpensive
work boots also do well. Few families are large enough
these days for much "handing down" of wilderness gear,

but sometimes several families can get together in a sort of pool. Then there are the invaluable thrift shops.

Most kids seem to enjoy carrying packs from an early age. The first "load" may be no load at all, or a favorite toy. Use a daypack or a summit pack with shortened straps. A large daypack, with sleeping bag tied on the outside, can hold a considerable amount of light gear. Kids of about nine and older have no trouble with a full load—that is, a load proportional to their weight; a small, cheap frame pack may begin to make sense at about this age.

Even after a child can walk pretty well, he may think of it as a chore. It takes some encouragement to keep a young hiker going. Though your range will be longer now, you still don't want to be in the position of *having* to get to a particular, distant place. You'll need to take frequent breaks to rest, to eat, to play a game, to look at something entertaining like a stream. It can be fun to look things up in guides to flowers, trees, rocks, birds—if you aren't too high-handedly "educational" about it. Some favorite playthings should be there to fall back on.

In matters of safety your judgment will have to substitute for the youngster's—and that can take a good deal of your time. Give him a whistle, pinned to his shirt. (You'll have to convince him not to blow it for the fun of it.) Keep the younger children in sight and the middling ones within earshot. Older kids may want to run ahead, but have them wait at a given point (a trail junction, the foot of a slope, whatever). This is not, for that matter, a bad idea among adults.

Tell them what to do if they lose you. The rule: sit down, blow the whistle a lot, and stay put. Talk to them also about the possible hazards of the land: snakes, bears, poison oak or ivy or whatever, falling rocks, rapid currents. It can be hard to do this without making the woods sound forbidding, but it's not a step to be skipped.

Discourage kids from eating while they walk. (Some of them can't hike and chew gum at the same time, and there's a risk of getting a food fragment stuck in a windpipe.) You'll have warned them, of course, against munching the unidentified leaf or berry; still, a handbook on poisonous plants is one good item to have along.

In general, watch out for problems children may be

having. Some, as you might expect, complain very readily; others, surprisingly, do not. Check now and again for developing blisters. You need to make sure that kids stay comfortably warm or cool; watch for signs of hypothermia, heat exhaustion, and the like (see Chaper 27). Be alert also for altitude sickness; it isn't always harmless. Fortunately even the relatively stoic kids don't push themselves so dangerously far as adults may sometimes do.

When you get to camp, check the site for its particular problems—a steep drop, a rotten snag—and point them out. Experienced parents set limits: kids don't go beyond that creek, that rock, that stand of firs. With especially adventurous youngsters, one adult may have to spend most of his time keeping watch.

Any animals you encounter will be fascinating to the young. Teach the kids to understand them, to like them, and to respect them. But be sure to tell kids not to feed them, not to get too close. Animals that seem oddly unafraid may have something wrong with them. *Hands off the cute and furry.*

Many or most kids like to do small chores at camp. This is fine, of course, and should be encouraged. (With the younger ones, it won't speed the chores up any: contrariwise.) Wood gathering is a pleasant assignment, and so is help with tent pitching. If the weather permits, they will probably want to lay out their own bedsites. (Older kids get a lot of pleasure out of a tent of their own.) Then there's help with the cooking—safest are those jobs, like mixing a cold water pudding, that don't get the small fry too close to fire or stove. (Be sure to tie back long hair when there's fire around.)

There's nothing special about backpacking food for these relatively grown-up children. If anything, the food you take on a trip with youngsters should be even simpler, even easier to prepare. (There is much to be said for the ease of stove cooking here.) Some foods—desserts, of course, and individually-packaged hot-cereal breakfasts, and such—have entertainment value. Happily, the problem of the fussy eater is likely to solve itself on the trail.

Low impact: entertainment versus wilderness?

Though kids may enjoy a trip immensely, they aren't at

first likely to enjoy it for "adult" reasons. They are more likely than adults to want to return to familiar ground. And when they're in a wild place, they look for the same sorts of entertainments they would find at home: things to *do*. Toys, cards, and games are valuable, especially for rainy days.

Since nothing can fail to be new to them, babies just coming alive to their surroundings are as fascinated by one place as by another. Older kids want places they can play in. Above all they like *water:* a stream, a pond, an ocean shore, mud or—best of all—snow. They tend to be unimpressed by the subtle detail of the forest. The appreciation of wilderness *as wilderness* seems to come later in life.

This can lead to certain problems, for some of the things that kids find most entertaining are also hard on the wilderness they play in.

Kids (and boys especially—by nature? by social example?) are *engineers*. The first thing they want to do when they find a stream is build a dam across it; the first thing they want to do with dirt is turn it into miniature roads, walls, and earthworks. Even when no special project is underway, children, moving around as much as they do, can accomplish much more than their share of meadow-trampling and path-beating. This makes it all the more important, when you have youngsters in your party, to select a resilient site. And some might say there is legitimate argument for *not* taking youngsters into the wild places.

And yet there is every advantage to doing so. The taste for wilderness is best learned early, and so are the habits that protect the land. Though it may not come easily, it's never too soon to start teaching kids those wilderness manners that consist partly of courtesy, partly of safety, and partly of concern for the fabric of the country. During the day's hike, try to persuade kids not to trample down trail edges, cut across switchbacks, knock rocks down the slope, and not to collect plants at random. In camp try to steer the games in harmless directions. Low impact can be taught as a kind of game or entertaining drama. Even adults find it sometimes useful to think of it that way, and kids have the ability to throw themselves into a fantasy without irony. *(The bad guys are after me. Did I leave any marks they can track me down by?*) At any rate it's worth a try. Think of it as an investment. You're training tomorrow's wilderness user to go gently in the fragile wild places.

The change

After all this there comes a time—a different time, for different youngsters—when the young person begins to regard the wilderness somewhat as the adult regards it. Reports vary, but clearly many children come to this change of attitude as early as eight or nine. Wilderness travel is, after all, more play than work, for anyone; the gap between child and adult is not so great here as it would be, for instance, on a visit to the office where a parent works.

Somewhere along the line, the youngster starts to see the land as a place to adventure in, to admire and value for its own shape, its own interest. At this point he has already begun to be a "real" backpacker, and this is the time that backpacking parents especially look forward to. At this stage some parents (fathers especially) can't resist forcing the kids to walk farther, carry more, and achieve more than they may really enjoy. This is a mistake that can just possibly spoil things. But most kids who discover for themselves the pleasure of the wilderness seem to be addicts for life.

A year or two later the situation changes again, and the kid, long-legged and energetic, will be waiting constantly for *you.*

Trouble and How to Deal With It

It must be poor life that achieves freedom from fear.

—Aldo Leopold

But it is a characteristic of wisdom not to do desperate things.

—Henry David Thoreau

25:
Trouble!

NOBODY LIKES TO THINK ABOUT TROUBLE. Still less does anyone like to think about trouble in the wilderness. The thought throws a shadow on the pleasant landscape of memory and anticipation that is "wilderness" in every hiker's mind. But there is a thing that, like it or not, you can very nearly count on: if you spend enough time in the wild places, you will, sooner or later, have some part in dealing with a critical emergency—someone else's or your own.

Make no mistake: the wilderness (and especially the winter wilderness) is full of danger. Granted, the risks, when you compare them with the hazards of driving a car or running a power lawnmower, don't look very large. But wilderness risks, because less familiar, are at first more daunting.

The way to stay out of trouble is to think in terms of trouble. This doesn't mean a hypochondria, a fretfulness, or even a conservative unwillingness to take *considered* risks (that's up to you). What it does mean is awareness. Don't go out underequipped. Don't go out underinformed. On the trail keep an eye on the world around you and on yourself.

Look for certain objective outside hazards: the approaching thunderstorm, the loose rock ready to fall on companions below, the hazardous ford, the rotten snag. Some of these you will avoid, others you'll have to confront and deal with. Either way, the great virtue is simply to know what you're about. Most accidents seem to happen to people who take risks *without knowing it,* casually, carelessly, unprepared.

Watch also for physical problems in yourself, or in your companions, that could become serious if not attended to. Deal with nuisances promptly, before they become more than nuisances. A cold, drenching rain, for instance, is only an annoyance—but if you don't deal with it properly, it can lead to a life-endangering chill.

Fast trouble, slow trouble

When we think of trouble in the wilderness, we think most often of the swift, the sharp, the instantaneous blow: the avalanche, the snakebite, the falling stone, the lightning flash. And all these dangers are real.

But there is a second kind of trouble, less dramatic than the first but deadlier. This we might call "slow trouble." It doesn't happen all at once; instead, it sneaks up on you, insidious. Most often it comes with bad weather and with weariness. Altitude sickness can add to it; so can unrecognized hunger; so can unrecognized thirst. Slow trouble tends to build up out of many small problems, many small errors. And it would be inaccurate to say that the trouble finally "strikes"; rather, there comes a moment at which, with a sharp jolt of fear, you recognize the trouble for what it is.

If there is one rule for dealing with slow trouble, it is this: *catch it early.* When someone's physical condition begins to break down, or a party's morale, it is time to turn back or make an early camp. Don't try to bull it through. If your companions seem ready to tough it out, don't be reluctant to protest; they may be terribly wrong.

Few small groups ever select a leader. It goes against the informality they want. And often two or three competent friends can work together by consensus. But if there is neither a formal leader nor a lively "steering committee," a bad situation is only likely to get worse.

Obviously, there's no rule that says you can't have both "slow" trouble and "fast" trouble at once. In fact, it very often works that way. A miserable, exhausted hiker doesn't think as well as a comfortable one. Many short, sharp accidents are the result of errors made by fumbling hands and fumbling minds.

First aid

Ideally, at least one person in a party should have first aid training. In fact, *every* wilderness hiker would do well to get some, and climbers and long-distance trekkers need more medical knowledge than typical first aid courses provide. However, there is a fair amount that the unpracticed first-aider can safely do. And when there's no "expert" within three days and fifty miles, you have to work with what you have and what you know.

One of the most important items in the pack is a booklet setting out, precisely and in order, the actions to be taken when you have a seriously ill or injured person on your hands. Several guides are set up in this idiot-proof fashion. One of the best is Fred T. Darvill's *Mountaineering Medicine*, a $1 pamphlet available from the Skagit Mountain Rescue Unit (see *Resources*) and at gear stores.

First aid instructions usually emphasize the treatment of dramatic injuries: wounds, broken arms and legs, and so on. They show you how to respond to sudden accident. Important though that knowledge is, it's well to remember that many wilderness illnesses are not of that sort at all. Such slow-developing yet life-endangering problems as hypothermia, heat stroke, and pulmonary edema are discussed in Chapter 27.

If the emergency is fairly minor—and most are—you will have time to consider, to consult the manual, to talk things over with the cooperative victim. It is the major injury, or the physical collapse, that is most frightening. Such cases are rare in the extreme but so serious that it pays to think about them in advance.

Details vary, but in general there are three steps in dealing with a major wilderness injury or illness.

First, you *save life*. Some problems are so dangerous that action must be almost instantaneous.

Second, you *stabilize things*. Chances are you won't be

able to treat a major injury in any fundamental way; all
you can do is make the patient as safe and comfortable as
possible and follow, with caution, the instructions in your
manual.

Third, you *get the victim home.* Sometimes an injured
person can get out under his own power, slowly, and with
help. When he can't, you'll have to send for outside aid, or,
in some cases, carry him out yourself.

The notes that follow here are not meant to substitute
for a first aid manual; still less for actual training. I've tried
to select, from the long list of things the hiker needs to
know a few that seem absolutely basic. Please do consider
learning more. An eight-hour multimedia first aid course is
yours for the taking, at minimal cost, from Red Cross
chapters.

The first stage: saving life

As a rule, you examine the victim where you find him.
You don't try to move him. (There are exceptions: an
immediate danger from falling rock or avalanche, for
instance.) You check him immediately for two problems
that mean instant crisis. *Is he losing large amounts of
blood? Has he stopped breathing?*

Bleeding. A person can bleed to death in a minute or
two. And yet, in almost every case, you can stop dangerous
bleeding simply by pressing on the wound with a cloth or
(if need be) with your bare hand. Ten minutes of firm pressure should do it. If the wound is on an arm or a leg, it also
helps to lift the limb above the level of the heart. Never
remove a bloodsoaked cloth; make it the basis of the dress-
ing you later apply.

Breathing. Make sure the victim is not breathing. Then
lay him on his back. Clean out anything (like snow or
vomit) that you find in his mouth. Place one hand under
the back of the neck to tilt the head back sharply—this
keeps the tongue from blocking the airway from the
mouth to the lungs. Then begin the often-pictured technique of mouth-to-mouth artificial respiration, by far the
best we have. Place your free hand on the victim's forehead and close his nostrils with finger and thumb. Seal his
mouth with your own, and begin. Start with four quick,
forceful puffs: this may shock his lungs back into action. If

Giving artificial respiration

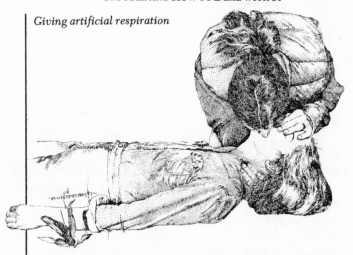

not, keep going, breathing deeply into the victim's mouth about once every five seconds. Remove your mouth each time to let him exhale.

Note this, however: neck injury is likely in any accident. If you even suspect such a problem, don't press up under the back of his neck. Rather, place your hands along the side of the lower jaw and draw it forward, closing the nose with your two thumbs. (This jutting of the jaw may help in any case where the airway remains blocked by the tongue.)

What if the heart has stopped beating? In that case, the chance of saving the victim of a wilderness accident is small. There is a technique, though, which sometimes succeeds. It combines artificial respiration with an artificial "heartbeat," supplied by pressure on the breastbone, and is known as cardio-pulmonary resuscitation (CPR). This complex maneuver is not usually taught in basic first aid courses; careful training is required to pull it off.

Three other problems can be listed with the instant emergencies. One is *poisoning.* No matter what was swallowed, the first step is to have the victim swallow water to dilute the substance. The second step is usually to induce vomiting. (Neither of these can be done, however, if the victim is unconscious, or if he is having convulsions.) For certain poisons—petroleum products (stove fuel!), strong acids, and strong alkalis—you do *not* induce vomiting.

No less perilous are *heat stroke* and *hypothermia.* In heat stroke the body loses its ability to cool itself and runs a deadly fever; in hypothermia, the body can't keep warm and chills toward the point of death. A person far along in either condition has little time to live. Each requires the obvious treatment—you cool the victim in one case, warm him in the other. For more on these problems, see Chapter 27.

The second stage: stabilizing

When the instant emergency is over, the next danger is commonly *shock.* Shock is a collapse of the circulation of the blood. It can occur with any accident, and is often a sole cause of death. Thirst and sharp anxiety are the first symptoms. The skin will grow pale and cold. The heartbeat will be quick but weak; breathing will be abnormal. The victim may get dizzy or black out. In the last stage of severe shock, blood pressure drops toward zero.

Treat for shock whether or not it has yet appeared. Lay the victim flat on his back. Unless he has severe injury to the head or torso, raise his legs. Loosen constricting clothes. Keep him dry. His body will have lost much of its power to maintain its temperature; depending on the weather, you must keep him either warm or cool. If he's aware, be certain to reassure him, to listen to him, to satisfy his requests where you can. If he's awake and does not seem to have major injuries of torso or head, give him sips of a weak solution of salt or salt and soda. Don't give fluids if he's vomiting or suffering convulsions.

If you have an unconscious victim, you must watch him carefully to make sure that the passage of air to his lungs remains open. Usually you can turn his head to one side. If he vomits or drools, or bleeds from facial injuries, be sure that none of the material accumulates in his mouth. Never try to get fluids into an unconscious victim.

Along with treatment for shock, do a second, more thorough examination. Look, touch, and listen. Get all the information you can from the victim. Try to find everything: wounds, fractures, burns, dislocations, frostbite.

Then decide, with deliberation, what happens next. That may be nothing more than signaling or sending companions for aid. Or you may need to apply whatever treatments you are fairly sure of, guided by common sense, a manual, and whatever training you've had. (The idea is not to "fix the victim up," but merely to prevent further complications. Don't do a thing unless you can tell yourself *why* you are doing it.) Do take notes on the victim's condition—even a cursory "medical history" may be of value later. And don't stop paying attention to him after the first crisis passes.

In the excitement, don't forget the welfare of the rest of your party. Among other things, it's often important to set up a safe and comfortable camp.

Third stage: getting out

In few of our wilderness areas is there much difficulty about swift rescue, at least in summer, and at least for hikers on busy trails. If the victim can't move under his own power, the problem is simply to attract the attention of rescuers, or of other hikers who can send for them. If there are several healthy people in your party, send one (or better, two) for help. Beyond that, the smoke of a fire is most likely to attract the notice of authorities. Be sure the party you send out knows how to describe your whereabouts, and what signal you plan to use to draw attention.

How do you decide if an injured person can walk out? It can be hard. On the one hand, you don't want to risk further injury. On the other hand, many accident victims *can* make it out, slowly and with help. Helicopter rescues are damnably expensive. (Who pays? Policies vary. In some cases the victim and his companions must pick up the tab themselves. If not, the public pays. Such a rescue should not be summoned lightly.)

One of the commonest injuries is a strained or sprained ankle. Some seemingly serious sprains will improve fairly quickly to the point where you can walk out with the help of an elastic bandage, leaning perhaps on a friend. In general, the pain you feel when you put some weight on the ankle tells you whether you're mobile or not.

If you travel away from the trails, or if you visit more remote areas in winter, it is a good idea to learn some rescue techniques yourself: how to make a litter, how to splint major body injuries, and so forth. These are set out in books on first aid, rescue and mountaineering medicine.

26:
Problem Animals and Plants

THE ANIMALS OF THE WOODS and the mountains are one of the things you come for. The word "wilderness," in fact, comes from roots meaning "the place of the wild beasts." Still, animals (and some plants as well) can make problems for the hiker. Seldom are these problems more than nuisances—the bugs have probably caused many times as much misery as the snakes and the bears combined.

Mosquitoes and flies

Mosquitoes lay eggs in shallow water or damp soil and hatch when days are warm and moist. In the mountains of the Southwest, where the soil is dry by August, they vanish early. Elsewhere, and especially in wet, temperate lowlands, mosquitoes may swarm much longer. Of various repellents, the best contain the chemical N, N, diethyl-meta-toluamide. In some months and in some regions, you may want not only repellent but also a headnet for walking. Netted tents and windy campsites away from water help on warm nights. Elsewhere in the world, mosquitoes are important carriers of malaria and other diseases, but this is no longer much of a problem in the United States.

Then there are the various stinging or biting flies, a whole tribe of flies. *No-see-ums* ("biting midges," "punkies"), found in low-lying areas over most of the country, are so tiny that they vanish in most lighting and can pass through netting. The *blackfly*, famous in the north woods, is found more widely under other names. The *deer fly*, medium-sized like the blackfly, has a similarly nasty sting. There are others: horseflies, elk flies, even a type known as "green-headed monsters." The standard repellents work against some, but not all, of these species.

Ordinary, non-biting flies can be a problem, too, especially in a camp with a latrine. Keep waste in the latrine well covered and keep food under cover as well.

Around marshes and lakes in low-lying regions, gnats can be an annoyance. The chigger, found in the eastern states, lives in grass; digging into your skin, it can cause an infuriating itch.

Ticks

These unpleasant creatures are bloodsuckers. Up to a quarter inch long and dark-colored, they are most numerous in the moist springtime of woodlands that dry out later in the year; in wet-summer regions they are a lesser problem for a longer time. Ticks climb onto you from foliage close to the ground. After riding on you for some time, they find bare skin and attach themselves painlessly. Repellents, at wrists, waist and ankles, help to discourage them. So do gaiters.

Once the tick is well attached, it's hard to get rid of. You can try packing oil or grease around it, so that its supply of air is cut off, dabbing it with repellent or white gas, or holding the glowing end of an extinguished match next to the creature. If it doesn't back out (and it may not) you will have to draw it out with tweezers. Grasp it as far toward the buried head as you can. Pull gently (some advise you to twist slowly; this may encourage the tick to let go). Don't press or crush—you don't want to force the tick's stomach contents back into your bloodstream. Do your best to extract the head and mouth parts. Wash the puncture with soap and water and put a Band-Aid on it.

If you're bushwhacking, you can head the creatures off

by examining your own and others' clothes every now and then. On a long bushwhack, hikers strip before bed and check each other for ticks. Parents should keep a close eye on children, especially very young children, for whom a tick bite can be somewhat more serious.

Unpleasant as they are, tick bites aren't generally dangerous. They can, in some places, transmit the disease called Rocky Mountain Spotted Fever (which, despite its name, occurs most often in North Carolina). Though this fever, untreated, can be deadly, antibiotics now control it easily.

Bees, wasps, and yellowjackets

Bee stings, relatively harmless to most of us, are very dangerous to some. Bees and wasps and yellowjackets cause several times the number of deaths each year that snakes do. If you have an allergy to stings, you probably know it; if you even suspect it, be sure to get a doctor's advice on how to deal with it. Desensitization is possible for some people; the injection of adrenalin is an often recommended emergency treatment.

If there is an allergic reaction, it will be unmistakable. In a few minutes the person will feel faint and giddy. His skin will be cool and moist. In severe cases the reaction will resemble an insanely exaggerated attack of hay fever. The tissues of the throat may swell so much that breathing is cut off. There is little the first-aider can do in such a case. Anyone with the allergy should carry a kit and be prepared to give himself the life-saving injection.

If you're stung by a bee, don't pull the stinger out with tweezers or your fingernails. The venom sacks cling to the stinger, and pressure forces more of the poison into the skin. Instead, *scrape* the stinger off with the blade of a knife.

Spiders

There's just one American poisonous spider worth mentioning: the black widow. There are several varieties in the United States. The familiar one, glossy-black and marble-sized has a red hourglass on the belly. But there is reportedly a northern type, which often has a broken or unclear hourglass, and a less venomous "brown widow" in Florida.

333

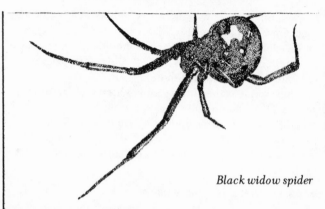

Black widow spider

One subspecies or another is found in every state south of Canada. You are most likely to find these spiders in woodpiles and in old buildings like outhouses.

Many people who are bitten by black widows have no greater problem than swelling or redness at the bite. Others suffer abdominal cramps. There may be some degree of paralysis, temporary but alarming, together with symptoms of shock. In about one case out of twenty there is danger of death; most victims are very old or very young.

Tarantulas, those big, elegant creatures furred like cats, have an insignificant sting. Infection of the bite is the one thing to be concerned about.

Scorpions and centipedes

Scorpions are eight-legged creatures, spider relatives, and sting with their tails. There are various species in the United States; most are found in the southwestern deserts,

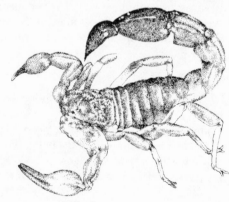

Scorpion

but they also are found as far north as Oregon and Montana. All are at least mildly venomous. Two species, found only in Arizona, can kill. The animal hunts at night. It's a good idea in any region to shake out your clothes and boots in the morning, though you seldom find anything inside them. In the daytime be careful when digging in sand or lifting rocks and logs. Though some scorpions are as long as eight inches, the dangerous ones are less than half that length; they're colored yellow to yellow-green. Scorpion venom attacks the nerves; when it kills, it is through paralysis of the lungs. Though cold packs are sometimes recommended, there's actually nothing you can do for a scorpion bite but wait it out.

Centipedes—many species—live under rocks and down wood. Some have a pretty good sting, though not many cases are at all serious. The harmless millipedes, sometimes confused with centipedes, have two pairs of legs growing from each body joint—the centipedes, only one.

The Gila monster

The Gila monster, found in the Southwest, is an almost harmless creature with a bad reputation. Though the bite can certainly be dangerous, the monster is not in the least inclined to attack, and almost every bite on record took place when somebody picked up a captive specimen. Incidentally, the Gila monster is an endangered species and has full protection. For its sake and yours, the rule is: leave it alone.

Gila monster

Snakes

We have four kinds of poisonous snakes in this country. Most important by far are the *rattlesnakes,* about thirty species, found somewhere in each of the forty-eight states, but there are other types: the *copperhead* in the East; the

335

cottonmouth or water moccasin in the southeastern swamps; and the *coral snake.*

Rattlesnakes, copperheads, and cottonmouths are all pit vipers. All have a thick, powerful body, a narrow neck, and, swelling from it, a large, definitely diamond-shaped head. The pit vipers inject through fangs a venom which attacks via the bloodstream.

The markings of rattlesnakes vary, but the rattles, at the end of the tail, are normally identification enough. Rat-

Diamondback rattlesnake

tlers seldom grow longer than five feet. The snakes thin out above 7,000 feet in the warm Southwest and aren't found much above 3,000 feet in areas near the Canadian border. In wet, cool regions, they prefer the drier sides of ridges, especially southern exposures.

The copperhead is found widely through the East as far north as New York State. It has, indeed, a copper-colored head, and hourglass markings along its body. The cottonmouth or water moccasin lives in wetlands from Vir-

Copperhead

ginia south, and west to central Texas. It is a thick, dark snake, up to six feet long, without obvious markings. Hikers aren't likely to see it, but waders and canoeists must be aware of it.

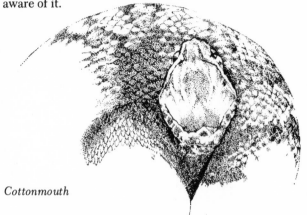

Cottonmouth

Alone of the venomous American snakes, the coral snake is not a pit viper. The snake is rather small, two to four feet long, and thin of body; it lacks the diamond head and secretes a poison which attacks the nerves. Coral snakes are handsomely marked with rings of yellow, black, and red. To distinguish a coral snake from other, harmless snakes that have red bands, remember that only coral

Coral snake

snakes have red rings adjoining yellow:
> *Red and yellow, kill a fellow;*
> *Red and black, scratch its back.*

Coral snakes in several species are found across the southern United States from the Carolinas to Arizona.

Now: how worried should you be about snakebite? Estimates vary, but it appears that about 1000 people

337

are bitten by poisonous snakes each year. Not very many of these victims are hikers, by the way. About two victims in one hundred die. While healthy adults are unlikely to die from snakebite, there are quite a few cases of permanent injury to a bitten hand or foot.

The risk, then, is not quite negligible. But it is certainly small. It is perfectly possible to blunder around the woods for years—even in good snake country—and never encounter a dangerous species at all.

Avoiding snakebite

Too much, proportionately, has been written about treating snakebite; too little has been said about the simple means of avoiding it. Different species vary in their readiness to strike, but none are out to get you. Snakes don't lie in ambush; they don't crawl into your sleeping bag. Threatened, they respond. You want to make sure that you aren't seen as a threat.

Snakes, cold-blooded animals, are active only when it is pleasantly warm. In some regions and seasons days are too hot for them, and they do their hunting at night. If only the morning and evening hours are temperate, snakes will be moving then. Torpid snakes, however, will still strike if stepped on.

Remember these simple precautions:

First, wear long pants and high-topped boots in snake country—and especially when you leave the trail. The feet and legs are most likely to be struck.

Second, make sure you can see where you're putting your feet and hands. Be especially careful in rock scrambling. Never thrust a hand over an unseen edge to grope for a hold.

Third, if you hear a snake rattling, stop dead still until you see where it is; then move away. Meanwhile, the snake will almost certainly be moving away from *you*.

Fourth, never pick up an unidentified snake. A large number of bites result from this.

Treating snakebite

Should you carry a snakebite kit? The experts are much divided on this question. Some feel that the risk is too slight to justify the expense. Some further argue that the use of a kit rarely helps much; and they point out that a kit, in unskilled hands, can do more harm than the bite itself.

But other voices, still in the majority, urge that you carry a kit and know how to use it—especially in known snake country, and in cross-country travel.

Snake bite kits—there are various brands—contain a small scalpel, a couple of suction cups, and a constricting band or ligature. More elaborate treatments can be obtained, but they are mainly for use in hospitals.

If a snake does bite you, try to find out what kind of snake it is. Kill it, if you safely can, to get a closer look. Look for fangs, rattles, the broad viper head, and the characteristic "pit" itself—a little crater between eye and nostril. Examine the wound also. If there are one or two deep, wide-spaced punctures—the fang marks—you know that a viper struck you. You do *not* know that you got a dose of venom—in about half of all cases, none is injected! If there's no pain, no redness, no swelling, you have no problem. Most sources say: do *not* start the treatment unless the symptoms appear!

When they do appear, your first job is to slow the spread of the poison, through the tissues under the skin, into the rest of the body. To do this, tie the constriction band around the leg or arm, between the torso and the bite, and about two to four inches away from it. *This is not a tourniquet and must not be tight.* It is not meant to cut off circulation. Make sure you can get a finger under the band; make sure you can feel a pulse outside the constriction; and remove the band entirely every few minutes. If swelling spreads out from the bite, move the band to stay a couple of inches ahead of it.

Your second job, begun immediately, is to get rid of as much of the poison as you can. Most bites are on foot, ankle, hand, or wrist. These are dangerous places to cut, because blood vessels, tendons, and nerves lie close to the skin surface there.

Wash the site with soap and water. (You may need to shave a hairy spot so that suction cups will work properly later.) Now take the blade from the kit and make short, straight, shallow cuts across the bite. These incisions must be parallel to the body member and to the "grain" of structures in the skin. Thus on a finger, or on the top of the foot, you would cut lengthwise to finger or foot. Cuts should be about half an inch long and no more than one quarter inch deep, sometimes less. There should be fairly generous bleeding.

Then take the suction cups from the kit, press the air out of them, and apply them to the bleeding skin. Don't pump, but re-compress them whenever they loosen. Keep up this process for an hour.

Your third job is to treat the wound, like any other injury; to ride out whatever illness the venom brings; and to get to a doctor. Find the doctor first, by all means, if you can—but often you can't. Don't exert yourself. Stay quiet in a cool place. Avoid coffee, tea, and alcohol. Depending on the amount of venom you've received, you may be very sick or scarcely sick at all. In very severe cases, a foot or more of the limb will be swollen and discolored, and there will be vomiting, giddiness, and symptoms of shock.

I have spoken, for convenience, as if the victim were treating himself. This can be so, but more often a companion does the job. If anyone in the party has special knowledge, he's naturally the one to handle the crisis.

Coral snake venom is entirely different from that of rattlesnakes and their relatives, and the cut-and-suck treatment is no use against it. Fortunately, bites by this snake are exceedingly rare.

Animal bites

Even a minor bite by a wild or domestic animal can bring three possible dangers. The first is infection; you fight it by ordinary care in treating the wound, and later, if they are needed, with antibiotics. Second is tetanus. Tetanus, though a dangerous disease, is easy to prevent. A tetanus immunization shot, plus one booster every seven years, protects you. Every hiker should have this insurance.

By far the most serious of the three dangers is *rabies*. Beware of any animal that acts oddly, including one that seems overfriendly. Raccoons, skunks, and bats are all occasionally rabid. Don't pet or encourage a raccoon that begs for food. There is no immunization against rabies (for human beings), and the disease is always fatal once it is underway. There is, however, a treatment that can prevent the disease from developing after a bite if it is begun quickly enough.

If you are bitten by an animal, try to catch it and kill it, if by any chance you can safely do so. Keep the body, or at least the head; then get back to civilization as fast as you possibly can. (If you can get the animal home without killing it, that's still better, but this is obviously difficult.) With luck, lab analysis of the animal's brain will show it not to be rabid and spare you the discomfort of the treatment. If the bite was below the neck, you have several days in which the treatment can be successfully begun. A bite on the head or neck gives you less margin.

Poisonous plants

There are many, many plants that are more or less poisonous if eaten. Know exactly what you're doing before you eat any part of any wild plant, including, most especially, any mushroom. The only general first aid rule for plant poisoning is to drink water and induce vomiting.

Much more common is another kind of "poisoning": the brief, inconsequential sting of nettle or the unbearable itch of poison oak and similar toxic plants. Poison oak is hardly a danger to life and limb, but it can certainly take the pleasure out of a wilderness trip.

There are various species of poison oak (including the one called poison ivy). They are found over most of the United States at lower elevations. Some species climb like vines; others form bushes; others do both. The best field mark to look for is leaves grouped in threes.

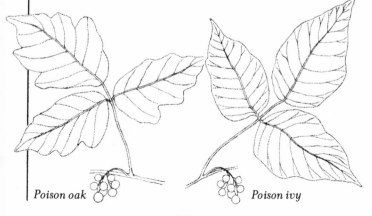

Poison oak   *Poison ivy*

Each group of three leaflets grows out at a different point along the stem; the clusters are "alternate," not "opposite." Sometimes the leaflets are hairy, sometimes smooth; their edges may be smooth, toothed, or lobed.

All species have the same poison, the same miserable effect. The sap, most plentiful in spring and summer, is the carrier. A few hours after you bruise or even brush a plant, the skin begins to itch and redden, and blisters rise. As time goes on, the irritation spreads. The problem will last for several days. You can often head off the eruption by scrubbing with strong soap and cold water right after exposure. (Since the irritant is itself an oil, don't use cold cream or any oily soap—it will only help spread the damage.) Once the reaction has begun, you can suppress the itching somewhat with poison oak lotions.

Poison sumac, a relative of poison oak, doesn't resemble it much in appearance. A shrub or small tree, it has smooth, pale gray bark and alternate leaves divided into seven to eleven leaflets, with smooth margins and a reddish tinge.

Poison sumac

This sumac is most common in the Great Lakes region and on the Gulf and Atlantic coastal plains. In the North it is shrubby and keeps to boggy places; in the South it is a tree up to twenty-five feet tall, growing in swamps and river bottoms.

Trumpet creeper is a woody climbing vine that grows in

woods and thickets throughout the eastern United States. Like the sumac it has divided leaves which however grow in opposite pairs. The leaflets are toothed at the edges.

Almost two million people each year come down with cases of poison oak and poison ivy. Only about half the population is allergic—maybe you're in the lucky half. There is a temporary immunization which some people find effective. For off-trail travel in low, wooded country infested with any of these plants, you need to carry strong soap and perhaps some lotion as well.

Nettles have a different kind of weapon. When you brush them, sharp hairs on their leaves and stems give you an "injection" of poison. There's a stinging pain, sharp but quick to pass. The plants have broad, soft leaves, rounded at the base and pointed at the tip, with coarse teeth. They are found especially along watercourses. The *spurge nettle* has the same effect but a different appearance. Its leaves are alternate, with spreading veins, and deeply lobed in three to five parts, maple-fashion. Various species are found, mainly on sandy soils, over most of the South and Southwest.

In Everglades National Park, which preserves this country's one fragment of subtropical forest, there are several irritant plants with poisons strong enough to be actually dangerous. You might inquire about them before hiking or canoeing in that region.

27:
Diseases of Heat, Cold, and Altitude

NEW BACKPACKERS ARE OFTEN too much afraid of wild animals. But they may be too little afraid of other, less obvious, yet sometimes perilous dangers: the heat, the cold, the wet, the wind, the alpine sun, the lack of oxygen at altitude. All these things affect the hiker. Some of them can make him very sick, and some can kill him. One of the "environmental" disorders—the disease called hypo-thermia—probably endangers more backpackers in a single year than snakes do in decades.

The body's heat machine

To keep working properly, the human body has to stay near the normal 98-99 degrees Fahrenheit. A very precise balance has to be maintained between heat gained and heat lost. If the balance shifts too far in either direction, the hiker becomes a victim, a person in trouble.

You generate heat just living. The harder you work, the more you generate. At the same time, the body loses heat, constantly, in the breath and from the skin. Survival depends on conserving this body heat when the weather is cold and getting rid of it when it's hot. There are natural mechanisms for doing each.

What happens when the problem is *cold?* First, given fuel enough, the body builds up its own fires. You burn more calories in cold weather even if you aren't doing extra work. If that isn't enough, shivering, that involuntary exercise of the muscles, begins. At the same time, the small veins and arteries near the skin, where heat is radiated to the outside air, close down. Less blood approaches the skin, and less heat is lost. In dangerous cold the body may cut off a large part of the circulation to the arms and legs, risking the limbs to keep the head and torso warm. After that the natural defenses are exhausted. To operate in cold climates, we depend on artificial ones. Clothing, our added insulation, has made us a species that can live in the Arctic as well as in the tropics where we evolved.

If the problem is *too much* warmth, there are different mechanisms. Vessels in the skin and in the arms and legs expand, bringing blood to the surface, where its heat is lost. Perspiration begins, and sweat, evaporating, takes still more heat away. Clothes only get in the way of the cooling, except when you need to block the direct heat and burning ultraviolet rays of a hot sun.

This, oversimplified, is the machine. The diseases of heat and cold—heat exhaustion, heat stroke, hypothermia, and frostbite—attack when this cunning system is pressed too far.

Heat exhaustion

Of the four disorders, this is the most common and the least dangerous. If you are working hard on a hot day—perhaps climbing a long, steep slope with a heavy load—the body's cooling mechanisms may actually do their job too well. The vessels at the skin may dilate so much that the internal organs, including the brain, get less blood than they need. Very suddenly, the victim will feel faint and nauseated. His heartbeat may be fast and irregular. He'll sweat a lot, and his skin will be oddly cool, his face pale. He'll feel like hell.

Heat exhaustion calls a halt; thus it makes its own cure.

Lay the victim down in the shade, with his head low. Loosen any tight clothing and give him salt water. In half an hour he should feel better. After that you can go back to hiking; you may need to slow the pace for a while and perhaps lighten the victim's pack. Make sure that he gets enough water, energy food, and salt.

Heat stroke

Heat stroke is a much rarer, much more serious illness. It is not just a flurry, correcting itself; instead, the body's temperature-control system breaks down completely. The victim runs a dangerous fever. The same hot day might bring on either heat exhaustion or heat stroke, but the symptoms are utterly different.

The stricken hiker feels unbearably hot. He stops sweating, almost completely. He will stumble, talk nonsense, and may even grow delirious or lose consciousness. His face will be flushed, not pale; his skin will feel hot and very dry, not cool and sweaty. Rest, by itself, won't help at all.

Heat stroke is an instant emergency. It will kill. There is a single treatment: get the victim cool. If there's a lake or stream nearby, lay him down in the water; if not, cover him with wet cloths. Massage his arms and legs to increase the flow of blood (and loss of heat). Keep doing these things until the victim is rational and steady again.

Heat exhaustion passes and is done; heat stroke has lingering effects and can recur. If you've had an attack in your party, it's time to go home and get the stricken person to a doctor.

What brings on heat stroke? It seems to be the result of excessive, uninterrupted sweating. The sweat glands get worn out, as it were, and can no longer do their very necessary job. The danger is greatest when nights, as well as days, are uncomfortably hot; even the respite of a cool night gives the body time to recover. When temperatures stay stubbornly high, be sure to drink quantities of water—more than you think you want. Get plenty of salt and potassium in your food. Wear a broad-brimmed hat and keep your head cool. Take rests in the shade, and, whenever you get a chance, go for a swim.

Hypothermia: the killer

Of all the diseases of heat and cold, hypothermia—it might be called "cold stroke"—has the ugliest record. In most deaths from what is called "exposure," it is hypothermia that kills. As in heat stroke, the body's defenses break down, struggling vainly not against an excess of heat but against a lack. The temperature of those organs that are vital to life—the organs of the head and torso—begins to drop. All the conserving mechanisms are tried. All fail.

The first warning is a vague, unpleasant feeling of general chill. With it comes increasing tiredness, irritability, general lack of morale. It can be hard to judge how much of this is simple weariness, but it is best to be very suspicious. At this stage hypothermia is easy to deal with; it may be enough to eat some candy and take shelter from the wind.

The second, and definite, sign of hypothermia is uncontrollable shivering. When this begins, the body temperature is already a couple of degrees below normal. This is no ordinary shivering. It is a convulsive, alarming shuddering, growing more violent as the body continues to chill. As it increases, coordination begins to fail; the victim will stumble, mumble, act illogical. And yet, if he doesn't know the signs, he may push on—"mastering himself" when he should not, wrongly convinced that he is only tired.

If the shivering is alarming, still more alarming is the moment when, after tapering off, the trembling *stops*. This means that the victim's temperature is down to 86 or 87. He has little time left. In the last stages the muscles grow more and more stiff and unresponsive, and pulse and breathing slow. Finally the victim will simply fall to the ground. If nothing is done for him, a coma will follow, and then death.

Once hypothermia is recognized, you have to get the victim warm immediately. Stop. In bad weather, get a shelter up. Here it pays to know how to erect a tent or natural shelter quickly! Strip him of wet clothes and get him under cover and into a sleeping bag. If the case is serious, a second hiker must strip and get into the bag with the victim. This life-saving trick has brought people back at almost the last possible moment. As soon as the victim recovers enough to handle them, give him hot, sweet liquids, and then energy food. (Never try to get food or liquid into an unconscious person, though—he may inhale it.) After the first danger is over, six or eight hours pass before full recovery. As with heat stroke, you have to assume that a person once afflicted is still in danger when he seems well again. Head for home.

Generally speaking, it is in winter that you have to be most constantly aware of the hypothermia danger. But a surprising number of cases also occur "out-of-season"—in the warmer half of the year. On New Hampshire's Mount Washington, four hypothermia cases once had to be rescued within 48 hours—in August! While Washington, one of the most weatherbeaten summits in the United States, is hardly typical, there is some risk in any cool region. Spring and autumn hikers in cool places are especially vulnerable, because, so often, they take gear and clothing suited only for midsummer.

Remember: it doesn't take bitterly cold air to make "hypothermia weather." The problem can arise even on a mild day if it is both *windy* and *wet*. A wet hiker, in cotton clothing, on a wind-swept ridge can die of hypothermia when the air temperature is in the 40s or 50s.

Frostbite

Frostbite is, essentially, freezing: the freezing of a part of the body. Fingers and hands, toes and feet are vulnerable; so are the chin, nose, and ears. Frostbite often accompanies hypothermia, because the body, gathering all blood and heat to the all-important organs of the core, cuts off supplies to the limbs.

Frostbite cases, like burns, come in three "degrees." Many people have had "frostnip," first-degree frostbite; this is alarming but not, in itself, serious. It is a freezing of only the upper layers of the skin. The part will feel burningly cold, and then numb. The skin will whiten and harden, but only on the surface; pressing it, you will feel the still-resilient flesh underneath. You can often deal with such slight frostbite simply and casually. If your hand is nipped, you can quickly thaw it in your warm armpit. If someone has frostnipped toes, there's the belly treatment. You stop, strip off the victim's shoes and socks and put his feet on somebody's warm belly—not nearly as uncomfortable as it sounds! As the nipped area rewarms, the victim will feel a painful prickling. The skin may be mottled and somewhat swollen the next day and may appear "stained" for a number of weeks. Be sure to protect the part from any further freezing.

Second-degree frostbite is hard to distinguish, when it occurs, from the first degree. The difference shows up after rewarming, when blisters form. This indicates that the freezing, while not yet dangerous, has gone somewhat deeper into the skin. The treatment is the same as for first-degree frostbite.

In third-degree frostbite the whole thickness of the skin is frozen, together with some of the tissue underneath. This is a much more serious matter. The entire member will feel stiff and stony. As the freezing proceeds, the original pain will give way to numbness, and then to an illusion of *warmth*, which is a real danger sign.

Once third-degree frostbite has taken place, you can't thaw out the flesh without great pain. Because of this, it is sometimes best *not* to begin the thawing until you get the victim nearer help. People can walk many miles, if they must, on frozen feet. If, for instance, you discover definite deep frostbite on someone's foot in the middle of the day, you should not stop but head as fast as you can for the roadhead, or to a place from which rescue will be easy. Once you make camp, however, there's no choice but to warm the frozen flesh.

If you must do this, the authorities now agree that it must be done *all at once*, rather than gradually. Soak the injured limb in a bath of tepid water, no hotter than about 108 degrees Fahrenheit. (If you don't have a thermometer, test the water with your elbow; it should feel pleasantly warm, not hot.) Keeping the water at that temperature, soak the part for twenty to thirty minutes. Never pummel the damaged flesh, rub it with snow, break the blisters that appear, or try to exercise the part. Never apply direct heat.

Frostbite is, of course, a winter problem almost exclusively. Winter campers, the first few times out, may worry about frostbite every time their hands or feet get unpleasantly cold. But mere chilliness, though by no means desirable, isn't frostbite. But it's better to be over-suspicious than to be too complacent.

One caution: overtight boots can lead to frostbite when you might not expect it. Overstuffing your boots with socks, in the attempt to keep your feet warmer, may actually cut off circulation and make them colder. Tight snowshoe or crampon straps, cinched over pliable boots, can do the same. If your feet feel chronically cold, try easing up on straps and laces.

Deep frostbite is another of those subjects that *have* to be talked about, because the problem is so frightening and serious when it occurs. But third-degree frostbite simply won't overtake any well-equipped and knowledgeable backpacker.

Preventing the diseases of heat and cold

We've touched, many times in this book, on some of the basic practices that should keep you safe from the diseases of heat and cold. Reviewing them quickly:

Keep comfortable. On cold days keep warm—on hot days keep cool. Adjust your clothing whenever you need to. Don't be so strong-minded that you let yourself suffer for hours—if nothing else, you'll be wearing yourself out, and that can lead to trouble.

Drink plenty of water. Thirst isn't a reliable guide to your need for water. Drink *more* than thirst would suggest, a gallon or more a day.

Get plenty of food. This is doubly important in the cold. Nibble all day long. The body can and will run on its own fat, but this is an inefficient source of energy unless new sugar and starch are coming in.

Don't push on to exhaustion. Some readers will laugh at this advice; climbers, and others with fixed ambitions, are unlikely to follow it. But whenever heat or cold is a problem, exhaustion can help precipitate heat stroke, hypothermia, or frostbite. It can complicate other health problems as well.

Be in good condition. This means reasonable exercise at home as a matter of routine, and a good diet. Some Americans, though technically healthy, don't have the reserves of strength they would need to call on in a wilderness emergency.

Avoid most drugs. Winter campers, snug and warm at nightfall, often take a swallow or two of liquor. No harm in that. But whenever cold is becoming a major problem, it's best to stay away from that and any other "stuff." Different stimulants and depressants have different effects, but they all seem to interfere with the normal working of the body's heat machine. (Coffee and tea are okay, however.)

Deal with trouble early.

Salt

Hikers have traditionally taken salt tablets to replace the salt lost in sweat, and to prevent or cure muscular cramps. Recently this practice has come into disfavor. Ordinary salt is only one of several necessary substances that are lost in perspiration—they are known collectively as electrolytes—and some sources call it pointless, or even harmful, to dose yourself with salt alone. Electrolyte-replacement drink mixes are available, and some people swear by them. Some people swear by their salt tablets, too. But in truth you can get all the electrolytes you need in the normal diet (see Chapter 12).

If you need supplements, it will be early in the season, before your body has adapted to the stresses of hiking, and on trips where you sweat a great deal. The body "gets used" to sweating and "learns" to conserve its salt—just as it "gets used," in time, to altitude, to cold, and to punishing heat.

Altitude sickness

"Altitude sickness" is a name for several separate physical problems. Naturally enough, it is mostly encountered in high western ranges. We're only beginning to realize how many people actually get sick at altitude, sometimes running considerable risk without ever knowing it. In a recent study, eighty-four percent of the people who climbed to the 14,000-foot summit of Washington's Mount Rainier were found to have at least some symptoms.

Altitude sickness is brought on by rapid rise in elevation. The farther you climb, the harder you hike, and the larger the loads you carry, the greater the chance of trouble. Though altitude problems rarely start below 9,000 or 10,000 feet, they *can* begin as low as 5,000. How fit you are doesn't seem to matter a great deal. Non-smokers don't have an easier time of it, either. Women are apparently somewhat more vulnerable in the days just before menstruation.

Ordinary altitude sickness, the kind experienced by thousands, is known medically as "acute mountain sickness." Coming down with it, you will probably notice first a headache, mild or intense. If you're hiking, you'll feel exhausted and short of breath. You'll lose your appetite and may feel nauseated. In more severe cases there is vomiting. Many people get a few symptoms toward the end of a long first day that ends above 9,000 feet, feel better when they stop hiking, and wake up perfectly fit in the morning. Others are uncomfortable for several days.

All of this is a nuisance at worst—for most of us, most of the time. But acute mountain sickness can develop, on the second or third day, into one of two other conditions, both highly dangerous. For either there is only one cure: *pack up and get down the hill*—if possible, while the victim can still move under his own power.

Cerebral edema, a rare but deadly condition, is an accumulation of fluids in the brain. The current belief is that ordinary mountain sickness is actually a very slight cerebral edema, but the more intense form is unmistakably different. The headache turns violent. The victim will be terribly weak. He may stagger, babble, hallucinate. If he isn't taken to lower elevations, he falls into a stupor, followed by a coma and then by death.

Almost as serious, and very much more common, is *high-altitude pulmonary edema,* an accumulation of fluid in the lungs. Over one hundred people die of this disease every year, some at elevations no higher than 9,000 feet. The symptoms are somewhat like those of pneumonia. There is coughing, shortness of breath, quickened breathing, and fast heartbeat. The lungs feel tight, stiff, constricted. There will be creaking or bubbling noises in the lungs, slight at first, and then increasing. As the victim gets worse, his cough will bring up a pinkish foam. Finally, the patient goes into a stupor brought about by oxygen lack. Essentially, he drowns in his own body fluids.

Again, the one real answer is to go down. Sometimes a drop of a couple of thousand feet will bring a cure. If you can't evacuate immediately, have the victim sit up, and try to keep him alert. Give lots of liquid.

Pulmonary edema is by no means unknown in adults, but for some reason the danger is much greater for people under 21. Hikers who have had it once must be on the watch for it afterwards. And here's a curious fact: people who spend a long time at high altitudes, return to sea level for several weeks, and then go up again, run the greatest risk of all.

Avoiding altitude sickness

The body has the ability to adapt, within limits, to the lack of oxygen at unaccustomed altitudes. On the typical short backpacking trip, however, this adaptation has barely begun when the party heads for home.

The more slowly you ascend, the fewer problems you will have. It's often recommended that you allow one day for each 1,000 feet you climb above the 10,000-foot line. If you must start high, try at least to get a full night's sleep at the high roadhead, and to schedule a fairly leisurely first day.

People with heart and lung problems should certainly ask a doctor's advice before setting out on trips in the high country.

Sunburn and snowblindness

About sunburn there is little to say. You know your complexion and your tolerance. In the woods, and in most American mountains when they are free of snow, suntan lotions will protect you, along with a broad-brimmed hat and perhaps a bandanna at your neck. Don't under-dress. It's safer to cover up if you aren't well tanned. Avoid particularly a burn on your shoulders, where the pack-straps ride.

The higher you climb, the more burning ultraviolet rays come through the filtering atmosphere. A moderate overcast does nothing to stop them. Be aware that burning rays bounce up from glittering granite, sand, water, or snow.

A mild sunburn is nothing to worry about. Your tanning lotion will also do for a salve. Severe sunburn, even though it heals, is actually a permanent injury and contributes to the apparent "aging" of human skin. In unusually bad cases there may be blistering, severe pain, even swelling, headache, nausea, fever, and chills. Such a burn can immobilize you. Moist, cool dressings will help somewhat.

There are many good suntan lotions and partial or total sunblockers; inquire at a druggist's or at a backpacking gear store. At very high altitudes and on snow you need the most total protection you can get. Most preparations wash off with sweat and must be renewed. The old standard, greasy "glacier cream," while not perhaps the most effective, has the great advantage of staying put.

One form of sunburn is very serious: *snow blindness*. Snow travelers must have dark glasses or goggles (and a spare pair in the pack) and wear them much of the time even under a light overcast. The higher you climb, of course, the more important it becomes to keep protection on your eyes. Glasses for use above timberline must protect the sides of the eyes as well, with tinted glass or plastic, or with solid barriers.

Snow blindness is nothing more than sunburn of the surface of the eye. The first symptom will be a scratchy, sandy feeling. That's the time to hurry off the mountain. In another six or seven hours the eyes will swell almost shut, and the touch of light will become a physical, painful thing. At that point, to get down the mountain, you have to be led. There are only two first aid treatments: cold packs, and total darkness.

The Wilderness Regions

They say, Rules change in the Reaches.

—Ursula K. LeGuin

28:
Wilderness in the East

MAGNIFICENTLY VARIOUS, THE WILD COUNTRY of North
America: low and high, lush and barren, flat and rugged,
dry and wet, warm and cool. Different, too, are the
requirements it imposes on the hiker. To the California
Sierra backpacker, accustomed to sunny summers, cool
granite, and dry air, much of America's wilderness seems
foreign, difficult even—a new and sometimes complicated
world.

   In most of the United States, after all, summer is not
dry and hot; it is wet and hot, or, in some sections, wet and
cool. Over much of the East, Midwest, and South, the summer months are actually the wettest of the year, and some
other season—commonly autumn, sometimes spring or
winter—is the driest time. Even in the western deserts,
such rain as falls may fall mostly in summer. And while
most hikers, in most regions, still take to the mountains in
July and August, more and more are learning the advantages of the other ten months of the calendar.

*Eastern wilderness regions,
including Northern Plains*

Eastern beach and wetland wilderness

Say *wilderness,* and the average hiker gets a mountain in his mind. But along the Gulf of Mexico and the Atlantic coast, the great wild places are not high and rocky; here they are flooded and flat. These are the wetlands: the swamps and marshes, freshwater, brackish, and salt.

One band of watery wilderness follows the shoreline: thousands of miles of pickleweed, needlerush, saltmeadow cordgrass, bulltongue and bulrush, spreading behind glistening barrier beaches from the mouth of the Rio Grande to the mouth of the Hudson and beyond. Barren the marshes seem when first you look at them, horizons of gray or green or dull pastel, laced with the bright arteries of tidal channels. Yet these are not poor lands: they are among the richest places of the continent. Much of that richness of life you don't see, but you can guess it from the throngs, the flocks, the incredible populations of birds: ducks and geese in the millions, ibises, herons and egrets, terns and eagles and ospreys and hundreds more.

357

The marshes, of course, have little for the booted backpacker. This is country for the boatman, for the paddling
canoeist. But between the marshes and the the open sea lie
long, shining barrier beaches, from Padre Island in Texas to
Monomoy in Massachusetts, and these can be hiked.
Beachwalking is travel unlike any other—hours or days on
beaches without crowds, hiking at waterline where the
sand is wet and firm, beside a noisy ocean or a quiet inland
sound. Fresh water can be scarce on these barrier islands,
and on long trips you may have to carry your own
gallon-a-day. When you walk the dunes, be careful not to
trample the fragile matted plants that stabilize some of the
drifting sands. Just a few careless hikers can alter a whole
landscape—so delicate is the hold of green plants on these
inhospitable places.

The climate of these coastlands is in general very mild,
but of course it varies greatly from the semi-arid southern
tip of Texas to the lush shores of Florida and the hard
capes of New England where the coastal wetlands end at
last. In many places autumn is the "season," the best time
of year to see the great migrations of the flocks.

Much of the continent's margin of marsh and island has
been lost, lost to dredging and diking and filling, lost to
urban development, fouled by oil spills and chronic pollution. But there are also large areas still pristine, and a few
of them, chiefly National Wildlife Refuges, are protected.
There are also several National Seashores. Within these
government-owned lands large sections remain wild.

Inland from the shore there is another series of places
both wild and wet. These are the swamps of the Gulf and
Atlantic coastal plains, and of the lower Mississippi Valley,
where rivers slow and spread on their travel to the sea.
They are not, for the most part, open marshes, but rather
great waterlogged forests of tupelo, bald-cypress, and oak,
hung with Spanish moss. Logging was never easy in the
swamps, and got a late start there. Thus they contain
today, if only by default, some of the grandest virgin forests in the East. Some of the best-known swamps are the
Great Dismal on the Virginia/North Carolina line; the rich
Congaree in South Carolina; the vast Okefenokee Swamp
in southern Georgia; Bradwell Bay in Florida. Certain of
these wetlands have a measure of protection in National

Wildlife Refuges and National Forests. Others are vanishing as lumbering and drainage projects advance.

The greatest of all the eastern wetlands is neither marsh nor swamp but something unique in itself: the Everglades. Here there flows a huge, rustling river without banks—a river of sawgrass and sluggish water, finally turning salt in mangrove forests on the shores of Florida Bay. Most of this great flowage is now protected in Everglades National Park and the Big Cypress National Preserve. Here is the largest wilderness of the East, and one of the most valued natural preserves in the world.

Scarcely smaller, scarcely less impressive, but without protection, is the huge Atchafalaya Basin of Louisiana, our largest river-bottom swamp—a thousand square miles of watery forest, another thousand of coastal marshland. The Atchafalaya is threatened, at this writing, by plans to channelize and drain its waters.

The swamps, like the marshes, have to be seen from the water. There are a few short nature trails in the parks and refuges, but very little chance for lengthy trips on foot.

Eastern mountains: general

The Appalachians, the Ozarks, the Adirondacks—all the eastern mountain masses—are wilder today than they were half a century ago. Even the National Parks in this region were repurchased from private owners after settlement and—not seldom—ugly exploitation; the forests within their boundaries are largely young-growth. But the East is a well-watered, mostly temperate region. Even in the mountains, the growing season is long—as long as ten months in the south—compared to a month or so in the high western ranges. Here it does not take geological time to heal scars. Already the signs of the human past have become more charming than disturbing in otherwise wild scenes: old roads now gone to trails, old orchards still bearing fruit, the stone foundations of old houses, the rock walls around old fields.

North Carolina's Mount Mitchell, 6,684 feet high, is the tallest peak east of the Black Hills of South Dakota. Considering the moderate elevations, it is easy to underestimate the ruggedness of these ridges. Five thousand-foot summits may still rise the larger part of a mile from valley floors below. Along with gentle trails, there are many that are steep, roughly surfaced, and demanding.

The eastern ranges are almost entirely wooded. Hardwoods—oaks and hickories, maples and beeches, birches and many more—grow almost to the summits in the southern mountains and cover valleys and foothills in the north. Above them grow coniferous forests of spruce and fir (though the hardwoods take over in this zone, too, in the first years after logging). When you travel under broadleafed trees in summer, you don't see out very often or very far. Under the trees, thick brush—especially the thickets, gorgeous in the spring, of dogwood, rhododendron, mountain laurel, briar—can make it hard to push your way cross-country. Even more than in the West, most eastern hikers stay on the trails.

If there is a time for cross-country travel, here in the East, it is fall and winter. When the leaves are off the hardwood trees and the stems of brush are bare, the landscape is transformed. You see out, see for miles, see where you are; away from the trails the going is not so hard. Besides, you'll be dressed for bushwhacking; in the warmth of summer, you may not be.

Though there are exceptions, most blocks of eastern wilderness are rather small. On long trips, hikers may traverse several of them, rather than choosing a single area to explore. In such regions as the Adirondacks and the White and Green Mountains of New England, whole clusters of wild areas lie close together. A great deal of hiking, too, is done on *extended trails*—pedestrian routes that traverse both wild lands and tame, and even cross (by arrangement with the owners) long gaps of private land. The Appalachian Trial is the most famous of these, and the great model, but there are a great many others: the Long Trail in Vermont, the Metacomet-Monadnock Trail in Massachusetts, the Shore to Shore trail in Michigan, and dozens more. Though this idea has been imitated in the wild mountains of the West, it seems most functional in semi-settled country, where the truly wild sections are few and far between.

The small size of most eastern wilderness areas does have its advantages. Access, undeniably, is easy. It is often possible to reach wilderness roadheads by public transportation. You can't get as far away from civilization as you can in the more favored western landscapes; thus, in the normal hiking season, you are not quite so totally on your own. However, this ease of access, this lack of great remoteness, can be deceiving. It can lead hikers to under-estimate the problems that will face them on the trails— and especially those problems that are caused by weather.

Anywhere in the eastern mountains you will want a tent year-round. A tarp might serve for the rain but not for the mosquitoes of summer. And even a cool, clear night can be so humid that you need cloth above your head to catch the heavy dew. You should choose your gear with almost perpetual dampness in mind. Boots should be well-coated with waterproofing. Unlined boots, which dry out faster than those with padding inside, may be preferable. Where it is very warm, some hikers choose the army's can-vas "tropical combat boots." In the mountains a polyester sleeping bag makes better sense than one filled with down, because it will still insulate if it gets wet. In lower areas of the more southern mountains, where nights in summer are often uncomfortably warm, you may not want a sleeping bag at all, but only something on the order of a wool blanket.

Throughout the East, and especially along the various long trails, you find shelters. Some of these are simple, three-sided structures without caretakers. Others, espe-cially in the Northeast, are much more elaborate. While these shelters can be very charming and highly convenient, it is better, all things considered, to leave them out of your plans. These refuges are often crowded. Too often they are littered, dirty, or vandalized. Some sit in deserts of trampled, eroded ground. And nuisance animals—bears, skunks, raccoons—naturally congregate at these sites. In some areas—Shenandoah National Park, for instance—the rangers now discourage the use of shelters except on day-hikes and in emergencies. In many other places you must reserve a spot in a shelter in advance.

It's absolutely necessary to carry a stove in eastern wil-derness. Fires are widely restricted, and in some places where they aren't, they should be. In the Catskills, around shelters maintained by New York State, acres have been stripped of all breakable wood, living or dead. It's an ugly scene and repeated in too many places. Don't be part of it. When the weather is wet—as it so often is—a stove may be the only practical answer anyway.

The southern Appalachians

These are the wettest of the eastern mountains. The peaks of the Smokies, with some ninety inches of annual rain, are in fact the wettest spots in the country outside the Pacific Northwest. March has the largest monthly precipitation; the summer, with torrential thundershowers, is only a little drier. Summer days are typically in the 70s or 80s, though temperatures may drop to 40 after a storm; humidity is almost always high. The typical hiking uniform in the heat is the minimum: shorts, perhaps a light shirt or net undershirt, and boots. (But you need long pants where poison ivy is dense along the trail.) On the lower slopes, nights may be only a little cooler than the days. Above 3,000 feet, however, nights drop to the 60s even in hot July.

September, October, and November are the driest and clearest months, really the best of the hiking weather. The trails are less crowded (except in popular hunting areas!) and the mosquito problem is past. In some years, the southern Appalachians get a display of fall color worthy of New England. Regular frosts begin in November.

In winter, snow is frequent but unpredictable. Since only the highest ridges stay white for very long, you will not generally have much need for skis and snowshoes. At middle elevations, rain mixes with snow and alternates with snow—it may snow at night and rain during the day. As anyone knows who has dealt with such conditions, they make for difficult camping. Freezing rain—glaze—is also fairly common. For all that, midwinter in this region is actually one of the drier times of year. Days are cool and often gray, nights subfreezing but seldom bitterly cold. Yet temperatures *can* go down below zero, winds *can* rise to gale force, and white-out conditions are not unknown on the higher ridges. Like all eastern woodlands, these are open and airy in the winter, full of the light that is turned away in summer by a million leaves.

On the slopes you find hardwood forest chiefly, or rather hardwood *forests:* there are several distinct, complex communities. (It has been said that the Great Smokies contain more species of trees than are found in all of Europe.) Spruce and fir appear above 5,000 feet. Summits may have "balds" of grass or heath, mostly rhododendron and mountain laurel.

In this southern part of the Appalachian chain, the federal government has considerable wild holdings. The most significant is Great Smoky Mountains National Park, a wilderness almost western in scale, and split by a single road. Other pieces of wild country—in Shenandoah National Park and in various National Forests—are a good deal smaller. A few are formally protected for their wildness; most, at this writing, are not.

The Northeast

North of Virginia, the Appalachians subside. In Pennsylvania there are rather few large blocks of publicly-owned land that is wild. When the land rises again in New York State, the character of the mountains has changed.

The weather is considerably cooler. While some summer days may be hot, warm nights are rare, and cold storms can come in at any time of year. Only three months—and less, in many places—are free of frost. In New Hampshire the 4,000 to 6,000-foot peaks of the White Mountains can get snow and high winds at any time of year, and the summer temperature, in bad weather, can drop as low as 20 degrees. Combined with wind and rain, such temperatures can make conditions very wintry—hypothermia weather, even frostbite weather, during summer. A surprising number of people get into trouble on summer hikes in the northeastern mountains.

Fall in the Northeast is an excellent time for the hiker. It has many crisp, clear days and is about the closest thing to a dry season. Winter is white, beautiful, and bitter. Snow camping, snowshoeing, and ski touring are all popular here. Winter hikers watch out for occasional storms out of the southeast, which can bring rain, usually followed by a shift of weather, subzero temperatures, and northwest gales. Everything gets wet, and then freezes solid. Zippers jam, tents seem welded to the ground. Experienced winter travelers do their best to avoid such weather.

The original forests of these mountains were almost entirely spruce and fir; only at lower elevations, as along the Hudson, did the hardwoods naturally predominate. But because almost every hillside has been logged at some point, the transition hardwoods have taken over almost everywhere. Above the zone of full-sized timber, there may be a thousand feet of dwarfed birch and mountain ash; then, as low as 5,000 feet in some sections, only tundra and stone. All of these ranges were completely buried during the last glaciation by the advancing ice; the numerous lakes of New England and New York are only the most obvious of the marks the icecap made on this country.

This is the only part of the nation where the bulk of the wild land is in the care of state agencies and private landowners rather than of branches of the federal government. The state of New York has given formal wilderness protection to almost 1,000,000 acres of its vast properties in the Adirondacks and proposes another 90,000 designated acres in its lesser empire, the Catskills. In Maine, too, it is the state that is responsible for the wilderness and semi-wilderness of Baxter State Park and the Allagash Waterway, and several million acres of private timberlands—open to limited public use—remain remarkably wild.

The U.S. Forest Service does manage most of the public land in the White Mountains of New Hampshire and the Green Mountains of Vermont. Even here there is an unusual setup. Much of the work of management—the trail maintenance, the staffing of backcountry shelters, even some of the planning—is done by private clubs, chief among them the Appalachian Mountain Club. The westerner may be taken aback at the relative luxuries he finds in some of these mountains (though he is at liberty to avoid them). Everywhere you see the traditional shelters, many of them with caretakers (and fees); there's even a system of eight elaborate backcountry hostels, or huts, where meals are served—reservations, of course, are required.

The Ozarks

West of the Appalachians, on the long, gradual slope toward the Mississippi, you find little wild land in public ownership. But beyond the great river, in the knot of low mountains called the Ozarks, there are quite a few spots where the original wilderness, once driven back, has been permitted to restore itself. There are National Forests here, and the National Park Service has narrow, linear parks along several of the major rivers.

In many ways the Ozark country resembles the mountains of the Southeast. It is only a shade more continental in climate—the summer a little hotter, the winter slightly less mild. Summer lacks the hot nights which can be so troublesome in the Southeast. Autumn is very pleasant. The wettest months are April, May, and June, and the driest (though by no means rainless) are the midwinter months of December, January, and February. There's some snow, but it doesn't last.

In the Ozarks proper, wild areas are often found on the rugged slopes between lowland valleys and plateau-like summit regions. Because the gentle highlands are settled and grazed by cattle, water in the streams below almost always has to be purified for drinking.

Lake-and-forest wilderness

Along the Canadian border, from the Adirondacks to the High Plains, there lies a great, flat tangle of blue lakes, bogs, potholes, and circuitous rivers. All this land was overwhelmed, four times in the last million years, by glaciers out of the north. Many American landscapes have the marks of glaciation. But in this flat expanse, so barren of other obvious "landmarks," almost every feature you see was put there by the unimaginable weight and power of the ice. Ice made this region the fascinating one it is. It laid down moraines and eskers and drumlins and erratic boulders; it shoved old rivers into their modern courses; it scraped some landscapes bare and covered others with rich soil. And most of all it made lakes, the modern Great Lakes themselves and uncounted small ones. It's handsome country; mostly gentle, mostly forested with hardwoods or various conifers, and in large part well-settled and civilized. But scattered across it are government lands, state and federal, where wilderness remains—or where it is being allowed to return.

Most of this is in small sections. The National Park Service has some of the larger properties, wild at least in part, around the Great Lakes: three National Lakeshores and a National Park, splendid Isle Royale, a 100,000-acre archipelago in Lake Superior. On state lands, Michigan and

Wisconsin have both chosen areas, within their larger State Parks, for protection as state-owned wilderness areas. Other fragments of roadless land remain in National Forests and National Wildlife Refuges.

But the greatest lake country wilderness lies west of the Great Lakes, in northern Minnesota. This is the famous Boundary Waters Canoe Area within Superior National Forest, about one million acres along the Canadian border. It is a wilderness of pines, red and white and jack; of waterfalls and bare rocks and waterside camps and portages; and of water itself: water in lakes, water in ponds, water in rivers, endless water. The struggle to preserve this region, not yet ended, has been going on for fifty years. Adjoining the Boundary Waters are parks in two nations: small Voyageurs National Park on the American side and the million-acre Quetico Provincial Park in Canada. Together these areas make up one of the chief wilderness reserves of the North American continent.

The climate of the lakes country is continental—hot in summer and cold in winter—but somewhat milder close to the shores of the Great Lakes. In the eastern part of the region, late summer is the rainiest time; but to the west, on the edge of the Great Plains, the rain peak comes earlier. Winters are gray and often bitterly cold. The Boundary Waters Area has six months of snow cover and some of the lowest winter temperatures recorded in the contiguous United States.

Wilderness on the plains

Little enough is left of the wild Great Plains, so little that it is almost painful to recount the fragments we have. Yet there are some, mostly in the northern part of the region, along the Canadian border.

The plains, though beautiful to the intelligent eye, lack obvious spectacle. Most of the protected areas in this vast region were set aside rather for wildlife than directly for recreation. The prairie states are spotted with wildlife refuges—some for ducks, for sandhill cranes, for pelicans, for other birds; some to preserve the bison and that other curiosity, the historic Texas Longhorn. Certain of these refuges have within them blocks of true prairie wilderness, varied sometimes by lakes, sometimes by streams, sometimes by stony hills, but always more than anything else a wilderness of grass.

In North and South Dakota, the Badlands, stark, eroded landscapes, interrupt the smooth ascent of the plains. Badlands National Monument, South Dakota, preserves a part of this country: tablelands, gulches, canyons and buttes, bright colors in the crumbling earth. The Monument also contains a very sizable chunk of rugged, roadless prairie. Theodore Roosevelt National Historical Park, across the border in North Dakota, has smaller areas of wild ground.

As you move west across the plains, the grass grows shorter, the weather drier, and the federal holdings more extensive. Here there are many "national grasslands," lands that were badly overgrazed in private ownership, then purchased by the government for restoration. In eastern Montana there are more than a million acres of public domain land, wild in part, around the backed-up waters of Fort Peck Reservoir on the Missouri. River-carved, eroded, semi-arid, these river breaks, like the Badlands, have a mountainous look. Part of this region has been named the Charles M. Russell Wildlife Range; it is one of the chief reserves of prairie wilderness.

But perhaps the most important remnants of the wild prairie are places, not in public ownership, at the greener, moister eastern edge of the plains, places where fragments of the original lush plant association have somehow survived the last century unbroken by the plow. There is hope that Congress will purchase one of these parcels as a Tallgrass Prairie National Park. It must happen soon. Once the deep, tough, original sod is turned, the land can never be brought back to what it was.

Only a few of the wild areas of the Great Plains are large enough to reward a long hiking trip. But there's a good deal here for the weekend traveler and the day-hiker. The fascination here is of the rare. So much of the whole wild center of a continent is reduced now to so little.

Over most of the Plains, early summer is by far the wettest time of year. As you move west and north, the annual totals of rain become smaller and smaller, and a larger and larger percentage of that moisture falls in warm-weather thundershowers. On the edge of the Rockies, the all-important summer rains—the rains from April through September—add up to less than fifteen inches. For the backpacker as for the farmer, this is, in practical terms, the edge of the true West, the beginning of what used to be called "The Great American Desert." On the northern High Plains, there can be a 150-degree range in temperature over the year, from 100 degrees above zero to 50 or more below. The Canadian borderlands, in particular, are known for their all-but-perpetual winds.

Rainfall from April 1–September 30

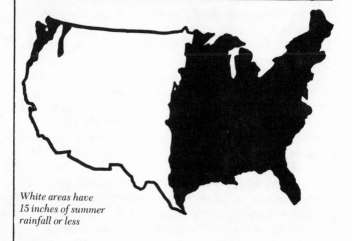

White areas have 15 inches of summer rainfall or less

29:
Western Wilderness

MOST OF OUR WILDERNESS IS WESTERN WILDERNESS. This is
the country that supplies, to most of us, the imagery of
wild places: the high lakes under glacier-gouged cliffs; the
fir- and pine-timbered valleys; the desert lands of carved
and colored stone. Wherever you are, in the eleven contiguous western states, there is wilderness not far away. The
problem is not to find it but to save it. Wilderness in the
West, though grand, is shrinking fast.

What possible summary is there for these lands, so varied that they might seem to belong on different continents?
It is almost hard to imagine at one time the rainforests of
Washington and the red-rock canyons of Utah—the spikes
of the northern Rockies and the chaparral mountains of
Southern California—the sagebrush steppes and the alpine
glaciers. To have all these things within a thousand miles of
each other would be astonishing enough. But often a mere
hundred miles of travel, or fifty, or ten, is enough to take
you from one world to another. There are places where
you can walk, within a couple of days, up through a luxuri-
ant forest, over treeless, snowy, windblown passes, and
down into desert basins on the other side.

Weather in the West

The variety of the West is very much a matter of weather; a matter of contrary climates. Many influences make these climates, but three things, in this region, are paramount. There is first the Pacific Northwest storm track, bringer of winter rain and snow. Second is the warm, moist air that rides up into the Great Plains, in summer, from the Gulf of Mexico, producing thunderstorms. And third is the shape of the land itself. Western mountains don't just endure the weather; they help create it, for themselves and for the lands around them.

The winter storms bring to the West most of its snow and rain. These storms take shape in the northern Pacific and sweep southeastward onto the continent. Though their centers strike the continent at various places, the storms bear down most often on the state of Washington. South along the Pacific Coast, away from the middle of this storm track, the winter rains grow steadily shorter and steadily more intermittent.

To the east the rainfall also diminishes, but in this direction the change is not gradual. It is dramatic, abrupt. For here the storms encounter the high mountain barrier of the Cascades and, farther south, the Sierra Nevada. These ranges force the clouds to rise; rising, they cool; cooling, they must let their moisture fall (chill air can't hold as much suspended water as warm air can). When the

Simplified view of mean annual precipitation

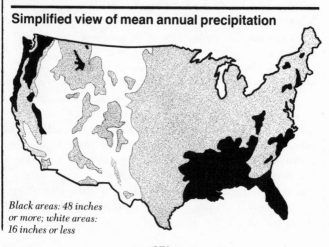

Black areas: 48 inches or more; white areas: 16 inches or less

370

clouds at last pass beyond the crests of the Pacific ranges, they have little rain or snow left in them. And so beyond the mountains the hinterlands are dry: wide steppes, vast deserts, hard and arid hills. Only the highest mountains in the interior ranges are tall enough to force more moisture from the depleted clouds. Look at a weather map of the West, a map that shows annual rainfall, and you can tell, almost as from a topographic map, where the interior mountains are.

If there were no rains in the West besides those that come down the storm track, the interior regions would be even drier, more extensively desert, than they are. But the West, like the East, has another kind of rain: the summer thundershower. To oversimplify, thunderstorms happen when moist air, heated by sun-warmed ground, rises straight up into cooler layers of the atmosphere. (This is why oceanic islands so often have all-but-permanent thunderheads above them.) The more moisture there is in the rising air, the more rain the storm will shed. The humid air that produces most of the nation's thunderstorms comes north, in the summer, from the Gulf of Mexico. Thus such storms are rather rare, and rather dry, toward the Pacific Coast but become much more important as you move inland toward the Rockies and the Great Plains.

So you could say, very roughly and crudely, that winter rainfall in the West depends on how far you are from Puget sound in the state of Washington. And you could add that summer rainfall depends on how far away you are from the edge of the Great Plains. Having said these things, you would immediately begin to see exceptions. The tangled mountains of the West create, within the larger pattern, a thousand local climates. Most of the time, high ground is wetter than lower ground nearby, and every mountain casts, on the side away from the prevailing winds, a "shadow," not of lessened light, but of lessened rain.

Significant though it can be in arid places, the summer rainfall seldom really amounts to very much. Except for parts of the Northwest and the Northern Rockies, you can safely say that the West is dry in the summer months. It may be dry and hot, as in the southwestern deserts; it may be dry and cool; but dry it remains.

Even when afternoon thundershowers seem to turn the air to water, this is only an interruption. Humidity stays generally low. Thus a hot day in the West is seldom as hard to take as a similarly hot, but muggy, eastern afternoon. It is for this western summer climate that much of the traditional wilderness gear is most suited. The down jacket, the down-filled sleeping bag, the tarp for shelter, the poncho against rain—they make sense for most of the West in the "normal" hiking season.

What about western temperatures? The pattern is simple. The farther north you go, the cooler it gets. The farther up the mountains you go, the cooler it gets. A rise of 1,000 feet, it has been estimated, much resembles a northward movement of 300 miles. In New Mexico, timberline—the line where it becomes too cold for trees to grow—lies at about 11,500 feet. In Montana it lies at about 7,000.

The forests of the West follow climate. You can divide them, with a certain neatness, into types that succeed each other as you climb a mountain slope, or as you move north

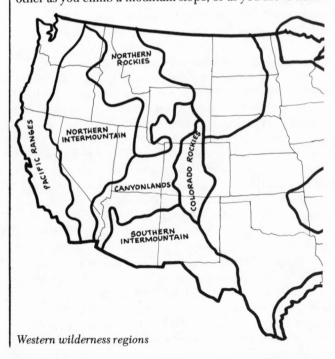

Western wilderness regions

into the cooler regions. There are typical (though not unvarying) forests of the lower, dryer hills; typical forests of the high and middle slopes; typical forests rising to timberline. On almost any long mountain hike you will watch the woods around you change—not once but several times—perhaps from ponderosa pine to Douglas fir, from Douglas fir to true firs, from true firs to the specialized trees of timberline. Wherever you go, however, you will find mostly the needle-bearing trees—spruces and larches, cedars and junipers and cypresses, pines and firs, redwoods and hemlocks and yews. These mix, at times, with broadleafed trees: oaks, bays, madrones, aspens, cottonwoods, maples, alders, and many more. But in only a few areas in the Far West, and then mostly in California, do the broadleafed trees make up a woodland by themselves.

The Pacific ranges

Along the Pacific Coast, just about all the remaining wilderness is found in the mountainous country. These highlands rise in two parallel north-south lines. Nearest the ocean are the tangled, many-ridged Coast Ranges. Typically rather low, these ranges nevertheless do rise, in several places, to 8,000 feet, and even to 10,000.

At the southern end of the Coast Ranges, in Southern California, summers are so long, so hot, and so dry that hikers are out in spring and fall rather than in what would elsewhere be the "normal" hiking season. Some areas are closed to public use in the rainless months because of the extreme danger of fire. Only the highest peaks are forested; lower and middle slopes are covered with the complex and typically Californian brushfields called "chaparral."

As you move north along the coastal chains, the climate becomes steadily wetter and cooler, the forests greener, and the dry season shorter. Summer turns pleasantly cool, especially in the higher elevations. But except in the far northern reach of the chain, there is always a distinct dry season—always a couple of months, at least, when rain would come as a surprise.

Parallel to the coastal ranges rise a second and greater mountain wall: the Sierra and the Cascades. The southern half of the chain is the famous Sierra Nevada. A single enormous fault block lifted as much as two miles above sea

level, the Sierra slopes gently on the west but breaks
abruptly to the deserts on the east in a scarp as much as
10,000 feet high. The Cascades of northern California,
Oregon, and Washington are built on a different plan
entirely. The basic Cascades are in fact a band of low forested hills or rugged mountains of middle height. But from
the green base there rise, spaced and isolated and spectacular, a dozen huge domes and spikes of lava, ice, and
snow: the great volcanoes of the Pacific Northwest. The
Sierra and the Cascades are cold enough, and wet enough,
to carry glaciers—small remnant icefields among the peaks
of the south, massive rivers of ice in the northern part of
the Cascades. Where there are glaciers today there were,
in the past, huge icecaps; these gouged out Sierra granites
and Cascade lavas to make the sockets of thousands of
modern lakes.

North of about central Oregon, summer too becomes
wet in the Pacific ranges. At the latitude of Puget Sound,
storm fronts come in from the Pacific not only in the winter but also, now and then, in summer. In the mountains of
northern Washington there is no longer even the ghost of a
reliable dry season (though even this rain-prone summer is
not wet by eastern standards). The Olympic Mountains on
the coastal side are the wettest in the forty-eight States;
they are lavishly green below timberline, hung with ice
above. The North Cascades, inland across Puget Sound, are
only a little drier. Hikers in this region, like hikers in the
East, go ready for rain, and count themselves lucky if they
do not get it.

There are two kinds of winter camping in the Pacific
ranges. First, there's travel below snowline—which means
anything below about 8,000 feet at Los Angeles, anything
below about 2,000 feet at Seattle. Here what you get is
rain, or snow that melts about as fast as it falls. Higher you
enter the snowy wilderness, colder, yet easier to deal with.
Perhaps the least friendly zone of all is the dividing line,
where the substance in the air seems neither water nor
solid snow but something clinging and clammy. All snow
in the Pacific ranges, though, is fairly wet; that is, it has
quite a bit of liquid water within it. Such snow behaves
quite differently than the dry, loose powder of the more
interior ranges. Slab avalanches, though a real danger

in snowy mountains anywhere, are less ubiquitous and devastating in this maritime region. An additional hazard, though, comes from wet-snow avalanches, massive amorphous slumps that occur when the temperature rises.

Winter hikers and campers have a somewhat easier time of it in the southern reaches of the Pacific ranges. In the south there are often long, clear spells between rains. But the closer you get to the Canadian border, the better your chances of running into endlessly bad weather (*Bad*, I say, but it is also beautiful). It isn't unheard of in the mountains of the Pacific Northwest for snow to fall every day, most of the day, for a month.

Scattered up and down both the Coast Ranges and the Sierra-Cascades are remnants, large and small, of the pioneer wilderness. They are not scattered evenly. If you plotted them all on a map, you would find, standing out from the scatter, three major clusters of still-wild lands.

In the southern half of the Sierra Nevada lies the scraped-granite country, the country of John Muir, the region of Yosemite and south. Several million acres in these mountains are still roadless, undisturbed. More remarkable yet, the crest of the Sierra runs 150 miles in this region without being crossed by a single highway, a single east-west road. Only trails rise to the high passes. It was a hundred years ago that the pioneer conservationist Muir began to lobby for the preservation of these mountains. Few of the great wildernesses that existed in Muir's time have survived so well.

A thousand miles to the north, near the Canadian border, the wild areas of the Olympics and the northern Cascades surround Seattle like so many magnificent suburbs. Here too the record of preservation has lately been fairly good.

Not as much progress has been made in the third great wilderness region of the Pacific ranges. This is the fascinating stretch of the coastal chain, partly in Oregon, partly in California, known as the Klamath Mountains. It's a rugged country, tangled, lofty, cut by rivers, and mostly forested. Botanists know it as one of the oddest corners of the United States for its rare trees and curious flowers; it has a wider, Sunday-supplement fame as a home of the man-ape "Bigfoot." Little of the extensive wilderness within the

Klamath Mountains has protection. Timbered wilderness is always hardest to preserve, and the virgin forests, not yet quite depleted in these mountains, draw the loggers on.

National Forests cover most of the higher, more rugged ground in the Pacific ranges. National Parks—Kings Canyon, Sequoia, Yosemite, Lassen, Crater Lake, Rainier, Olympic, North Cascades—give more total protection to certain spectacular stretches.

The Great Interior

We've seen how the western mountains organize the rain. The Pacific ranges make the lands to windward wetter than they would be if the continent were a featureless plain. The lands to the east they rob of water. The deep Southwest might be desert in any case, but because of the mountain barriers, an incomparably vaster area—the whole hollow center of the West—is dry. Nine states have part of this arid domain within their boundaries; one—Nevada—is almost entirely within it.

It is common to think of this enormous region as a basin, confined as it is by the Pacific ranges on the west and by the Rockies on the east. But that can give a false impression. Whatever else this country is, it is not *flat*. It is broken endlessly by mountain ranges, some rising to 12,000, even to 14,000 feet. It is broken by deep-carved canyons, where rivers run as much as a mile below the surrounding plateaus. And though all the region is more or less arid, it is full of the variety of low and high places. Mountains, cooler and wetter, are covered with forests of pinyon pine and juniper, of ponderosa pine, even of white fir and Douglas fir; summits may have timberline species like Engelmann spruce and the gnarled and undying bristlecone pine. These greener places may be *in* the desert, but they are not truly part of it.

Here in the hidden lands, dry and not-so-dry, are some of the most compelling wilderness landscapes of the continent. Certain of these landscapes are as famous and admired as they deserve to be; others are almost perfectly unknown; few of them are, as yet, protected.

Lord knows the opportunity is there. Even now settlement in this country is sparse. Most of the land never passed out of the public domain. The government has so much property in the intermountain region that it is simplest to think of it as a great federal reserve, interrupted, here and there, by lands that are privately owned. Some of the higher mountains have timber and are classified as National Forests; some of the grandest landscapes are National Parks; some portions, habitat for the desert bighorn sheep and other endangered animal species, are National Wildlife Ranges. But the bulk of the land is controlled by the federal agency known as the Bureau of Land Management (see Chapter 30).

Through the center of the intermountain deserts, the Colorado River and its tributaries have cut a ten-thousand-mile web of precipitous canyons in rock now gray, now black, now red (that famous southwestern rust or rose) or yellow. Some of these gorges are gigantic, like the Grand Canyon itself, where the Colorado cuts its unimaginable slot into the layered rock of northern Arizona. Others are closed-in, convoluted, narrow. In the greater gorges, travel is by water. The hiker may walk down to the water's edge, but there is no path along the waterline. The lesser canyons, though, are footways. And above the canyons rise mesas—isolated, flat-topped mountains, left behind in the general erosion, some of them high enough to be forested.

The canyon country has its superb wilderness; it also has its river narrows, possible damsites that entrance the engineers. Several of the most exciting stretches of the Colorado and the Green have been flooded by enormous government reservoirs (this is one of the most heavily developed river systems in the world). Even the Grand Canyon itself was almost so flooded. Some of the finest remaining stretches are protected in National Parks.

The Colorado canyon system, cutting across the intermountain region from the northeast to the southwest, divides the desert into ragged halves.

Northwest of the canyons, between the sunken rivers and the Pacific mountain walls that block the rain, lies the most primitive part of the Great Interior. Here hundreds of separate mountain ranges rise from the desert floor. Most of them run north and south, parallel, ranked and regular: the state of Nevada looks like one great washboard from the air. When the difference in height is enough, the valley floor and the mountain crest are con-

trary worlds. Standing in desert scrub, you look up as much
as a vertical mile into green mountaintops that seem to
have no right to be part of the same landscape. From the
peaks the effect is reversed; the plain below becomes the
other country. There are no other views like the views
from a desert mountain, and there are few that are
half so long.

The northern and larger part of the washboard region
is known as the Great Basin Desert; it covers most of
Nevada and parts of Utah, Idaho, Oregon, and Washington. Here the valley floors themselves are rather high
above sea level; the typical vegetation is sagebrush. At the
southern tip of the region, mostly in southeast California,
lies the lower and hotter Mojave Desert, famous for its
curious Joshua trees and for the desert climax of Death
Valley.

In the Mojave several large areas have been set aside
for preservation: Death Valley and Joshua Tree National
Monuments, California's Anza-Borrego Desert State Park,
and, in Nevada, the Desert National Wildlife Range. But
outside this one small corner of the washboard country,
very little land has yet been set aside. Until quite recently
there seemed scarcely a need to set land aside in so remote
a region, for it had the greatest advantage a beautiful landscape can have: it appeared to be useless. No longer.
There's a new mining boom in the West, a needlessly
destructive one. The speculative prospector, riding not a
burro but a bulldozer, is at work in these mountains,
gouging out the ground so slow to heal. And the off-road-
vehicle rider, the motorcyclist, the jeeper, is claiming all
this country for his own—his own to scar.

East and south of the dividing canyonlands there lies a
second vast reach of desert and desert mountain: Arizona
south of the Grand Canyon, most of New Mexico, and
much of western Texas. Here too the highlands rise above
arid basins. Most important is the long band of mountains
called the Mogollon Plateau. Ruggedly eroded, the Mogollon swings across the Southwest in an east-west arc from
the Colorado to the Rio Grande. Timbered, cool, cut by
canyons of its own, the Mogollon highland is attractive
country. Several wilderness areas have been set aside
within the National Forests that cover its spine. One of

these, the Gila Wilderness at the eastern tip of the plateau, was the first such area ever set aside, explicitly, with formal boundaries. It hasn't done so well since—the protected area, like an ice block thawing in southwestern heat, has been trimmed back repeatedly.

On each flank of the Mogollon Mountains—north to the canyons and south to the Mexican border—the true deserts return. To the north lies the Painted Desert; to the south, the Sonoran; to the southeast, the Chihuahuan. Each has its strange and characteristic plants, its unmistakable scenes, and its natural reserves. In the Sonoran Desert, in southern Arizona, lie Cabeza Prieta National Wildlife Range and National Monuments named for the saguaro and for the organ pipe cactus. In the Chihuahuan the one large reserve is Big Bend National Park, in Texas, on an arid, spectacular bight of the Rio Grande.

Across the intermountain West the climate varies, and not only according to the height of the mountain you are standing on. The land north and west of the great canyons gets almost all its meager rainfall in the winter. But as you move east and south, the thunderstorms of summer become more and more important. In the canyon country there may be as many as sixty thunderstorms a year, and these drop a fair amount of rain—though even this falls mostly on higher ground. Southeast of the canyons, the thundershowers, though not so numerous, are even more significant. In the peak rain months of July and August, the mountains of central Arizona are among the wettest places in the West! Still farther south and east, in the Chihuahuan Desert, it is the winter storms that scarcely matter, summer that brings the whole supply of rain.

In the lowest, hottest parts of the desert—in Death Valley, for example, or along the Arizona-Mexico border—winter is the pleasant hiking season; spring and fall are reasonable; summer is impossibly hot. Farther north and at higher elevations, spring and fall can be delightful. In the canyon country, April and May, cool and clear, may be the best months of all. Water is comparatively abundant then, while the thunderstorm season, with its flash flood danger, has not yet begun. (Never camp in a streamcourse, especially in the narrows of a canyon, during the high-risk months.) In the northern reaches of the intermountain

379

deserts, summer travel is conceivable, though uncomfortable at times; winters, especially in the lofty mountains that rise between barren basins, can be very snowy and bitterly cold.

The wilderness Rockies

Beyond the deserts rises the second mountain wall: the Rockies. No simple line of peaks, the Rockies are many ranges, tangled, branching, offset one from another—a world of mountains, not a single chain.

The barrier they make is not a solid one. In New Mexico at the south, and again in southern Wyoming at the middle of the range, the Rockies subside. In each place the desert and semi-desert country sweeps across the Continental Divide and merges into the dry western edge of the Great Plains. The dramatic Wyoming gap divides the Rockies into two very different mountain regions: the southern, or Colorado, Rockies, and the northern Rockies of northern Wyoming, Montana, and Idaho.

The southern Rockies don't really get started much south of the Colorado–New Mexico border. When they do rise, they go up all the way: Colorado has fifty-four peaks over 14,000 feet. The Colorado Rockies, for all their height, for all their forest cover, have a flavor of the desert still around them. They belong to the Southwest. They have the same dry spring, the same dry autumn; many parts of the region have the same summer thunderstorm season, in July and August.

The northern Rockies have a different pattern. As you move toward the Canadian border, the winter wet season grows longer and wetter. At the same time, the summer thundershower season has its beginning earlier and earlier in the year. In Idaho and Montana the warm-weather wet season arrives at the end of the spring; June is likely to be a very rainy month. July, August, and September are drier and clearer, but by no means free of rain. Since the northern Rockies lie in the summer storm track east from Puget Sound, long-lasting frontal storms can come in at any time. It can even snow. While some hikers rely on tarps for shelter in this region, many others insist on solidly built tents.

The northern Rockies are cooler than the Colorado

mountains, and wetter and greener. They were far more
extensively glaciated, and a few icefields still linger. There
are swarms of lakes, especially where the bedrock is of
granite. But the northern Rockies are also lower, and this
somewhat mutes the contrast between them and the more
southern ranges. In neither section can you count on *any*
night of the year being free of frost in the high country. In
Colorado, most areas can be hiked without skis or snowshoes in late June; parts of Idaho and Montana have deep
snow on the ground to the end of July.

Winter in the Rockies is an exciting season. While the
Pacific storms do reach these mountains, they are weak-
ended here. It can be fiercely cold and windy, but not even
in the northern Rockies is winter so implacably wet as in
the coastal mountains. Between storms, you can look for
many days of cold, bright, bitter sun—for the winter camper,
the ideal. Though night-time temperatures can go far below zero, the mountain climate is, if anything, a shade
milder than that of the adjacent plains. Snow is that dry,
cold, luminous stuff that skiers love—and fear, for this is the
snow best suited to avalanche formation.

The Rockies are full of wilderness even now. These are
timbered mountains, and where there is timber, in the interior West, there are National Forests. Concerning these
wild areas the usual debate is going on: save the wilderness, or cut the trees? Or, to put it more precisely: just how
much of this land do we log? And just how much do we
save?

In Colorado and New Mexico the virgin areas, though
numerous and grandly scenic, are, by western standards,
only moderate in size. It is in the northern reaches of the
Rockies, from Yellowstone to the Canadian border, that we
have the most remarkable treasures. The region is familiar
for its sizable National Parks, Grand Teton, Yellowstone,
and Glacier; less known are the vast wilderness areas, protected and unprotected, that lie in the National Forests
around the parks. Leaving aside Alaska, these are the largest areas of wild land that remain to us in the United
States. They have the splendor of the things within them—
river-gorges and fierce rapids, elk and grizzly, lakes, bright
forests, and difficult peaks, walls of granite and layered
sedimentary stone. But most of all they have the splendor

that comes simply from their size. Here, if anywhere, you can imagine yourself, for a few days, in the continent-spanning wilderness that was. At least five of the wild areas in these mountains are larger than the state of Delaware.

The Politics of Wilderness

We are not fighting a rearguard action, we are facing a frontier. We are not slowing down a force that inevitably will destroy all the wilderness there is. We are generating another force, never to be wholly spent, that, renewed generation after generation, will be always effective in preserving wilderness...We are working for a wilderness forever.

—Howard Zahniser

30:
Battle of the Wilderness: An Orientation

IN THE UNITED STATES TODAY we are making a decision—a decision which is all but irrevocable: how much of our remaining wild country, with its woods, its trails, its animals, its waters, will we preserve as wild? And how much will we log and mine, tangle with new roads, and scatter with new scars?

We are deciding. But this vast decision is not being made all at once nor in a single forum. It is being made on the maps and charts of the federal land-use planners. It is being made in crowded, noisy public hearings. But most of all it is being made in the Congress of the United States.

How much wilderness?

We have been assembling the American answer, piece by slow piece, for decades now. Some wild land we have preserved explicitly, in parks and such, and we allow ourselves to think that it is out of reach of exploitation. Much more land—many times that amount—we have developed or tamed (or in too many cases, ruined) so thoroughly that we cannot imagine it returning to the wild. But there is a third great stock of lands: the wild places that have neither been saved as such nor finally lost. Their future state is undecided. Still wild now, but without guarantee of wildness, they are subject to invasion, objects of debate.

For these debatable lands time is running out. The pace of decision is quickening. So is the pace of loss. And it will not be too many years now before we are able at last to add up our two columns and say: *This much our society chose to preserve. This much it chose to dominate and change.*

How will the balance look, I wonder? Will we be reasonably happy with the choices we have made? When the debate has lost its immediate heat, will we be glad of the compromise the opposing pressures brought?

The pressures that work for the reduction of wilderness are strong, stronger perhaps now than they have been for decades. The timber industry, facing the depletion of the forests on its own western "tree farms," is lobbying incessantly for the right to cut more, cut faster, in the forests of the public lands. The miners, pointing to resource shortages, demand that no land be off limits to their bulldozers—and indeed there is not very much land that *is.* Motorcyclists and jeepers, pursuing their new and hugely popular recreation, resent any limit on their often destructive use of public lands. But as the supply of wild country lessens, more and more people are moved to speak out for the preservation of what remains. So wherever the future of the land is being chosen—wherever wilderness survives but has no shield—these two large informal coalitions meet in contest.

I follow tradition and call this contest a *battle.* I do this despite a certain reluctance; journalists have a habit of giving to every dispute the color of a war. But in this case the analogy is almost too useful to be spared. For here indeed we have the clear, opposing sides. We have strategies, tactics, dispositions of power. There are fronts and theaters. You can mark the progress of the contest on a map. In one respect only the analogy misleads; these "engagements" seldom end, for either side, in total victory, or clear defeat. The result is always one version, or another, of the inevitable compromise.

In any case call it a battle. And no one who cares for the wilderness, or who travels in the wilderness, or who finds comfort in the knowledge that the wilderness is there, can afford to be ignorant of the outlines of that conflict, its rules, and its chief protagonists.

The turf: the state and federal lands

Wilderness can be almost anywhere. Even in private ownership, in this country, there is quite a bit of land that remains wild. But as a practical matter, it is only on government-owned land that significant blocks of wilderness can be protected; only on government land that preservation can be made to stick in law.

State-owned lands have some share of the American wilderness. In state parks across the country, away from park roads and campgrounds, there are still odd corners of virgin land. In several states there is much more than that. The New York State Forest Preserve in the Catskills and the Adirondacks contains most of New York's wilderness; Maine, California, Michigan, Wisconsin, Alaska all have sizable pieces of wild state-owned land. But in most of the nation, it is on *federal* property, and only there, that very large areas of land have been left alone.

What and where are these federal lands?

At one time or another the federal government owned the bulk of the land in almost every state outside the original Colonies (the greatest exception was Texas). As a rule, when the nation annexed new territory, the federal power was not only sovereign, it was also the owner of all the unoccupied land. Toward that vast domain the nation, in its first hundred years, had a very consistent policy: *get rid of it.* In theory, the Great West was to be given to small farmers; actually, much more of it went to the railroads, to speculators, and to state governments which, in turn, sold it for profit. But the point is, it *went.* By 1890 only a few small enclaves of federal land remained between the Atlantic Ocean and the first upthrust of the Rocky Mountains.

Beyond that mountain barrier, though, the surface of the continent was sterner, not quite so readily platted out and disposed of. Well-watered agricultural lands, such as there were, went into private ownership early. So did some of the finest and most accessible forests. But for the other land—the steep, the rugged, the hot, the cold, the water- less, the remote—the demand was not so high. And mean- while, slowly and painfully, the national policy began to change. Yellowstone National Park, first of all, was set aside, off limits to private claims. Then followed Yosemite, and then, faster and faster, whole systems of federal reserves. At last the public lands of the West came to be seen, not as an expendable currency, but as a precious and permanent federal domain.

We are lucky in this. We are doubly lucky that these lands, poor though mostly they are in economic value, con- tain so much of the splendor of a splendid continent.

Even now the bulk of the federal lands lie in the West. But in this century there came a new development: a movement to purchase some private land in the East for watershed protection and for public parks. Most of this massive re-purchase program was carried out during the Great Depression (though it has never entirely ceased). Now the East, too, has a certain share in the federal domain: a scatter of National Parks, National Forests, and National Wildlife Refuges.

Today, in most states, at least five percent of the land is federal, if you count military reservations; in the West the federal percentage is vastly higher. In the forty-eight con- tiguous states, the federal government owns some 406,000,000 acres altogether—about one-fifth of all the land. Only a portion of this land, it should be understood, is wild, and most of it is quite properly open to timber- cutting, mining, and other commercial uses.

Such is the empire. Within it there are four main fief- doms, four types of land reserves, each managed under a different charter by a different government agency. These are the *National Parks*, the *National Wildlife Refuges*, the *National Forests*, and the mostly desert *National Resource Lands*. They are controlled, respectively, by the Park Service, the Fish and Wildlife Service, the Forest Service, and the Bureau of Land Management.

The Wilderness Act of 1964

Before 1964, each of the four land agencies made at

least a token effort to preserve examples of its wilderness. The Forest Service did most, the Bureau of Land Management, least. But as the years went on, it became clear that the job, all in all, was not getting done; the pressures to develop land were too great for the agencies, acting alone, to resist.

And so came about the Wilderness Act of 1964.

The Wilderness Act is an extraordinary law. Before it descends into the necessary mechanical detail, it is readable; it is even stirring. *"It is hereby declared to be the policy of Congress to secure for the American people . . . the benefits of an enduring resource of wilderness . . ."* A wilderness (the Act goes on) is a place *"where the earth and its community of life are untrammeled by man, where man himself is a visitor who does not remain."*

In the Act, Congress created what is called the *National Wilderness Preservation System.* Simply put, it is a national roster of protected wild areas on the public lands. Only Congress can place areas on that roster; only Congress can remove areas from it. The boundaries of each preserve are defined with legal precision; for instance, from this peak down that ridge to this survey marker to that stream. Within those boundaries, wilderness is made as safe as, in a changing world, it can be. Roads may not be built; timber may not be cut; jeeps and motorcycles may not enter. (Grazing is permitted in certain areas, though, and even mining, under strict controls.) Each such protected area is known as a "Wilderness." "Wilderness" in a legal sense, "Wilderness" with metes and bounds, "Wilderness" with a capital "W."

When Congress creates a Wilderness, the designated area remains part of the National Park, National Forest, Wildlife Refuge, or other named reserve in which it lies. The same people continue to manage and control the land. Nothing changes. But changes that might otherwise take place are prevented. Strict limits are set on what the managers can do with the land—or on what they can do *to* it.

Ever since the Wilderness Act was passed, debates about wilderness have gone to Congress for their ultimate settlement. Both sides have been lobbying hard. One faction seeks to have the largest possible amount of land placed in the formal Wilderness System; the other faction seeks to keep the largest possible amount of land out of that system.

The cast of characters changes from case to case. But among the consistent opponents of wilderness are the timber industry; the mining industry; the off-road vehicle lobby; the concessioners in certain National Parks; dam-builders and power companies; and Chambers of Commerce and local governments in rural parts of the Far West. Speaking for maximum wilderness are the various conservation groups, national and local, and—much more significant—their individual members and others with similar concern. There are many tactics in this debate, but in the end it always comes down to a simple test of strength: which side can pile up the most mail on the legislators' desks? Not many Congressmen, when you get right down to it, know very much about wilderness, or care very much about it; they vote according to what they hear from their constituents. And, by the record, it seems fair to say that the pro-wilderness public is the larger. It may take time, but once a proposed wilderness begins to be seriously considered by Congress, the area almost always makes it into the system. Though the boundaries are usually settled by compromise, the compromises tend to be more generous than miserly.

So the process, in outline, is simple. But it works a little differently for National Parks than for National Forests, a little differently for Resource Lands than for Wildlife Refuges. So let's take a brief look at the record of the Wilderness Act in each of the fiefdoms that make up the public lands—the different theaters, so to speak, of the wilderness campaign.

Please note that the scene is rapidly changing. Much of what you read here may already, as you read, be out of date. But this is the story so far as, in late 1976, it had gone.

Theater #1: The National Parks

The National Parks have in them some of the grandest landscapes of the continent. They were established to preserve the land—to preserve it absolutely. And yet they were also partly intended to be showcases, tourist attractions, "pleasuring grounds." So no National Park is entirely wild, and most are laced with roads and spotted with buildings. There has been a great deal of controversy, over the years, about just how tame the parks should be allowed to become.

The Wilderness Act instructed the National Park Service to study every large wild area in the parks and come back with a recommendation to Congress and to the President. This was done. Sometimes the planners proposed that no wilderness be classified, that lands be left open for developed use. Most of the time they suggested wilderness, within specified boundaries. The President has passed these reports on to Congress, and Congress has most of them before it now. Rather few wilderness areas, so far, have been created in the parks, but many more will come. In several cases Congress, by drawing more generous wilderness boundaries than the Park Service wanted, has prevented the Service from building controversial roads.

There are about 20,000,000 acres of National Parks in the United States south of Canada. (Many parks are known as National Monuments, National Recreation Areas, National Seashores, or by other names.) Probably eighty percent of that acreage is wild. Wilderness in the parks is not a very hotly-debated matter, since the land can't be logged or mined in the first place. The greater conflicts lie elsewhere.

Theater #2: The National Wildlife Refuges

Like the National Parks, most National Wildlife Refuges are highly protected areas. They don't get as much publicity (which is probably all to the good), and they are, on the average, less spectacular. But the refuges are managed for the welfare of wild animals, and for many species, welfare means wild habitat.

Altogether there are about 11.5 million acres of refuges outside Alaska (some are known as National Wildlife *Ranges*, or by other names). The Fish and Wildlife Service has some very large desert areas in the West, maintained for rare species like the desert bighorn sheep, but also smaller wetland refuges all over the country, set aside for the ducks and geese that travel north and south each year along the four continental "flyways." The refuges have been going through the same wilderness study process as the National Parks. As with the parks, Congressional action has not been especially rapid, but the situation is quite stable. The prospect of wilderness protection has helped to discourage over-development. Not much is being lost.

Theater #3: The National Resource Lands

When the U.S. government stopped disposing of the public land in the Far West, it stopped by stages. First it set aside certain National Parks. Then it established National Forests. Then it began to reserve Wildlife Refuges. Each of these systems has grown over the years. But all of these named, designated reserves still add up to less than half of the federal land in the West.

What is left has been called simply the public domain, or, more recently, the National Resource Lands. These lands are chiefly (though not entirely) desert: desert plain, desert hill, desert canyon, desert mountain. It is rare for the Resource Lands to have much timber. They are rugged and rough and dry and little-known—and they are full of spectacle. For years they were undervalued, under-protected, and overgrazed to the point of devastation. Only gradually has the situation improved.

The agency in charge of this vast empire is the Bureau of Land Management. The BLM has never had the budget of the other land agencies, nor the staff, nor the sophistication. It has been a passive custodian, handing out grazing permits, handling mineral leases, and doing what it can to prevent vandals from destroying the priceless petroglyphs and Indian artifacts that are scattered across the intermountain West.

It is hardly surprising that the BLM has done very little by way of protecting wilderness on its lands. In 1976, however, things began to happen. In that year Congress passed a law designed to strengthen and define the agency. As part of that law, it instructed the BLM, like other agencies, to make an inventory of the wild areas under its control, and to study each of them, making reports to Congress. How this will work out is not clear at this writing, but it seems possible, now, that many wilderness areas will be set aside on the National Resource Lands.

These lands amount to some 175 million acres in the West outside Alaska—nearly half of the public lands in the forty-eight States. Nobody knows, yet, just how much of this land is really wild. Plainly the untouched areas have been shrinking faster than ever in the last ten years, notably in the regions where off-road vehicle use is heavy. But there may be as much as sixty million acres of wild land to be found on the resource lands even now. This is a new frontier of preservation, and we can be certain that efforts to set aside this land, or any part of it, will be controversial indeed.

Theater #4: The western National Forests

It was in the National Forests of the West that the preservation of wilderness areas began. It was mainly on their account that the Wilderness Act was later written. It is in these forests that most of the controversy has been focused ever since. And the timbered western mountains probably contain fully half of the wild country we have left—Alaska always excepted.

In 1922, a worker in the U.S. Forest Service, a southwestern ranger named Aldo Leopold, began urging his superiors to set up wilderness preserves. While an abstract admiration for wild places had long been current, this thought of protecting them by zoning within fixed boundaries was still novel. Beginning in 1924, the Forest Service set a number of such areas aside. In the 1930s another federal forester, Robert Marshall, made it his personal cause to see vast areas of wilderness preserved. In 1937, Marshall became one of the top officials of the Forest Service. The list of protected areas was swelling. Things were moving fast.

Then, a few months after his new appointment, Marshall died. The job he had undertaken was unfinished, indeed scarcely begun.

Unfinished it remained. Only a little additional land was put into protection by the Forest Service in the next twenty-five years. Indeed, much land that had been protected, under Marshall, was now opened to logging. And each time this happened, pressure for an Act of Congress, a new way of saving wilderness, grew. In a sense, the Forest Service was itself responsible for the Wilderness Act of 1964.

Again leaving out Alaska, there are about 166 million acres of National Forests. Unlike the parks and the refuges, the National Forests have a complicated job to do. They are

supposed to provide something for everyone: timber, minerals, pure water, wildlife habitat, forage for cattle and
sheep, and recreation of several competing kinds. It's no
easy thing to balance these demands. There is one whole
group of purposes that are best satisfied when the land is
left wild; another group that require roads and development. Many critics feel that the Forest Service has failed
to find the balance, and that timber obsesses the agency
while every other use drags on behind.

The Wilderness Act of 1964 confirmed the areas which
the Forest Service had protected for their wildness, under
the agency program, and made them units of the National
Wilderness Preservation System. Congress also instructed
the Forest Service to study certain other wild areas and
come back, to Congress, with proposals: should there be
formal wilderness there, and how much? Since 1964, Congress has created many wilderness units of Forest Service
lands. Often the lawmakers must choose between a smaller
wilderness advocated by the agency and a larger protected
area proposed by conservationists, or come up with an
alternative of their own.

However, there is one problem unique to the National
Forests. Each of the other three land agencies is required
to inventory *all* its wild lands, study them, and make
reports to Congress. While all this is going on, the lands in
question cannot be developed. But the Forest Service was
required to study only certain specified areas—adding up
to a mere fraction of the total wild land. Later, of its own
accord, the Service resolved to study a second set of areas
and to protect them, in the meantime, from conversion to
other use. But even with these additional study lands, the
bulk of the wild country in the National Forests is unprotected entirely; the Wilderness Act does it no good at all.

Because of this, the western National Forests have
remained the greatest focus of the wilderness debate. All
over the West, the Forest Service is now making new plans
for the use of its holdings. Such plans have been made
before; they will be modified in future years. But because
development is proceeding so fast, the current cycle of
planning appears to be decisive. All over the West, local
groups of conservationists are urging that wild places be
protected, in some manner, in the plans. All over the West,

commercial interests are lobbying for maximum development. It's the familiar argument, but not, in this case, before Congress. And when the agency officials make their decisions, there is little chance for appeal.

Yet *little chance* is not the same as *no chance*. True, Congress is not ordinarily involved in these planning issues. But it can take action on them if it likes. Congress can step in and protect a wilderness anywhere on the public lands, whether the managing agency requests it or not. In practice, lawmakers have been somewhat reluctant to intervene in this fashion. Nonetheless, they will do so when public demand is high enough, and several wildernesses have indeed been set aside without an agency report or agency approval. In other cases Congress has ordered study of wild areas the Forest Service would have preferred not to single out for attention.

For many wild places in the West, including some of the finest, this intervention, this direct Congressional action, appears to be the one survival chance.

Theater #5: National Forests in the East

The story of wilderness in the eastern National Forests is somewhat different. For the thirty years after Bob Marshall died, the Forest Service maintained that none of its land in the eastern United States could be called wild. Almost all of that region, they pointed out, had been logged. Green the eastern mountains might be; lovely they might be, as the resilient forests closed over the stumps and the scars. There might be areas that seemed wild; that were, for practical purposes, wild. But in truth, the Forest Service argued, they were forever altered, damaged, changed.

It is, or was, an interesting question. Does "wilderness" mean only land that has *never* been disturbed? Is it strictly a description? Or is it rather essentially a promise: "This land will not, *henceforth*, be disturbed"? Though there has been some disagreement within each camp, conservationists mostly prefer to regard "wilderness" as a label of intent.

After years of argument Congress decided the issue. In 1974, it began adding National Forest areas east of the Rockies to the National Wilderness Preservation System, and it has instructed the Forest Service to prepare reports on many more. So the job of protecting eastern wilderness is well begun. In the East as in the West, however, there is plenty of opposition from commercial interests and from the off-road vehicle lobby—somewhat surprising when you consider the small size of the areas concerned. It's been suggested that the total of Forest Service wilderness in the East might reach a million acres, but no more.

Theater #6: Alaska

In everything that has gone before, I have deliberately left out the most important part of the American wilderness: the state of Alaska. Indeed, this book has said nothing of Alaska—a huge omission but a necessary one; the subject is so vast. There is certainly more wild land left in Alaska than in all the other forty-nine states of the Union combined.

Until 1971, nearly all the Alaskan wilderness—nearly all of Alaska, in fact—was unreserved public domain, controlled (but mostly ignored) by the Bureau of Land Management. The state government was entitled to select a large chunk of this federal land for its own use—this was a provision of the 1958 Statehood Act—but an ownership dispute with Eskimo and Indian groups had held up the grant to the state. The situation was paralyzed.

Then, in 1971, the logjam broke. Congress worked out, at last, a settlement of the native Alaskans' claims. At the same time it set up the rules for the greatest land rush in American history—a many-sided competition, among state and federal agencies, to cut out pieces of Alaskan territory for their own. What is happening is very complex indeed, but it boils down to a two-sided tug-of-war. On the one side are the National Park Service, the Fish and Wildlife Service, and, outside the government, the conservationists; all seek the largest possible acreage in parks and wildlife refuges. They argue that the land is simply too cold, too fragile, too magnificent, to sustain any other use. On the other side of the question, broadly speaking, are the Forest Service, the Bureau of Land Management, the state, and various industries; all hope to keep the largest possible amount of land open to development and to the extraction of minerals and timber.

The conservation faction is proposing that more than 100 million acres of Alaska, or about a third of the land in question, be placed in such highly protected areas as National Parks. If Congress accepts this proposal, much of that vast acreage will someday be part of the Wilderness System.

How much wilderness is there?

The United States is a big country. Setting Alaska aside once more as a special case, we have, in the other forty-nine states, about 1,900,000,000 acres of land within our borders—just short of two billion acres—about three million square miles.

How much of that is, in fact, still wild?

It isn't all that easy to tell. But it's possible to make a guess. There are probably something like 145 million acres of wild land left on federal lands in the lower forty-eight states and Hawaii. If you add in state-owned pieces of wild land, the figure might be 147 million. That sounds impressive, and it is. It is a treasure. But compared to the total acreage of the forty-nine states, it is not quite so imposing—something between seven percent and eight percent of all the land. At the moment about fifteen million acres—

Growth of the National Wilderness System, 1930-76

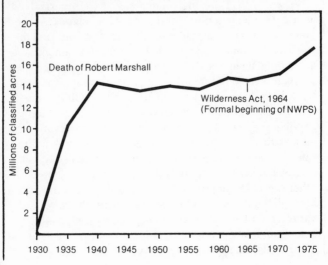

one-tenth of the possible total in these states—are in the Wilderness Preservation System.

When you add in the huge wild sweeps of Alaska, of course, the figures change. Including the Alaska wilderness, it seems likely that about one-fifth of the total acreage of this country is still roadless and undisturbed. That's a lot. Much of that amount, clearly, will never even be considered for wilderness protection; even the most ardent preservationist can scarcely hope for more than about 275 million acres of classified wilderness, or just over one-tenth of the land in the United States

How much wilderness should there be?

But perhaps the reader has had enough of this haze of numbers, this alphabet soup of agencies. How much wilderness should we set aside? How much do we need? How much can the nation afford?

There is no "scientific" answer to this question. This is, above all else, a matter of the value that we choose to place on wild things. With Congress making the major decisions, the American people will probably get about the amount of wilderness they ask for. They will make the answer themselves.

But there is a point that needs to be made.

It is tremendously important to remember that the American wilderness is, by definition almost, *poor in natural resources*. The public lands, after all, were the lands left over after settlers and commercial interests had selected the best and richest country for their own. And within the public lands themselves, most of the richer sections were developed long ago. With a handful of precious exceptions, the densely-timbered, easily loggable areas were not left wild. Nor were the areas of obvious mineral wealth. Nobody has the comparison down in numbers, but this is very certain: if one-fifth of the United States (Alaska included) remains wild, that one-fifth contains nothing like as much as one-fifth of the commercial resources of the nation. By and large, wilderness is *cheap*. You don't give up very much, in other kinds of wealth, when you put wild lands aside. And you gain, besides the wilderness itself, some very practical benefits. The clean water that flows from undisturbed mountains, and the fish that live or spawn in those clear streams, may have more dollar value than all the timber, all the minerals, all the grazing land those mountains contain.

Even when our wild areas have resources in them that attract exploitation, there are many cases where the temptation ought to be resisted. And it should be resisted whether or not we care for wilderness itself. On many millions of acres the penalties of exploitation are simply greater than the gains. In the West, for instance, there are certain mountain slopes that are richly timbered, waiting, so it seems, for the saw. And yet, under the green of timber, these slopes are steep, unstable, easily eroded. When the trees are cut and the land torn up by logging roads, some of these hills will slip, slide, and lose their soil to erosion. Soil loss, on the historical scale of time, is permanent. Moreover, the sediments, clogging the streams below, can cause them to undercut steep banks and start a whole new cycle of destruction. In such a case the land is not merely being *used*, it is being abused, impoverished, attacked.

This, then, is the question we must ask first of all: "How much of our public land is actually *suited* to development?" Surely the land that is too poor, or too fragile, for such development, ought to be left more or less alone— left for its wildlife, its watershed, its recreation value. You might think this would be almost automatic. But of course it isn't. People disagree on what the land can do. There is always someone making the case for a road, a clearcut, or a mine.

Yet it's well to remember, when you hear someone complain of wealth "locked up" in wild places, that much of that wealth is an illusion. We take it, if we do, at an unacceptable price to the land and to its future.

Wilderness advocates sometimes speak in terms of black or white; of preservation versus destruction; of "wilderness or wasteland." There is an element of exaggeration here and an element of rhetoric. And yet the rhetoric has its basis in a plain, unpalatable fact; what happens to the American wilderness, when it is "converted to other uses," is often an ugly, an unfortunate, even an appalling thing.

What you can do

Has this ever happened to you:

Have you looked for a remembered trailhead in a mossy forest—only to find it vanished in a clearcut's tangle of slash?

Have you found, instead of a fir-shaded trail on a ridge-top, a new-carved logging road?

Have you gone back to a familiar vista of desert mountains—and stared for wordless minutes at the endless scrawl of dirt-bike tracks on the vulnerable ground?

Have you looked for the streambank flat where you once had lunch in a wilderness valley—and found not a place but the wreckage of a place, torn up by a prospector's wandering bulldozer?

Or maybe you've felt dismay at the sight of a line of survey stakes along a wild trail—marking the course of an invasion to come.

For years, backpackers, returning (as they thought) to well-loved unchanging places, have been finding this return denied them; finding that the landscapes they recall are no longer there.

It is one thing to speak, in the abstract, about the dwindling of the American wilderness. It is quite another to watch it dwindle, to see the same piece of land in both conditions; the before, and the after—the wild, and the overrun.

People react to this experience in many ways. Some are angered. Some are grieved. Some are resigned. Some make it a project to see as many beautiful places as they can "before they're all spoiled." But these people have in common—too many of them—the belief that these changes are inevitable; that they belong to some inexorable Master Plan and that nothing anyone can do will stop them. If you can't even (as the old saying goes) fight City Hall—then what hope can there be in taking on a large and determined government agency?

The feeling is quite understandable.

But it also happens to be dead wrong.

If there's anything we should have learned from the history of American conservation, it is that, if you have to, you *can* fight—or at any rate, influence—City Hall. *Any* City Hall—whether it's the one across the street, or one of the many power centers in Washington, D.C. "Inevitable" processes can in fact be changed, or turned aside. And the force that does it is usually nothing more—and nothing less—than the letter of opinion, written by the citizen to somebody who has the power to decide.

So: if you have a strong opinion about what's happening to wilderness, don't sit on it. Write. An opinion letter can either be very general—simply a statement of your feelings on the subject—or very specific. Here are a few possible courses to follow.

• *When you get home from a trip,* take the time to write a letter to the agency about the place you explored. Do this even if you have nothing in particular to write *about.* It is valuable simply to express your admiration for the land, to build up a record of interest. It can be surprisingly important, when controversy develops, to be able to prove that people *do* care about Indigo Creek, or Silver Prairie, or any of a hundred fine, endangered places. If you saw things happening you didn't like, by all means comment on them. (Calmly. Abusiveness, of course, can only do harm.) Make a point of inquiring about the agency's plans for the landscape you traversed—is it to be logged or otherwise developed? Protected, and in what way? Is planning perhaps going on right now? Ask to get on the mailing list for any announcements that appear.

(How do you know who to write? Get the address if you stop off at a local agency office, for instance to pick up a wilderness permit. If you're using an agency map, you may also find an address on that. Typically, you'll be contacting a particular National Park or Wildlife Refuge; or a National Forest; or a sub-state District of the Bureau of Land Management. If you're missing the address, you can contact the regional office of the appropriate agency—see *Resources* section.)

• *Write your Representative in Congress,* and your two Senators. Tell them of your interest in wilderness in general. If you've written to an agency regarding a particular area, send your legislators a copy of that, too. You may not get a very promising response, but don't let it bother you—politicians do keep a close eye on their mail (see addresses, *Resources*).

• *Locate an environmental organization* that is interested in the same issues you are. If you don't have contacts in this direction, the national offices of the Sierra Club and the Wilderness Society can help; so can some gear stores. In many states there are "Wilderness Coalitions," alliances which bring together different groups with an interest in preserving local wilderness. These Coalitions generally publish newsletters, with very up-to-date information about what is going on in specific areas. Then there are more local bands of wilderness advocates. You may find it worthwhile to join one of these organizations, for a few dollars. Hooked into such a grapevine, receiving news-letters, you know, at a minimum, who to write your letters to, and when, in order to get the largest possible effect.

- At this point, of course, you can go on to get as involved as you like. Every conceivable job is waiting to be done: exploring unprotected areas, monitoring timber sales, attending hearings, and much more. But it isn't nec-essary to go beyond the almost effortless project of writing that occasional letter. And if only a small proportion of today's wilderness users did speak up, their common voice would be very loud indeed.

There is more than a little satisfaction in doing some-thing, however slight, to protect the future of a place you have enjoyed. It is as if you had paid a small and proper fee for the use of the land. And if there is a tiny, unavoidable impact on the wilderness, whenever a hiker goes into it, his letter, written after the trip, can more than wipe out that debt.

31:
The Backpackers:
Who Are They?

WHO ARE THE BACKPACKERS, ANYWAY?

We know, in a general way, what they do. But what kind of people are they?

Since about 1960, researchers have been querying the users of wilderness to find out what backgrounds they have, what their values are, and what reasons they have for leaving the motorized world behind. The results of this research are still spotty, still emerging, still somewhat contradictory. But certain patterns seem well established.

Clearly, most backpackers get started young on the trails—usually in their teens. Most of those who do get this early start continue to backpack; people who take up the sport later have a much greater tendency to drop out.

Most wilderness travelers are young or youngish. This may change somewhat as today's large generation of new converts grows older; people who have backpacked all their lives don't quit the trails at some arbitrary "retirement age."

Most wilderness users are married, and most of them have one or more children. Very many of them begin taking their children into the backlands as soon as the kids can walk, if not before. This is a fact that the makers of packs have taken optimistic note of.

The backpackers would seem to be an educated lot (or at least they have spent a lot of time in school). Two out of three, judging by most surveys, have college degrees. In the over-all American population, only one out of ten have attended college. Not surprisingly, backpackers tend to work at professional or white-collar jobs.

The people who head out with gear on their backs, though choosing about the cheapest possible vacation, come mostly from the higher-income half of the population. This is true, not of wilderness travelers only, but of outdoor recreationists in general. Car camping, too, is a pursuit of the upper middle class. But the truly wealthy don't seem to be much drawn to the outdoors.

Some studies find that backpackers are disproportionately city dwellers, city bred. Others disagree. It seems to depend largely on where the questions were asked. But it does appear that the city-dweller is more likely to value the wilderness *as wilderness*, to resent intrusions on it, and to think carefully about his own behavior there. City people seem to be most keenly aware of wildness as something special, something fragile; it's not just "country" to them.

When people head into the backcountry, they go mostly in small groups—sometimes the family, sometimes three or four friends. These latter groups are usually male. The larger organized parties are comparatively rare. Surprisingly rare, also, is the hiker who sets out alone.

Most backpackers and hikers would prefer not to have any company but the company of their own party. If they must meet other groups, they prefer to meet small ones. Thus the large organized parties are resented somewhat by the rest of the backcountry travelers, the vast majority that move in threes and fours. This is clearly a problem. And yet the larger groups appear to serve a particular and important purpose. In them you find many more children, many more people over fifty, and many more people who are venturing into the wilderness for the first time. For many, the organized trip is the introduction, the open door. And while many of the small parties are made up entirely of men, the larger groups are composed of men and women equally.

If there is wild country close at hand, hikers tend to take short trips adding up to about three weeks a year. It is surprising to find that, on most trips, people walk no more than ten or fifteen miles, altogether. Day-trips, there-and-back-again excursions on which no camp is made, account for a very large proportion of wilderness use.

Indeed, most wilderness areas are most visited by local people. Only a few well-known attractions draw people from more than a couple of hundred miles away. Nor do the hikers and packers spend a lot of money on their excursions: the average, according to one survey, is under $10. For longer trips, it is undoubtedly much higher, but seldom over $50. Not many people, these days, take horses or hire the help of professional outfitters. Though there are regions in which the use of packstock and paid helpers is traditional, this style of camping seems to be on the decline.

When they aren't in the mountains, what do back-packers like to do with their free time? According to one report, "cultural activities" (whatever those are) stand at the top of the list. At the very bottom: spectator sports, television, non-wilderness sightseeing, and other kinds of travel.

Knowing these things, it is interesting to look at the picture of the wilderness traveler that is presented, at times, by opponents of the wilderness idea. This image was reflected recently by the president of the Nevada Chamber of Commerce, as reported by the *Tahoe World:*

Hermann said that *"only the rich few who have money to hike out with very expensive equipment"* were able to enjoy the Forest Service's public campgrounds. The Nevada Chamber President added that camping out was something that *"none of us working people have the time, money, or patience to do."* Hermann also referred to the Forest Service's recent purchase of the Meeks Bay resort as useless for vacationers *"unless you can afford to be a hippie and go out and live in the woods."*

According to such notions, the wilderness people come only from the cities (and generally from cities a long way away); have weeks and months of free time to spend in wild travel; are uniformly husky and ambitious; are filthy rich (although at the same time hip) and, indeed, must be wealthy in order to pursue their expensive notions of good fun.

The real picture, obviously, is more complex. The back-packers do tend to have money (or parents with money), and good gear is indeed a substantial cost. Yet even the finest set of wilderness equipment costs much less to buy, use, and maintain than a dirt bike, a camper, or a snow-mobile. The difference is not one of means; it is a difference of taste, of attitude. As for the other points, wilderness users most definitely do *not* come from far away; they do not have more free time than other people; and if they are in fact much "hipper" than the population at large, the studies to date don't reflect it.

Researchers, adding up what they know so far about the backpacking public, see one large and unavoidable conclusion—the wilderness boom is not about to stop booming. They discount any notion that this long-building enthusiasm is a passing fad. The backpackers, they say, come from exactly those groups that are growing fastest in the American population—the professionals, the highly-educated, the upper middle incomes, the young adults. Further, the love of the wilderness is clearly something easily learned in youth and only with difficulty put aside thereafter. And today's trail travelers are diligently raising another generation of like mind.

Why do they come?

This is not a question that troubles the backpackers much themselves. But it does interest the researchers, and they have surveyed, probed, and theorized for years. They have defined and traced two dozen motives, at least, for "wilderness behavior."

There is the escape from the pressures and routines of life in the city. There is the pleasant, impersonal simplicity of the jobs to be done, the challenges to be met. There is the pleasure of exertion. There is the hunt for a trophy: the peak you "bagged," the fish you caught, the photograph you took, the miles you walked, the lofty passes you crossed. There is sometimes the chance to compare notes

about gear (that inexhaustible conversation) or to trade sto-
ries about past adventures. In the wilderness, as everywhere, there are games people play.

But if many different attractions bring the hiker to the
wild places, some of those attractions matter more; some
matter less.

Except, perhaps, for some of the climbers and river-
runners, people don't seek out the wilderness with the idea
of proving themselves, of testing themselves against adver-
sity. They don't go there to meet other people, nor to add
to their personal status. Even exercise and better health
count only as benefits gained on the side. And while it
seems certain that wilderness travel does something for
balance of mind, for sanity even, it is the rare backpacker
who is self-consciously "into" wilderness as people are
"into" biorhythms or encounter groups.

In short, it appears that people do not treat wilderness
travel, in any fundamental way, as a means to some other
end; as a setting merely, for some personal drama, therapy,
or display.

So we come back to seeing the taste for wilderness as
nothing more, and nothing less, than that—a wish to be in
the wild places; to know the places themselves. The
researchers have not found it easy to analyze this basic
affection for wilderness into simpler, more explainable,
desires. Still, they have made the attempt. Generally, they
have tried to divide the attraction into plus and minus
sides: are we drawn to these places because they *are wild*—
or do we admire them rather for their contrast value:
because they *are not tame?*

At this point (I can't help thinking) the analysis reaches
the stage of diminishing returns.

32:
Problems in Wilderness Management

WHEN, AFTER DOUBT AND DEBATE, a wilderness is finally
"saved"—when Congress draws around it that protecting,
legal line—there's a feeling of comfort, of a thing accom-
plished. And the feeling is quite justified. When Congress
has acted, you know that the land is safe, in its wildness,
from most kinds of invasion. That is no small thing.

But when a wilderness is set aside (and sometimes even
earlier than that), a whole new set of problems begins to
appear. So great is the public interest in wilderness these
days, so dramatic and so open is the process by which wild
places now gain protection, that every classified area
becomes somewhat notorious. The more controversy there
has been, the better-known a newly-designated wilderness
becomes. It's a familiar pattern: the season after a legal
wilderness is established, people begin coming to the place
in record numbers.

And so we encounter the other half of the wilderness
challenge. How, in the face of always increasing use—welcome though that use must be—can the wilderness stay
wild?

It may take decades. But someday, sooner or later, the last large area of unprotected American wilderness will be spoken for. Perhaps it will get protection, perhaps it will be given over to some other use, but the indecision will be done. Long before that final allocation, we will have to shift our attention to the related problem: how to manage the wild land we have already made up our minds to preserve.

This book has said a good deal about wilderness management, as it looks from the backpacker's point of view: the annoyance (and the plain necessity) of wilderness permits; the problems caused by badly laid-out trails. And we've spoken incessantly about good practices to follow in the wild country, and how they differ from the bad.

Now it may be useful to turn the question around, to look at the problems of managing wild country as the *managers* see them. The backpackers come and go, but the professionals are always there. The Park Service, the Forest Service, and the other agencies have the wild land in their care. These people have been watching the changes that take place, year after year, in their domains. Much of what they see they do not like. They are searching—though "groping" would sometimes be a better word—for ways of handling the problems of the land. And the backpacker has every right, and every need, to keep an eye on what is being done, on what is being proposed. More than anyone else, it concerns *him*.

The problem

What do the managers see that worries them so? Just what any concerned backpacker observes, but they see more of it.

They see the eroding, gouged-out trails and, across high meadows, the multiple, beaten tracks, like freeway lanes.

They see campsites turning into fields of scarred and barren ground; garbage pits and drainage ditches; grasslands pockmarked with old tentsites; trailsides and lakeshores littered with the blackened circles of old fires.

They see areas stripped not only of dead, down wood—but also of standing snags, so important to wildlife, and of all green branches small enough to break by hand.

They see the careless disposal of human waste, and the

possibility of grave water pollution in wild places—a possibility their tests confirm all too well.

And, hard though it is to believe these days, they see (and pick up) an astonishing amount of old-fashioned, unforgivable *litter.*

There are subtler effects that the backpacker may not himself be aware of. Too much human traffic, at certain places or at certain times of year, can disturb or drive away such animals as bighorn sheep, can interfere with their breeding, or keep them away from scarce desert water supplies. For other animals, human presence is actually too much of an attraction; it makes nuisances, scavengers of them. Consider the bears.

Finally, quite distinct from these effects on the land and its native species, there's the matter of "over-population" in the wild country—"overpopulation" as judged by the backpackers themselves. Generally, wilderness travelers prefer not to have a lot of company on the trail. Increasingly, though, they find it. For many, this by itself damages the pleasure they came for and makes wilderness inadequately "wild."

It is easy to exaggerate these troubles. As yet they are obvious in rather few places. We are not yet in danger of "loving the wilderness to death"—not much of it anyway. But the problems are there, and they are growing. Now is the time to get them under control.

Put yourself in the position of a wilderness manager. What do you have to do? What are your choices? If you want to reduce the "impact," the total wear and tear on a piece of wilderness, how do you go about it? There appear to be three distinct approaches that you, as manager, can take.

● First, you can concentrate on lessening the impact each individual hiker contributes.

● Second, you can build facilities to handle heavier use than the land could take without them.

● Third, you can actually limit the number of people you allow in a particular place at a particular time—and you can do this in various ways, subtle or direct.

In fact, of course, the wilderness manager uses all these methods constantly, relying sometimes more heavily on one, sometimes on another. The variations are endless as the land is varied. But these are the three basic lines.

Lessening individual impact

The easiest target is the obvious, outright abuse. When somebody cuts across a switchback on a trail, or builds his fire against a boulder in an unscarred meadow, or uses a streambank for a toilet, or sets up camp ten yards from another party, he is obviously doing something drastically wrong. Almost certainly he is doing it out of ignorance. The people you meet in the wild places seldom lack a genuine affection for the land, but they may not understand what its limits are. So the problem is largely one of getting the message across.

Beyond the obvious bad practices, there are others, like the building of fires, that are fine in some places, very destructive in others. No one set of rules can be applied everywhere. A backpacker entering an unfamiliar area may need to be told what the particular problems of the region are—education again.

This is one of the functions of the "wilderness permit." When the hiker picks up his permit, he gets, or should get, some necessary information. Rules and recommendations are printed on the permit, and the ranger on duty is supposed to be careful in explaining the reasoning behind them. All this should be having an effect. And yet, in the backcountry, you still encounter the most blatant abuses. Clearly, a still better job of education must somehow be done, and it has to be done much faster. It took a decade for the constant campaign against litter to change even slightly the way people behave. We can't wait that long to stop the deterioration of the wilderness.

One educational trick (a controversial one) is the "wilderness entry test." In a few places backpackers are required to pass a multiple-choice test to show that they understand the recommended local practices. In certain other wilderness areas people are asked to take such a test if they plan to abandon the main trails for more remote travel.

Formal regulations can, of course, be enforced. In most areas of heavy use there are "wilderness rangers" who can talk to people, and, if necessary, issue citations. But wilderness areas are too big, and rangers are too few, for this

410

traffic-cop approach to accomplish much. It's absolutely necessary that people understand the problems on their own and without coercion do what they can do to solve them. There's no other practical way.

Even when there's no question of outright abuse, some travelers contribute more impact than others. Other things being equal, the builder of a fire is taking up more room, so to speak, than someone who uses only a stove; the horseman takes up more "impact room" than the hiker. In little-used or resilient areas, these differences may scarcely matter. Elsewhere they can be crucial. One researcher has ranked the different types of parties, going from the smallest impact to the largest:

Least impact: small parties of day-hikers
    Small parties of campers who build no fires
    Large parties of day-hikers
    Small parties of campers who do build fires
    Large parties of campers
    Small parties using horses
Most impact: large parties using horses

Some would quarrel with this ranking, but the principle is there. So a manager might well want to discourage some kinds of parties and encourage others; this is one use to which quotas (see below) can be put.

The matter of small parties versus large is sometimes more complex than it seems. There are situations in which large parties are clearly downright destructive. On the other hand, a well-run but sizable group may actually be gentler on the land than an equal number of hikers who arrive in many small parties.

Develop to preserve?

Now we come to the second of the roads the manager can take. Along with trying to reduce the impact of people on the land, he can set out to make the landscape itself capable of handling more people. He can do this, oddly enough, by building things.

It seems paradoxical, this notion of "protecting" wild land by making it less wild, but to a limited extent it always has to be done. Even a simple trail is already a compromise with perfect wilderness; it is, in the planners' jargon, a "hardening." But a well-designed trail carries many more people than the land could support if they all scrambled cross-country. A marked and definite campsite is another kind of "hardening": barren already, it can come to little additional harm. About the next step up is the latrine. Then comes the more elaborate backcountry toilet. Taken to its extreme, this "hardening" can give you cement fireplaces; paved or graveled trails; huts and lodges; and even (as at Yosemite) backcountry sewage treatment plants.

Many of these facilities have been built merely as luxuries. But they can also have a function in protecting land. The more people a manager decides to accommodate, the more facilities he finds himself building. By concentrating use at "hardened" sites, he can at least in theory take some pressure off the rest of the land, the land he leaves alone. Reasoning partly this way, the National Park Service, in particular, used to be a busy builder. In Yosemite National Park, five "High Sierra Camps" provide meals and beds in summer; the White Mountains of New Hampshire have their own system of hostels. If all the people who use these lodges were instead camping out on the land, the total impact would arguably be greater.

So why not go the whole distance? Why shouldn't we imitate the Europeans and build whole constellations of huts and lodges? Why not "harden" the wilderness to the point where any number of people could be taken in at once?

There are several good answers. First, and most obvious: a "hardened" wilderness is always a lessened wilderness. And every time you go beyond the most basic improvements, you make the wild places markedly less wild. Second, each new wilderness development is, in itself, an impact. Around a backcountry lodge, you'll probably find a ring of heavily-used land, with various kinds of damage taking place in it. These facilities don't merely accommodate use—they also attract it. They may indeed lessen the impact of each person they attract, but the total effect on the wilderness can only grow as the population does.

There seems to be growing agreement that elaborate facilities are simply out of place in the deep wilderness.

Backpackers themselves seem to be almost unanimous in turning down the thought of new developments in remote landscapes. As one Forest Service study concludes: "Most visitors like to take their wilderness pretty straight."

Most—and yet not all. When researchers interview wilderness travelers they find a certain number who really are not even looking for wilderness as it's generally understood. Rather, they want *places to hike*, pleasant places, away from roads, but not necessarily truly wild. Moreover, quite a few of them would welcome the conveniences not widely found in genuine wilderness. They'd be just as happy to have outhouses, stone fireplaces, surfaced trails, picnic tables, and whatever else the managers decided to install.

And so there arises the notion of compromised wilderness, or, as it is sometimes labeled, "Back Country." In Back Country you might have quite elaborate facilities— even perhaps service roads, closed to private cars, but open to the vehicles of the managing agency. Trails and camps would be "hardened" as required, to take very heavy use. The land would be "gardened" to repair inevitable damage, and considerable impact would simply be accepted. These Back Country areas, it is argued, could attract a lot of hikers—the ones who aren't really wilderness buffs—and thus take some of the pressure off of the deeper wilderness.

It's an attractive idea. In fact, it's an unassailable one. We will certainly need some of these less-than-wilderness zones. Indeed, we have a few, especially in the East; the long trails and hut systems of the Appalachians amount to a kind of Back Country. (It is one of the great failures of land-use planning in America that we don't have more such areas. When we exploit land, we exploit it so thoroughly that the middle ground, the pleasant accessible land neither totally tame nor totally wild, disappears.)

And yet conservationists have not been in a hurry to support the Back Country concept. Not, at least, as it is usually put forward. The suggestion is most often brought up by the U.S. Forest Service; the Forest Service generally proposes to set up these compromised areas by cutting them out of larger regions that are, in fact, true wilderness, prime and pure. Thus Back Country becomes an *alterna-*

tive to formal wilderness, rather than a complement to it. Where one wins the other loses.

Limits on use

In any landscape that is used for recreation—no matter how much it has been "hardened"—there comes a point of saturation. Mountain valleys, like movie theaters, can only hold so many people. How many depends on how much damage you're willing to accept. In the wilderness, by its nature, the "carrying capacity" cannot be terribly high. As one Park Service document bluntly puts it: "If use continues to escalate, it is doubtful if *any* management activities can perpetuate the park resources . . . even with endless research and funds." There comes a point where no amount of care, no amount of personal conscience, no amount of "gardening," can keep the land from showing signs of wear. Exactly where the limit lies can be hard to decide. It depends on different things in different places. But everyone agrees that it exists.

What do you do (as a manager) when the line is crossed? What do you do when there are simply more people in a place than a place can gracefully hold? Of all the questions that the wilderness managers have to answer, this is the most difficult and most pervasive.

There is more than one way to control the amount of use a particular piece of land receives. The most obvious (but not always the best) is the formal, flat-out *quota*. In a quota system, each wilderness, or portion of a wilderness, is judged to be capable of handling a certain number of people at one time. If more than that show up at the trail-head—most likely to happen on some sunny August weekend—some of them will be turned away, asked to take another trail, or to come back on another day. There are various ways of deciding who gets in and who doesn't: reservation systems, wilderness entry tests, lotteries, or some combination. The simplest and most usual arrangement is first come, first served.

When the land agencies began, in the early 1970s, to introduce these quotas, they did it with more than a little hesitation. They no doubt feared that the backpacking public would resent them, bitterly perhaps. Indeed there has been some resentment. Some hikers, offended by the regulation, have begun to avoid the well-known wilderness areas where these measures are being taken. Some have moved on to other wild places, unprotected and unregulated; others may simply be staying home.

And yet most hikers, a vast majority, seem to have accepted the quotas calmly, and even with some favor. Some people are frankly pleased; they find that they can now go back to old places, favorite places, that they had abandoned as the population grew.

Other ways

Despite the seemingly broad acceptance of quotas though, there's something intrinsically unattractive, inhospitable, about the wilderness numbers game. If crowding damages the wilderness experience in one fashion, regulation impairs it in another, subtler way.

That formal use limits are often necessary, often the only answer, is clear. And yet the quotas are not the only tools that can be used to guide where people go. There are several other ways of distributing use without actually turning people away.

What are they?

One of the tools is *publicity*, which can encourage people to try one place and discourage a trip to another. Suppose, for instance, you warn the backpacker that certain areas are heavily used. Since backpackers don't like a lot of company, it seems possible that many will change their plans. They will, at least, if they have the needed information well enough in advance. With this in mind, the agencies have begun publishing maps, for some areas, showing zones of heavy use. How well this will work is not yet clear.

Publicity, misused, can harm instead of help. One National Forest in Oregon made the mistake of publishing a map illustrated with a photograph of an attractive lake, a steep cliff above it, an obvious campsite, and a caption naming the place. "That's the most overused spot in the whole area, now," say the local officials.

So publicity is one key. Another, still more important, is *access*. If a fragile site is getting too much use, you can lessen the problem simply by making it a little less easy to get to.

To do such a thing is to reverse the trend of decades. The wilderness, of course, has been shrinking. And every time a road cuts deeper into country that was wild before, the remaining wild land becomes that much more accessible, that much less remote. Places that were two days away from the roadhead may now be one day away, or one hour. When the border of the wilderness moves inwards, so does the zone of maximum use.

This shrinking is always significant to the wilderness manager; it increases the pressure on the inner lands. But most of all it matters when new roadheads appear within easy hiking range of places that are both interesting and fragile. A timberline lake basin is exactly such a place— especially if the lakes are stocked with fish. When such an attractive landscape becomes easy of access, managers will either have to limit use by quotas or let the land deteriorate.

The easiest wilderness to manage is a large one, with the most sensitive portions near the center and buffers of less fragile country surrounding that core on all sides. There used to be many blocks of wild land that fit that pattern almost exactly. But in our rush to open up access to high, spectacular places, we have built many roads that reverse this convenient natural zoning. Too often it is the most vulnerable landscape that is now most accessible of all.

Only recently have we realized that easier access has a price. Part of that price is more, and bossier, regulation.

But lately, in a few special places, wilderness managers have dared to reverse the trend. To great public astonishment, they have actually *closed* a few established roads, restoring wilderness, or at any rate *distance*, where it had disappeared. The Park Service has been the leader in this, but the Forest Service has begun to consider closing down logging roads that lead to the edge of wilderness—once the logging is done.

When roads get closed, some backpackers approve heartily; others protest. (There has been much controversy concerning road closures at Mount Rainier National Park.) It can be annoying—no question about it—to give up an easy access you're accustomed to. The annoyance is less when there's a decent, parallel trail, out of sight of the road, on which you can walk. Nobody wants to hike on a roadbed. (Couldn't you have an open road, and, in the woods beside it, a trail for people to use who want the extra miles? You could. The problem is that nobody would use it. The hiker who has wilderness in mind doesn't get much fun out of walking to a place that other people are reaching, ten times as fast, by car.)

Better than closing roads, of course, is not to build them in the first place; it's cheaper, easier, and less controversial. From the point of view of the wilderness manager, it's important above all that his wilderness not shrink any further. For many large but dwindling wilderness areas, we still have a choice: we can use the land itself to filter use, so that not too many people arrive at once in vulnerable places; or we can remove this natural buffering and increase artificial control to compensate. Each method has certain advantages. But the natural sorting-out is less destructive of the freedom one hopes for in the enjoyment of the wilderness.

A special issue: disperse or concentrate?

There's a basic question that comes up again and again in wilderness management. Briefly, is it better to *concentrate* human use in certain places, leaving the rest of the landscape more or less untouched? Or should the goal be to *disperse* human presence, and human impact, as widely as possible over the land?

This question comes up in several forms. The planners must answer it, one way or another, when they set up rules on campsites and camping. In some wilderness areas dispersal is the rule. Except for certain zones that are, for some special reason, off-limits, the hiker can make his camp where he chooses. But in other areas, you are encouraged, even required, to settle on certain established sites. Sometimes the managers of a wilderness will shift abruptly from one policy to another—confusing, surely, to backpackers who return to a place and find last year's *Thou Shalts* transformed into this season's *Thou Shalt Nots!*

On the face of it, concentrated camping seems foreign to the wilderness. Heavily-used sites have some particular problems too. It is near such sites that you're most likely to find pollution problems and woods exhausted of firewood.

417

But if dispersed camping seems more the natural order of the wilderness, it has this drawback: it takes skill and attention to choose a suitable campsite on fresh ground and use it in such a way that no scars are left behind. The camper in the established site avoids this problem.

Of course there are intermediate policies. For instance, people who light fires are often required to use the definite sites, while people who use only stoves can camp where they like. (Some areas are closed to all camping, even to all hiking, for good reasons: for the welfare of endangered species; for scientific study; for watershed; or because of extreme fire danger.)

The same question—disperse or concentrate?—must be asked in a larger context. At present, backpackers and hikers use some wilderness areas, and some portions of wilderness areas, very much more than others. Certain trails are main highways; others are traveled little; trail-less regions may get only a few visitors a year. There is a parallel variation over time. Certain summer weekends bring out fantastic crowds; certain weekdays leave the mountains almost vacant. For the informed backpacker, this is all to the good. Unless he is set on some particular destination, he can simply choose to go to the emptier places—and (if his schedule allows it) he can choose the less populous times.

Now if the demand for wilderness keeps on increasing—and there are good reasons to think that it will—more and more people will be turned away from the best known and most populous areas. Presumably they'll learn to go to other sections. And so, as one result of regulation, use will probably spread out somewhat more evenly over the land and perhaps also over the calendar.

There's wide agreement that this will happen. But there's some question as to whether the spreading-out should be promoted actively. Should the less-used areas be made more easily accessible? Should access roads to such areas be improved? Should new trails be built through trail-less regions of wilderness? Should little-used areas be given strong publicity?

Many wilderness management people are cautious about wholesale plans to "open up" these backlands. After all, there's no reason to want every corner of a wilderness

418

to be visited equally. On the contrary, there's much to be said for having both the busier and the more quiet corners. In some ways the least used parts of a wilderness are the most valuable parts. As wilderness use increases, we can expect to see the setting aside of *no use zones* within them—areas where the natural regime is preserved absolutely. As every corner of the world environment is modified, subtly or grossly, by the presence and technology of the human race, scientists search with increasing frustration for places to examine the original. A non-recreational zone inside a formal wilderness answers this need about as well as anything can.

One thing is clear: if dispersal is going to be the rule, it's important to have plenty of wild land available to disperse people *into*. The problem of *managing* wilderness is in no way separate from the problem of *preserving* wilderness. The more we have, the easier it is to manage; the more the supply diminishes, the greater the manager's difficulties become.

And the first order of business is to set aside for the future as much as we can of our still-grand wild inheritance. We need a generous wilderness, not a narrow, cramped, and superregulated one. We need to guard our freedom in that wilderness, and freedom, in the wilderness, means *room*.

Appendix:
Resources

1. Conservation/wilderness travel organizations

Appalachian Trail Conference
Box 236
Harpers Ferry, West Virginia 25425
(contact for information on member organizations)

Federation of Western Outdoor Clubs
4534½ University Way, N.E.
Seattle, Washington 98105
(contact for information on member organizations)

Sierra Club
530 Bush Street
San Francisco, Calif. 94108

The Wilderness Society
1901 Pennsylvania Avenue, N.W.
Washington, D.C. 20006

2. Federal and selected state agencies which manage wilderness land

Bureau of Land Management (BLM)
Office of Information
Department of the Interior
Washington, D.C. 20240

BLM—Arizona
Federal Building
Phoenix, Ariz. 85025

BLM—California
Federal Office Building
2800 Cottage Way
Sacramento, Calif. 95825

BLM—Idaho
Box 042
Boise, Idaho 83724

BLM—Montana
Federal Building and U.S. Courthouse
316 N. 26th Street
Billings, Mont. 59101

BLM—New Mexico
Box 1449
Santa Fe, N.M. 87501

BLM—Nevada
Federal Building
300 Booth Street
Reno, Nevada 89502

BLM—Oregon and Washington
Box 2965
Portland, Ore. 97208

BLM—Utah
Box 11505
Salt Lake City, Utah 84138

BLM—Wyoming
Box 1828
Cheyenne, Wyo. 82001

National Park Service (NPS)
Department of the Interior
Washington, D.C. 20240

NPS—Mid-Atlantic Region (Del., Md., Pa., Va., W. Va.)
143 South Third Street
Philadelphia, Pa. 19106

NPS—Midwest Region (Ill., Ind., Iowa, Kans., Mich., Minn.,
   Mo., Nebr., Ohio, Wisc.)
1709 Jackson Street
Omaha, Nebraska 68102

NPS—North Atlantic Region (N.Y., N.J., the Northeast)
150 Causeway St.
Boston, Mass. 02114

NPS—Rocky Mountain Region (Colo., Mont., N.D., S.D.,
   Utah, Wyo.)
Box 25287
Denver, Colo. 80225

NPS—Pacific Northwest Region (Ida., Ore., Wash., Alaska)
601 Fourth and Pike Building
Seattle, Wash. 98101

NPS—Southeast Region (Ala., Fla., Ga., Ky., Miss., N.C.,
   S.C., Tenn.)
1895 Phoenix Blvd.
Atlanta, Georgia 30349

NPS—Southwest Region (Ark., La., N.M., Okla., Texas)
Box 728
Santa Fe, N.M. 87501

NPS—Western Region (Calif., Ariz., Nev., Hawaii)
Box 36036
San Francisco, Calif. 94102

U.S. Fish and Wildlife Service (FWS)
Department of the Interior
Washington, D.C. 20240

FWS—Denver Region (Iowa, Mo., Kansas, Neb., the
   Dakotas, Colo., Utah, Wyo., Mont.)
Box 25484
Denver Federal Center   Denver, CO 80225

FWS—North Central Region (Minn., Wisc., Mich., Ill., Ind., Ohio)
Federal Building
Fort Snelling
Twin Cities, Minn. 55111

FWS—Northeast Region (Va., W. Va., Pa., and the Northeast)
U.S. Post Office and Courthouse
Boston, Mass. 02109

FWS—Pacific Region (Calif., Ore., Wash., Nev., Ida., Hawaii)
Box 2737
Portland, Ore. 97208

FWS—Southeast Region (La., Ark., Tenn., Ky., and the Southeast)
17 Executive Park Drive, N.E.
Atlanta, Ga. 30329

FWS—Southwest Region (Ariz., N.M., Texas, Okla.)
Box 1306
Albuquerque, N.M. 87103

U.S. Forest Service (FS)
Department of Agriculture
Washington, D.C. 20250

FS—California Region
630 Sansome Street
San Francisco, Calif. 94111

FS—Eastern Region (the Northeast and the Great Lakes states; Missouri; West Virginia)
633 West Wisconsin Ave.
Milwaukee, Wisc. 53203

FS—Intermountain Region (Nevada, Utah, southern Idaho, western Wyoming)
Federal Building
324 25th Street
Ogden, Utah 84401

FS—Northern Region (Montana, northern Idaho, N. Dakota)
Federal Building
Missoula, Mont. 59801

FS—Pacific Northwest Region (Oregon, Washington)
Box 3623
Portland, Ore. 97208

FS—Rocky Mountain Region (Colo., most of Wyo., S. Dak.,
    Nebr., Kans.)
Box 25217
Denver, Colo. 80225

FS—Southern Region (the South, incl. Okla., Ky.)
1720 Peachtree Road, N.W.
Atlanta, Ga. 30309

FS—Southwestern Region (Arizona, New Mexico)
517 Gold Ave., S.W.
Albuquerque, N.M. 87101

Maine Department of Conservation
State Office Bldg.
Augusta, Maine 04333

Michigan Department of Natural Resources
Box 30028
Lansing, Mich. 48926

New York Department of Environmental Conservation
Albany, N.Y. 12233

Pennsylvania Department of Environmental Resources
Box 1467
Harrisburg, Pa. 17210

3. Maps and publications mentioned in text

Backpacker Magazine
65 Adams Street
Bedford Hills, N.Y. 10507

Backpacking Equipment: A Consumer's Guide
William Kemsley, Jr., and Backpacker Magazine
$4.95
"Backpacking Stoves"
Backpacker #15, #16 (June and August 1976)

"California Wilderness Resources"
California Wilderness Coalition
Box 429   Davis, Calif. 95616

(Comprehensive map of California roadless areas.
Invaluable for hikers and conservationists. Should be
imitated in other states.)

Composition of Foods
Agriculture Handbook #8
U.S. Government Printing Office
Washington, D.C. 20402
$2

Medicine for Mountaineering, 2d. ed.
James A. Wilkerson, M.D.
Available from: The Mountaineers
    719 Pike St.
    Seattle, WA 98101

Mountaineering Medicine: A Wilderness Medical Guide.
    7th ed.
Fred T. Darvill, Jr., M.D.
Mount Vernon, Wash., 1975
Available from: Skagit Mountain Rescue Unit, Box 636,
    Mount Vernon, Washington 98273

Stoves for Mountaineering
Available from: Off Belay Magazine, 15630 S.E. 124th St.,
    Renton, Wash. 98055
$1.00

Topographical maps

U.S. east of the Mississippi:
Branch of Distribution
U.S. Geological Survey
1200 South Eads Street
Arlington, Virginia 22202

U.S. west of the Mississippi:
Branch of Distribution
U.S. Geological Survey
Federal Center
Denver, Colo. 80225

Canada:
Department of Energy, Mines, and Resources
615 Booth Street
Ottawa, Ontario

(USGS maps now cost $1.25 for 7.5- and 15-minute quadrangles; maps of larger areas sell for $1.50 and $2.00. Canadian maps range from 50¢ to $3. The USGS provides state indexes free.)

Wilderness Camping Magazine
1597 Union Street
Schenectady, N.Y. 12309

Wilderness Digest series
Boy Scouts of America—High Adventure Program
Box 989
Lone Pine, Ca. 93545
(Each digest describes current regulations for travel in designated wilderness areas. Volumes now available: Southwest, Northwest.)

4. Gear Suppliers

(This list is partial, thus probably unfair. It essentially omits stores which merely retail gear by other makers; it omits many small-volume companies that do work of the highest quality. Special recommendation is not implied. However, many of the listed outfits publish very useful catalogs. Please note that addresses may change.)

Alpine Designs
6185 East Arapahoe
Boulder, Colo. 80303

Browning
Route One
Morgan, Utah 84050

Bugaboo Mountaineering
170 Central Avenue
Pacific Grove, Calif. 93950

Camp 7
802 South Sherman
Longmont, Colo. 80501

Camp Trails
Box 23155
Phoenix, Ariz. 85063

Cannondale
35 Pulaski Street
Stamford, Conn. 06902

Class 5
2743 9th Street
Berkeley, Calif. 94710

Coleman
250 North St. Francis
Wichita, Kans. 67201

Eastern Mountain Sports
1041 Commonwealth Ave.
Boston, Mass. 02215
(mail-order repair service in the Manufacturing Dept.)

Eddie Bauer
Box 3700
Seattle, Wash. 98124

Eureka Tent
625 Conklin Road
Binghamton, N.Y. 13902

Gerry
5450 North Valley Highway
Denver, Colo. 80216

Himalayan Industries
Box 5668
Pine Bluff, Ark. 71601

Holubar
Box 7
Boulder, Colo. 80302

JanSport
Paine Field Industrial Park
Everett, Wash. 98204

Kelty Pack, Inc.
9281 Borden Ave.
Sun Valley, Calif. 91352

Kreeger and Son
30 West 46th Street
New York, N.Y. 10036

L. L. Bean
Freeport, Me. 04032

Moor and Mountain
63 Park Street
Andover, Mass. 01810

Mountain Safety Research
631 South 96th Street
Seattle, Wash. 98108

The North Face
1234 Fifth Street
Berkeley, Calif. 94710

Pacific/Ascente
Box 2028
Fresno, Calif. 93718

Paul Petzoldt Wilderness Equipment
Box 78
Lander, Wyo. 82520

Potable Aqua: see Wisconsin Pharmacal

Recreational Equipment (REI)
1525 11th Ave.
Seattle, Wash. 98122

Rivendell Mountain Works
Box 198
Victor, Idaho 83455

Sierra Designs
247 Fourth Street
Berkeley, Calif. 94607

The Ski Hut
Box 309
Berkeley, Calif. 94701

The Smilie Company
575 Howard Street
San Francisco, Calif. 94105

Snow Lion
Box 9056
Berkeley, Calif. 94701

Synergy Works
255 Fourth Street
Oakland, Calif. 94607

Wisconsin Pharmacal Co.
New Berlin, Wisc. 53131
(a mail-order source for Potable Aqua water purification
tablets)

Index

Notes

Notes

Notes

Notes

Notes

Notes

Notes

Notes

Notes

Notes